CW01572878

The Spanish Cheese 'Sanwish' Without Bread

Chris Wright

authorHOUSE®

AuthorHouse™ UK Ltd.
500 Avebury Boulevard
Central Milton Keynes, MK9 2BE
www.authorhouse.co.uk
Phone: 08001974150

First published by AuthorHouse 3/30/2010

ISBN: 978-1-4490-7396-1 (sc)

This book is printed on acid-free paper.

"How vain it is to sit down to write when you have not stood up to live."
Henry Thoreau

"I have been a fortunate man. Nothing in my life has been easy."
Sigismund Freud

"After the completion of our early films, Gene Hackman and I firmly believed that we would never make another one. The trouble was that we were totally in love with failure."
Dustin Hoffman in a BBC interview

"A man is a fool who, finding himself in a crisis, honestly believes that the situation could not become any worse."
Reggie `The Fish´ Bowler, on discovering the third bar was also closed.

Introduction

Being possessed with an insatiable appetite for reading material I have long since relegated the dog as being man's best friend, to second place. For me a book has always been my foremost companion. Not, I hasten to add, that I have anything against the canine community, much less. In fact there are several four legged friends of mine with whom I share more in commune than with their egotistic owners'.

So for me there is nothing to compare with a good book and nothing I like more than to be rooting around at rummage sales, contemplating car boot sales, or just chancing my luck in charity shops in search of a good read.

One cold and rainy January day I was in full swing and wandered into an Oxfam shop somewhere in the south west of England intent on gratifying my literary lust at a minimum price before returning to Spain. I ignored the normal variety of knick-knacks on display and made a bee-line for the book section. There, for some reason, my immediate attention was drawn to numerous copies of the English bible, hymns of praise and prayer books mixed in amongst the many novels. Such publications I had never normally come across, even at church rummage sales. Curiosity compelled me to take a peek at one of the smaller leather bound editions marked 'Hymns'. Inside, written in beautiful script, I discovered a dedication which read as follows:

> Olive,
>
> *from her affectionate Father*
> *1939.*
> *- her Mother's book.*

Another edition of 'Common Prayer' revealed the inscription '*To Dear Daddy from Evelyn and Eric. Xmas 1923.* And yet another 'Holy Bible' simply stated, *Ethel Morton 1902.*

As the traditional rummage sales are mostly held on church property such personalized religious publications would no doubt be considered by possible local buyers as prying into the private life of a friend or neighbour. However, the detached charity shop would easily absorb such material where it would remain, if not a potential sale then for the most part anonymous. An overwhelming sense of sentimentality that here I should encounter such intimate and surely treasured belongings, that for just over one pound sterling, I bought the four copies; my reason being that their owners surely deserved some kind of continuity in respect of recognition, even though it be posthumous and installed in the house of an ex-patriot.

And so it was to be a similar situation with Doris Wilson.

*

Paul Bennett, a friend of many years, arrived at my local bar one evening and placed in front of me and envelope containing a closely typed manuscript. "Here," he said, "this just might interest you. It's the life story of my Aunt Doris."

"It must have been a pretty short life, Paul," I commented, removing the A4 sheets and leafing through them. There were just fifteen in all.

"Wrong there, Chris. It's just that she died before she could write anymore."

I ordered a couple of beers and returned the manuscript to the envelope promising Paul that I would read it through. It took very little calculating that this would take around fifteen minutes in all and at the same time provide me with possible soporific reading matter that night before switching off the bedside light.

And it was just like that.

Those few pages gave me a brief insight into the life of a woman who was born in London's Bermondsey area some years before World War II. Having had more of a zest for life than the average person, she seemed to have been constantly on the move. There were detailed descriptions on trips to the seaside, picnics, coach excursions and cinema. Also included were details on how her dress fashion changed. But above all these activities one sensed that her Saturday nights' out at London's dance halls were her favourite. Apparently Doris just loved dancing. In the last few pages of the manuscript it was obvious that she was making plans for trips abroad but I was not to know about this as here the story ended.

I put out the bedside light and dropped the manuscript on the floor thinking to myself, "So what? There must have been thousands of girls around that time behaving exactly like Doris and all doing the same thing."

I could not have been more mistaken.

Some weeks passed before I saw Paul again. "Here, take a look at this," he said sitting down beside me in my local bar.

I sighed, "Not more stories about hyper-active Aunts, Paul?"

"No, Chris. It's just that I came across this snapshot the other day." And so saying he produced a rather faded black and white picture showing a group of around thirty people in all, posing in front of an old motor coach. The vehicle was squat nosed and all curves fondly known as a 'Charabanc'. It appeared that the group was on some sort of an outing as several wore 'Kiss me quick!' hats. The weather could not have been anything to write home about as many of those present were wearing mackintoshes or the occasional overcoat. Most, that is, apart from a small figure of a woman on the front line. Alongside the others it was easy to calculate that she was little more than five feet two inches in height and could surely be termed as a 'tough cookie' in that she was the only one who wore a flowery patterned, summer dress. The way she stood there immediately struck me as odd. Facing the camera, head a little on one side she was providing the photographer with her best, bright, smile. However, the rest of her body from her shoulders down appeared to be angled off to the right creating an impression of being slightly twisted.

"I suppose that is your aunt Doris," I said jokingly to Paul, stabbing a finger at the woman.

"Right in one Chris," he grinned. "Just take a real close look, will you?"

I did so and noticed immediately that one of Doris's legs, being somewhat shorter than the other, had committed her to wearing specially designed footwear. My attention was then drawn to her handbag, well not so much as the handbag that she was holding in front of her, but that the hand clutching it had only two fingers, giving it a claw like appearance.

"You see," said Paul's voice in my ear, "my aunt Doris was a complete wreck."

At a loss for words I was silent for a moment. I then asked, "Well what's all this stuff I've been reading about her getting dolled up and off here and there?"

"Well it's all true."

"What do you mean, it's true?" I stared at him. "Are you telling me that your aunt Doris, who was totally handicapped and a 'gad about girl' as well, decided to write her autobiography without even a whisper of her physical disability?"

"That's about it, Chris. There was no stopping Aunt Doris. She was into everything and to her the handicap seemed never to exist."

"Even Saturday nights dancing at the Palais de Dance?"

"Especially Saturday nights at the Palais de Dance."

I then thought of all the other personalities who had become well known for overcoming their personal disabilities. People like Douglas Bader the legless fighter pilot and others like paralysed Christy Brown who had written books just with the use of his left foot. Now here was someone who believed that she had a story to tell and the fact that she was very much handicapped did not even enter into it.

"Well I must say I'm very much impressed," I said to Paul. "But why bring it along to me?"

He thoughtfully moved his glass around on the bar, then said, "Don't really know, Chris. It's just that you once said that you collected interesting items like ties and books from people who had passed on."

Oh, yes. I had forgotten about the small tie collection in my wardrobe. These ties, around five or six, had belonged to friends, many long gone and occasionally I would chose one to wear saying, "Alright, Frank Nixon (or whoever), let's you and me go out today."

I looked at Paul, "So you just thought that Aunt Doris might be of interest to me. But why, you have no idea. Is that right?"

"Yes, that's about right."

"Well I must say I will have to think about it, Paul."

He waved to the passing barman and ordered two more beers. Then placing a hand on my arm said, "Listen Chris, I just thought it might be of interest to you; nothing more than that."

"Well if it is any consolation, Paul, I will think about it. Alright?"

"Fine with me."

"Sure?"

"Absolutely."

It was a few days later I saw the programme about a one legged man on the Spanish television. And that is where it all began. The one person that I had never known had influenced me to such an extent that in only fifteen pages she had stimulated me, personally, to write my own story.

So before we begin I would very much like to put the records straight by confirming that this book is firmly dedicated to someone I neither knew nor met...... Doris Wilson.

*

Naturally it would be an injustice to all the other personalities to be found in this book not to include them as without any one of them this chronicle would have been found somewhat lacking in that 'little something'. I mention Pany 'The Greek' Darlas whose ability in languages was only superseded by his sense of humour and ability to spellbind the female sex. My dear friend and partner, John (Mac) MacPhee who, together with Tony Strodder, became a cornerstone in the dreaded FU triangle. Also Stan Perkins, Gedo van der Weij, John Stepney, Geoffrey Dobson, Ken Martin, Steve the 'Ford', Joe Lucas and Ron Bartlett of the 'Jim Beam Club', Reggie 'The Fish' Bowler (impressive raconteur on stories involving his friend, late author, Ernest Hemingway), Big Ted from Doncaster, Vicente Montoya from the Spanish customs authorities, Horst Amon, Irish Tony, Edmundo (Mundi) Gomez, Paco Lerma, Brothers Mike and Brian Hill, the 'Special' Mavis Venables, Betty Anne and Gomar Davis, Bob Cooper, Tony Patterson, the Swiss family Bouchard, Ivo and Francoise Leemann, Isabel Ruiz, Jacky Higgs and, of course, Vicki Lynn.

There are many others friends, including my dear family, who have made this possible and in some instances, without whose help, the book would probably have been completed a couple of years earlier. Never mind I love you all.

Chris Wright
Valencia, Spain.

Chapter 1

Programmes on one legged men are not usually to be expected, least of all on Spanish television. But there again, I suppose, it serves to demonstrate that the country still remains even until this day, somewhat 'different'.

At the time I saw this particular programme it did occur to me that in this day and age it was possible to have an artificial leg fitted. However, perhaps this particular man just liked being one legged. Anyway, he was complaining to the attractive lady interviewer, who looked as though she would be better employed by a toothpaste company judging by her brilliantly white mouthful of dentistry, that it was extremely difficult to come across a shop that sold single shoes. I, personally, cannot recall ever actually seeing anywhere that was in the market for single shoes. But there again I am one of the many that are blessed with the normal amount of feet.

The way he described his predicament made me wonder that perhaps there just might be an opening for such a shop. However, on second thoughts, the problem of stock maintenance made me dismiss the idea immediately. I mean do people have a tendency to lose their right legs more as opposed to their left legs? I don't know. The disabled man went on to say that, apart from the fact that life had treated him badly in the loss of a limb, it was even more unfair that he should be condemned to buying pairs of new shoes when one shoe would suffice. I felt sorry for him, because he did not seem such a bad sort of fellow, as he sat nervously tugging at the one empty trouser leg. Never mind.

This time, I am glad to say, the happy ending arrived when a footwear manufacturer, on hearing about his predicament, immediately mailed him a large selection of shoes for his one foot. If my memory serves me right the exact amount was twenty-six in all. They had this array of footwear lined up toe to heel all around his living room. He said that life had much improved as most mornings were spent happily hopping around the room deciding on which shoe to choose.

*

This short television program took me back to my childhood. It was a time when, although not being favoured with a great deal of intelligence when it came to academic studies, I was in the front row when they handed out imagination. I have tons of the stuff, mainly instilled into me by one of my English masters', a certain Pop Mercer. He made a great impression on me, in more ways than one. Now half a century later I still have occasion to look up at the sky and shout in true Oliver Hardy style, "Hi, Mr. Mercer. Look at the fine mess you've got me into now!"

Before the start of each class Pop used to run his fingers through his shaggy main of white hair then glare at us over his precariously perched reading glasses.

"One thing you must have in life, boys," he growled, "is imagination. Without imagination you are lost. In fact, your life without it would be totally unimaginable."

I spent some time pondering on this observation, not really understanding what it was he was trying to impart to a bunch of illiterates that most of us were. Then one December, towards the end of the term, Pop was put in charge of organising the Nativity play. If I remember correctly it was 'Tobias and the Angel'. After the second or third act on the opening night the whisper travelled around the audience like wildfire that Pop had absconded with the school secretary. This plain, sharp edged, unattractive woman, at least twenty years his junior, was renowned for her favourite catch-phrase when being presented with a problem. "The headmaster will fit the matter," she would announce firmly in her high pitched nasal voice. Now who the hell used to use those words, 'to fit the matter', even fifty odd years ago? Anyway it was at that moment that the light of understanding dawned on me and I could see what he had been intimating each time that he had expressed his views on 'imagination'.

Naturally, rumours were rife at the time amongst the older boys and these varied from missing school funds to unwanted pregnancies. However even those fizzled out in the end when neither of the errant couple made any reappearance. I, personally, liked to believe he really had used his creative mind and was living comfortably on some desert island. He with his imagination, and she graced in a grass skirt with plenty of beads but still sporting her national health spectacles. I could even hear her intoning every now and then that the Headmaster definitely would have fitted the matter!

*

So there I was one sharp, finger tingling, morning around eight or nine years of age and on my way to school. I had awoken early and with that strong intuition felt by all boys around my age, had the feeling that there was something different about the coming day. And sure enough this was quickly confirmed. As I stood shivering in my pyjamas taking in the view from my bedroom window it was obvious that winter was definitely on the way. A glistening white covering of hoar-frost lay on the lawn, the vegetable garden, the roof tops, in fact, everywhere. The hot breakfast, topped off as usual with a spoonful of Lyles Golden Syrup to keep out the cold for some reason, was consumed rapidly. Then well encased in warm clothing by my mother and warned of what might befall me if I lost one or both of my gloves, I was released to the elements.

Barely had I reached the end of the road when I spotted them. There they were perched snugly on top of a mound of earth in front of a construction site. A new house it was, to be precise. I remember clearly because I heard my father commenting to my mother that it was a bad place to build; something to do with the drainage, I believe. Anyway there they were in all their tattered glory. Two shoes standing steadfastly side by side on a table cloth of white frost. One small rather drab, mustard coloured shoe still sporting a fine looking black lace and the other, a large almost boot size one, mud splattered but otherwise quite smart with the upper part in reasonable condition but sadly, without a lace. They looked to me rather like the Laurel and Hardy of the footwear world and I could almost visualise them breaking into a jolly little song and dance routine.

I glanced around and seeing nobody within the immediate vicinity, was tempted to take a run up the mound of earth and deliver a goal scoring kick just to see what would happen. But something, I know not know what, stopped me. Perhaps it passed through my mind that it would be a cruel action to take. I don't know. But what I do know is that when I continued on my way to school that morning, the thought of those odd shoes occupied my mind during most of the lessons.

By lunchtime I was anxious to see if they were still there and it came as a minor relief to find that indeed they were. This was lucky because a plan of action had already formed in my mind. Hurrying home I dashed upstairs and removed the old box camera we had on top of my parent's wardrobe, where all the Christmas presents used to be hidden. Then once again out into the road, oblivious of my mother calling out that lunch was ready, I took a photograph of the two odd shoes. It turned out to be an excellent picture mixed in, much to my father's surprise, with holiday snapshots taken at Lowestoft where we used to spend each glorious August holiday. From that day on I have added similar photographs to my collection of cast off footwear.

*

Sources for coming across boots and shoes were as varied as the items found. Beaches, I discovered, were fascinating locations for my expeditions. The majority of interesting footwear I came across as I scuffed my way along the shoreline, ignoring the usual attractive sea shells, were water sodden sandals or soft shoes with the occasional unusual city type shoe thrown in to add interest. These city shoes were mostly well worn and rotting, having succumbed to the salt water. It was on such occasions that my thoughts turned to wondering how on earth they had arrived at that particular spot. Pop Mercer would have been proud of me. It might have been that the owner had been drowned, possibly during the Dunkerque evacuation, and that his ghost was condemned to wandering the seven seas in search of his other Clark's size nine brogue. So I carefully took photographs, made notes as to where I had found them and under what circumstances.

One of my prize coups was a plimsoll. Remember those canvassed topped rubber soled shoes that we wore for physical education at school? Well this particular one, hanging by its lace and swinging gently in the breeze, caught in the branches of one of the willow trees that line the river Dee, by the old stone bridge at Llangollen, North Wales. That anyone could have placed it there deliberately was impossible and it certainly could not have arrived there due to any great flood. I mean it dangled at such a height that it could only have slipped from Noah's Ark. That was one of my accomplishments that defied even my wild imagination.

So each of the photographs were placed in an album I was given one Christmas and on each print I wrote the date together with a few details as to how and where I had come across the shoe. It was a non-time consuming but interesting hobby that was, I suppose, akin to keeping a diary or such. Large cities usually turned up a selection of more dilapidated cast off footwear, while the countryside produced a variety of newer shoes that sometimes made me wonder how anybody could walk away from them and wearing one shoe only. Could shoe robbers exist? I mean would it be possible to be walking along minding your own business and suddenly someone brandishes a gun in your face and demands to know, "Is that a size eight and a half Italian styled Lotus you're wearing?" Maybe.

*

Journeys to the continent revealed a treasure trove of interesting abandoned footwear; apart from Spain that is, which is another story. It didn't take long to discover that there the chances of coming across the odd shoe in that enigmatic country, was almost impossible. Many years later I was to be informed that the reason for this was that at that particular time, in the late fifties that is, there was only one principal manufacturer producing footwear for the national market; designs and colours being very much limited. This, of course, also restricted things somewhat in respect of my hobby. However it must be said that this pre Common Market land that lay slumbering to the south of the Pyrenees Mountains produced an incident, involving my pastime that probably sparked off my interest in this country. At that time Spain was very much a closed shop, governed by a short moustachioed dictator who never really came to terms with the fact that not everybody loved him. "After all," he was quoted as saying, "I am the father of all Spaniards."

Early editions of the Guinness book of records had little to say about the country and it was only later that statistics included bullfighting, poisoning people with oil and mammoth sized Valencia paella rice dishes that exceed one hundred thousand portions.

The particular episode that stimulated my interest in this almost wild land, that it was then, took place at a time some twenty odd years after the end of the Spanish civil war. It was a time when the country was still licking its social and economic wounds from the terrible effects of family against family, brother against brother. The rugged Costa Brava with its cliffs and coves was only just becoming a commercially viable glint in the eyes of the British tour operators.

The travel company that arrived at the same time as myself that year was Wallace Arnold, based somewhere in the north of England. Their clients looked as though they had missed the turn off for Blackpool and had driven straight on to Spain by mistake. The beach at Tossa de Mar was scattered with groups of middle aged to elderly people with cloth caps, braces and large ladies in their stiff boned corsets commenting on the water, unusual food and the toilet situation. I believe that Wallace Arnold still exists today. Well done!

It was a time when I realised that Spain had managed to grab a monopoly on two combined features that no other European country had or would ever have, that of unlimited sun and space. Around twice the size of Great Britain and with a population density much less, it was a place were one could breath and commune with an unbelievable variation when it came to scenery and general living. Of the former it had absolutely everything from snow capped sierras to flat dry arid plains, to lush green pastures in the north.

And, of course, let us not forget the Mediterranean. As a potential holiday resort Tossa de Mar on the Costa Brava was then still very much in the early stages of development by today's standards.

With only an inkling of an idea on how to cope with tourist influxes the infrastructure of the town was very limited, to say the least. I still have a photograph of bed linen from the hotels spread out to dry on the beach and held down by stones. There were a few reasonably good hotels where two people could stay, have a double room with full board for just two to three pounds a day with all the comforts. All the comforts that is, apart from being woken up in the early hours by the noisy donkey carts that were collecting the entire town's rubbish. Then one hour later this being repeated by the sound of an appalling, evil smelling, sewage lorry that sucked out the septic tanks from the hotels. It was around that time that the town authorities were laying pipes so that the effluent could be directed straight into the Mediterranean at night.

It was totally forbidden to stray onto the beaches after dark because smuggling was rife, mainly cigarettes and booze from the Canary Islands. Nowadays, however, all that has changed. The Mediterranean coast is now subject to the arrival of 'Pateras' or open boats loaded with illegal immigrants from African countries and incredibly fast, multi engine, launches carrying drugs. So in the nineteen fifties the night revellers, being full of the local cheer did not notice the perfumed fragrance that insidiously wafted in from the sea. It was the early morning bathers next day that were the first to receive the good news as they came into contact with all sorts of undesirable things floating around in the sea. By the amount of diarrhoea sufferers I encountered in those early days this form of pollution was, to my mind, a primordial form of recycling. Still, everyone seemed happy and the town's chemists and two doctors were delirious.

*

One evening, with the idea of avoiding the bars and becoming legless before midnight, I wandered over to the Rueda club on the outskirts of the bustling town, paid my meagre entrance fee and fell head over heels in love with a gypsy flamenco dancer who was billed as 'La Sigla'. It took about fifteen minutes for this to happen. The moment I set my eyes upon her I realised that she epitomised all I had read about that veiled mysterious land. In La Sigla I could physically hear in her voice and see in her dancing something beyond my normal being and in that brief instant all that I had read about Spain became a reality. Dark, olive skinned with wide, innocent, eyes, high cheek bones and long jet black, almost blue, hair down to her waist.

Her fine long slim fingers were made to express the intricate movements of flamenco expressions and seemed to hypnotise the audience as she flourished them above her head while beating a tattoo with her wooden heeled shoes on the small stage. She was, perhaps, around eighteen years of age when I stepped into her young life. A slip of a girl who looked as frail and as light as the specks of dust that rose around her from the boards at the same time giving the impression that she would have difficulty in lifting a kilo of apples or facing a strong wind. But could La Sigla dance, play the guitar and sing? To me she was absolutely sensational; out of this world. The amount of energy her young body exuded at each megahertz performance could have lit up the town during one of the blackouts, and believe me, with those wild summer storms that had a habit of appearing during the summer months, blackouts were a very frequent. That first night the sound of her insistent vibrating tattoo as she stamped and gyrated, made me light headed, dizzy and followed me back to my hotel where I spent a sleepless night.

I returned again and on the third night, plucked up courage, went along after the show and in stumbling Spanish presented her with flowers and a box of Swiss chocolates. Well from then on that was it. I was allowed behind the stage every night and could watch from the wings. Her back up guitarist was an unhealthy sallow faced individual with bad teeth and pock marks. She called him 'Tio' but whether or not he actually was her uncle I never found out. When the curtain came down after each stage shaking performance she would fall into my arms completely exhausted and I would hold her until she sufficiently recovered and was able to drink one of those San Miguel special beers that they kept in the ice boxes, fridges still being an item yet to arrive. At night, in her lodgings, she would snuggle childlike to my chest as we lay on her narrow bed and sipped Fundador brandy while she whispered secrets about her brothers and sisters in that irresistible lisping Andalusia accent.

It was La Sigla or my little 'Siggy as I called her, who pleaded with me to take her to Barcelona in my new company car. How could I refuse? She was like a child, bouncing about, pointing things out and waving to people as we passed through parched white washed villages with me manipulating the steering in sometimes futile attempts not to fall into the pot holes that littered the roads like jigsaw puzzles.

Arriving in Barcelona, Spain's second largest metropolis, we parked right by the fountain in La Plaza Catalonia at the top of the Ramblas. The charge was just three pesetas, less than two pence at that time, for the whole day. The official attendant on duty, complete with a cap and an arm missing, explained to us that he was a casualty of the Civil War.

He then offered me a 'Peninsulares', one of the Spanish government cigarettes which sold at just a few pesetas for a packet of twenty. I politely accepted and spent the next five minutes coughing much to the delight of Siggy. Then hand in hand, which was allowed in public, but not kissing as that could result in being charged with creating a scandal and a stiff fine, we wandered down the Ramblas, past the flower stalls to the Plaza Real. There we sat on small wrought iron chairs at a table under the high grey stone arches sipping dry Moriles wine from Jerez and toying with warm toasted almonds. Then it was on to 'Los Caracoles', signifying 'The Snails'.

One of Barcelona's best known restaurants it was initially owned by 'El Tuerto', meaning the one-eyed, who used to be seen driving his horse and coach like crazy around the city many years before. Possibly to stimulate the customer's taste buds, the only entrance to this fascinating dining venue lay through the noisy, hectic, atmosphere of the kitchens. Once seated under the constant swishing of the ceiling fans in one of the many dining areas, we ate in an authentic Spanish atmosphere surrounded by wooden panelled walls covered with autographed photographs of every imaginable world famous personalities who had at one time or another visited the restaurant. Here was Enrique Caruso to Frank Sinatra, from Yvonne de Carlo to Humphrey Bogart, Rita Hayworth, and Maria Callas and so on. And what a feast! We savoured succulent roast legs of lamb, drank the heavy red wine from the Rioja region and laughed at each others little jokes as only true lovers can.

On retrieving the car, some two hours later, I was delighted to find that the extra two peseta tip had resulted in the vehicle being washed, polished and was now free from the dust and grime that came with travelling on Spanish highways. Delving into the boot I pulled out a packet of Senior Service cigarettes and gave it to our one armed attendant. The toothless smile it produced and the guttural Catalonian, "Gracias Señor. Gracias!" was rather embarrassing but everyone seemed happy.

*

It was then on the way back to Tossa tired but happy that the incident occurred. Night was coming on rapidly as we followed the uneven asphalt through a barren forest of dry leafless cork trees, their grotesque, misshapen, limbs projecting at seemingly impossible angles. So engrossed was I at this almost macabre backcloth that when we came to a sharp bend I almost failed to notice the two armed figures that stepped out from the side of the road and waved us down. Siggy cried out and my foot hit the brake pedal.

"They Guardia Civil, Chris," she whispered agitatedly as I pulled over. "Do not something do silly."

"No, I not something do silly," I said, as we sat waiting for them.

The men in their green, dishevelled uniforms and tri-corn hats waved their guns and motioned to us to get out of the car. And so we did, as casually as possible. Although I was well aware that my papers were in order and that I had committed no offence, to my knowledge anyway, I still felt a nervous stirring within me. I remembered reading somewhere that these were the poison dwarfs of Spain and that there was a saying that implied that where they tread no grass grows.

For some moments we just stood looking at each other, Siggy clinging to my arm. I know little about firearms but the rifles they were brandishing looked as though they would prove more damaging to the person firing them than to anyone they were being pointed at. However there was no way I was not going to argue. The older of the two, who sported an untidy Pancho Villa moustache beneath a spectacular nose that looked as though it had been designed with the London Underground in mind, turned and peered into the car while the other leaned casually against the bonnet leering at Siggy.

Realising that the steering wheel was not on the normal side of the vehicle, moustache turned to Siggy and let off a stream of gruff unintelligible words of which I only managed to interpret 'Ingles' and 'Papeles'. Dutifully

I reached into the car and produced the required documentation. He seemed only interested in the insurance green card which he examined with great concentration while checking and repeating carefully the registration number.

The younger one of the two had now begun to grin at Siggy who moved closer to me, gripping my arm even more so. I could still feel her nervous trembling. This seemed to animate him, his grin grew wider and he muttered something about 'Novio', signifying fiancée or promised one. Siggy nodded but said nothing.

It was only when I was asked to open the boot and we all trooped to the rear of the car that I noticed their footwear. I honestly could not believe my eyes. I was mesmerised, speechless. Both men were wearing different coloured shoes, one brown and one black. It was unreal. I opened the boot with difficulty as Siggy refused to let go of my arm. The first thing that came into view was the carton of English cigarettes.

"Muy bueno," said the older one nodding at the packets of Senior Service at the same time returning my documentation.

"Give them a cigarette," hissed Siggy.

I reached down, removed four packets and offered them while staring at their shoes. The atmosphere immediately changed. A lot of "Gracias, Gracias," and lighting up of cigarettes and once again everyone was happy. Apart from me that is whose eyes remained transfixed on their footwear. Both men looked about the same size so why could they not just change shoes. But then I realised that the combination was wrong. Siggy was saying something to them and the word 'Novio' was again mentioned. Everybody laughed and I thought it prudent to join in for appearance sake but my mind was still elsewhere. I was almost temped to ask them if they had similar pairs of shoes at home but thought better of it.

A short while later, after much handshaking, we drove slowly away, leaving the two men waiting for the next victim and I mulled over what I had seen. I said something to Siggy but received no reply. Now relaxed, she had dozed off, slumped comfortably against me.

*

During that journey my thoughts turned to what had brought about my just being there. About Siggy, about everything I had experienced within the last few weeks. For some reason the image of Pop Mercer floated towards me. Until that point, this kindly old gentleman had been completely correct, imagination was necessary when one was committed to being in the same place where all was too familiar and one desired that something just a little bit different. But here in Spain, well each day produced something out of the ordinary. Go on, tell me. How many people have you seen wearing a pair of shoes in two different shades? I would say practically impossible. Especially if confronted by two officials together wearing footwear of different colours. No way! If this could happen within a space of twenty-seven days what else was out there waiting? "Pop Mercer," I thought, "Forget it. Life without imagination is possible. It is here!" Now let us be honest, we all know that in front of every silver lining there sometimes lurks a very nasty black cloud and in my particular case it was to be at times more of a cyclone. However at that particular moment I was convinced it would not be anything that I could not safely handle. When Siggy eventually awoke neither of us was inclined to talk much as both of us were well aware that this was to be our last day together.

On that particular night, the memory of which has remained with me until this day, Siggy danced as only those with Moorish blood and 'Aficción' can dance. More dust than usual billowed up in clouds from the bone dry floor as she hammered it with her wooden heels. And each time she swung around to face me where I was standing to one side of the stage I could see the expression on her face. A combination of love and accusation that tomorrow I was to betray her by my leaving.

"This is for you and you only my Englishman. Remember it is you who are deceiving me by your going."

Even the grizzled old guitarist looked surprise at the ferocity of her dancing. Then, as the sound of the last chord faded and died she turned towards me, fell to her knees bowing her head in my direction. Her hair cascaded over her face obliterating her features as though irrevocably drawing the curtain on our relationship. Both arms reached out towards me, palms upwards, as though in final supplication. I felt faint and the hairs on my own arms rose. There was a moment's silence when it seemed that the whole world had stopped and then the applause began assaulting my eardrums until I recovered my senses. Still in a daze, I automatically moved across to her, gently raised her exhausted form and with her head pressed to my chest and sobbing silently, carried her out, ignoring the protests of the club owner and even more the demands of the audience for the usual encore.

Later, in the soft shadowy glow of one small candle in her tiny room we drank too much Fundador brandy, made passionate love and cried clinging to each other, swearing fidelity and she pleading with me to take her to England. I would not admit it, even to myself, but knew deep inside that this was probably the last time we would be thus. Then, as the pale morning rays of the Mediterranean sun began to filter through the wooden shutters, coward that I was, I slipped quietly out of the narrow bed, dressed and left with the gift of her sharp tangy lemon cologne still clinging to me, together with the salty taste of her tears on my lips.

*

I made the frontier at Le Balou and stopped to drink a coffee-cognac. Then coming down out of the mountains felt the comfortable warm green blanket of the Gallic countryside enfold me. But as I drove through the limitless vineyards full of heavy ripening bunches of grapes awaiting the September harvest, instead of the hoped for tranquillity my mind remained a hive of restless activity, as complex, yet at the same time as clear as the images that Siggy's dancing had created. I began attempting to reason with my feelings about this last corner of Europe where everything seemed contrary to my way of living. There, compared with the rest of the countries, even under the thumb of a dictator, life seemed to have more distinct values as regards day to day existence. Or if you like, more significance that is, than tilting at the windmills of the usual problems together with the lousy weather awaiting my return in England. The same spiritual awakening had occurred with some books I had read in the past. At that moment I knew I would never be quite the same as before.

Then looking back on the whole incident, for what was the hundredth time and as crazy as it might seem, I knew that I should have remained with Siggy.

Stayed and faced whatever was to come. No, even with my twenty odd years was I under any illusion that there would be a happy ever after ending but I was damned sure that during the time spent together I would have been more alive than I possibly ever would be in my whole life. However such is the conformity that we are, almost obliged to adhere to for the sake of society and personal commitments, I continued driving north towards Calais. That night I stayed as usual at the Hotel du Perron, south of Orleans and in the morning bid farewell to the stuffed bear in the reception area and feeling just that little bit better, headed for Rouen and Calais.

My mind was made up at that particular moment. Apart from returning to Spain one fine day, hopefully, in the not too distant future, I would go, if at all possible, on a more permanent basis. Escape or adventure? We would have to see.

This time, however, it was only to be some months later that the opportunity for a short break occurred and I grasped the opportunity to return. In the meantime I had written to Siggy but apart from a picture postcard just after my return to England, had received no reply.

*

As I drove into Tossa de Mar I could see that little had changed apart from a large amount of construction going on. With the news at home being a mixture of the American pilot, Gary Powers being held in Russia, the Eichman Nazi trial and holiday makers arriving in Spain to find their hotels still at ground level, I hoped that these particular ones that were being built would be ready on time as it was already late spring.

As soon as I arrived I booked into my hotel then hurried along to the lodgings where I had selfishly abandoned Siggy in what seemed a lifetime ago. There I was confronted by a grossly overweight concierge who, on close proximity, appeared to have cornered the market on body odour. He politely informed me that Ziggy was, indeed, still in residence.

"However," he leered at me, "if you want to see her you had better get in line. There are several other customers before you, Inglés."

I stared at him open mouth not knowing quite what to say then turning stumbled out from the dark, cool, hallway into the bright sunshine.

I did not know what I was really anticipating but certainly was not what I expected. I was devastated and in a daze just wandered around the streets desperately trying not to be enticed into any of the bars with their cheap booze and possible false comfort.

It was later that I succumbed and somewhat exhausted found myself at the 'Chiringuito' bar on the beach. There I commandeered one of the precarious stools and ordered a gin and tonic. The owner apologised saying that the only gin he had at that moment was 'Green Fish'. Knowing that this particular gin was made out of fish bones and was sickly sweet I opted for a Bacardi and coke. No need enhance my demise too rapidly.

Then, as coincidence now played an important part in my life, I found myself sitting next to a young blond, blue eyed, German around my own age, also looking as though he had lost five pesetas and found one. Naturally after the second 'Cubalibre' it was not long before we fell into conversation.

13

In excellent English he introduced himself as Gunter and went on to explain that he was a representative of a branded drink called 'Suze', which seemed to be advertised a great deal in France. He then said that his first visit to Spain had been made the previous year. We fell silent for a while then for something to say I asked him how he had arrived in Tossa. Casually, he ordered another two drinks then inclining his head towards the promenade where there appeared to be a small group of people gathered.

"In the Cruiser," he explained, nonchalantly.

"The Cruiser?" I queried rather puzzled.

"Yes," he said, patiently taking a mouthful of 'Cubalibre', "it's my car."

Then carefully replacing his glass on the bar he added, "My catch the girls' car."

Naturally my interest heightened.

Next, after a few minutes silence, he drained his glass in one spectacular swallow, pulled out his well padded wallet and said, "Come, I show you. Let's you and me go catch girls!"

We paid Paco, the bar owner, who insisted on giving us several of his home made cigars called 'Caliqueños', then strolled up the beach, my mood lightening somewhat with the drinks and the company. Skirting the white bed linen laid out to dry from the hotels we stepped onto the promenade. I could now see why the group of people had been gathered there. Before me was the most beautiful white, open topped, American Ford Galaxy that I had ever seen. Immaculate red leather seating, together with every imaginable extra plus white walled tyres and an excess of bright shining chrome. It was a dream.

"Absolutely fantastic!" I said. Then, "Do you catch many girls?"

"Oh, yes, of course," he grinned. "But last year was the very best of all."

"Oh, really?" I said, following his example and climbing into the car, to the delight of the several admirers, without opening the door.

"Yes. Last year, I was with very special young girl," he explained, manipulating the starter so that all the cylinders growled into life causing the onlookers to step back a few paces.

"Ya," he continued, putting the beast into gear and burning rubber as we pulled away. "A very nice girl who dance at the Rueda night club. She loves this car."

"Good, God!" I thought, as my stomach did a double somersault, "Was it possible?"

Then, "Of course it was possible." I could almost feel Siggy sitting next to me there and then, bouncing up and down, waving to all and sundry as Gunter drove the Cruiser around the town.

"Did you take her to Barcelona?" I asked, attempting to keep my voice casual.

He glanced sideways at me at the same time waving to three Swedish looking beauties that were smiling at us as we rolled by.

"How the bleddy hell you know that?"

"I bet you went to 'Los Caracoles' restaurant as well," I added, unable to resist the impulse.

He braked and pulled sharply over to the side of the road, cut the engine and turned to me,

"Well?" he demanded.

"Because the same thing happened to me!" I explained.

For a moment we stared at each other then climbed out of the Galaxy laughing like a couple of idiots and began pounding each other on the back. Now the passers-by not only had a magnificent vehicle to admire but a spontaneous show with an Englishman and a German falling all over the place doubled up with laughter.

"You know what?" he said, between guffaws. "All the way to Barcelona in this bleddy car." Here he took a kick at one of the white walled tyres. "Cost me a bleddy fortune in gas!"

Needless to say the rest of the holiday was spent together and every night after that we took on the town in the Cruiser accompanied by as many girls of different nationalities as we could cram into the vehicle. Gunter would negotiate the narrow streets, every now and then shouting "Oh, Laaaaay!" and returning the waves of the other holiday makers meandering along the narrow sidewalks. Unable to help myself I kept glancing at the crowds possibly hoping for glimpse of Siggy but I never saw her again. It also appeared to be an unspoken agreement between Gunter and myself that neither her name nor El Ruedo club was ever mentioned after that first day of our meeting.

However after all these years the moment that I catch the fragrance of lemon cologne I am, for one brief second, immediately transported back in time and can almost hear the relentless strumming of Tio's guitar and the compelling tattoo of Siggy's wooden heels on the boards.

*

That particular month the Costa Brava suffered from some terrible storms and I remember seeing cars floating out to sea, two of them Volkswagen Beetles, as the water poured down from the hills carrying everything before it. I also recall exchanging blows with a hefty looking Nordic type who had become abusive about the fact that Gunter and I appeared to have a monopoly as regards females. This situation sometimes arose in the small dance bars where many of the girls were still chaperoned by their mothers and the Spanish boys did not really go for foreign tourists wishing to dance with their possible future wives. On the night of the brawl it was absolutely bucketing down and as usual all the town's lighting had given up. The rainwater was gushing down the centre of the unmade street and we stood like a couple of drunken fools exchanging blows, wet through and with the lightning streaks providing the only illumination. In the end, too exhausted to carry on, we both went our different ways. I think in a way that proved a minor way of relieving me of the frustration I felt over Siggy. Even that particular incident ended amicably when the Swede and I happened to meet face to face the next day in a bar and ended up apologising and buying each other drinks. Eventually the holiday came to an end with Gunter and I promising to keep in contact which neither of us ever did.

Chapter 2

On my return to England I concentrated on my work, entered into a form of marriage with both a wife and a building society and apart from the occasional holiday thought less about Spain.

It was around that time that I began to visit, Lobb's Wood, a private gaming club near Farnham in Surrey. Comfortably situated in enchanting grounds cosily surrounded by pine trees, this friendly half timbered house had, at one time I was told, belonged to the J.M. Barry, writer and author of Peter Pan, whose work everybody should read again when they reach middle age as the book takes on a completely new significance.

James Barry's solid writing desk and commodious chair were still in place and many is the time I just sat there day dreaming with the clicking of the roulette wheel in the background and the soft but light hearted conversational tones of the players interspersed by the more serious voice of the croupier chanting the numbers.

As with most members I became quite friendly with the club owner, Tony. A charming, good looking Spaniard who, when he was not flying with Iberia Airways, ran the club and acted as a competent croupier.

One evening, after dining at one of the splendid buffets that Tony's vivacious wife Isabel had organised, he asked, "So where do you go for your holidays this year, Mr. Chris?"

"Oh, I don't have any plans at the moment," I replied, through a fork full of delicious fresh salmon. "Spain again, I suppose."

He smiled his passenger flight steward smile. "Why not go to my home town?" he suggested and then went on to explain that his particular home town was Valencia, located some two hundred miles south of Barcelona on the Levantine coast. Always on the look out for something original I said that I would certainly consider his proposal, although the thought of all those extra miles did not really sound encouraging.

*

I read somewhere once that to a man of imagination, a map is a window to adventure. And so it was that my free time in the following weeks was dedicated it to that of pouring over maps, judging distances and timing trips. Here, I hasten to add, these calculations were firmly based on my experiences of the best places to stop for dining or accommodation purposes. Not for someone such as myself am I attracted to those thick red lines denoting fast stretches of boring concrete motorways with their occasional stop off places that dispense coin operated coffee, fast food together with apathetic piped music.

No, my preferences are the spidery thin secondary roads that pass through out-of-the-way villages with their jealously guarded secret restaurants, tabacs, bakeries and small shops. Over the years I have accumulated a wealth of knowledge on these 'little gems' and will travel far out of my way to visit anyone of them. For example, a small village in the heart of the old Gascony region, France, keeps a tight hold on one small 'Charcuterie' which is, in fact, not your normal shop by any means but a small cottage. To enter, one opens the precarious garden gate and passes through a totally neglected, weed strewn, garden.

First time visitors would begin to wonder if the exterior was such utter chaos then what could one expect within. However once through the door when the sight, smell and taste senses come into play, it is a virtual gourmet's paradise. Foie gras sausages, truffled poultry galantine, rillons and superb rabbit galantine are set out before you. Another very run down station hotel to the north of Toulouse provides an extraordinary Pot-au-feu where the meat is prepared the previous night and left to simmer on the open fire with hardly a ripple on the surface until the following day when it is so tender that it has to be removed with such precision as it will disintegrate immediately. And yet another warm hotel in the Auvergne region where the wife of the 'Patron' would, at my request, stealthily sneak down to the cellar where her husband hid his personal 'Camembert' and bring me a portion that had been blessed by the gods'. These and many others that boast equally gourmet adventures all grace the routes I will chose and at times wondering whether, instead of continuing to my destination, it might just be a more sensible idea to seek out the nearest Estate Agent and set up home there and then.

My original enthusiasm for leaving England on a more permanent basis some years before and seeking those castles in Spain, had diminished somewhat, perhaps to some primitive instinct at the back of my imaginative mind warned me that with such a drastic move all would not be plain sailing. How right it was. I wonder what I would have done if, when examining those Michelin road maps and tracing those multicoloured lines south towards the Iberian Peninsula, I had caught the merest glimpse of what was in store for me. But at that moment it was impossible to visualise and probably if I had even a mere suspicion I would surely have laughed as much as Gunter and I had laughed that day in Tossa.

Who would believe that in the year nineteen eighty-three, I would be promised to be shown the whereabouts of precious stones buried in the Pyrenees on the condition that I withdrew one of the charges against England's notorious jewel thief, Robert Chatwin, owner of Sutton Jewellers.

That one of the first rules in prison was not to eat the ends of the bread.

That a negotiation over Elvis Presley's head would lead to a series of adventures that would involve the distribution of cursed key rings and result in such a run of bad luck the formation of a company under the name of FU Incorporated (Fuck You Inc.), would be initiated.

That it would be possible to be asked whether or not I required bread to go with my cheese sandwich in one of Valencia's best known cafeterias.

The hairdresser who carefully shaved my hair from just one side of my head, leaving the other side with locks over my ears, and then, because it was lunchtime, insisted on inviting me to eat in one of the town's best dining venues with the promise that he would complete the job afterwards.

The request by the local police to interpret for them as they had arrested the largest, hairiest man, I have ever set eyes upon, sporting an incredible shaggy red beard, on charges of impersonating a woman.

Seeing the dog that wasn't and the more than two metre tall negro resplendent in full dress uniform that consisted of ankle length, bright scarlet coat complete with black military styled beret, who turned up at the bullfight and was later seen stalking the streets of Valencia.

Trying my hand at 'bootlegging' and as a result nearly coming to grief when a tyre on the car exploded, with four hundred and twenty-five litres of pure alcohol on board.

Being unable to meet a friend at the Metropol Hotel, Valencia, as he had been banned for life some years before when he and the author Ernest Hemingway had squirted the city's Mayor with gin (Gordon's of course) fired out of water pistols.

Being asked to take charge of a friend's ashes in the event of his death, to be placed in Boddingtons's beer cans and tossed into the English Channel before the ferry arrived in Plymouth.

Having my own spontaneous protest, 'Lie in' at the American Embassy in Madrid.

Writing articles for 'Las Provincias' newspaper, distribution 96.000 copies daily, covering the Valencia Community which stretches from Castellon to Alicante.

To discover at first hand that a country which has been welcomed to the European Community and is happily publicising its commitment to democracy to all the world can receive a sentence by the United Nations for abuses against human rights and totally ignore the situation.

To present a cookery program on the Valencia television channel and help run a radio station on the Costa Blanca.

To learn of a most amazing fail safe method by which the Holy Scriptures can be imparted to one.

Separation, births, deaths and disappearing swans. Yes all this and many other incidents were to befall me, to frustrate me, to make me happy, often to frighten me, to excite me and to really screw up what would probably have been an otherwise extremely pleasant, but somewhat dull existence, back in England. Well would you or anyone else have honestly believed even one tenth of that, if somebody had predicted it? I certainly would not. Yet it really was going to happen, is still happening and that following trip to Valencia was about to play an important part that would help set the whole thing in motion.

*

Eventually holiday time arrived and on the elected day my wife, Marilyn and I set off south towards Dover and France. This time we approached Spain by travelling down the western side of France via Le Mans, Poitiers and Tours. Then, after becoming frustrated with the lunchtime traffic in Bordeaux, we drove inland to the elegant city of Pau.

After Pau we headed for the frontier passing through the enchanting village of Laruns nestling in the Valle D'Osseau or valley of the bear, below the magnificent Pyrenean mountain range that separated the rest of Europe from the Iberian Peninsula. Winding our way slowly upwards through the Portelet pass towards the Spanish frontier post situated at the ski resort of Formigal, we were treated to some of the most spectacular scenery I had ever set eyes upon. Occasionally, on the pitted, narrow road, we were obliged to slow down and often brought to a standstill by the presence of captivating, free range, tan coloured cows, with their jangling mountain bells that strolled along the highway oblivious or disdainful of all passing traffic.

Later, and without any significant hitch, we dropped silently down into Spain passing by the Biescas campsite where in some later years there would be a tremendous flooding that would tragically claim around eighty lives.

The next town of any note was ancient Huesca. Like Laruns this also enjoyed the solid backcloth of the mountain peaks, at the same time heralding the beginning of the vast dustbowl of the Aragon plain.

Then it was on towards Zaragoza with road surfacing that really tested the cars suspension. And was it hot? To say that you could fry an egg on the bonnet would have been an understatement. At that moment I was sure you could have added a couple of sausages and a tomato as well. No problem. It was impossible to drive with the windows down, due not only to the unbearable temperature, but also the continuous dust clouds enveloping the car as other vehicles passed in either direction. Naturally in those days air-conditioning was unheard of so we just sweated along over uneven cobbles hoping for some relief, as it was now late afternoon and the sun appeared to be slipping towards the horizon to our right. It was then through the shimmering heat haze way out in front that I caught a glint of the sun's rays reflecting off some distant object. I blinked several times and stared out ahead.

Then, almost leisurely as if to enhance my reasonably optimistic mood that there just had to be something better than what we were passing, the magnificent, and many spired cathedral of Zaragoza became visible. As we approached an old stone bridge that spanned Spain's largest river Ebro, we saw by the roadside a large sign, somewhat dilapidated, but proudly announcing 'Zaragoza Ciudad Inmortal'. Sadly that has long since gone. A shame really as together with the cathedral and the majestic lie of this metropolis this simple beacon induced in me the warm sensation that I was arriving somewhere comfortable and secure.

The high ceiling, plant potted hotel with its echoing mosaic tiled floors, we discovered was much in keeping with this Goyesque city and the room provided one of the largest baths I have ever had the fortune of climbing into. As the plumbing clanked and gurgled away I lay back and watched the somewhat tanned water pouring forth from the huge taps and had a delicious feeling that things were now on the right track and Zaragoza was definitely going to be placed on my list of favourites.

Next morning, rested and refreshed, we set out again, passing the famous bullring where years later I was to receive a short lesson at the Taurino School from one of Spain's most famous bullfighters who has since died of his injuries suffered at a 'Corrida' in France.

*

The road south crossed an arid, ash grey, moonscape leading to Daroca and Teruel beyond. The town of Teruel that figured in one of the most prominent battles of the Spanish civil war lay in a deep cool valley and as we drove up and away from its high red, tiled roofed, ornate buildings we were once again subjected to the blistering, oven like, temperatures. Pressing on we eventually stopped in the small village of Barracas. Here we lunched on slices of smoked ham and Manchego cheese together with a salad that included what appeared to me like half eaten olives.

I remonstrated with the waiter, not really understanding his reply. Then, when I became a little angry at the thought we were possibly eating already chewed olives, he marched off to the kitchen to return brandishing an enormous jar full of them.

"You see, Señor," he explained, while raising his voice so others at the nearby tables could hear. "They what we call 'olivas partidas'. They are all like that. They have been, how you say, crushed. No, not eaten. Crushed!"

My wife muttered, "Fool," and I mumbled something inadequate about wanting to check, smiled and continued eating, at the same time wishing that I was anywhere else but there. However, apart from the occasional glances and whispered comments from our fellow diners, all was fine.

Once again outside the temperature seemed to have risen even higher and what little tarmac there was on the highway had melted so much that the tyres were actually sticking to it. It was impossible to carry on so we stopped again at another cafeteria cum restaurant just less than one hundred yards from the previous one and there we sat sipping iced water and cold San Miguel beer under large electric fans that spread the hot air around so that everybody had their share. Eventually I mustered my courage, went outside and confirmed that it had cooled off sufficiently to carry on. I did this by walking across the road and arriving at the other side with my slip on shoes still intact. From then on it was all down-hill through miles of dark green orange and olive groves with the occasional lemon tree thrown in.

Arriving at the coast, both of us felt a little more animated when we saw the placid blue and green Mediterranean stretched out before us. A joint decision was made and we decided to pass straight through Valencia and head a little further south until we came to somewhere we could settle for the rest of the holiday. In those days there always existed the minute possibility of coming across a small idyllic Spanish fishing village but sadly all that has since disappeared.

*

The holiday resort of Cullera, some twenty kilometres from Valencia, was akin to the shock of diving into a freezing cold pool. It was early evening when we arrived and 'walkabout' time for the locals. The place was absolutely heaving to put it mildly and I am sure that if I had been nearer to middle age I would immediately have high tailed it out of there, but fast. However we were hypnotised by all that was happening. As this was one of the coastal points nearest to Spain's capital Madrid, it seems that everyone from there descended on the place each summer. Later I read a statistic which quoted as saying that there were more people per square metre there in August than anywhere else in Europe.

I am certain it was correct. The fault that most of them seemed to have was that as they walked along the pavement they all appeared not to be looking the way they were going but over their shoulders to where they had come from. It was only until we had accustomed ourselves to this flaw that it things became easier. Also eight hundred years of their Moorish background was in full evidence in the way they dragged their feet. Almost none of them lifted a foot to walk a single step. Talk about a soft sand shuffle; it was fascinating.

Most of the buildings were ugly high rise blocks of apartments and as there appeared to be little in the way of hotel accommodation we went along to a nearby estate agent and rented one for the following three weeks. The proprietor, Pepe Crespo, who spoke excellent English, conducted us to one that was available on what had to be competing for the noisiest street in Europe statistic. Before handing over the keys Pepe assured us that the owners of the place would be along within the hour to provide all the necessary bed linen.

Now this was to be a critical point where Manolo and Conchin became involved in my life. Both were of a similar age to us. Manolo was a short, cheerful, round man, prematurely losing his hair. With a wide, ready, smile he gave the impression that if it were possible to unscrew him you would find chocolates inside. Employed at one of the large banks in Valencia, he took his profession seriously but sometime in the not-too-distant future he would be retiring early as with the demise of General Franco, the dictator and the onset of democracy, the bank where he worked was to be subjected to several armed attacks Looking down the wrong end of a sawn off shotgun on different occasions, naturally caused his health to suffer. I did ask him why it appeared that robbers had a definite preference for banks as targets and he came back to me with what I thought to be a very logical answer.

"In Valencia alone there are a multitude of banks," he explained, "all with a varying amount of branches. In fact I do not think it is possible to be in any main street in Valencia where you cannot see a bank. Everywhere you look there is a bank of some kind."

He grinned and spread his hands. "So, tell me, Chris, what place has more money than most and above all you don't have to go far to find one? A bank, of course!"

Conchin, his dear wife, was a high spirited elegant woman with that Latin charm one so often finds in educated Spanish women heading towards middle age. With an infectious laugh she seemed to have the ability of being both serious and flippant at the same time. When talking to her she would, elbows on her knees and hands cupping her chin, devote her entire attention to what was being said, although I am certain that in those early days she did not understand half of what I was trying to impart.

When we were with her she always carried an enormous textbook full of graphic pictures with English equivalents.

"Mi Biblia," she would explain, clutching it to her ample breast.

So her 'bible' would be referred to at each slight verbal misunderstanding and conversation would cease until she had consulted her manual confirming or otherwise the correct word.

One thing that was brought home to me was that while Marilyn and I had been born around the outbreak of World War II, Manolo and Conchin had been born at the outbreak of the Spanish civil war. Whilst Manolo's mother, whose husband was fortunate enough to be on General Franco's side, was awarded a comfortable pension, Conchin's mother, whose husband fought with the Republican army, was still castigated many years later by not receiving any type of remuneration whatsoever for her old age. Anyway they both made you feel good to be with and nearly forty years on we still live within a stone's throw of each other. These immediate, no nonsense, kindly friends, took charge of us and made it their business to introduce us to all that was truly Spanish. This, I was happy to find consisted of mainly a vast variation in food, fascinating sights and of course, Las Fiestas.

*

Naturally the fiesta that evoked an important interest for me that particular year was the 'Vendimia' or wine harvest celebrated annually in Requena, some fifty miles north west of Valencia.

Would you believe it? They actually had wine gushing freely out of the local town fountain for a whole week there was so much of it. Heavy blood red fermentation that had the strong earthy flavour of the region, made your hair stand on end and could put you to sleep after a few glasses. The atmosphere was sensational.

Stands selling every imaginable cold cuts including white sausages, black sausages with and without rice, with or without onion, red sausages, whole hams, smoked and boiled. In fact everything that caused my mouth to water. And while on the subject of 'mouths' much to my amazement I even came across a stand that was selling second hand false teeth. People were actually searching through the stock and sampling them for a comfortable pair of 'choppers'. Whether or not the owner was supplied by the local dentist or the local undertaker I thought it prudent not to ask.

Manolo also took us to a nearby village, Corbera that was holding their own local fiestas which included the inevitable young, long horned, cows and, of course, bulls. These were supplied especially for these occasions on a rental basis, paid for by the town hall. At this particular 'fiesta' there was a makeshift ring in the village square made up of horse carts and iron railings fixed into place as best as possible in the hope that the animals could be contained within; an assumption that did not always appear to work.

Naturally having taken copious quantities of the local wine I decided to do what might be termed as 'have a go'. I had already seen quite a lot of professional bullfights in the past and thought I had the general idea with the cape. That was my first mistake. Forget it! These animals are used time and time again and are in no way drawn towards flapping cloths, red or otherwise. It is, as I immediately found out, the two legged human being holding the cape that is the real target to go for. Taking to the air and performing what could well have been a triple somersault, following what felt like a Henry Cooper body blow, I was subjected to laughter, cheers, jeers and spontaneous rude remarks, most of which passed me by in the dazed state I was in. Staggering to my feet I was hustled out by well meaning youths full of the local cheer. My dear wife laughed hysterically, Manolo looked grim and shook his head sadly, while Conchin, the only one to care, placed her arms around me making clucking noises as though consoling an errant child who had taken a simple fall. As they say time has a habit of dimming the memory, especially so if one was, at the time of the incident, well oiled, under the influence, or blotto. The same thing was to reccur in the future but, I am pleased to relate, under circumstances nowhere near as violent. This happened when I was actually living in Valencia. It was a time when my friend and partner in a small jewellery business was due over from the UK.

Chapter 3

It would be difficult to forget that particular summer, almost to the actual day that it began; somewhere around the middle of June, if my memory serves me correctly. There was no leading up to it as in previous years. No two days cool and three days fine and well perhaps tomorrow, but better take something else to wear, just in case. That year was different. It just happened. People looked out of the window one morning and there it was. Summer had arrived like a thief in the night to steal our complacency and give us a sharp kick from behind. Not just a nudge. Oh, no! A good solid kick. A real whack. You stepped outside and you said, "Whew!" and you really meant it.

The long days went by and as it drew nearer to August things became almost impossible. It was then that Mac arrived. The BA flight from London was due in at two fifteen on another suffocating afternoon. I cursed my way out to the airport wishing that my old car had, at least, some sort of air conditioning apart from open windows. At the airport there was the usual wait and I treated myself to a cold can of beer. Eventually they announced that the plane had landed and a little later he came striding through from the customs, his usual cool self mixed in amongst all the general hustle and bustle. Taller than most and blessed with craggy Celtic features he looked more suited to sporting a kilt than the light coloured sports jacket and trousers which he was wearing. He spotted me and with that deliberate but casual walk he always uses when approaching the first tee at the golf club, he came over. No emotional, Latin embracing and back slapping that was going on around us. No. Just a formal handshake which said it all.

"Hello there, CJ. How are you?" I smiled up at him as he marked a good couple of inches more than me.

"Fine thanks, Mac. Good trip?"

"Yes, no problems, old chap."

We passed through the electronic doors, grabbed the illegally parked car from under the noses of the airport police and were soon heading back to Valencia. Airports are always a few degrees cooler than the cities they serve and Valencia was no exception.

Mac struggled to remove his jacket. "Bloody hot, CJ."

"Yes, but it will be a lot cooler where we are now heading," I said fixing my seat belt.

My apartment is pretty large by any standards, with an office, four bedrooms etcetera and a ceiling three metres high. The lounge-cum-dining room faces south and the opposite end north. So with the windows open at both ends it usually guarantees a reasonably cool atmosphere.

We deposited the cases in his room and quickly made our way out again and across the road to the local bar where the air conditioning was humming away in top gear and the first breath was like inhaling icicles after the heat outside. It was, for a change, quiet in the place and we commandeered a couple of stools at the bar. I ordered two lagers which were served in tall glasses that had been kept in the freezer. We both sat there looking at them, and Mac ran his finger down the outside of the glass as I had seen John Mills do once in a film years back called, 'Ice Cold In Alex.'

"Cheers, CJ." Decision made he raised his glass.

"Cheers, Mac. Nice to see you. To see you nice."

We chatted about nothing in particular. Just bringing each other up to date on what we had been doing. The afternoon passed pleasantly with just enough conversation interspaced with laughter and moments of silence, a true sign of companionship. My wife, Kathy, had prepared an evening meal and later over a couple of nightcaps we went over the various points for our business meetings that would take place during the coming days.

"Well, what's on the agenda first thing tomorrow, CJ?" Mac asked, sitting back and relighting his Martin pipe for about the tenth time.

"'Bye Bye Rat', at Commercial Almi," I replied.

"Bye Bye what at where?" he asked, meticulously damping down his favourite tobacco mixture.

"It's a new machine that this company wants us to market for them," I explained. "Apparently it makes a supersonic noise out of the human hearing range that drives rats crazy."

"Really, CJ?" He sounded most impressed. "And where do they want us to locate these machines. In the local town halls?"

"There are many who like to see that," I agreed, laughing. "But really they are built for bakeries, warehouses that store food stuffs. Those sort of places."

So I refilled our glasses, we drew up a list of possible outlets and then retired to bed.

*

At eleven the following morning we presented ourselves at the offices of the commercial organisation. The two brothers who ran the company were there to welcome us and following the introductions, together with the inevitable coffee, we sat through a short feature film on the effectiveness of the 'Bye Bye Rat' machine. It was pretty horrifying with frightful scenes of the vermin trapped in wire cages attacking each other in an effort to get away from the diabolical black box nearby which was producing some sort of supersonic noise completely out of our hearing range. Of course all present agreed that if it was that effective then there would be no problem on the marketing side of things.

The two Almi directors also discussed the various possibilities of our promoting in the UK a selection of jewellery items that were manufactured locally.

Towards lunchtime the usual aperitifs of wine and smoked ham appeared and then at around two o'clock all four of us headed towards one of the more prestigious restaurants in the neighbourhood, of which there were many. Mac, I think, enjoyed it all and would try most things that were placed in front of him. However after several days of this and on being presented with an array of more appetising dishes than usual he commented, "The business part is not too difficult, CJ, It's just the bits in between like this that are tiring." And so the week passed and we managed to place 'Bye Bye Rat' in several bakeries and a food warehouse that belonged to a well known Valencia food chain. At last the weekend arrived.

"Fancy a bit of bull fighting?" I asked, as we sat in one of the local bars.

Mac's bottom lip protruded slightly as it always did when he was considering a serious point. "Can't say that I really agree with it, CJ," he replied. "But having just said that, it might… well be an interesting experience."

*

The village of Siete Aguas or Seven Waters derives its name from the natural drinking   fountain in the centre of the 'Pueblo'. There are seven

29

outlets, set in an array of decorative ceramic tiles, from which pours a constant flow of mineral water from the mountains. This particular fountain enjoys its popularity for the fact that in the hot summer months the mineral water gushes forth at a teeth aching freezing temperature, whereas in the winter, for some reason, it comes out warm enough to bathe in. Opposite this fountain the village boasts one of the finest ponds in the Valencia Community. With its spotlessly clean ducks, geese and swans it is the centre of attraction for all visitors, particularly the younger ones.

The permanent population there is usually around fifteen hundred but in August and particularly during the 'Fiestas' this figure increases to a noisy several thousand or more many of whom arrive from all parts of the world for the local marathon held on a long hard course through the mountains to the north west. One of the regular winners of this competition was from Kenya and when a friend, one of the organisers of this gruelling competition, was showing him the route on his first visit, the competitor requested confirmation that there were no lions around the area.

The small annex to one of the older houses that I rented on an all year basis was certainly not much to look at but had a spacious terrace at the back that faced down a long green valley completely devoid of any roads or buildings.

Here my wife and I would sit for hours sunbathing, listening to music or grilling local sausages and chops on the barbeque.

*

So that special weekend we all arrived on the Friday evening and settled in. After a brief snack on the terrace Mac and I wandered around the village watching with interest the preparation for the following day's great event. The whole square was being invaded by horses and mules drawing carts and wagons. These were formed into more of a square than the usual circle but still, however, reminiscent of the Wild West films. The animals, after discarding their burdens, were then led away noisily protesting at the amount of unaccustomed activity. As spectators watching all this happen, it naturally evoked a thirst so that a visit to the local bar was called for. After many introductions and much handshaking Mac and I settled ourselves in a corner with a couple of chilled San Miguel beers.

"Plenty happening, CJ," he observed, looking out of the window at several men hammering and roping together huge wooden posts to form a barrier.

"Yes," I agreed. "They cut the street off at each end, let in the 'vacas' or young calves, that apart from wide spiky horns appear to be blessed with an extraordinary amount of bad temper and antagonism towards two legged humans who goad them by waving rags at them, poking them with long poles or anything else that takes their fancy. That's in the morning.

The afternoon is when they get down to the serious business with a real full grown bull and talking of that I did hear that the beast they have lined this year is a real baddy."

I pointed down to the square which, as they had cut the traffic, was now a wonderful playground for what seemed all the village children. "They let the beast loose in the square down there, made up of those wagons. And you see that platform in the middle?" I indicated a square wooden flimsy looking stage about five feet in height. "That's where the young bloods take refuge from the animal. Of course," I added, "a height of five feet to half a ton of very angry pot roast is not at all difficult to jump. So we should see some action."

*

Next day dawned as it should be with bright sunshine and that sharp tang of mountain air to brighten everyone up after the night before celebrations. At around eleven o'clock the traditional rocket was fired and together with the rest of the clients we hurried outside of the bar to watch the release of the first young cows into the street.

There was a lot of "Hu! Hu! Toro!" accompanied by shrieks and screams from the girls when one of the animals made any sign of movement in their direction. It was early on when one calf, with wide spread horns, managed to force its way through the beaded curtain of a house whose negligent owner had failed to secure the door. The crowd went quiet for a moment, anxiously listening to the banging and crashing sounds of splintering objects that were coming from within. Then much to everyone's delight the errant owner leapt out of the window and ran to the barricade accompanied by the shouts and cheers of the onlookers. There were even more cheers when the startled animal put in an appearance some moments later. And, of course, the wine flowed. Wine skins were passing from hand to hand and anyone who did not throw back their head and participate in swallowing the dark brew was regarded with suspicion. Mac, I could see, was enthralled.

Lunch consisted of 'bocadillos de tortilla'. The crusty bread, still piping hot from the oven which used wood gathered from the local orange trees as fuel. The rolls, stuffed with potato and onion omelette, melted deliciously in our mouths. We savoured these back at the apartment sitting comfortably under the sunshade whilst watching a family of eagles gliding high above the Sierra de Los Pinos on the far side of the valley. It was all very pleasant.

At around five o'clock I suggested that we make a move.

"Lead on, CJ," said Mac, curious to know what was happening as a sudden violent explosion rent the air together with a high pitched sound of the local municipal band bursting into action.

I personally think it was the next part of the proceedings that led to the incident that is still clear in my mind even today. However, I cannot remember whether it was Mac or I that actually found the temporary bar that was selling half pints of Mr. Gordon's beverage mixed with tonics at ridiculously cheap prices. Anyway, both of us anxious to avail ourselves of this delightful discovery rapidly consumed several of these explosive mixtures. We might well have stayed there but at one point a mighty shout went up followed by more cheers.

"Come on," I urged, "it's started!"

"Wait a minute. What about the drinks?" asked Mac, as usual having his priorities in their correct order of things.

"We take 'em with us, of course," I said, pushing him out into the street.

Blinking in the dazzling sunlight after the dark interior, we could see people everywhere. They were behind the carts and wagons, on the carts and wagons and even under them peering through the wooden spokes. All intent on watching the action unfold before their eyes.

I then spotted a space on one of the wagons. "Come on, Mac. Up there!" I shouted above the din.

So up we climbed still clutching our drinks and making ourselves comfortable, at the same time feeling reasonably safe. The sight before us was breathtaking. Quantities of yellow sand had been spread over the area and the wooden platform was absolutely packed with youngsters mostly sporting bright red handkerchiefs signifying their 'Afición' for the bulls. At that moment all eyes were riveted on the horse box that had been reversed into the far side of the arena. An expectant hush descended on the crowd as two men in blue overalls appeared and started wrestling with the heavy ramp to the rear of the vehicle. A third, his arm in a sling and large plaster across his face, stood by shouting instructions and I heard someone say, "That's Paco, the owner. He got that lot when he turned his back on the bull last week."

Finally the ramp fell with an almighty crash and for a moment nothing happened. The blue overalls ran for the barrier and stood next to Paco. Everyone seemed to be holding their breath. Next a heavy thump, thumping noise from inside the vehicle and the whole thing started to sway back and forth. As the bull had been pushed into the box head first it came out backwards, slithering down the ramp and falling onto the sand. Then struggling to its feet it stood squinting in the strong light after the darkness inside the vehicle. Next, without any warning, it was off like an express train accompanied by enthusiastic encouragement from the crowd. All muscle it would have topped any scale at six hundred kilos. But what stood out more than anything as it careered around the ring was that it lacked one horn. Where it had been at one time there was just an ugly stump. The other one, however, was an almost perfectly formed, sharp deadly instrument that the animal was making full use of, hooking and slashing at everything that came within range. The one word that came to my mind when I saw the beast was, 'mean', very mean. Several times the bull almost overturned the platform on which the boys clung together. And the girls shouted and screamed even more so as several of their boyfriends nearly came to grief caught by the savage brute.

Mac and I watched fascinated at the spectacular enfolding before us from our privileged position. The atmosphere was charged to fever pitch of expectation. And, of course, the sun now being high in heavens ensured that the heat took care of our drinks.

"What about a refill, CJ?" Mac asked, waving his empty glass.

"Good idea," I agreed. "Let's do it!"

Now that was the easy part. The difficulty came as a disaster, brought on by the effects of Mr. Gordon's gin. It hit Mac like a sledge hammer. He stood, staggered to the side of the cart and then toppled gracefully onto the crowd below.

When I eventually arrived down by the more conventional route people were helping him to his feet, brushing him down, slapping him on the back at the same time offering their wine skins for revival purposes.

"Think I hurt the old back a bit, CJ," he said, groaning and at the same time rubbing the affected part.

"Well if you want to we can return to the flat for a rest."

"Good Lord no, dear chap. I wouldn't miss this for anything. And besides that a refill is called for."

We found our way into the now quiet bar, presented our glasses and asked for a couple more half pints of G & T. There in a reasonably quiet corner we sat discussing the events.

"Ready for another-basin full, Mac," I asked.

"Lead on, CJ."

Once again outside we saw that our places on the cart wagon had been commandeered by others. "Where do you want to go, Mac?" I asked.

"Seems less crowded over there," he observed pointing to the other side of the square.

"Don't like pushing our way through this crowd," I ventured. "Especially all the way over there."

"Who says anything about pushing our way through that lot, CJ," he scoffed. "Right across the middle we go. That's what I say."

"You're mad!" I said. "Complete suicide."

"Well not quite right across the middle, CJ. Let's say just a little bit to the left."

"It's still in the ring, Mac, and that bloody animal doesn't look at all happy."

"Come on, old chap," he persisted. "Won't take a couple of ticks and the beast is down there by the church."

"Alright," I relented, "but let's make it quick!"

We eased our way through the crowd carefully carrying our glasses that were full to the brim and launched ourselves across the arena. Initially, what with all the movement we did not attract much attention as there were always people jumping in and out from behind the barrier shouting, "Toro!" But after some steps many eyes turned in out direction. And that, unfortunately, included the bull's. Next it was all happening. A roar went up as the animal came charging across towards us. Dropping my drink I just ran and from behind the barrier turned horrified at what I might see. Now I have never seen Mac run in my life and this was no exception. What I saw I could not believe, and remember there were several thousand witnesses. Instead of taking to his heels, Mac just stood stock still and faced the bull. Feet together, glass held in his left hand he raised his right arm, palm towards the animal. And believe it or not the animal skidded to a halt.

That massive half ton of flesh stopped some five metres from where Mac stood. The only thing that gave any sign of movement from him was his lips.

"Probably praying," I thought.

Then the bull was off once again, flying across the arena to where several spectators were flapping cloths. Mac then turned and strolled casually over to the barrier where I stood trembling. It was quite unnecessary for him to force his way through the crush of spectators as the people moved respectfully to one side as he passed.

"Near thing, CJ," he said, raising the glass to his lips from which, I was willing to swear, not a single drop of liquid had been spilt.

"Near thing," I gasped. "I can't stop shaking."

"Anyway," I asked, "I thought I saw your lips moving. What the hell did you say to it?" His eyes reflectively turned towards the bull as if an old acquaintance had just bid farewell.

"Oh that, CJ," he replied slowly.

Then dismissing the whole ghastly incident with that insufferable air of nonchalance, he smiled.

"I just said, "We are not going to hurt each other are we?"

*

Actually the event was not as surprising as most would like to believe. In the last century, around the nineteen thirties and forties, there was a famous matador, Rafael Gomez Ortega, who made his name by placing a chair in the middle of the ring and just sitting there while the bull was released. His theory in that the bull does not normally attack an inanimate object must have been correct in that he died in retirement at the age of seventy-eight.

At the moment that this particular bull charged there was a great deal of movement, particularly on my part, whereas Mac stood completely still and did not attract the bull's immediate attention. Anyway suffice to say that, apart from a bruised back and a monster of a hangover, Mac was alright and we returned to Valencia on Sunday evening. It was on the Monday morning that the phone calls began coming in from where we had placed the 'Bye Bye Rat' machines. Apparently the customers confirmed that although there were no signs of any rats, the machine had resulted in attracting a fair number of cockroaches and the odd cat or two. So it was, at that time, really 'Bye Bye Rat' machines.

Chapter 4

Back at my first 'Taurino' attempt in Corbera, Conchin had sympathised with me over my bruised body and pride. It was from then on that we decided that the rest of the holiday would take on a more relaxed form and that the following weekend we would visit one of their relations somewhere up in the wilds of Almansa region, towards Albacete. I was told that Almansa was famous for some obscure battle involving Austrians, French, and of course, English, several centuries ago but for what I never found out.

Again it was a sweltering hot day when we set out and as there was a group of us we used two cars with me following Manolo's Seat. Some sixty miles from Valencia he turned off the main road and wound his way over to what appeared to be semi desert land, totally lacking in any type of trees, vegetation or even a road that I could see. Keeping well back because of the huge dust cloud kicked up by the other car we eventually arrived at what can only be termed as a ramshackle farm that looked as though it required the services of a Sam Seven missile to put it to rights. It appeared, mainly, to be constructed of earth and stones. Here and there I could see an interesting selection of grasses and plants actually growing out of the walls. Nature, it seemed, was making an all out attempt to reclaim what must have been the last farm for miles been around. In fact, only some two years later, I received the news that the place had actually succumbed and fallen down around the family's ears, precipitating an unwanted move to the nearest town. To one side of the main building there were several, equally derelict outhouses and one solitary tree, beneath which stood, believe it or not, the inevitable donkey.

"Looks like someone has been in touch with 'Rent-a-Set-up', especially for us," I commented to no one in particular.

I do not remember much about the family but can recall that there were numerous children, possibly due to the absence at that time of

Spanish television. The meal that they were preparing for us was 'Gazpacho Manchego', a speciality of the region. Totally different from the cold tomato soup 'Gazpacho Andaluz', this one consisted of rabbit, chicken and partridge together with flat torn off chunks of unleavened bread all together in a sauce that you could almost stand your spoon up in. It was prepared in a clay and brick oven next to the huge fireplace, rather like a good size 'Inglenook' in which one could sit very comfortably with feet outstretched towards the glowing embers. With no door the oven was liberally stuffed full of dry wood which was then set alight. When the crackling blaze died down the hot ashes were brushed to one side and the cooking was done on the hot, flat, slab base. The thick combination of meat and sauce together with the bread was delicious.

While we were eating, seated around a heavy wooden table on various rickety, what appeared to be home made, chairs and quaffing the equally home made wine, one of the shepherds came in and sat apart from us feeding in the fireplace. I was told later by Manolo that we were the first 'foreigners' he had ever set eyes upon. The woman of the house, who Conchin introduced as her sister, then prepared a large thick slice of the flat bread onto which she spread the mixture of Gazpacho and wrapped it up rather like an outsized Cornish pasty. The lean, wiry old shepherd's face broke into a toothless grin as she handed it to him. Then removing his cap, he said, "Gracias, Señora. Muchas gracias." Next carefully stowing the package away into a large, battered leather satchel in which, I assumed, he carried all his belongings, he slipped away as silently as he had appeared.

Manolo nudged me as the door closed behind the old man. "There's enough food here for three days out on the hills with the goats," he said.

Later, after the meal, I was ushered up the narrow staircase to one of the many bedrooms set under the eaves and as I fell onto the extremely lumpy mattress, befuddled by wine, I looked up at the ceiling which had no plaster whatsoever and examined the dry canes and grass sticking through like some vast vegetable collage. Moments before drifting off into a dreamless 'Siesta' I remember seeing a pair of young lizards chasing insects in one corner of the room.

*

The holiday drew to a close as my bruises healed and we said our goodbyes a few days later, promising to keep in contact and return the following year. It was on the day that we left that Manolo took me to one side.

"Listen, Chris," he said seriously, "if you have any ideas about moving over here, permanently that is, then I promise that I will help you all I can."

That short explicit sentence I was later to find out was true. What I also found out through hard earned experience, was that when there were complications with official matters, two phrases were constantly employed. One was, 'There is no problem' which I rapidly grew to learn signified, 'There is going to be a problem, and a big one at that, and the other, 'I have influence in that direction.' This I learned to read as the claimant had no influence at all and certainly not in that particular direction. The best ones were those that quietly said, "I can't promise anything but will see what can be done." These usually came through with something positive.

*

Once again in England my wife and I returned to our respective professions, grew steadily apart from one another and were finally drawn into a stormy divorce. Fortunately no children were involved so we went our separate ways although it could not have been said 'satisfactorily' by either party.

It was around that time that Mary appeared on the scene. She has never ceased to remind me that my first words as she climbed onto the bar stool next to me in one of Woking's popular clubs. I remarked, "Hello. I'm not usually this tall. I'm sitting on my wallet." You know, believe it or not, she actually laughed and had me laughing as well. I thought that if anyone can do that and without any effort they must be great company. Mary was divorced and had no ties, so after a few weeks of going out together we eventually decided it would be more convenient and even more comfortable if we set up home. So this was done and we continued living in the Surrey area until around a year later, for my work purposes, we moved to the Midlands.

*

The first year of living in the delightful village of Kibworth Beauchamp to the south of Leicester, Manolo and Conchin came over to visit us and as sometimes happens in such cases, I was treated to seeing more London sights that I had ever set eyes upon before whilst living in Wimbledon years previously. After two pleasant weeks all four of us returned to Spain by car and passed another agreeable holiday there. Actually this one served to unsettle my UK life style and stimulate my imagination as to what type of business would suite me in Spain. Not being absolutely conversant in the language limited the possibilities. However, having said that, I was prepared to consider anything that would release me from driving back and forth to Birmingham most days and visually coming across the awful amount of traffic accidents that occurred with the fog and ice on the motorway around Spaghetti Junction. This was not helped by the fact my duties included visiting the Birmingham Accident hospital and personally seeing the resulting injuries.

*

In the spring of that year a curious incident occurred. One restless evening, after arriving home having witnessed a multiple pile up on the M.1, I wrote letters to various breweries expressing an interest in taking a pub with the idea that in the event of finding one I would not be travelling anywhere for at least six days a week. At that time I was led to believe that tenancies for pubs were at a premium and thus dismissed any positive response. However one morning the phone rang and Mr. Worth from Watney's Brewery, Northampton invited us to attend an interview the following week.

"No harm in that," I thought, agreed and made a note in my diary.

The next morning at exactly the same time Mr. Worth telephoned again and asked if we would be interested in attending an interview.

"I thought we agreed yesterday to see you next week?" I said, rather surprised. There was a silence at the other end and then he said, "Oh, really. What day did I say?"

After confirming the details as the man had obviously no recollection of our previous conversation, I said to Mary, "That Watney's sounds awful good beer."

The following Tuesday morning we drove down to Northampton and having time on our hands, stopped at a charming but rather run down inn not far from Market Harborough. With its old world appearance it looked as though with a bit of money there could be possibilities. An hour later you can imagine our surprise when we were actually offered that particular pub.

What a coincidence we thought. Then both of us being of an adventurous nature we accepted the offer, married, sold up our lovely home and moved into those grotty premises. Never will I forget the first morning when I staggered down stairs into the bar nursing a king size hangover after the previous night's celebrations.

"What the hell have I got myself into now?" I asked myself, seeing the mess and breathing in the stench of old beer and stale cigarette fumes.

It took only a short time for me to realise what I had, indeed, got myself into. The term to be applied would be 'Instant problems'. As the breathalyser was coming into full force at that time I requested that the brewery grant me a licence for a dining room. The answer was negative as this would distract customers from consuming their products and there would be little or no benefits from the food sales. This certainly curtailed our business .In a village of no more two hundred and fifty inhabitants much of our trade was derived from outsiders and the prospect of travelling any distance just to drink was daunting to say the least, Can you imagine it nowadays trying to run a pub without food? Australia's Slim Dusty's song about the pub with no beer could now equally be applied to the pub with no food.

So after a couple of years arguing with the brewery and some pathetic structural alterations which included a set of shelves that would only accommodate Gordon's gin bottles and nothing else in the spirit line, we decided that now was the time to seek sea, sunshine and new pastures to the south of the Pyrenean mountains. Here I would mention that the Stag's Head, Maidwell, Northamptonshire where the brief interlude took place, is now a thriving free house and far removed from those bygone days.

*

While waiting to sell the tenancy I drove over to Spain with an architect friend, Graham Batty, and completed the purchase of an apartment in Cullera. It was at the time the UK, was undergoing a monetary crisis (when was it not?) and we were all subject to the 'Dollar Premium'. I never really understood why it should have been named after another currency when it was our problem, but there we are. Everyone going abroad at that time was limited to taking with them only a certain amount of sterling. Everyone that is who did not have the facilities of transferring money to accounts in other countries under the guise of business commitments. So the ordinary people were the 'fall guys' as usual.

At that time a friend's wife discovered that her husband had invited another woman to travel with him to their chalet in Marbella for a short holiday. But instead of the usual immediate confrontation that would normally have occurred, the wife telephoned the powers that be at Dover. Then when her husband arrived, the welcoming committee asked him to step out of his car and removing the carpets, discovered to his dismay and their joy, as the informant had been correct, around five thousand pounds. Duly confiscated and with a heavy fine it put paid to that particular amorous adventure. Me, I stuffed my boots with bank notes and on arrival at the `Banco de Madrid´ in Valencia, removed them, placed them on the counter and asked that they be deposited into my account. The staff, being full aware of the UK situation fell about laughing. On that particular trip I met Reginald Bowler who, due to his involvement in buying and supplying fish through a Valencia company, we renamed Reggie the Fish. And it was through Reggie that I came across an unusual rarity that existed in Spain at the time and does so even today, but to a far lesser degree of effectiveness.

Chapter 5

If June could be hot in Valencia, then July and August could be murder. One required plenty of nerve, stamina and a tough constitution to step outside between the hours of one and four in the afternoon. The heat picks you up, spins you round, and then slaps you down, leaving you gasping for breath. Nowadays, of course, the large department stores have modern air conditioning which encourages you to linger just that little bit longer and spend just that little bit more. However sooner or later, richer or poorer, you are going to have to make that decision to chance an Olympic sprint across to the shady side of the street. Apart from the disorientated tourist just nobody walks on the sunny side, at least not at that hour. Newcomers to the city consult their watches and nod knowingly to one another in the belief that the astronomical temperatures, often up to and over the thirty degrees centigrade mark, cannot be expected to continue right through the afternoon and into the early evening. It really must ease off around five o'clock. Relief is on the way. No chance! That is precisely the moment when the 'Poniente' announces its presence. This blistering, peppery, dust laden, West wind that comes storming across the plains of La Mancha, turns the city into one vast concrete tumbler dryer. Grit flies into your eyes, clings to you hair and turns your throat into sandpaper. Of courser, if you work in an office or shop, then you make the journey to and from home as painlessly as possible and forget what is happening out there. If, on the other hand, your livelihood demands you be outside, then it is a very different matter. This is the case with the 'Limpiabotas' or the shoeshine boys. For them there is always business to be had in bars and cafeterias, amongst the senior citizens enjoying their 'Tertulias' or coffee meetings. Never the less the extra pickings are that much more acceptable if they are prepared to brave the elements out along the sidewalks. For them the

'Poniente' is a pain in the neck, but certainly not lethal as it can be for others.

Apart from the national holidays the people of Valencia celebrate their own 'Fiestas' in March and July. The 'Fallas' in March, estimated to rate amongst the world's largest festivals is, naturally, the most important. Valencia has a whole industry dedicated solely to this 'Fiesta'. Supported by the numerous factories producing fireworks of all types, the city has maintained its position as possibly the noisiest place in Europe in the week leading up to Saint Joseph's day on the nineteenth of March. Lines of giant sized squibs are strung out along the city streets then detonated at midday and the evenings. Even larger fireworks, that on the decibel scale that would rate alongside eight inch shells, are launched into the air at specific times with extraordinary effects on dogs, cats, pigeons and unwary pedestrians. The catastrophic impact on ones hearing leaves little to the imagination.

The second most important Valencia 'Fiesta' takes place in July and it was during this particular month that I was there when the 'Poniente' blew with a savage force that few had encountered before. Celebrations were in full swing and every afternoon before the magic hour of five o'clock, the 'Aficionados' gathered in their hundreds to see the bullfight or 'Corrida'. The three matadors on that particular afternoon's program were quietly anxious about the 'Poniente' which came in short sharp gusts swirling the grains of sand and tugging at their capes. Everything was being done to weight these 'Muletas' with copious quantities of water being poured onto the bottom of the cloth.

This, it was hoped, would lessen the risk of the cape being blown against the matador at the crucial moment when the bull charged. Everyone knew that when this did happened the beast instantly follows the lure and this could mean big trouble for the matador. He could find himself sailing through the air and if he were lucky enough not to be hooked onto one of those deadly horns might suddenly find himself beneath a half ton of angry bull intent on staking him to the ground.

So we all watched and waited expectantly. I was seated on the popular side surrounded by the most ardent of fans. My ticket had stated optimistically 'Sol y Sombra' indicating that by about the third bull I should be sitting in the shade and be able to discard my paper hat. It was the second bull of the afternoon that created the most excitement. Antonio Ordoñez, principal matador, had just executed a series of beautifully slow artistic passes and was completing the 'faena' with a classic 'paso de pecho' or chest pass, when the wind plucked at the cape. Fortunately the wide set of horns on the huge black Pedro Domenech bull were past but the muscular shoulder of the beast caught him. Ordoñez felt the side swipe of one thousand two hundred pounds in weight travelling at the speed of an express train. The man sailed into the air enveloped in the cape then landed heavily onto the sand. The bull pivoted with the agility of a polo pony and was on him. Ordoñez could do little more than cover his head and pray that the back-up team would not be slow in coming out. Striking wildly to the left and the right those razor sharp horns sought the man.

The crowd leapt to its feet, women screaming and men aghast at what was happening to their idol. But as fate does sometimes decree, the bull distracted by the flapping capes of Ordoñez's 'Cuadrilla', the danger was past and he survived with a severe bruising, a ripped suit of lights and a slight dent in his ego. Minutes later he went on to kill cleanly with a fine 'estocada' and received two ears. I remembered that moment some years later when in nineteen ninety five when this stylish bullfighter was able to lay claim to being the first ever matador to receive the French 'Legion d'honneur'.

So it was at that moment when the crowd was breathing a heartfelt sigh of relief that, for some reason, I glanced across the ring and saw the man for the first time. Perhaps it was because he, amongst all the continuous movement, remained completely motionless, that drew my attention. However, having said that, it would have been most difficult for him not to have drawn anyone's attention in the crowd. An imposing figure, dressed in a bright scarlet, fully buttoned, ankle length coat the colour if which accentuated his Negroid features and on his head a black military styled beret.

Seemingly oblivious as to what was happening in the ring, he stood like something carved out of stone, gazing fixedly at a group of people nearby. Below Ordoñez was sighting the bull for the kill and two minutes later I looked up and the man had gone. That brief incident struck me later as being completely unreal, so much so that I almost began to believe that in all the excitement of the moment I had imagined the whole episode. However, only four more days were to pass before I saw him once more.

It was just after eight o'clock in the evening when some of the shops and offices were closing. Traffic was nose to tail along the Colon edging its way slowly forward in the direction of the bullring and the railway station. Then out of the blue there he was again. Still in that outrageous attire he was striding purposefully along the crowded pavement looking neither to the left nor to the right. Closer to him that I had been on the previous Sunday I was able to observe the intenseness, the same impassioned expression of concentration as he strode along. However what struck me most of all was that nobody, absolutely nobody, was taking the slightest bit of notice of the man. In fact it was quite amazing to see that as he advanced furrowing a path through the tide of citizens, they just simply moved to one side averting their eyes elsewhere, almost as though the figure was some harbinger of bad news and not to be looked upon. I eventually lost sight of him as he abruptly turned off in the direction of the Gran Via. "That," I thought, "was that."

And so it was, until I called Reggie the Fish one evening who much to my delight, gave me the good news. He had managed to come by two free tickets for the bullfight the following Sunday. This in itself was a feat, in that the principal matador would be the now very popular Manuel Benitez or to many 'El Cordobés' and even more so as 'El Beatle' by virtue of his particular hairstyle. Free 'Entradas', for this particular Corrida, were gold dust.

"That's really great news," I said, enthusiastically and meaning it. "Where shall we meet, Reggie? How about the Metropol?"

This grand hotel was situated directly in front of the bullring and had been for many years the place for the 'Aficionados' to gather, be seen, wrangle over the various merits and more often to criticise, the matadors, the bulls, their respective breeders and the 'Corrida' in general.

"No, not the Metropol," Reggie's voice crackled over the phone. "It's a no go area for me."

"A what area for you?" I asked, puzzled.

"A no go area, Chris. Banned for life and all that. Understand?"

By the tone of his voice something serious had happened at sometime or other. "What went wrong, Reggie?" I asked.

There was silence for a moment and I thought we might have been cut off. Then he said, "That author fellow, Hemingway and myself. Well you know how it is?"

"Sorry Reggie. I don't know how it is," I persisted, knowing that he had, at one time, enjoyed the famous writer's friendship over the years both in Spain and Africa. "You tell me how it is, or rather was, Reggie."

He coughed and I could imagine him sucking on one of those awful 'Peninsulares' cigarettes. "Well," he explained, "Ernie and I had been down to the beach for a paella at the Pepica restaurant and you know that old

Chinaman who has been around the area for years. The one who sells toys and things?"

"Yes," I said, my curiosity now thoroughly aroused, "I know the one you mean."

Reggie coughed again. "Well, Ernie insisted on buying a couple of water pistols from him."

"And...?" I ventured.

"And," went on Reggie, "when we got back to the Metropol, Ernie had the barman fill them with gin."

Another lengthy silence. Then digesting what he had said I asked, "Who did you spray, Reggie?" visualising him and Hemingway, well into their cups after a lunchtime session at the beach, charging around Valencia's most prestigious hotel with water pistols full of gin. A moment's hesitation and the voice at the other end came through lamely, "The Mayor, Chris. Only the Mayor."

"OK," I said, stifling a laugh. "Let's forget the Metropol and make it the Barrachina in the Plaza Caudillo." So we agreed on a suitable time and said our goodbyes.

*

Nowadays Spain's developers are dedicated to satisfying the untouchable car manufacturers and with the construction of supermarkets, hypermarkets and super hypermarkets etcetera in the suburban areas, it has contributed to the demise of many city centres, Valencia included. What used to be the very core in respect of business, commerce and entertainment has now turned into a walkabout area for pedestrians on Sundays.

During these redevelopments and inevitable changes of the nineteen eighties the city was deprived of many of its popular eating and meeting places, both pastimes being an essential part of Spanish living. Lamentably these venues included the Barrachina, the Balanzar, the San Remo and the Cafe Lauria. They all offered everything anyone could wish for in the realm of food, drink and impeccable service. It was, however, the Barrachina which was considered by many visitors to Valencia as being the most celebrated rendezvous in this south eastern corner of Spain. Some years later, when I was actually living in Valencia, many a time I have had friends telephone me from as far away as Germany, Switzerland, Denmark and other countries, of course, including the U.K, who would be passing through or staying and always the conversation would terminate with the enthusiastic cry, "See you in the Barrachina!"

As steadfast as the rock of Gibraltar the Barrachina was firmly placed next to the town hall and a virtual Aladdin's cave for lovers of good food and wine. Long marble topped bars displaying an incredible selection of snacks or 'tapas'. Baby squid prepared in its own ink, 'patatas bravas' (parboiled potatoes afterwards fried, then covered in a hot garlicky mayonnaise sauce), large succulent anchovies, giant red king prawns, small delicate shrimps and many other mouth watering dishes. A second bar offered, baked on the spot, hot crispy rolls with more than fifty different fillings. Then yet a third and fourth counters catered for clients wishing to buy gift wrapped chocolates, glazed fruits (oranges in particular), jars of peaches from the north of Spain, more jars of 'embutidos' or sausages and meats preserved in oil from the high plateau of Teruel, to smoked 'Jabugo' ham from Huelva in the far south next to Portugal, all on sale from six in the morning until two o'clock the following night.

*

That festive Sunday afternoon I headed for the Barrachina anticipating what could be an exceptional 'Corrida'. For myself there is nothing that can compare with the expectation that precedes a possibly exceptional 'Corrida'. It starts in the pit of the stomach and gradually works its way upwards until you feel that your head will burst and only subsides when you are presented with that great yellow circle of sand and the mass of colour surrounding it. On the downside however there is no feeling worse than when, after the fourth bull, you realise that this might be the moment when you are going to leave knowing that this was another bad 'Corrida' and that you have been cheated.

Pushing my way through the swing doors of the Barrachina I was confronted by the most extraordinary sight. The place was heaving at the seams. Customers milling around, waiters shouting out orders, plates and glasses rattling above the excited conversations of people, all discussing the coming event. But there, slap bang in the middle of all this mayhem, was the most unbelievable oasis of tranquillity. Seated at the far end of the bar was a smartly dressed Spaniard, wearing an immaculate white shirt, buttoned up to the throat but without a tie, together with the traditional black suit and one of those black wide brimmed hats favoured by bullfight fans. Perched on a bar stool he was sipping what appeared to be a glass of dry sherry or 'manzanilla' wine and with a small fork was spearing at some kind of 'tapa' on a small dish. Whilst I, personally, was having difficulties in forcing my way to the bar, around this individual was a clear space. In fact it was easy to calculate that he had four or five times more elbow room than anyone else in the place.

And there, standing rigidly to attention behind him, head and shoulders above everybody else, was the immaculately attired Negro in his full length scarlet coat and black berry. Arms rigidly straight down by his side, shoulders set squarely back, he stood motionless, eyes planted firmly on the man at the bar. The other was very obviously aware of his presence but was vainly trying to ignore him. However his exaggerated casualness as he raised his glass to his lips and picked at the dish in front of him, betrayed his nervousness. Once again I was astonished to see that all the nearby customers must have been well aware of their existence but were taking great pains not to notice them both. In fact everyone was looking elsewhere. Examining the 'tapas'; the Señoritas in their traditional dresses energetically manipulating their fans. Absolutely anywhere, but at the two men. With difficulty I managed to organise myself a beer and moments later Reggie the Fish put in an appearance, struggling gallantly through the tumult. I called for another San Miguel and thrust the ice cold bottle into his hand as he came up to me.

We shook hands and Reggie said, "Sorry about not being able to meet you at the Metropol but after the incident with that author fellow, Ernie, they made it quite clear that we wouldn't be made welcome there ever again."

"Not to worry, Reggie," I grinned. "I don't think there is a lot of space around here for firing gin filled water pistols." Then inclining my head towards the tableau at the end of the bar I asked, "What's all that about over there?"

Reggie smiled. "Oh, that," he said. "That one sitting at the bar is in big trouble. At the moment he has not friends and nobody will be seen anywhere near him."

"What sort of trouble, Reggie?"

"Listen, Chris," he smiled, "apart from serious illness there is only one real sort of trouble in this world. When I had my twenty-first birthday my father said to me, 'Son, never get yourself into any problem that you cannot resolve by paying money.

Secondly never make love to your wife in the morning as you never quite know what you might meet during the day.' The second has always been a possibility whilst, in my case, the former has always been an inevitability. So the main problem in life is money trouble."

Tipping back his head he took a long swallow of beer straight from the bottle and then brushing his military moustache with the back of his hand, said, "You see, the chap at the bar owes money to someone and whoever that someone is has employed the services of 'El Colorado' or the Coloured one. That's the tall fellow behind all dressed up like the doorman from the Ritz."

I glanced across and could swear that the Negro had not moved so much as a muscle whilst the man at the bar continued sip his drink and toy with the 'tapa'.

Reggie continued. "There is no way he will let him alone. Wherever he goes, the Colorado will be with him. Won't do anything but just follow him. The other might give him the slip during the day but you can bet your bottom dollar he will be there tomorrow, waiting outside his house."

He extracted one of his 'Peninsulares' from a packet and lit the cigarette, inhaling with relish. "Of course, the moment the debt is settled he'll be left alone, have all his friends back again and all will be well."

Later that afternoon when we were settled in our seats I occasionally glanced around the ring but the scarlet coat and black beret were nowhere to be seen. Perhaps the Spaniard had decided not to go after all. At the moment of writing this an acquaintance of mine, Enrique, is employed in a similar position and can be seen steadfastly going about his duties dressed as 'El Zorro', complete with mask, cape, boots, all topped off with a saucy wide brimmed hat sporting a magnificent feather. A while back there was also a Pink Panther loping around Valencia. But it is not the same now and I do not suppose it ever will be when I think of 'El Colorado'.

*

With the purchase of the apartment in Cullera completed, decorated and furnished Graham and I set out on the return journey to England. We decided to leave to at around one o'clock at night after dinner with Manolo and Conchin at a restaurant called La Venta Montiel. It was, as expected by recommendation of our friends, a first class spread topped off by a flaming speciality of the house, baked Alaska. Nowadays, naturally, we would have retired to the nearest hotel and slept off the effects of the evening's celebrations but not being of faint heart and no breathalyser enforcements to contend with, we set out for Paris.

I was driving the MGB at the time and as the weather was favourable, the top was down. It was on one of those long stretches in France, the following morning, where the roads are lined on either side with elegant trees, that we had the incident with the wasp. This vicious insect, showing total disregard for the occupants of the car, flew straight into the car on my side, sought the lowest point and then decided to exit by travelling up my trouser leg. Needless to say there was, on my part, immediate panic. I braked sharply, pulled over to the side of the road and leapt out of the car. My companion, who happened to have been reading a several days old English newspaper instantly aware of my predicament, also jumped out. As the inconsiderate insect was now threatening my most intimate parts I quickly dropped my trouser. Graham went into action and with the rolled up newspaper began to pound away at the trousers around my ankles. Now normally that would have been the end of the story as the wasp took off for pastures new. However at the moment my trousers were down and my friend was flailing away with the rolled up newspaper, there happened to pass a rather grand, English registered, Rover car. I will never forget the expression on the driver's face as he went by and then, gracefully, left the road, missing the trees with the precision of a formula one driver and ending up very much shaken, but unharmed, in a nearby field. Later explanations were offered and apologies accepted, as we ably assisted these gentile people back onto the road. Whether or not the reason for our rather unusual behaviour sounded credible to them I do not know.

*

Once again in England I was to be greeted by the news that a friend of mine for many years, Stan Warby, wished to take on the pub. That was the good news, the bad being that I had contracted some infection whilst in Spain (probably swimming in the wrong place) and was admitted hospital for a week. My recuperation was rapidly assisted by the joint idea that Mary and I buy a motor caravan, rent the Cullera apartment and travel around Spain for a while and at the same time deciding what business potential was in the offing. Actually I will be honest as the latter was only a blind really because with our limited knowledge of the language, possibilities were certainly restricted and that was in the direction of the catering trade. Not, that I hasten to add is there anything wrong with that honourable profession. Anyway we selected a Bedford Dormobile which was, I decided, as much then as now, and excellent choice. Before actually taking off for Spain the formalities had to be observed as regards the transfer of the business to Stan. This was achieved without too much difficulty although he did seem a little reluctant to take on 'Muffy', Mary's pet donkey, which occupied the paddock with around two dozen hens and an oversexed cockerel. The latter, not surprisingly, staggered out of the hen house one morning and expired at my feet. Even this incident was not without its humour as I immediately took the bird into the bar and much to the delight of several farm hands present, attempted to revive it with spoonfuls of cognac. Without any success I would add. Never mind, the following week I visited Melton Mowbray market in the Bedford and being somewhat carried away by the bidding at the auction finished up with another cockerel and a delinquent goat.

Whereas the cockerel was quite happily installed with the twenty or so hens, which must have been missing their deceased husband, the goat insisted on adopting me as its mother. Being short of stature, the goat that is, I put the animal into the stable and only closed the bottom half of the stable door. For some reason I was delayed in the kitchen of the pub until my attention was drawn to the fact that there were howls of laughter and general shouts of encouragement coming from the public bar. This was not at all unusual around closing time but early evening certainly not normal. On investigating I discovered that the animal had escaped from the stable, found its way into the bar and was consuming huge quantities of cigarettes in their packets, crisps and packets of peanuts. In fact anything it could reach. Naturally it was receiving adequate encouragement from all those customers present in the place. Finally this ungrateful beast was disposed of at a price (myself paying) to a nearby lady farmer who promised to look after it, in the manner to which it was accustomed. How long that lasted I have no idea and am not particularly interested. What did interest me however were the innumerable uses to which the Bedford motor caravan could be put. Our favourites included excursions to local gymkhanas and point to point races. What with all the comforts of space and an adequately stocked fridge, it was magic. Not too long afterwards the change over of the pub was concluded and Mary I together with our Bassett hound, moved out. Then two weeks later, after possibly outstaying our welcome at my parent's home in Leicester, we set out for Spain.

Chapter 6

The Bedford Dormobile opened up an entirely new world for me. Whereas before it was very necessary to start searching for a reasonable hotel in France at around six o'clock in the evening, we could now cheerfully continue until we found a suitable stopping place for the night. This usually involved being placed strategically near to any restaurant with an eye catching menu. One night we parked in the centre of a charming French village and after a splendid meal involving aperitifs, a couple of bottles of wine all followed by a glass of Calvados each, we fell contentedly into bed not even bothering to move the vehicle. The following morning proved most embarrassing as when we awoke it was to find that we were entirely surrounded by market stalls and with no way out. So to offset this minor problem, as most of the stall holders were not at all pleased, we set about buying various items from all the stalls within the immediate vicinity and then establishing ourselves in the nearest bar to while away the morning until the market closed at around two o'clock. This time we approached Spain via Andorra, stopping only to replenish our supplies of duty free booze and tobacco at one of the enormous supermarkets, before continuing down to Seo de Urgel and the border.

Night was coming on rapidly as we drove towards Lérida. Very few vehicles were approaching from the opposite direction and the ones that did were extremely scarce. So with the road being quite narrow I was tending to cut the corners and keeping to the centre of the highway. This was fine, until after several miles we came upon two Civil Guards motor cycle police who energetically waved us down. I pulled over and they indicated that we should both get out of the Bedford. Obviously they were well aware as to what I had been doing and remonstrated with me, all the time casting sidelong glances at Mary. I apologised profusely and they seemed to accept my reasoning that at that hour there was little or no traffic. Then the older one, much to my surprise suddenly asked if we would care for a drink in the nearby cafeteria. Needing little encouragement I parked the Bedford in the car park and all four of us wandered over to the cafe. Mary appeared even more stunning in the interior lighting of the place with her tight blond curls and blue trouser suit. Both policemen became more and more affable, especially after several cognacs. Conversation was extremely animated and anyone seeing us would have presumed that we had been friends for years.

Eventually one of them checked his watch and there was a rapid exchange of words with his companion. He then turned to me and said, "Would you like to go to a dance?"

I looked at a rather surprised Mary who played her part well by shrugging her shoulders as if to indicate that she had nothing of immediate importance on her agenda, so I said that it sounded a good idea.

"But where?" I then asked, more for something to say.

"Just a few minutes down the road at the next 'pueblo'," I was told.

So I paid for the drinks, which seemed to be expected and received my change from a grinning barman who was obviously accustomed to this situation and I we all trooped outside. The 'guardias' mounted their motor cycles and lights flashing we were escorted to the next village and the local dance hall.

The noise was overpowering and the orchestra, being more accustomed to marches, was sweating away as hard as it could go, churning out 'Cuando Caliente el Sol' and 'La Yenka'. Mary obliged our newly made, uniformed, friends by taking to the dance floor with each one in turn. One of the barmen had taken care of their headgear, and they were jigging around the floor, complete in pistols on their hips. Thinking back on the incident nobody amongst the revellers appeared at all surprised at our presence, although there were very few there who actually cared to acknowledge us. Later as the jamboree came to a close, these two very merry traffic policemen, spoke to the owner of the establishment and we were given permission to park up there for the rest of the night. Not that there was a lot of it left. "Quite a blessing," I thought, as all of us were getting quite legless and I was becoming somewhat concerned as about their ability to ride their motor cycles. However there was no need to worry as one again in full uniform they became most officious and set off with only the slightest of wobbles.

*

The following morning both of us had to contend with the most awful of hangovers and I instantly became one of Spain's most careful and considerate drivers. "Well," I thought, "if this could happen through bad driving, I really had better take it easy."

Thinking back to that incident it did occur to me that a court sentence for traffic offences that included a half bottle of one of the country's cheaper brandies to be drunk at one sitting might well reduce the amount of accidents and traffic offences.

So without further incident we made Cullera and were soon in our apartment. Final touches were added in preparation for our first rental clients who eventually arrived on time. It was then that all the information I had considerately written down for them became worthless when I found that their primary interest related to where they could buy tins of baked beans, fish fingers and hamburgers. This threw me somewhat as at the beginning of the nineteen seventies these items were not generally available. However I assured them that 'Paco's' supermarket sold cod 'croquetas', a reasonable substitute for fish fingers. So this seemed to please them.

As it was now towards the middle of summer and the heat was becoming quite intense, even during the night, we parked on the top of the mountain that lies to the rear of the town. There it was considerably cooler especially for sleeping purposes. On the very first morning we were treated to a visit by a most enormous and beautifully coloured butterfly which flew purposefully into the Bedford, settled here and there as though checking out the place, and then after some moments nonchalantly flew off again. I mention this as what appeared to be the same insect that visited us on each occasion that we chose to this overnight spot. Although my knowledge of these charming insects was limited to recognising a 'Red Admiral' or a 'Cabbage White', apart from that I was quite ignorant on the subject of entomology. However at that first morning I sensed that this occurrence was something out of the ordinary but was not to know it at the time how much these delicate creatures were to influence my spiritual sensitiveness later on in my life.

*

Having read Cervantes, and that was no mean feat when one had been weaned on Steinbeck, James Joyce, Raymond Chandler and the likes of Mickey Spillane (even now I have two copies of Spillane's 'My gun is quick!'), we decided to head towards La Mancha and Don Quixote country. On the way there we passed the turn off that I had made some years before and remembered the 'Gazpacho Manchego' feast with Manolo and Conchin. Albacete came and went and then we spotted a sign that read Muñera, Tomelloso and Toboso. Possibly for the reason that the latter was where Cervantes Dulcinea in Don Quixote de la Mancha originated, I turned off. Immediately we found ourselves following a straight cobbled road which reminded me, for some reason, of Judy Garland's 'Yellow brick road' and had me singing 'Somewhere over the rainbow'. It went on for miles and miles through fields blanketed with bright yellow sunflowers for as far as the eye could see and, as I had been forewarned, the temperature became almost suffocating. My vocal aspirations became pathetic and finally disappeared in a whisper that even the tepid bottle of spring water we carried could not relieve. It was then with no sign of any real shade whatsoever, that I saw up ahead one solitary, rather dejected tree. There I pulled up, turning into the little shelter it offered. Both of us attempted to rest on our bunk beds in the back of the Bedford, but it was hopeless. With the windows down, we were subjected to the blistering flow of hot air and with them up were left gasping for the lack of it. So once again we pressed on passing through Alcázar de San Juan, which seemed a deserted and rather sad town, until we came eventually to Campo Criptana. There, not having the strength or the inclination to go any further, we stopped.

*

Now late afternoon we found that the only place that we could find succour was the 'Casino'. Contrary to what we understand the word 'Casino' to signify in English, the Spanish also use this to denote the village club or general meeting place. And of course, as all clubs and meeting places have bars, this was fine by us.

Parking the Bedford in the largest shadow that we could find we then crossed the road and walked thankfully into this spacious bar. A multitude of fans on the high ceiling hummed, droned and swished, spreading what little air there was around the immediate area. What seemed a vast amount of tables and chairs were set out in neat rows and to the back, behind the long high, intricately tiled bar, stood the only barman as large and as solid as the surroundings. We were the only customers in the place and as though pleased just to have the company the man welcomed seemingly as though we were old friends.

"Something simple to eat and drink, por favor," I replied, when we had passed the normal pleasantries and he had asked what we wanted. Seeing that we were obviously foreign tourists he then went on to explain that La Mancha was famous for the best cheese in Spain and the wine was not too bad either. As if confirming the latter he turned and indicated two enormous, blackened, oak casks behind him.

Taking him at his word I said, "Right, a plate of 'Manchego' cheese and a litre from the cask."

There are certain times in life that one can look back on with affection when it comes to food and drink, simple as it might have been. And this was one such occasion. Sitting in the middle of this deserted, but most solidly comfortable place, we dined on chunks of hot bread and cured Manchego cheese that tickled the palate and demanded more. All this encouraged down with the heavy, velvety red wine of the region.

I must admit that when I asked him to refill the terracotta jug he looked somewhat surprised but did so with myself detecting what might have been a slight shaking of his head. But by this time we had the flavour and were happily passed the point of no return. Just that little bit more bread and a little more cheese and we felt that all was right with the world. The next stage of the proceedings involved both of us in unison resting our heads on the table and falling asleep or succumbing to the feast might be more appropriate. I remember dreaming that I was in a seemingly endless dark tunnel carrying a piano on my back. It was not so much the weight of the instrument but the fact that the ground beneath my feet was in constant motion. Each time I thought that the exit was within a few more faltering steps I then found myself back at the beginning again. And so it was that at least two hours later that we surfaced and to what a surprise.

The whole place was a complete mass of people. Every single table was occupied with families, friends and above all children who seemed to be everywhere at once. The resulting pandemonium was overwhelming and it goes without saying that many pairs of eyes were fully turned in the direction of the two foreigners who, bleary eyed and with the expressions that they were supporting sacks of coal on their heads, gradually sat up and took stock of the situation. How we had slept while that entire racket was going on could only have been thanks to the local beverage. It was during the time we were out for the count the considerate barman must have removed the jugs, glasses and plates from our table, therefore virtually covering our tracks in respect of the afternoon's fiesta. However by the smiling faces I am sure something had been said. Next, choosing the right moment when the least amount of people were staring and children pointing in our direction, we teetered over to the bar, paid and leaving just a little more than the normal tip, made our way back to the Bedford.

*

I mention that about the tipping because in Spain's interior even today to over tip would be considered rather vulgar. A couple of years before I had stopped for the night in Morella, the fortress town in the Maestrazgo region some forty miles inland from the coast.

There after having a first class evening meal, followed by a good night's sleep and breakfast the next day I was presented with a bill that amounted to the equivalent of around five pounds for the two of us. Wishing to express our appreciation I included a tip of thirty pence. The manager was most upset.

"Sir!" he protested, sliding it across to me over the reception desk, "you have paid quite sufficient. Thank you."

Needless to say I felt most disconcerted as my expression must have shown and we left feeling that we had committed some gross offence against the man's hospitality. Since that memorable lesson I have become very wary as to the amount I should leave, calculations being based mainly on the service received. In fact, a gesture really, albeit in modern times, particularly along the coast, a rude one.

*

So after retreating from the local 'Casino' and still very much woozy from the Manchego wine we climbed into the Bedford and drove up the one small hill at the back of the village. Here we parked amongst a huddle of silent windmills, almost squat human figures with their sail like arms outstretched as though waiting patiently for a kindly wind. Beneath the bright stars and into the quiet stillness of the night we sat outside at peace with ourselves and the world as it was at that moment. It must have been well after midnight when, feeling the temperature fall a little, we finally fell into bed knowing that we were being cared for by those kindly and vigilant sentinels nearby.

One of the difficulties I have found in life is not having the ability to actually realise when I am experiencing the moments that are truly important to me personally. I am certain that not one single person has not at one time or another looked back and said, "I remember what a very good time I had," doing something, seeing something or whatever. The art though, is to have an actual awareness at the actual moment that you are experiencing something extra special, the memory of which will remain with you always. That is what counts in life. And such it was with myself on the following morning when for some reason I awoke very early.

Slipping out of bed I pulled on my shorts and jumper for the air outside still carried that sharp, but not disagreeable, nip to it and slowly made my way over a carpet of pebble strewn ground, past those pale white windmills, towards the eastern side of the small plateau. Here I stood with the scent of another hot day in the offing and my attention, tinged with anticipation, drawn towards the east and the coming of the dawn. Above me the stars were slowly surrendering their lustre and like small lanterns disappearing one by one while the previous night's new moon became a fading thin semi circle of light suspended in the heavens. In front of me the sky began to change almost imperceptibly, giving forth indistinct pastel shades of lemons, greens and blue greys. These in turn succumbed to warmer rosier hues as the sun gradually announced its presence on the distant horizon. Standing there gazing out over this vast Manchego plain in the company of my windmill friends to the rear, their sturdy limbs outstretched, welcoming the new day as they had done for hundred of years, I suddenly felt spiritually at one with nature, the universe, part of all that had passed, all that was present and everything that was to come. For many people the epitome of Spain is represented by the castles, the palaces, the bulls or the flamenco dancing. However, if anyone now asks me my own particular choice I always say, "Those few kindly windmills standing on that small knoll behind Campo Criptana, in the midst of Don Quixote country." Later, before setting out that morning, we plucked up courage and drove to the 'Casino', where with a welcoming smile from our barman friend, we fortified ourselves with hot coffee and croissants.

*

The sun was well into the heavens and promised a further scorching hot day as we drove towards Toledo, passing Consuegra, which translated means the relationship between two sets of in-laws whose sons or daughters are married. What a name to give a village; it evokes all sorts of ideas as to where it originated. It was there on a lofty ridge that looked as though it had been modelled on the humps of the Loch Ness monster that we were treated to seeing a line of eleven windmills like little old men, also vigilant and waiting.

A little later we rolled into Toledo and began our tour of the city by becoming almost stuck in one of the many narrow streets. With some difficulty I managed to reverse out we found a car park and took to walking.

El Greco's house, now a museum, was high on our list so assuming, correctly, that it would certainly be cooler inside there than out in the dusty streets, in we went. It was a delightful place with wooden floors and plenty light. Although I am not a dedicated admirer of the artist, too many elongated faces hands and feet for my liking, we found the atmosphere most pleasant and choosing one of the smaller rooms, sat on a seat and silently admired the artist's work.

All was well, which for some reason until that moment had remained closed, the door was thrust open and in trooped an elderly uniformed guide followed by an enormously fat American. He was an incredible sight, almost as though he had stepped straight out of a Giles cartoon in the Daily Express.

Open necked multi coloured shirt to rival Jacob's coat was tucked into his Bermuda shorts, the belt invisible beneath his bulging stomach. A pair of sandals, together with almost knee length socks, came up to his ample knees. All this was topped up by a grinning, many-chinned red face and over all, perched on his head, a huge Stetson hat. Around his practically none existent neck hung a multitude of objects. There were cameras, extra lenses, binoculars and a large satchel. He was unbelievable, unreal. Not in Pop Mercer's wildest dreams could his imagination come anywhere near to what presented itself in El Greco's house, Toledo, on that particular day. And, of course, to top it all the man possessed a voice to go with his image.

"Ya see!" he was speaking to the guide, his voice raised to its loudest pitch, as though the man were a deaf imbecile.

"Ya see! Right der off da coast o' Florida!" he bellowed, jowls wobbling frantically.

I was convinced that the guide had no idea what he was talking about, however the man smiled and nodded.

"Yup!" went on the American, his face beaming, "A Spanish galleon. Reckon 'bout ten miles from der coast an' in 'round a hunred, ya a hunred foot, o' water."

At that point he glanced around the room and spotted us. To his great joy he now had a ready made audience and this discovery animated him to raise his voice to an even higher pitch.

"Ya know whaat?" he went on. "Doubloons. Stacks o' them. All down der whaat youse guys left behind!" Here he dug a podgy finger into the guide's chest. The other just smiled again and nodded, probably thinking about his expected tip.

"Waddya tink a dat? Just waddya say hu?"

The man was grating on my nerves now and I could not resist responding. "Possibly," I said, "but all those doubloons could not buy one of these works of art." Here I nodded to the paintings.

He looked around the room as though suddenly surprised at the fact the walls were covered in works of art.

"But ders millions o' bucks down der, I'm tellin' ya, Mister. Millions!" He glared over at me.

"Yes, but all of that could not buy just one of these pictures," I repeated.

He was silent for a moment, just staring at me, his beady eyes assessing the situation. Then suddenly his face broke into a huge grin, his bulbous lips parting as he called, "Ah get ya now, Buddy Boy. They jest 'aint fer sale!"

Later outside both of us fell about laughing and every now and then one of us would say, "They jest 'aint fer sale, Buddy Boy!"

*

With me having a tendency towards being a latter day Dickension McCawber, the next 'something to turn up', happened very quickly. Being attracted to a small bar from which floated the strains of a deep baritone voice singing a fair, but slightly distorted, version of 'Paliacci,' we met Gomar and Betty Ann Davies. In we went and after a few glasses of the local wine I was tempted to participate in this spontaneous entertainment and both Gomar and I received considerable applause together with several refills from customers who, if their hearing was not sound, there generosity was.

This captivating couple, it turned out, came from Swarthmore, (No we hadn't heard of it either), Philadelphia, USA, and were touring Europe. Gomar, who would have made a great prop forward in any rugby team, was a dark handsome chap whose family originally heralded from Wales. Apart from being the wrestling coach at Swarthmore University, he was doing everything possible to cling to his Welsh roots. He proudly explained that the Welsh valleys, to the rear of Cardiff, were on their list of 'musts' this time round. Betty Ann was a sweet trim, petite, woman blessed with an irresistible Irish smile. Her maiden name was Mulligan and her brother the jazz saxophonist, Jerry Mulligan. Betty Ann's strict Catholic mother was going to be sorely troubled when, a couple of days after our meeting, Gomar insisted on taking photographs of a nearby, rather sleazy, establishment called the 'Jesus Bar' and mailing them to her. So we made immediate friends and decided to travel around together in the Bedford for a few days.

Segovia was another of our first ports of call. And what a pleasant surprise awaited me. Until that memorable moment I had only seen storks on margarine packets and to my joy there on the chimney tops were the real things For me it was fascinating to see these gangling, awkward birds on their stilted legs tending their nests and taking clumsily to the air every now and then in search of food. I could watch them for hours. Needless to say we took photographs of both the storks and the viaduct. But even that was not quite like the windmills of Campo Criptana.

Another joint trip took us to Avila and as we approached the walled city of Santa Teresa we found ourselves looking out for the gap in the ramparts that was the result of the magnificent efforts of Gregory Peck, Sophia Loren and Frank Sinatra in the film 'The Pride and the Passion'. That particular evening we dined in a basement restaurant not far from the cathedral in front of which was the fountain onto which Gregory Peck placed Frank Sinatra's body at the end of the film. The region's speciality was 'Chuletas de Avila' or as we know them, T-Bone steaks. There together with the neighbourhood wine both Gomar and I felt in fine fettle and treated the customers to a varied selection from our repertoire. However, much to our disappointment, we found that our spontaneous operatic entertainment was not so well received there and were politely asked to pipe down or hit the road by the owner.

Then following more halcyon days it was necessary that Mary and I return to Cullera for the purpose of organising the apartment in readiness for the next lot of visitors. Sadly we said our 'goodbyes' to our new friends and promised to meet up in Cullera at some later date.

*

It was midway between Madrid and Valencia that we decided to visit the Parador at Alarcón. This state run hotel was a small but magnificent castle which contained all the trimmings worthy of such an establishment. Suits of armour, selections of colourful flags, each with their intricate coats of arms and all around the place good solid Castilian furniture that weighed heaven knows how much. Accommodation wise there were just five bedrooms which were nearly always booked.

We arrived late afternoon with the idea of having a wander around, a couple of aperitifs followed by dinner and a night's sleep parked somewhere nearby. As we pulled up I noticed a young couple standing next to a splendid, all chrome Harley Davidson motor cycle that they had parked on the drawbridge. Climbing out of the Bedford we stood nearby drinking in the wonderfully wild scenery and at the same time admiring the fine old castle. Next thing a voice called out.

"Hi there! Youse guys English?"

Then without waiting for a reply the leather bedecked man called out again as if feeling the need for and explanation, "Ah was just checkin' out yu' plates."

Here he inclined his head in the direction of the Bedford.

"Right," I confirmed. "Yes, we're English."

Tall, fair haired, probably not quite thirty-five years old but still maintaining a boyish smile, he was dressed in all the appropriate biking gear including a pair of knee length boots that you see the American cops' wearing in the films.

"Ya hear that, Sue Baby?" He turned to the girl who had probably not yet seen her thirtieth birthday and was very much shorter than he. I looked at her and thought for a moment that she was carrying one of the cannon balls that were piled up nearby next to old pitted cannon, but it turned out to be her motorcycle helmet.

"Ah said, these guys was English, didn't ah, Honey?"

Sue Baby nodded her head but did not look too pleased to see us. She then reached into her jacket and drew out a packet of Camel cigarettes.

"Sure did," she confirmed but, I noticed, a note of despondency in her voice.

The man came striding over and thrust out his hand. "Real nice to meet youse guys."

Then before I could say anything he added, "My name is Mickey. Mickey as in Mouse dat is!" He burst out laughing and I smiled politely at the same time wishing I had a dollar for every time he had cracked that one.

"Chris," I said, taking the hand and returning the vice like grip. "And this is Mary."

"High there, Mary." I saw my wife visibly wince as he grabbed her hand.

"Sue Baby, come on over and meet these nice folks," he called over his shoulder.

Sue Baby came over and offered around the Camel's.

"Hi!" she said. "Are you the guys that have the reservation at this place?"

"Waat!" exclaimed Mickey as in Mouse, before I could answer. "Wid dat trailer. Don't reckon so honey."

"Quite," I confirmed, "we have the...er trailer."

Sue Baby's freckled face broke into a smile. "Gee. That's great. Then I reckon the room must be ours." She sounded relieved.

"Don't never stayed in a real castle before," explained Mickey. "We're kinda doin' Europe yu know? A year off. Sabbatical and all dat." He indicated the Harley and we nodded making the appropriate comments.

Then Mickey said, "Tell ya wat. Let's all go take a drink."

"Now that seems a most reasonable suggestion, "I said, also smiling.

"Hear dat, Sue Baby. Da way youse guys talk. Just like da movies. Really slays me."

*

Later as we consumed drinks at the bar, Mickey went off and booked in then returned saying he would be 'mighty pleased' if us 'guys' joined them for dinner. We accepted and after a couple more drinks went out to change for the meal. The Bedford, not being on the same scale as the American 'Trailer', we took it in turns to organise ourselves and while I was standing outside admiring the arid surrounds Mary called out. "What do you think Mickey Mouse does for a living?"

"Don't know," I mused. "But he seems a dead ringer for a New York taxi driver. Remember he said they were from the Big Apple?"

Parador Hotels are state run establishments in Spain and unlike the equivalent in many other countries that usually lack something or other in respect of food, service or whatever, here they are great. The meal was superb. Just to be sitting there in that imposing dining room was in itself a pleasure.

It was when we had reached the coffee and brandy stage, with Sue Baby lighting up one of her inevitable Camels, that Mickey suddenly said, "So waddya do fer de filthy lucre, Chris?" Remembering my encounter with Americanisms through Mickey Spillane, I told him that we had just sold the pub in England and before that I was with MSD, the large American drug Company from New Jersey, USA; he seemed quite impressed by this.

"Sue Baby here is a teacher," he offered. Then looking pointedly at Mary and me asked, "Waddya think I do?"

We were silent for a minute not really knowing what to reply so he pressed on.

"Some people think I'm a teacher as well. Others think I'm a lawyer or CIA, a cop even. Waddya t'ink?"

More silence. Then unable to resist I said, "I think you're a New York cab driver."

His mouth dropped open and thrusting back his chair he stood up,

"How da hell you'd know dat?" he exclaimed staring down at me. "Der ain't nobody never got it right!"

Sue Baby was grinning and Mary hid her face in the table napkin after delivering me a sharp kick on the shins. I then mumbled something about seeing a film recently and that he resembled one of the main actors who was a New York cabby. He sat down again but I could see that he was still very much astounded.

After breakfast next day with Mickey and Sue we said our 'farewells' and the last I saw of them in my rear view mirror was Mickey staring after us with a puzzled expression on his face and Sue lighting up a Camel.

"Ah reckon ah could really get t' likin' this sort of thing Mary Baby," I said, as we made tracks for Valencia.

*

Manolo and Conchin were the first to welcome us. Smiling more than usual, Manolo said, that he had found some ideal premises within walking distance of Benidorm centre. Great for the barbeque business in which we both envisaged.

"The only trouble," he went on to say, "is that the agent handling it is an American and a bit of a smooth character. But he seems fairly straight forward on the formalities. Must be doing alright. I made some enquiries and he has just bought another newer aeroplane."

"Aeroplane?" I asked, puzzled.

"Yes, a Piper Comanche or Cessna, one of those. Keeps it down in Alicante."

"No problem," I said, "we just play it carefully. You keep an eye on our apartment and in the next couple of weeks when we return from England we go straight to Benidorm and see the man."

"Fine," agreed Manolo, "but just one thing."

"What's that?"

"You'll need a much larger size in shoes if we are going into business."

Chapter 7

On our return to England we reluctantly parted ways with the Bedford by selling it to a friend, Brian Phillips, who lived south towards London. Together with vivid details of our adventures in Spain that went with the sale, Brian was most impressed and determined to visit the country himself.

However for Brian the opportunity did not arise until sometime later as he had a young family, a business to run, and was very much involved in the local town council activities. When he finally made the memorable trip it certainly was not the adventure that he had envisaged. What lay in store for him I would not have wished on my worst enemy.

It happened something like this.

When Brian came to pick up the Bedford we had naturally done everything possible to make the vehicle look attractive. In fact it was immaculate. Already a caravanning enthusiast Brian was used to dealing with the problems of towing another vehicle so from now on this was to be very different. He eventually arrived home, parked in the drive, and a little later was dutifully showing his family this latest acquisition.

"Look, it has everything that 'Old Slowcoach' had, and more besides," he enthused to his not so eager wife, Barbara. 'Old Slowcoach' was, of course, the previous non-motorised caravan the children having christened it thus because it was always trailing behind them.

"Fridge, cooker, large cupboards, loo, shower, plenty of electric plugs and a TV, point."

Barbara sniffed irritably. "So we still don't go away from home. We take the damn place with us as usual!"

"Don't swear in front of the children," Brian reprimanded and turned his attention to them. Michael and Jane were, naturally, most excited by the new addition to the family. Even more so when their father promised them that they could sit in the rear at the table and play games, whilst he drove.

"You wouldn't let us sit in 'Old Slowcoach' and let us play, Daddy," said Michael, the eldest at nine years of age and quick to point out any adult shortcomings.

"That was because 'Old Slowcoach' had to be towed behind the car," explained their father, "and it is not allowed. Now this......," here he ran his hand fondly along the side of the Bedford, at the same time looking meaningfully at his wife. "Now this is different. In future you two kids will not be sitting in the back of the car fighting like cat and dog. No, you can sit at the table and play games. And what is more, if you are good." Here he hesitated to let the words sink in before continuing. "Very good that is, you can even help yourselves to the occasional ice cream from the fridge"

"Yippee!" cried the children in unison and Brian was pleased that he had a majority support, even if it might turn out to be only temporary.

"I hope we are not going down any muddy tracks near that smelly old farm where the man charged you for pulling us out of the ditch that time," put in Jane. "And afterwards you wanted to stop and kick one of his cows, but mummy wouldn't let you."

"No, certainly not," said Brian, a little dismayed at his daughter's ability to remember such disturbing incidents. Then casting a sidelong look at his wife who appeared to be taking a little more interest in the interior of the vehicle, he said, "No, in fact I was thinking that as this is like driving a normal car and nothing like towing 'Old Slowcoach' then we just might, sometime, in the future that is, consider going to Spain."

"Yippee!" they chorused again and immediately began lobbying their mother to agree.

Later after the initial excitement had died down and with Brian being involved in his business and council duties, trial long weekend runs involving Devon and Cornwall were the focus over the next few months. Then one winters evening as they sat warming their toes in front of the fire the subject arose again about where to go that particular year and Barbara's answer was, to her husband's suggestion that Spain might be the place.

"All those bulls and nothing but paella to eat."

"Come on darling," Brian encouraged, "it's not like that at all nowadays. Look here." He rapidly produced, to his wife's surprise, his sales aid in the form of the latest caravanning magazine.

"Look at this," he stabbed a finger at some of the photographs. "Sandy beaches, campsites with everything laid on like supermarkets, hot showers, swimming pools. And here," he pointed to a colourful map, "Costa Brava, Costa Azahar, Costa Blanca...."

"And Costa 'Fortuna'," sniffed Barbara, interested but not at all convinced.

Ignoring the pun Brian continued. "No, they don't tiddle about down there like they used to. They know that with the good rate of exchange the Brits are the big spenders."

A minutes silence and then he added as an afterthought, "And of course half the price of a holiday in Torquay."

"And what about the kids?" persisted Barbara, still far from being won over. "What if they catch something, have upset tummies or get.... what's it called, Montezuma's revenge?"

Brian reached over and placed a reassuring hand over hers, "Look, darling, we take all the usual precautions like Harry and Marge across the road. Last year they went all the way to Italy with their four kids and here was not problem. Anyway Montezuma's revenge is what you catch in Mexico and I don't fancy driving across the Atlantic." Barbara allowed him a smile which was, at least, to Brian, some sort of encouragement.

*

There was a meeting of the local Caravan Club the following evening and Brian, who had been looking forward to hearing the guest speaker voice his experiences on 'Twenty-five years of Continental Caravanning,' realised that it coincided with a council meeting. The latter, naturally taking preference was to be about the proposed spur that connected the town with the new motorway some three miles distant. Brian could see that the meeting would be terminated fairly quickly, or so he hoped. The only other item on the agenda of any significance was the official announcement of Hamish Dagliesh's retirement. As chairman of Broughton Wesley town council, Hamish had decided that his business, together with his wife's failing health, took precedence over his official duties in respect of the town's future.

A dower, anglophile Scotsman, fondly referred to as, Citizen Kane, he owned and ran the local newspaper with a high principled Presbyterian rod of iron. His rough cadaverous features, together with his habitual tweeds, were an indication that he would just as well be at home tracking highland deer as organising the town's only daily publication. None-the-less, even with his staid right wing views, the local socialists and SDP disciples begrudgingly agreed that over the last decade or so Hamish had interpreted both local and world news, at the same time helping to guide the town towards a commercially successful new twenty-first century. Brian had already been collecting signatures and other details for the proposed OBE, and all had agreed that it would be a foregone conclusion.

*

Towards the end of his speech Brian said, "And as we go about our daily business, let us be ever mindful of Mr. Dagliesh's dedication to making our town a better place for everyone."

Even as the words fell from his lips Brian observed the increasing smiles on the faces of his fellow councillors and realised that he sounded as though he was rendering grace more than bidding a formal farewell to Hamish.

The chairman responded warmly to their applause and warned that whereas he might be forsaking most of his ties with the council he would, however, still be very much present in a vigilant capacity through the Advertiser. He then did as he had habitually done over the years when making a point, removed his spectacles and let his gaze pass over all present as though challenging them to dispute his words.

"Let us look forward to having some new blood, gentlemen," he intoned. Then in order to demonstrate that Brian's biblical tone had not gone unnoticed he added, "I personally feel there are those amongst us who are hiding their lights of initiative beneath that proverbial bush. Thank you very much gentlemen."

He naturally received a standing ovation and Brian, in the capacity of secretary, a few minutes later declared the meeting closed. He then joined in the small talk that followed after which, judging the time right, bid everyone good night and headed towards the door at the same time as Hamish.

As they stepped out into a light drizzle that had come on, Hamish placed a fatherly arm around Brian's shoulders. "You've done a first class job over the last couple of years, my boy, which has given you a good insight into how things work in our community and I personally feel you would make a good chairman, even if you are a bit young and impetuous at times."

Brian held his breath and resisted moving to put up his umbrella. They walked towards the car park and Hamish continued, "You see, most of the others, although they have the town's interests at heart, they still tend to treat their duties more as a political game of chess."

Brian smiled inwardly as that was exactly the way Hamish behaved at times. They had now reached the chairman's old Jaguar car parked alongside Brian's Bedford and Hamish releasing his arm, turned to look at the younger man. "Take Arthur Allard," he said. "A nice enough fellow but the way he behaves at times."

Brian nodded without saying anything.

"The thing is," went on Hamish, "he has a lot of popular support from the others. A capable man in his business, I understand, but not the sort of fellow I would choose."

He glanced around as though Arthur Allard might be lurking somewhere nearby. "Divorced twice you know?"

"So I believe." Brian allowed himself, at the same time thinking, "It's not that Arthur is divorced or that he spends time at the races. No, it is because at that time Arthur was studying the form of an eligible local filly in the shape of Shirley Honeyworth. And it just happened that Shirley, senior reporter on the Advertiser was, by coincidence, Hamish's precious niece. Apart from this, being single and in her late twenties, she was a favourite runner in the Broughton Westly marriage stakes.

"Anyway, my boy," Hamish was saying as he pulled out his car keys, "better get yourself organised, get into gear and encourage more support."

Brian put up his umbrella with a forceful, "Yes, Sir. You can rely on me."

The old man climbed into the car but before closing the door said, carefully, "And keep your nose clean, Councillor, especially if you are thinking of gallivanting off to foreign parts in that machine." He nodded towards the Bedford that appeared to be standing nearby with a rather smug expression.

The Jaguar's engine burst into life, the window came down and as the car moved slowly away.

"Don't let that Allard put a spoke in your wheel, Brian," he called, as the other stood there watching the car swing out of the car park, the exhaust leaving a significant vapour trail and left Brian, wondering how Citizen Kane managed to have such an insight into things.

*

The Bell Hotel, Broughton Westly, was a large rambling place that some two hundred years ago might have laid claim to being a successful coaching inn. It had two massive wooden doors that had been open for as long as anyone could remember. Behind these a cobbled courtyard served as a car park, in one corner of which stood a stone horse trough and on this provider for now non-existent thirsty animals was inscribed 12.04.30. Nothing whatsoever to do with the hotel's historical background it was just of the many curiosities that had arrived with the present landlord. The date just so happened to be his date of birth.

The hotel's eight, rather drab, draughty, bedrooms were in the main frequented by commercial travellers who appreciated good beer, good food and preferred a pleasant atmosphere more than elegant surroundings. The Bell hotel was also the adopted venue for a very enthusiastic group known as the COAL club. Not, as some might think, a gathering place for the town's coal merchants, but a pre breathalyser circle of friends, firmly dedicated to the Consumption of Alcoholic Liquor. The main bar was, indeed, comfortable with a worn faded carpet and the inevitable stone fireplace. Upstairs a large wood panelled room served for functions, having a stage at the far end. And it was here that the Caravan Club held their meetings.

Brian's luck was still in as he found a parking space in the courtyard and was soon pushing open the door to the warm, friendly atmosphere within. Then nodding to a few friendly faces he climbed the creaking staircase and was just in time to hear an enthusiastic round of applause. Swearing under his breath he realised that he had totally missed the main event of the evening. The place was crowded; possibly because with summer not being far off many members had the urge to flee the doubtful English climate and so had come along to see what it was all about. Brian stood by the door unsure whether or not to return to the bar when a flash bulb exploded and he saw that the Broughton Advertiser was in evidence with the charming presence of Shirley Honeyworth.

*

People were moving around and gathering in small groups, most clustering about the speaker of the evening, a tall spindly, balding man, whose shiny pate reflected the overhead light like a beacon beckoning the pro continental caravaners to better holidays. Making his way over to Shirley, Brian, received acknowledgements from several of those present. As he approached her he could not help admiring her slim tanned legs that disappeared into a neat grey skirt. Head purposely bent over her notes her naturally wavy hair insisted on toppling into her eyes so that every now and again she would reach up and push it firmly back in place. Her nose could have been that little bit smaller but her lips compensated. They were generous lips made for kissing and had a little pencil line around them as if to indicate to the lucky partner their exact location. Fine, almost invisible eyebrows arched over grey green eyes that reminded Brian of the old film star Googie Withers.

All in all Shirley was a very attractive woman. However as with some physically attractive women there was a catch and sadly Shirley's shortcoming was aptly portrayed in her voice. Not only was it pitched just that much higher than normal, almost to the tone of an old record played at speed, but also there was an added burden of a speech defect. No matter how she tried Shirley had certain difficulties with her pronunciation. After a while one became accustomed to this and in its way it was almost endearing. But initially it could be most disconcerting.

"Hello, Shirley," said Brian, touching her on the shoulder. The head rose and the grey green eyes looked up at him. "Hello, Counshillor," she said.

This reply would not normally have bothered anyone else but as Brian had always, in his premarital past, secretly hoped that their relationship just might have developed into something more than just 'good friends', Brian was irritated.

"Oh, come on Shirl; don't be like that with me. The name's Brian. Remember?"

She laughed and reached up to push back her hair. "Wash the matter. Do I embarrish you?"

Brian stuck his hands into his pockets and hunched his shoulders. "You might have done in the past," he said gallantly, "but it would take more than titles to embarrass me now."

Relenting a little she moved her handbag from the chair next to her and patted the seat.

"Come on then. Sit down."

He obliged saying, "Tell me about the talk. I've just arrived." Here Brian winked, "Citizen Kane and all that." He then smiled and they both laughed.

"Won't be a tick," she said. "Chust finishing my notes."

Brian sat quietly wondering if Arthur Allard was, in fact, dating her. "If so," he thought, "Arthur was certainly a lucky devil."

Eventually closing her note pad Shirley turned her attention to him. "Tell you what," she said, "invite me for a beer downstairs and I will reveal all."

"All!" exclaimed Brian faking a look of amazement at the same time letting his attention fall onto Shirley's ample bosom. "And in the bar at the Bell hotel to boot! I can't wait to see the Advertiser tomorrow."

"Alright, Brian," she said smiling, "you can make that a large gin and tonic."

"Ouch!" said Brian, coming to his feet and clasping his hand to his forehead. "Come on then before I get waylaid by someone with problems."

"Too late," hissed Shirley looking over his shoulder, "I can see Shyril Outhwaite heading thish way." Brian rolled his eyes at the ceiling.

"Oh! I really don't deserve this!"

"'fraid so Brian. See you in the bar."

Gathering up her things she stood, moved away acknowledging the approaching Cyril with a friendly nod.

Brian turned and was immediately immersed in a dense cloud of smoke issuing from an old pipe that Cyril seemed to have permanently clamped in his mouth.

"Evenin' there, Councillor," said Cyril. "Didn't think you 'ad made it 'ere tonight."

Brian accepted the proffered hand. "Hello, Cyril. I just arrived actually, so I missed it."

Then in an effort to divert the other's attention from any problem he might have in mind, Brian said quickly, "Shirley was just telling me how interesting it was. What did you think, Cyril?"

Cyril sucked earnestly on his pipe. "Well weren't too bad ah suppose. That's if yer like it. Ah personally don't 'old much wi' them forin places. Not afta wot 'appened in Spain, any road up."

Brian was suddenly all attention, ignoring the fumes that were issuing from Cyril. "Spain?" he said, "What happened in Spain?"

"Tha'll not 'ave me near ruddy place agin'," Cyril replied, puffing furiously and sending out more smoke signals than ever. "Dusty, 'ot, flies and ruddy police wi' shiny 'ats t'every corner."

"What made you go there in the first place?" enquired a puzzled Brian.

Cyril leaned forward and lowered his voice, "Mi missus and mi daughter," he confided. They both went an' fell fer a ruddy 'and kissin' ruddy waiter at Orchard 'otel. Said 'is family 'ad a big farm near Barsi-ruddy-lona."

Brian was intrigued. "And did they have a farm?"

"Naaaa!" went on Cyril. "Not what you'd call a real farm. Rabbits, that's wot they 'ad. 'Undreds of t'little buggers all t'over place. All in big wire cages. 'Orrible it was!"

Brian realising the conversation was not quite going the way he would wish asked, "Did you find any decent campsites. I mean did you stop at any of those places along the coast?"

"Aye, lad wi did that. An' what 'appens? Tha' little sod of a daughter o' mine wanted t' run off w' site manager. Ah knew summat worrup t'way he kept cummin' up t'see all wa' alright wi' lass. And her wantin' ter go barbe-qu-in an' dancing t'every night."

Brian concluded that the intrigues of Cyril s family affairs was not going to be in the least bit of help as regards his intended holiday so he commiserated with Cyril a little more and under the guise of urgent council business took his leave.

"Wot abaart mi drains?" shouted Cyril, realising he had been duped, as Brian headed towards the door.

"All under control," called Brian over his shoulder. "All under control."

*

The cosy hum of conversation welcomed him in the bar and the COAL club members were happily sampling a new brew from Flowers Brewery. To Brian it would have been even more comfortable if John Brooker had not been monopolising Shirley's company. As he eased his way towards them Brian saw John lean over to whisper something in Shirley's ear and they were both laughing when he arrived.

"Well, hello there. Hope I'm not interrupting anything special," he said.

"Not at all, old son," said John, offering his hand. "Just having a chat with Shirley here. So what's your poison?"

Brian nodded towards the COAL club group who were now whooping it up at the far end of the bar. "Whatever they're having. By the noise it should be pretty good stuff. And anyway I need it after fifteen minutes with Cyril Outhwaite."

"Two pints of what the lads are drinking, Ted," called out John.

Ted Walker, the ex-RAF landlord, sported a wonderful well trimmed handlebar moustache under a large nose that was now showing signs of dedication to his trade. Always impeccably turned out, Ted usually wore a black blazer complete with the expected badge and trousers with knife-like creases. Apart from his dry sense of humour, customers were attracted to him by his manner of speech. No, not an impediment like Shirley's. Ted's pronunciation was fine but he had the habit of intermingling his conversation with, "Ho!"

So naturally, when John ordered the two pints Ted automatically came up with "Ho! Two pints for the use off coming up. Ho!"

Then nodding towards Brian, Ted asked, "Ho! And how are we this evening, Councillor?"

"Lay off the Councillor bit, Ted," responded Brian. "I'm getting enough flack from Shirley here."

The two pints were placed in front of them. "Just a little respect. That's all. Ho!"

Then Ted turned to Shirley. "And anything for Broughton's Ace reporter? Ho!"

"Yea," said Shirley, "Counshillor Phillips ish inviting me to a large gin and tonic."

"Is he indeed!" cried Ted. "Ho! Then a large G and T it will be."

Ted went to work and when Brian was about to pay John produced a healthy looking wallet and placing a well meaning hand on Brian's arm said, "I'll see to this round."

Nobody argued but Shirley glanced at Brian meaningfully as if to remind him that their agreement was still on.

Once his fist had curled around the pint glass Brian said, "If I remember correctly you went to Spain last year, John?"

John, a few years older than Brian, possessed a pale serious face, belaying a wicked sense of humour and clear blue eyes permanently framed in a pair of horn rimmed spectacles. Brian could never really determine if these were for his eyesight or convincing people that he had genuine intentions.

"Sure did, old son," said John. "Way down the Med. coast. Got as far as Tarragona. Actually, come to think of it, just past there."

"Tarragona?" repeated Brian.

"Yep, past Barcelona. Reckon about a sixty miles further down. Bloody marvellous."

He grinned at Shirley. "Found a great campsite," he continued as if anticipating Brian's next question. "Place called San Carlos something or other. Nice little fishing village. Lovely beaches and not a lot of Brits. Mainly Spanish, some French and a couple of Germans. Really magic."

His eyes twinkled behind his spectacles as if re living the pleasant memory. Brian's interest heightened and he made a note of checking out San Carlos something or other.

"Any nudish beaches?" asked Shirley, out of the blue.

And it was then that Brian realised where Shirley cultivated her healthy tan on her arms, legs and heaven knows where else. He had heard rumours that she was a subscriber to a naturist camp in the next county, but found it hard to believe that anyone related to Hamish Dagleish would indulge in such things. At that moment he was tempted to say, "I bet Citizen Kane wouldn't like his niece asking such questions," but instead said, "Naughty, naughty!"

Shirley stuck out her tongue. "Counshillor, Fuddy duddy."

Brian repented. After all he needed all the help he could get for the council campaign.

John was smiling at the exchange. "Actually there is one I believe," he offered, "but a little bit further down the coast."

"Tell me," demanded Shirley, "I'm all earsh."

"And the rest," thought Brian.

"Nothing much to tell really," said John. "Just some bumph we picked up at the tourist office."

"Photos?" persisted Brian.

"What of the nudist camp?" asked John.

"No, of course not. Just photos in general. Of the holiday."

"Yes. But I think that Beryl might have taken them when she went back to her dear old mother."

"Why?" asked Brian taking a swallow of his beer.

John looked puzzled. "Why did she go back to her mother?"

"No, Idiot!" said Brian. "I just thought that if you had any photos of the trip then I was thinking of inviting you around for dinner next Saturday. I'm sure that Barbara would love to see them."

"On my own you mean? John's eyes moved in the direction of Shirley, who was now sharing a joke with Ted.

"Of course not. Bring Shirley along. That's if she is not already spoken for next Saturday."

They both looked at Shirley who, in keeping with her profession was quite capable of carrying on a conversation whilst listening to another at the same time.

"Achually," she said, turning to the two men, "I've already been invited out."

Then when their expressions changed, she added, "But I can always speak to Shitizen Kane and put it off if you like."

All three laughed, two of them for more reason than the third.

When Brian arrived home the house was in darkness. Quietly he let himself in, climbed the stairs and after checking the children's room, silently undressed and slipped into bed next to Barbara. "Awake, darling?" he tentatively enquired.

A low mumbling from beneath the sheets added encouragement.

"Would it be alright if John and Shirley come round for dinner on Saturday night? Council support and all that."

A sleep befuddled and somewhat resigned reply rose from the depths. "Alright, Councillor. Good night."

*

The following day was a fresh, late spring Wednesday and Brian drove happily to work. His loans and insurance agency was thriving and having recently taken on an enthusiastic, capable partner, in the form of young Alan Cartwright, Brian found that he could devote more time to his important accounts at the same time ensuring watchfulness in respect of council activities. Towards mid morning he telephoned John. "O.K. for Saturday then?" he asked brightly.

A rather hung-over husky voice answered, "I think so, old son." Then after a brief silence it added, "My teeth itch."

"Really," said Brian, not following the others train of thought.

"Head aches as well," said John.

Brian laughed, "I suppose you stayed on last night with the COAL, club?"

"I think so. Or must have done."

"You mean you cannot remember?"

"Vaguely, old son." Then a little more lively, "By the way I've found those photos we talked about."

"Great," said Brian, "Will you confirm with Shirley or shall I?"

"Don't worry, old son. Leave it with me." I just hope that she hasn't had a call from the AA."

"AA?" repeated Brian, somewhat puzzled. "Alcoholics Anonymous?"

"No, Idiot. Arthur Allard."

*

At the same moment Brian was talking to John, Barbara was making a call to her mother. "Look, mother. Brian is still hoping to get the nomination for Chairman of the Council."

"I could think of a few and far more practical nominations for that husband of yours," interrupted her mother.

Barbara ignored the comment and continued. "Anyway we are having some people around for dinner on Saturday and we wondered if you would be a sweetie and put up with Michael and Jane for the night?"

A heavy sigh found it's was down the line.

"But darling, you know that I normally have people around for bridge on Saturdays."

"I know, mother. But this is really important for us. Do try and understand. You know they won't be any problem."

A silence, then, "Alright, darling. But tell Michael not to pick his nose in front of my guests."

"Mother! Michael never picks his nose in front of anyone!"

"I know darling. But I'm just making sure. Bye!"

*

Early Saturday evening saw Brian industriously preparing an exceedingly large jug of Martini. This consisted of two bottles of dry vermouth and one bottle of gin, with plenty of junky cubes of ice and slices of lemon.

"A pre dinner aperitif to make everyone happy," he observed enthusiastically.

Barbara, who was hard at it in the kitchen, had heard this on many previous occasions, finished this comment for her husband by adding, "And it keeps them from hammering the brandy afterwards."

"Quite correct, my dear," confirmed Brian, ignoring the sarcasm.

Not so easily put off Barbara asked, "Does it ever occur to you, dear husband, that 'Hello and would you like to try my speciality that produces what is know as 'Legless guest syndrome,' which in turn encourages them to drink everything in sight, including the after dinner cognac?"

Here she rattled some dishes in order to make her point while Brian, unable to come up with any suitable reply, remained silent.

Eventually John and Shirley arrived, the former still a little frayed at the edges from the previous night's session at the Bell whilst the latter looked as radiant as ever. Brian's Martini hit the right spot and soon all four were looking forward to the meal. For the main course Barbara had prepared a Beef Wellington which was to be accompanied by a bottle of red Spanish Cotino.

"I'm assured that this particular Rioja wine should be more than adequate," observed Brian, pouring a little into each glass, after they had seated themselves at the table. Then maintaining the momentum for the Spanish project, he turned to John and asked his opinion. John, adjusting his spectacles, smiled and theatrically prepared his palate by dabbing his lips with his serviette. Then raising the glass to the light he gently swirled the liquid around. "Certainly full bodied," he murmured. "Clings well and definitely a good colour."

Next he buried his nose into the glass and sniffed. "Fine elegant bouquet. Aroma of dried plums with overtones of toffee." Then tilting the glass against his lips he took in a fair amount, moving the contents around and making the appropriate noises. Finally he swallowed, and again wiping his lips with his napkin said, "Tempranillo grape, matured in oak. Well balanced flavour with just a slight suggestion of liquorice."

Here he reached for the bottle and placidly filled his glass. "Definitely a first class wine but at around six pounds per bottle, a little on the expensive side."

Apart from Brian who looked a little taken aback, the others all chorused, "How did you know that?"

"Oh!" said John lightly, "Quite easily really. I just followed Brian into Westminster Wines this morning and the fellow gave me the same sales pitch!"

At a loss for something to say while the others were laughing, Brian asked, "So it's still a good wine then?"

John winked at Shirley. "In fact," he replied, "I think I would be quite justified in awarding it, at least seventy-five points on the CPI rating."

Brian's eyebrows rose. "And just what the hell is that?"

John grinned. "Councillor Phillips Incentive rating, of course. Has something to do with the town council committee. Right Shirley?"

"Yesh, definitely," agreed Shirley. "You could buy shum good shupport with a wine like thish." Carefully she picked up her empty glass and examined it thoughtfully. "Speshially if there was a bit more of it."

Later, when the two women were clearing the table, feeding the dishwasher and organising coffee, Brian poured himself and John a large Martell each.

"Thanks, old son," said John. "Feeling much better now."

As they were both sampling the cognac Brian asked, "Got the photos then?"

The other withdrew from is pocket a thick yellow envelope and placed it purposely in front of them.

"There you go, old son. They're all there. Sorry but quite a few of Beryl and her mother," he said, unable to conceal a little bitterness in his voice. Then, raising his glass, he took another drink as if attempting to drown unhappy memories while Brian opened the envelope and spilled out the contents onto the table

"P'raps that's where things went wrong between us," John nodded towards the brightly coloured images.

Brian not wishing to go too deeply into his friend's marital affairs, still could not resist commenting, "Nothing to do with me, John. But taking your mother-in-law on holiday with you in the first place was a bit much, I thought."

John sniffed. "Well it didn't seem such a bad idea at the time. Particularly as she was paying for half the trip."

Brian persisted. "But camping, John."

At that moment the coffee arrived and while it was being handed around Brian slipped into his office and returned with a large map of Spain. Holiday snapshots for most women seem irresistible and soon Barbara and Shirley were happily sorting through them commenting and asking questions.

"Here's one of John's mother-in-law with a donkey," said Shirley.

"And it's got a hat on!" cried Barbara.

"Yes. That's her on the right," John acknowledged, unable to miss the opportunity.

Then Shirley asked, "Wash thish lovely old building?" at the same time waving the photograph in John's direction.

"Ah, that photograph," said John awash with nostalgia. Then after a moment's hesitation he added, "Once through those hallowed portals all will be revealed to you."

Brian glanced at Shirley and she smiled back at him, enjoying their own private joke.

"That my dear, Amigos," John intoned, solemnly, "is where they produce nectar for the very God's themselves."

"Well go on then," prompted Shirley.

John smiled, adjusted his spectacles, closed his eyes then said wistfully, "Priorato."

"And who or what is Prio something or other?" asked Barbara studying the photograph.

John placed his glass on the table, looked around at his friends and said slowly, "Pri-or-ato," savouring each syllable. He then continued. "This exceptional, elegant, superb wine can, without doubt, be blamed for the unusual increase in British residents in region of Tarragona." Here he waved a finger in the air. "And mark my words, dear friends; I can only predict that the way Priorato is growing in popularity they are soon going to have to build a bloody great wall around the area to keep people out!"

Next smiling thoughtfully and lowering his voice as if about to impart some great secret, so much so that the others had to lean forward to hear, he said, "You see Priorato is the lotus fruit of the Mediterranean. Once, only once, a single drop has passed your lovely lips," here he gazed pointedly at Shirley, "then you are a goner!"

"A goner?" repeated a mystified Barbara.

"Yes, dear lady. I shall repeat myself, a goner."

Retrieving his glass his glass John swirled the amber liquid around, drank deeply before continuing. "That photograph is of one of the very few sacred 'Bodegas' where they produce the sensational, the marvellous the dangerous, and I mean dangerous my friends, 'Priorato' wine!"

"And would you now consider yourself a goner?" asked Brian, smiling.

"Yes, old son. Definitely. Without doubt." Then once again lowering his voice he continued. "As one foolish enough to sample this.....this seductive potion, I freely admit....I'm a goner." He then raised his eyes to the ceiling and intoned, almost to himself, "If there be a superior being I pray that one day in the not too distant future, my feet will carry me there once more and my very soul will find succour within those sanctified walls."

All was quiet for a moment then Shirley said, "Wow! All that and a nudish beach!"

Breathing a long drawn out sigh John sat back and gazed reflectively into the glass answering the various questions that arose as the others sifted through the photographs.

A while later Brian unfolded the Michelin map of Spain and Portugal at the same time inviting his friend to point out San Carlos before John's vision became impaired. John obliged.

"There's Barcelona and down here," he ran his finger south along the coast, "and if I am not mistaken, is San Carlos de la Rapita. Yes here we are. Further down past Tarragona, near the mouth of the Ebro."

"The Ebro?" somebody questioned.

"Yes. The largest river in Spain."

The two women clustered around, leaning over to examine the map.

"Not very much of San Carlos is there?" commented Barbara.

"And thank God for that," said John quickly. "We don't want the word getting around. If the tour operators find the place," Here he clasped his hand to his head, "we're sunk dear lady!"

"And the Bodega?" from Brian.

"Back up the coast and inland a bit."

Brian carefully inspected the map. "Which way did you arrive in Spain, John?"

"Through Andorra, old son. Duty free and all that. I reckon that part was the end for Beryl and me. Her mother was quite upset by all the booze we took on board from the duty free shops."

Brian rested a finger thoughtfully on the paper. "Andorra, Barcelona and down the coast," he said.

John nodded. "But you don't actually go into Barcelona. You by-pass it."

"How long did it take you to get down there?"

John ruffled his hair, "Three or four days. Can't remember exactly. Beryl's mother wanted to keep stopping for some reason or other."

And so the conversation continued thus, until it was time for the visitors to go when finally Brian, together with Barbara's help, poured them into their taxi. Soon afterwards as the husband and wife were climbing into bed, Brian tentatively asked, "Well, darling. What do you think?"

"What do I think what?" came the sleepy reply.

"About a trip to sunny Spain, silly."

"Oh, that," Barbara yawned. "Could be a laugh I suppose. You might just finish up a goner."

Leaning over he kissed her lightly on the shoulder and waited for the warm blanket of sleep to overtake him. Drowsy thoughts turned the largest river in Spain into blood red Priorato wine. Perhaps if, at that moment, he had even inkling as to what kind of 'goner' he was going to be, then no doubt he would have returned downstairs and happily shredded the Michelin map.

*

As the month of May gave way to June and the rain became a little warmer, Brian went about his work diligently and spent his somewhat limited time, preparing for the family adventure. He also managed a drink now and then in the Bell which was the ideal place for any local gossip and at the same time a barometer for news and views on Broughton politics. Early one evening he found Ted polishing glasses ready for the early evening imbibers.

"Evening Ted," Brian said, nodding towards the Bass beer pump.

"Ho! And a very good evening to you, Councillor Phillips," Ted responded.

Manipulating the pump he then produced a perfect pint of 'Bass' that looked to Brian as though it were topped with cream. "You just missed Miss Honeyworth and Arthur," the landlord remarked, gently placing the pint before his customer.

Brian's interest heightened. "Really and how are they both?"

Ted obliged with a sly wink. "They said something about setting up some sort of nature camp down by the river. You know, that wooded area just past the Red Lion. Old Morris the landlord will be thrilled."

"Not as thrilled as Citizen Kane, I bet," said Brian, momentarily visualising Shirley and Arthur dancing through the woods like a couple of nymphs with Hamish Dagliesh in hot pursuit.

"Won't help much with his nomination for Chairman of the Council," he added.

"Perhaps his flight plan is directed in another direction," said Ted carefully rearranging his moustache with the back of his hand.

*

It was a few days later that Brian saw Shirley again and she waylaid him with the question.

"What wash the name of that plashe in Shpain where John went?"

"San Carlos de la Rapita. Why?"

The green eyes twinkled up at him and the lips, with the pencil mark, smiled. "Nothing really. Nothing at all. It's jusht that a friend wash ashking."

Brian could not resist saying, "How is Arthur these days. Haven't seen him around for a while?"

Shirley looked vague and then again smiled up at Brian. "Oh, Arthur. He'sh fine, I believe. I think he ish looking to buy some land down near the river."

"Really? How interesting," said Brian refraining from mentioning Ted's comments. "Bit difficult to get building permission down there. Not for me to say but I think there is some ruling on the development side."

"Don't think it ish for building," said Shirley but declined to say anything further.

So the matter rested there and after a general exchange of other local gossip each went their own way. The days passed by until the end of the school term eventually arrived for Brian's children.

"Your kids are becoming impossible," said Barbara as the holidays became nearer.

"How is it they are always my children when something is wrong?" asked Brian, but the silence was an answer in itself.

*

On the Sunday before they were finally due to leave for Spain all the family gathered for lunch during which Brian was to experience a slight feeling of panic.

"Mother. Why don't you come along with us?" asked Barbara suddenly out of the blue.

Her mother's knife and fork, which were on the point of engaging a particular juicy slice of roast beef, halted in mid air. Then looking carefully around the table at each of them in turn she said in her finest theatrical voice, "My dear children. I love you all very much as I am sure you are all aware. And there is nothing that I would not undertake in order to ensure your happiness. However...however, if you think I am sufficiently deranged as to partake in some sort of travelling circus for three whole weeks, you must all be bananas!"

The children howled with laughter, Barbara looked a little sad and Brian offered up a small prayer of thanks.

The appointed day of departure duly arrived with plenty of sunshine to see them on their way. The previous day Brian had passed by Arthur Allard's imposing service station on the outskirts of town and filled up with petrol. On asking for Arthur he was told by the pump attendant, "Boss 'ain't in. Went on 'oliday yesterday." So thanking him Brian drove home.

*

The motorway rolled out before them and Brian was at the helm of the Bedford. "Brian the clever one," he was thinking. "The calculating one; the scheming one; who, with a little influence from his friends, was about to enjoy a memorable holiday."

Even as the vehicle sped along he allowed his imagination to wander and visualised himself at the head of the long council table conducting his first meeting as chairman in a manner that would make Hamish Dagliesh proud of him.

"So this is what we do about Cyril Outhwaite's drains," said Brian to himself.

"What was that?" Barbara's voice broke in.

"Er.... nothing dear. Just thinking out loud."

"Well driver you had better start concentrating a little more. That's Dover up ahead."

The crossing was exceptionally smooth and Brian, persuaded by the children, much to his surprise more than anyone else's, won ten pounds on one of the fruit machines that were scattered about the boat. Awhile later they clattered down the ramp onto French soil and were soon following the signs towards Paris. Barbara sat dutifully with the map spread out before her while the children squabbled as usual and stared out of the window.

"Where do you think we might end up tonight she asked?" more for something to say than interest.

"As far as possible," replied Brian. "Somewhere south of Paris, I hope." He then added, "And tomorrow we should be in sight of the Pyrenean Mountains."

"Shame mother wouldn't come, wasn't it?"

Brian lifted his eyes towards heaven. "Yes, dear. A real shame."

That night they found a neat, clean camping site near to a small river amidst rustling birch trees. Brian and the children strolled around savouring the tangy scent of wood smoke mixed with the occasional Gauloise aroma, while Barbara prepared the evening meal. Later, when they fell into their bunks, it was to fall asleep to someone's radio playing an old Edith Piaf song. And Brian felt that they had truly arrived on Gallic territory.

Next day after a hurried breakfast they were once again out on the N20 road south towards Limoges and Toulouse. Passing through well kept, neat, villages, most displaying a colourful abundance of flowers, they stopped at one in particular shop that offered a selection of mouth watering cakes and pastries. Encouraged by their father the two children went in and in their school French successfully negotiated a fine assortment of goodies. The trim while haired elderly lady dressed in a high necked frilly blouse with a stiffly starched apron looked, "Just like Mary Poppins," said Jane.

Later they pulled in for a picnic lunch near Toulouse and as they sat munching sandwiches agreed that the sun was becoming that much warmer by the hour. As they left Toulouse a prominent traffic sign announced Foix and Andorra, so it was in that direction that Brian drove.

*

None of the family had actually experienced seeing the Pyrenean range of mountains separating the Iberian Peninsula from the rest of Europe and to Brian, in particular, this first time was to be an unforgettable encounter. For admirers of this region the anticipation that precedes the actual sighting can be likened to the expectancy that comes before a gastronomic feast for the gourmet, or the knowledge that Christmas is imminent and that we will soon be reunited with our loved ones. A special feeling that something warm and comfortable is about to happen.

The actual time of day is not important.

The coming begins when you first notice that up ahead all is not quite the same with the skyline. A daub of smoky grey sweeps across the horizon from the left to right as far as the eye can see. Then gradually, as the distance lessens, the viewer can begin to distinguish the varying contrasts in colours and shades. Not one yard of road exists where this spectacle remains constant. Overhead high majestic clouds, sparkling sunlight, rain, time of the day, the season, all contribute to the pleasure of this memorable sight. Nearer still, pale hazy smudges become lighter and dark smears become indistinct and mysterious. Eventually you can determine outlines of precipices, high spiky metallic peaks and here and there as though scattered at random, white toy sized villages perched, seemingly, on the edge of nowhere. The swirling ever changing cloud formations jealously envelop many of the summits and even in the months of August you can glimpse parcels of grey white snow crouching in prison like gullies condemned to never feeling the sun's warmth.

On they went past villages with quaint sounding names like St. Jean-de-Verges, Paul-de-Jarrat and Ussar-les-Bains, many with flag flying on road side stands offering local produce of fruit, honey and the rich Pyrenean cheeses together with selections of heavy red wines. As the afternoon wore on the sun moved west in the direction of Bordeaux leaving lengthening shadows and a cool breeze in its wake.

Eventually a smart road sign said that they arrived at Ax-les-Thermes and here on the outskirts of that tidy, spruce town they found another first class camp site.

"Tomorrow up to Andorra and from there all down hill to the sea," Brian explained.

"Will we see any snow?" Michael asked with boyish enthusiasm.

"Certainly hope not," interrupted his mother. "We have enough of that at home."

After their evening meal they strolled around and joined other visitors who were happily dangling their bare feet in the hot springs in the town centre. Then later they sat on the terrace of the popular Cafe-de-la-Paix, the children enjoying Coca Cola while their parents sipped small glasses of velvety smooth Armagnac from the Gers region.

*

Andorra was certainly not quite what they expected. A hotchpotch of high rise apartment blocks with here and there small individual building seemingly lost in the development race. There were shops, warehouses, stores, all selling every imaginable type of products and according to the huge signs displayed, at tax free prices. Shoppers were everywhere, hurrying, scurrying, clutching packets and parcels of every shape and size. Others in groups were approaching the situation from a more concise point of view, waving pencils and papers, calling to one another and comparing information as to where the best quality was available at the best prices.

To Brian the atmosphere was almost bordering on panic. He could sense the tension in the air, almost as though the crowds were expecting that at any minute a gigantic bell might ring out and a hidden voice would announce that Andorra would be closing shortly.

"Incredible!" he said as they stood on the steps of a giant superstore. "It's just like one huge January sale."

The family drifted aimlessly about finding it strange to be rubbing shoulders with people frantically tapping out rates of exchange on their calculators. Naturally the children were wide eyed with all they saw and eventually their father allowed them some money to spend as they wished. Barbara insisted on 'something for mother' and a bottle of her favourite perfume, for far less than it would have cost at home. Then, while she was selecting some cold meats and pâté for their lunch, Brian slipped away and remembering John's suggestion treated himself to a bottle of Armagnac and another of calvados. Later a joint decision was made to lunch early and be on their way as soon as possible.

"Three countries in as many hours," observed Michael as they finally crossed into Spain at Seo-de-Urgel, turning left towards Barcelona.

"Black shiny 'ats," said Brian a little later, doing a fair imitation of Cyril Outhwaite's voice, at the same time inclining his head where two caped Civil Guards stood silently at the roadside.

"That's wot Cyril Outhwaite sez any road up. Black shiny 'ats at t'every corner!"

They all laughed happily.

Villages with even stranger sounding names came and went, Baga, Berga and Pui-Reig. Some while later Barbara pointed out a sign that read 'Martorell'.

"That's the place," she said. "We follow that sign, by-pass Barcelona and then on to Tarragona."

It was well into the afternoon when they finally turned onto the main coast road and Brian calculated that they should be somewhere near Carlos-de-la-Rapita in around two to three hours. However the heat became quite intense, the children became irritable so they decided to stop for a well deserved break. Much later than Brian had anticipated they continued and he was immediately obliged to switch on the Bedford's headlights. The name Tarragona constantly appeared on the road signs but it seemed an age before they came anywhere near to the town.

"If Tarragona doesn't come soon," said Brian, "I reckon I'll be a goner."

Eventually, to the parents' relief, it did appear and they sped on thankful that they would soon be there. Possibly because they had travelled for many miles and were obviously very tired, they missed the first turn off to San Carlos. However all was not lost as a second exit appeared some five miles further on.

"There!" said Barbara, now wide awake. "To the right."

Brian dutifully slowed and took the slip road then turned back over the bridge towards the coast. Some ten minutes later a brightly lit sign came into view announcing, 'Camping Solymar'. Brian swung the Bedford into the entrance.

"It's very late, Daddy," said Jane. "Do you think they will be open?"

"'course darling. Bound to be. Can't have Councillor Phillips being turned away at this time of the night."

To the left was a little red brick office displaying a sign saying, 'Bienvenido a Camping Solymar'. Brian climbed stiffly down from the Bedford, walked over and knocked on the door. Someone inside shouted something which Brian took to mean 'Come in'. So followed by Barbara he opened the door and in they went. A round middle aged man wearing a wide smile and tee shirt on which was emblazoned 'Benidorm Costa Blanca', sat behind a desk, on which was the obvious remains of his supper.

"Muy buenas noches, Señores," he said, grinning at them both.

"Er....Good evening," responded Brian.

The grin grew wider revealing several missing teeth. "Inglish." More of a statement than a question. "Me, Paco. Fife yars in Benidorm," he pointed at the tee shirt. "Spik bloody good Inglish. Hallo!"

"Hallo to you," Brian replied.

"You wanta stay?" asked the man. "There are prices."

He pointed to a list pinned to the wall. A glance at the section marked 'Autocaravanas' did not require a calculator to determine that the costs were going to be more than reasonable.

"OK," Brian confirmed and was presented with a simple registration form to complete.

"You 'ere ten days, said Paco examining the form. "Bloody good. Fine time fer all."

Brian paid and apart form the receipt received a little booklet in Spanish containing a map of the site and general details which passed over to Barbara.

"OK, you fola Paco," said the Spaniard getting to his feet. "An' don't ferget regla sevin."

Here he pointed to his tee shirt again and winked.

The red and white pole was raised and they trundled through. While they were waiting for Paco to lead Barbara turned to Brian. "What was he talking about 'regular' something or other?"

"Well he was pointing at his tee shirt. Possibly that was his size," Brian laughed.

"Or he fancied yours," Barbara returned.

They both laughed and followed the little round figure of Paco along the wide path marked with white painted stones. Either side were shadowy outlines of tents, all shapes and sizes, some almost as large as a small bungalow.

"Wow! Just look at those!" cried the children excitedly.

"A bit different to what we saw in Cornwall," said Michael.

Their allotted place turned out to be near a log constructed building which Paco, after assisting Brian in manoeuvring the Bedford to its resting place, explained was the camp club house which had an entrance on the far side. The sea, he pointed out, was just beyond the tree line.

"Why can't we be nearer the beach?" asked Jane.

"Because we would be fried to a cinder in tomorrow's heat," explained her father.

"OK!" shouted Paco satisfied that they were well parked. Then with a wave and, "Bloody good night," he disappeared back down the path.

Barbara glanced over her shoulder to see the two children were rapidly losing interest and were curling up on the back seats.

"Husband dear," she yawned, "I'm all in. What do you say if we just made up the beds and sort everything out in the morning?"

Brian leaned over and gave her a peck on the cheek. "You know what? I think that's the best idea that you've had all day."

So around half an hour later they were all tucked up in their bunks and falling quickly to sleep.

Brian was dreaming.

He was kneeling in front of the Queen who in turn was waving a very large sword in one hand whilst in the other she was clutching a terracotta jug from which she quaffed huge quantities of red wine.

"Rise, Sir Goner," she laughed hysterically. "Rise and be counted by my subjects of Broughton."

"No!" shouted Brian, defiantly raising an arm to protect himself, "I'm not a goner."

"No?" said the Queen hesitating in mid swing. "Then together we shall drink Prio something or other."

"No, please no," protested Brian struggling to get out of the way, "I'm not a goner!"

Then someone was shaking him, hauling him up from his imperial nightmare an urgent voice was calling,

"Dad, wake up!" And Michael's face came into focus.

"What is it, Michael?" he mumbled. "Can't it wait?" Here he pulled the blanket over his head, blessing the ensuing darkness.

"No, Dad. It can't," said Michael insisting. "There are people out there with no clothes on."

"What?" Brian was instantly awake now.

"Yes," whispered Michael, as though he might be overheard, "out there. Walking around."

Brian pulled himself up and lifting the curtain peered out and saw to his amazement two beautiful beautifully proportioned, tanned, and long legged, girls walking by completely naked.

"Good, Lord!" he exclaimed, not quite knowing how to react. "Wake up your mother."

"Mother's already awake," came a sleepy voice. "What's all the fuss about?"

"People with no clothes on," repeated Michael.

Soon Barbara was looking through the window. "We missed the turning last night," she said. "This must be the camp site that John mentioned." Then she added meaningfully, "The one that your friend Shirley wanted to know about."

"That's as maybe," said Brian, "but what are we going to do about it?"

"Perhaps we just leave," from Barbara.

Brian rubbed the sleep from his eyes. "But we've paid for ten days. I just can't see them handing back the money for our mistake. And besides it would seem......well silly."

"What's the matter?" Jane asked now awake.

Again Michael repeated the story. His sister yawned, "And what's wrong with that. If it's warm?" Then seeing their expressions asked, "Is it bad then?"

Brian and Barbara looked at one another.

"No, Jane," her mother explained, "it's just well...sort of different. That's all."

"Then if it's not bad Mummy can we go to the beach?"

"Better ask your father."

"Look you can see the beach over there and there are people already on it," chimed in Michael.

The family followed his pointing finger to where the tree line ended revealing a wide expanse of smooth golden sands with an inviting stretch of blue Mediterranean Sea.

"Don't know. Better let your Mother decide." Brian flopped down onto the bed again.

"Well if it's not bad, why can't we? For one day at least?" pleaded Jane.

Barbara didn't take too long to make a decision. After their long journey the last thing she wanted was to be on the move again. "Well alright," she said. "We'll give it a try."

Needless to say the children were delighted and hurriedly took turns to wash, while their father lay there wondering what the day was to bring.

"I won't be running around on the beach. That's for sure," Brian said to Barbara when the children had gone. "It would look ridiculous."

Later when Barbara had followed them armed with the sun lotion, Brian busied himself tidying up the Bedford before plucking up enough courage to walk the hundred yards to the beach.

"Rather like swimming. Once you're in the water it's not too bad," he commented to Barbara as he settled himself on one of the sun beds.

And so the family enjoyed themselves, building sandcastles, collecting shells and swimming in the warm sea. All along the beach were rush covered awnings sufficiently large enough to provide shade for an average family which suited them admirably as too long in the heat of the morning's sun would easily prove a problem.

"What about lunch, husband dear?" asked Barbara as Brian, for around the fifth time, came out of the water and flopped down beside her.

"What about it?"

"Nothing dear. Just that soon we shall have at least two hungry mouths to feed and some shopping has to be done. And someone has to do it."

"I suppose it's me that has to volunteer?" said Brian.

"Quite correct, Councillor. List and money in the top draw next to the sink."

"But what am I going to carry the money in?" asked Brian, indicating that there were no hidden pockets in his skin. Barbara smiled,

"In your hand Councillor and when you get there buy one of those waist belt bags that you see everyone wearing. Alright?"

Brian climbed reluctantly to his feet.

"Yes Sergeant. Immediately!"

At that precise moment Michael appeared. "Can I go as well please, Dad?"

"Glad to have you along partner. See you gals back at the old homestead in around twenty minutes," he said as they both moved away gingerly treading on the hot sand.

With no problems to contend with at the little camp supermarket they were both soon returning weighed down with plastic bags and each sporting one of the small elastic waist money holders. In the meantime Barbara and Jane had laid out the table under the Bedford's awning and everything looked set for an appetizing picnic lunch.

"And apart from soft drinks and beer, what do have here?" cried Brian, waving one bag that clinked interestingly at the same time threatening to come apart with the weight.

"Wine," offered Barbara, immediately.

"Twenty thousand points for the lady," said Brian. "But what kind of wine? And don't forget this question is for forty thousand points."

"Prio something or other," chimed in Jane not to be left out.

"Near enough, Señorita," conceded her father. "You win the bonus."

The children cheered wildly.

"Do you think it is really wise to drink that after what John was saying?" Barbara asked.

Brian laughed as he produced two bottles.

"Come on. It might be good but it cannot be all that potent, sufficiently to keep me here forever and being the next chairman of Broughton Council."

Another spontaneous 'hurrah' from Jane and Michael to which their father responded with an exaggerated bow. Then the meal began with Brian opening one of the bottles.

"Like some, dear," he waved it in Barbara's direction.

"Well perhaps," she said, brandishing her glass. "Just to try."

Brian obliged then placing the bottle on the table took a serviette and daintily dabbed his lips. Then raising the glass to the light swirled the liquid around and examined the results carefully. Then after a few moments concentration smiled round at the family. "Full bodied," he began. "Clings well to the glass. Cherry coloured."

Barbara laughed and the children joined in.

Then gently he sniffed at the contents. "Fine bouquet. Matured in oak barrels for at least six months."

Next he tentatively took a sip and rolled the liquid around his palate and closed his eyes. "MMMmmmm!" he crooned. "Very nice in fact. The stuff dreams are made of."

A further cheer rent the air and Barbara, after tasting hers, said that she would really prefer white or rosé wine. Brian put on a suitable hurt expression.

"Light of my life," he said, "I did actually think that you might just say that."

"And so?" asked Barbara.

"And so, my dear," smiled Brian, "your son and I took the appropriate measures."

"Did you indeed," said Barbara spreading a liberal helping of foie gras onto a crusty slice of bread.

"Indeed we did. And if you care to mosey over to the fridge and let those beautiful eyes of yours take a look inside, you will see why. Because I have bought, for those lovely lips of yours, at some expense might I add a bottle of your own and for you only. A bottle of...."

"Of what?" interrupted Barbara.

Brian leaned over and kissed her on the cheek. "What else?" he cried, "What else, but champagne!"

"Real champagne?" she asked.

"No. Not exactly French champagne but, I am assured by the powers that be, a good as and in some cases better than the French. Anyway that is what my friend Pepe said from the supermarket."

"Dad was talking to a man who spoke English in the shop," explained Michael, "and he said that Penedés, near here, was the place for champagne."

"Anyway," added his father, "at one pound a bottle we weren't going to argue, were we partner?"

So their lunch continued with Barbara enjoying her Spanish champagne and Brian his Priorato. Whereas the level of the former bottle descended slowly it was equally compensated by the rapidity with which the red wine disappeared. Next, Brian held out that a large piece of Manchego cheese warranted the opening of a second bottle.

"Your father's a goner," remarked Barbara to the children.

"Sure will be," said Brian. "A goner for the Spanish custom called a 'siesta'."

"Fine husband dear but after clearing the table."

"No problem," he replied coming to his feet and suddenly taking into account that things did not quite seem the same as they had been an hour before. Then with those deliberate actions of someone who has had just that little too much, he cleared the things away and washed up. Finally his voice floated through the window to where Barbara and the children were sitting outside under the awning.

"Adios amigos."

This was followed by a long drawn out sigh as he stretched out on his bunk. Together with the wine and a combination of all that had occurred over the last days deemed that Brian was to sleep for sometime. Then when he eventually did awake it took him quite a time to realise where he was. Lying there quietly waiting for his head to clear he could hear the sound of voices coming from the beach. Gingerly, when he thought the moment right, he pulled himself into a sitting position, dropping his legs over the side of the bunk and sat there nursing his head in his hands.

"Good, Lord," he said to no one in particular, looking at his watch. "Nearly eight o'clock. Must have been out for hours."

When Barbara put in an appearance he was swilling his face with water.

"Alright, Batman?" she asked.

"Will be when I can drink something really cold," replied Brian.

"Sorry, but while you were snoring your head off the kids seem to have high jacked all the drinkies. Unless you would like some beer, that is. Oh, yes and there's some champagne left."

"I don't think that's funny," groaned Brian, gently rubbing his face with the towel at the same time reaching for the waist bag he had bought that morning.

"And where might you be off to now, Councillor?" asked Barbara.

"That place over there." Brian inclined his head in the direction of the club house. "I'm going to indulge myself in a large bottle of ice cold mineral water. Then as some general or other said, "We will return.""

Now accustomed to his nudity Brian set out for the club house. The path ran around the side of the building and his confidence grew as there was nobody else in sight. Then turning the corner he saw an elderly man, dressed in denims, tending the flower beds. As Brian passed, he nodded casually to the gardener who quickly responded by pointing excitedly at his overalls.

"Regla siete," he cried out excitedly.

"Regular nice guy," returned Brian, pointing to himself.

Then fortified by the first class lunch; the excellent wine and more than anything a life restoring siesta, the next chairman of Broughton council skipped up the steps, pushed open the door and strode purposefully into the club.

The Oxford dictionary describes the word 'Paralyse' as being unable to act or move normally. In other words to bring to a standstill.

And was Brian unable to act or move normally? Was he brought to a standstill?

You bet he was. Not momentarily. No. He just could not move. His brain had seemingly and totally disconnected itself from his limbs the moment that his eyes conveyed to it what they were seeing.

Alright, so there was nothing extraordinary about there being twenty-five or more people in any bar on a nudist camp or anywhere else for that matter. But given that Brian was as naked as the day he was born and all that were gathered there were fully clothed, made all the difference. The situation then took on even more horrific proportions.

"Counshillor Phillips," called a well known voice. "We didn't recognishe you without your closhes!"

And there at the bar though the horrendous mist of embarrassment was Shirley Honeyworth. And to make matters even worse, next to her, his face split from ear to ear in a hideous clown like grin, was Arthur Allard.

Behind Brian the door opened.

"Señor, Señor," an urgent voice was saying, "Regla siete!"

Brian slowly recovering his control turned to see Pepe from the supermarket.

"W…..What?" he asked, still in shock, not being able to grasp the full significance of what was happening.

"Rule seven," repeated Pepe urgently, placing a gentle hand on Brian's shoulder and leading him out of the clubhouse with the patience of a nurse.

"Rule seven in the book you got last night say that after seven o'clock in evening, everyone must dress normal. You understand, Señor?"

"Understand?" said Brian slowly, still in shock. "Yes, I understand."

But by that time it did not really seem to matter. Head down, Brian slowly made his way back to the Bedford with Shirley's voice slowly fading in the distance calling out something about, 'All will be revealed'.

Then, as the reality of the situation began to dawn on him, Brian wondered if there just might be that perfect little fishing village a few kilometres further down the coast where the family could continue their holiday. "As to the nomination of the chairmanship for Broughton Wesley Council," he thought miserably, "that possibility seems in line with the chances of Shirley doing a striptease in the Bell in the presence of Citizen Kane."

Chapter 8

After the sale of the Bedford, we invested in an old Vauxhall saloon car together with a larger size in shoes. Apart from other initial necessities that we crammed into to the vehicle we also included a new rotary clothes line: this being a novelty at the time. Manolo who had come across the article in an 'Innovations' magazine wished to patent it in Spain; a misguided idea I duly found out, because legal action against any pirating manufacturer could take years to resolve and was not worth it. Some considerable effort was spent to organise all the necessary papers for Worthington, our dog, and we were most surprised that just nobody at the French or Spanish frontiers were in the least bit interested. The rotary clothes-line, however, would be considered by Spanish customs officers to represent some kind of secret weapon that might possibly be employed to overthrow President Francisco Franco's regime and thus warranted much explanation and demonstration before it was allowed into the country.

*

Manolo and Conchin provided the usual warm welcome when we arrived in Cullera. After the initial 'Hello and how are we' it was noted that Manolo had received some kind of coaching from his wife.

"How you say in English?" he said brightly. "The bird has flied."

I looked at him in surprise. "You mean the bird has flown. What bird has flown?"

"The Benidorm bird," broke in Conchin. "The one with the aeroplane. He has flied off in it." She then added quickly in order to dispel any misgivings we might suddenly have, "No, he not flied off with our money."

I sat down while she went on to explain that two days before our arrival Manolo had driven down to Benidorm and found the estate agent's office closed. There were several, obviously, very angry people hanging around outside and on enquiring as to what was the matter he had been told that Mr. Silaby had, after drawing out all his cash, simply taken off in his aeroplane from Alicante and just disappeared.

Manolo, at this point, shrugged his shoulders as if to indicate that he was not surprised as similar incidents were happening at that time all along the coast. So after discussing the matter a little more all of us decided that a further trip down to Benidorm might be in order to see if there was any remote possibility of tracing the owner of the property Manolo had found.

*

The following day we set off in Manolo's Seat 850 car, which was an experience in itself after our roomy vehicle. On arrival in Benidorm we went directly to the castle like building, 'Byblos', which he considered would be of interest to our barbeque project. From what little we could see from the outside, Manolo had been quite correct on his choice of location. It would be ideal. Then, as there did not appear to be any signs of life in the immediate area, we left and drove into Benidorm. Next we made some enquiries at other local estate agents as to whom the owner might be, but nobody seemed to know. After an hour of this, we decided on some more positive action, that of taking some refreshment at one of the many watering holes available in the town. Parking the Seat, which in those days was certainly not a problem; we chose a lively looking bar and went in. This simple move was to prove for me, the beginning of a series of even more coincidences that were to follow me for the rest of my life.

Once installed at the place I found myself listening to three Englishmen talking animatedly about the disappearance of the elusive Mr. Silaby. One of them, who turned out to be a plumber from Benfleet in Essex, England, was complaining bitterly that he had been on the point of selling the lease of a property called the 'Byblos'. He was explaining to the others how Silaby had told him that he had an Englishman and a Spaniard that were interested in taking this large place off his hands but he had no idea who they were or how to contact them. So you can imagine his surprise when we interrupted the conversation and introduced ourselves.

At that particular moment this, for all of us, was the good news. The bad was soon to follow a few minutes afterwards when it was explained that the agent's asking price for the lease was at least fifty percent less than what the plumber was asking. Apparently Silaby had been offering properties to potential buyers at prices far less than what their owners were counting on. This, from a buyer's point of view, obviously made the offer very much more attractive. He had then, it would appear, been collecting considerable deposits from the purchasers and had, at the most appropriate moment, decided he had accumulated sufficient funds for an early retirement and had left rapidly. And how much more rapidly could one leave than by their own private aeroplane?

No, Manolo and I agreed that the new asking price for the lease was way beyond what we had anticipated so after a couple of drinks and some apologies we left it at that and returned to Cullera. It was only a few days later, when explaining to my family in England, what had gone wrong when my father said that the estate agent's name was familiar to him.

"How come, father?" I asked, rather surprised that he should be interested in such matters.

He was silent for a moment then said, "I remember now. It was the 'Silver Sands Park' scam a few years back."

"Good Lord, I remember that one!" I exclaimed. "Back in the sixties, wasn't it?"

'Silver Sands Park' had received considerable publicity at that time. When the tide of Mediterranean tourism had really begun to flow and people in rain swept Britain were thinking about how they could escape to the south and sun, for the minimum of investment, the possibility of buying their own small plot of land near the sea was almost irresistible. Especially made more interesting when these plots were located in a park where the buyer could arrive together with their caravan, park up and after an enjoyable vacation leave the caravan on their own plot and return to England safe in the knowledge that it was there anytime they wished to use it. The bad news came a little later when Spanish government officials quite rightly announced that a caravan constituted being a vehicle and as thus it could only remain in the country for six months in any one year otherwise, import duty, at that time being around eighty percent of the value of the caravan, was payable. The sale of the land plots was quite legitimate but, of course, the use of the patch was the owner's responsibility as was soon to be discovered. Our wily estate agent was not to be taken lightly by any means.

*

Mary and I were sitting comfortably on the apartment terrace the following morning. Above us the heavens were so clear and bright with sunshine that it seemed almost impossible to remember rain. "So what do we do now?" Mary asked.

"I suppose we could return to England," I said, not at all enthusiastically.

"But even that won't be easy, Chris. Not with the dog having to go into quarantine."

We both glanced across at Worthington who was lying stretched out in the shade looking as though he was enjoying his particular form of early retirement. Then after discussing the limited alternatives available to us we decided that as we had the apartment in Cullera we would look into what possibilities lay there.

At that time and probably even more so now, the road leading down to the beach, on which we had our top floor apartment, boasted no less than seventeen bars and restaurants. There were two ways of viewing this situation. One was that there were too many places to think of installing a similar business or secondly that they were all there because there was the business to be had.

"Rather like bees round a honey pot," remarked Mary. "They must be there for some reason. They can't all be on the road to going broke."

Anyway the decision to join them was made and after several days, without too much difficulty, we found some empty premises around one hundred square meters in size and at a reasonable rent. Now there were going to be seventeen bars and restaurants plus the first pub in the whole of the south eastern region of Spain.

As usual the property agent was Pepe Crespo who we had met on our first visit to Cullera. He was most helpful and did not, to our knowledge, own an aeroplane. We completed the paperwork involved in record time. That very same evening, as we were having a pre dinner-aperitif, someone rang our door bell and on opening it I was surprised to discover one of the local policemen in full uniform.

"Señor Wright?" he enquired, most formally.

I nodded, wondering what was coming next and feeling just that little bit nervous.

"I understand that you are going to open a bar in this street?"
Again I nodded.

"You will require two toilets," he explained, "one toilet for the Señoras and the other for the Caballeros. That is the law."

Still puzzled I agreed and waited for the punch line. "And......?" I ventured

"Señor, Wright," he said firmly, "I am the plumber that you will require."

So that was the beginning. Followed by the policeman plumber we quickly had two further police officials call on us who claimed that they were not only brothers but competent brick layers. There was even a third who claimed to be a professional electrician. The only one that did not appear was a carpenter, the local police force being somewhat lacking in this respect. So this one we had to source for ourselves, which again, was not too difficult

Needless to say with the Dictator's regime still being well in evidence there were complications in respect of the necessary paperwork. So here we employed the services of a local 'Gestor' or business administrator who undertook to do this side of things. He explained that as 'Residence Permit' was not possible to obtain without a 'Work Permit' and the latter was not possible without the 'Residence Permit'. A chicken and the egg type situation. However he confidently said that applying for them both at the same time this would resolve the problem. Next we were informed that these permits would arrive at the main police headquarters in Valencia within a few weeks.

As the Christmas season was now fast approaching I went along to the police HQ in Valencia one day and asked if the documentation, including our 'Residence' permits, had arrived. "No," I was informed by a severe looking police official in the foreign department.

"But we wish to go home for Christmas and return with our belongings," I explained in the nicest possible way.

"It would be most unwise to leave the country before the documents arrive from Madrid," he said, seriously. "It would mean that the whole process would have to be repeated again when you return. And if you bring any domestic goods with you it would also be a problem; importation charges and things. You understand?"

I nodded, feeling once again let down by Spanish red tape. Then, as I was about to turn away he suddenly asked, "Do you happen to go anywhere near London?"

"I beg your pardon?" I asked very much surprised by the question.

"I said do you happen to go anywhere near to London?"

"Yes," I replied stopping and wondering where this was leading to, "we pass right through London."

The tone of his voice softened a little. "Un momento por favor."

Next, he ducked down out of sight below the high counter only to reappear a few seconds later with an enormous cardboard box that he could hardly lift it was so heavy. Placing it firmly in front of me he looked me straight in the eyes. "Could you deliver this to my daughter who lives in Denmark Hill, London?" he asked. "It's for Christmas."

I peered into the box and was horrified to see that it was full of bottles and foodstuffs. Spanish champagne, brandy, liquors and an incredible assortment of smoked meats, and sausages together with plenty of other goodies including a large box of de Havana cigars. In fact it represented a British customs officer's dream and to me, personally, a nightmare.

"But...." I began, "This would be smuggling."

"Would be what?"

His dark, beady, eyes stared up at me over the top of the box.

"Contrabando, illegal," I explained lamely.

"You could tell them it was from the Valencia police," he suggested, smiling. "That would make it alright."

"Fantastic," I thought, "That would just go down like the proverbial lead balloon."

"But what about our permits and things?" I asked, hedging.

"Don't worry about them," he said reaching out, clasping my hand and taking it for granted that I would do him the favour. "I will arrange everything."

"Thanks," I said, wondering why it was me who was being grateful.

I staggered out to the car with the box and on arrival in Cullera reported the good news to Mary who became nervous as to what the consequences might be.

"We just tell them it's from the Valencia police," I explained feebly and for some reason she went into hysterics.

*

Two days before we set off I got in touch with Reggie the Fish and we arranged to meet one evening in Valencia. Both Mary and I drove up to the city that morning and being around lunchtime we decided to have a snack at the Barrachina cafeteria. When we walked into this hive of activity the first thing I spotted was a very large sign which read 'SANWISHES'. This, I took correctly to indicate that the humble English sandwich had at last arrived in Valencia. Encouraged by this innovation we crossed over to the bar and I asked the waiter for two cheese sandwiches.

"Certainly, Sir," he said, cheerfully," with or without bread?"

Naturally, we were both taken aback by this seemingly pointless question. However in those days I was fairly quick thinking. "Without bread, please," I said confidently and I heard Mary groan at the thought of what might be the results.

"Certainly, Caballero," he smiled, nodded and went off to the kitchen.

After a few moments he was back again. "Sorry, the chef says that it is not possible," he apologised.

I looked suitably puzzled. "What's not possible?"

"A cheese 'Sanwish' without bread, Caballero."

Putting on a pained expression, I persisted. "I'm sure that it is possible."

So off he marched again returning after a little while. "No, Sir," he apologised, "The chef says that a cheese 'Sanwish' without bread is definitely not possible."

"Look," I insisted, "Have you got bread?"

"Certainly, Sir"

"And have you got cheese?"

"Of course we have cheese, Sir."

"Then please bring me a cheese sandwich without bread."

By this time the noise level in the kitchen had increased and most of the customers could hear the argument going on. Eventually out of the kitchen came the waiter carrying two plates, one loaded with crusty bread and the other with several hunks of cheese. He laid them down in front of us. "The chef's compliments. Please work it out for yourself!"

And so we did: enjoying both cheese and bread together with a couple of glasses of excellent wine. When the time came to pay, I called the waiter over and on settling the bill complimented him on the cheese sandwiches without bread. He took the money and leaning over the bar spoke in a low confidential voice. "Thank you, Sir." Then he added, "I would just like to say that the chef was not at all happy. He will be out in a minute to speak to you and," here he looked me up and down slowly and continued, "he is very much bigger than you and he just wants you to know that only one week ago he returned from Brighton in England after completing a cookery course which included preparing 'Sanwishes'."

Needless to say after leaving a healthy tip both of us beat a hasty retreat before the giant sized chef could make his appearance.

Worthington was left to spend Christmas in the capable hands of some friends we had made in Cullera and we returned again to England for the festive season. I was somewhat nervous as we negotiated the ramp off the ferry at Dover but, fortunately, on this one occasion, luck did smile on us as we passed through customs and the enormous box of Christmas goodies was safely delivered to Denmark Hill.

Chapter 9

Following the Christmas celebrations I traded in the car for an old Austen van. It was a large, diesel engine, vehicle with a wooden floor and plenty of space to accommodate most of our household effects, apart from large furniture. The weather, of course, was lousy being the month of January and we were both anxious to shake off the snow from our shoes and return to a much warmer climate.

Mary was fortunate to fly directly to Valencia while I set off in the Austen. Having already been warned that I would possibly be charged import duties on the goods, I prepared a list itemising our things and putting a very meagre value on each one. There was no problem on leaving Dover but once on the other side in Calais I was instructed to line up with the other goods vehicles. When it came to my turn the French customs officer was horrified when I presented my list and nothing else.

"You must realise that this is not official," he said, staring at it.

"What do you mean?" I asked in all innocence.

"You should have gone to a custom's agent in Dover before arriving in France."

"What for? These are my things and I'm taking them to Spain."

He glared at me. "How do we know that you are not going to sell them in France? You should have deposited the money with an agent in England and then when you arrive in Spain it would have been returned to you."

Feigning more innocence I said, "But why would I want to sell my own things?"

But this time he wasn't having any. "Don't be smart with me, Monsieur, or you will be back on the boat."

I apologised saying that I just did not think that there was anything worth selling anyway and he went away. After at least an hour and a half he reappeared once more and asked which frontier post I would be passing when I crossed into Spain.

"Urdos, near Oleron-St.-Marie in the Pyrenees," I confirmed.

He made me write it down and then said something to me in French which sounded very much like, "OK, fuck off. You've caused me enough trouble!"

The old Austen van went extremely well and the further south I drove the weather responded. I timed my arrival at Urdos, this small frontier post in the mountains, for around ten o'clock at night. The cunning idea was, or so I thought, that both French and Spanish customs officers would be tired and there would be fewer problems, if any. When I eventually did trundle up, it was to find the frontier completely closed and no signs of life. So reluctantly turning round I found a small hotel nearby. Then, after a comfortable night, presented myself at the frontier around nine o'clock the next morning. The French customs officers just waved me through and I did not stop to argue.

Then it was the turn of the Spanish authorities.

There were two of them in their black tricorn hats. The red and white barrier was raised and I drove through with just a little bit of hope that they would wave me on. But no chance. I was instructed to park the Austin to one side. Climbing down I then produced my home made list and one of them, after examining it closely, removed his hat, rubbed his forehead and groaned.

"What's the matter?" I asked. "Is there a problem?"

"No, not for us, Inglés," he said, "but for you, yes."

"Why?" Again I put on my 'little bit innocent if not stupid' expression.

"Listen, Inglés. It is nine o'clock on a Sunday morning, right?"

I nodded, shuffled my feet and gazed at the pebble strewn ground as might a child, guilty of something but not knowing quite what..

"Well, I now have to telephone my chief who lives some forty kilometres from here in Jaca and believe me Inglés, he is not going to be at all happy."

I just shrugged and said that as there was no alternative I would have to take the consequences.

It was around a couple of hours later, an official car arrived came rattling up the hill with the customs officer accompanied by a very large and very nervous German shepherd dog. Fairly tall for a Spaniard and fully decked out in his official uniform he stood listening to his juniors explain the situation. Then clutching my list he turned to me. "Right, Inglés. Let's have a look at what you've got."

I opened up the back of the van and meekly showed him all the things I had stuffed inside before leaving the UK. It looked like I was heading for a junk yard. His face registered total surprise and he began examining the inventory in earnest.

Then finally he noticed the pathetic price valuation I had written down. "Not really a millionaire, are you?" he asked, looking up from the list and studying my expression as if seeking some hidden reason behind my being there under these circumstances.

"Listen, Señor," I said firmly, "if I were a millionaire do you honestly think I would be driving this old wreck across these mountains with all my worldly goods?" With a wave of my hands I pointed up at the forbidding snow covered peaks surrounding us.

His face registered a slight smile, obviously in agreement with my reasoning. "Come on then," his said making his decision, "close up and let us sort out the paperwork."

Inside his office it was warm and comfortable and he went about filling in the various forms at the same time muttering about leaving his comfortable bed on a Sunday morning to come up and deal with some crazy Englishman.

Finally another rubber stamp was placed forcibly onto the remaining form.

"Right there you are, Inglés." He passed over the papers with a flourish.

I nodded, took them and was just about to get up when he said, "That will be five hundred Pesetas customs duty."

Now in the early seventies five hundred Pesetas represented around three pounds sterling which even at that time could not be considered an exorbitant amount of money. The fact was, however, that until the banks opened on the following Monday morning I just did not have it. "Er.....," I began now feeling definitely embarrassed.

What now?" he asked pushing his chair back and climbing to his feet.

"Er...," I tried again.

He looked at me hard, sat down again, then elbows on the desk, dropped his head into his hands. "Por favor. Please, please don't tell me you haven't even got five hundred Pesetas?"

I nodded slowly. "I really am sorry....," I began.

"I just don't believe it!" he groaned again and sat there looking at me.

The dog became aware of its master's tone and seemed to move strategically between myself and the door. I looked what I hoped was suitably-shame faced and gazed at the large photograph of General Francisco Franco hanging on the wall behind him. Even the Dictator stared back at me with an expression of severe disapproval.

"Really, I am very sorry," I began again.

All was silent for a few moments while he considered the situation muttering, "I just don't believe all of this. And on a Sunday morning."

Then after a few moments staring at me he suddenly shouted out for one of his colleagues to come in.

"Here," he said to the younger man who presented himself and stood casually to attention, "I want you to witness this."

Next thrusting his hand into his trouser pocket he withdrew a five hundred Peseta note. "I am loaning El Inglés this money. Alright?"

The other's mouth dropped open as this certainly had not been in the training manual. "Si, Capitán," he said, not really certain that this was not some set up to undermine his patriotism.

A further rubber stamp was produced and I was handed the official receipt while the chief pinned the five hundred Peseta note to the papers and filed them. After the young Guardia had been dismissed I asked the captain his name and promised to return the money as soon as was possible. He nodded doubtfully at my good intentions and a little while later as I drove away I saw all three officials standing there together with the dog and the Capitán shaking his head, still muttering, "And on a Sunday morning. I just don't believe it"

*

On previous occasions when something mechanical went wrong with whatever vehicle I was driving I had become angry and distraught. All that has now changed. If something, anything, like a puncture or a breakdown occurs nowadays, my curiosity is aroused and I wonder what sort of adventure I might be on the point of experiencing. So far, I have never been disappointed and this particular time between Teruel and Valencia was to be of no exception.

It was late on Monday night, south of Teruel and around one hundred miles from Valencia that the Austen van decided that it had had enough for one day. Fortunately, for me, at the time, I realised that there was something amiss and was able to pull into a lay-by. It was now dark and I was miles from anywhere except for a large building opposite that sported different coloured neon strip lights outside, flashing on and off, together with an even larger sign that read, 'Club'.

Now in Spain in those early years, just before the demise of the dictator, there was a popular demand for what were known as "Wiskerias". These were establishments that employed girls to sell high priced drinks and sometimes themselves as well, for services rendered. Usually discreetly placed outside of towns and cities they were thriving businesses and some still are today on a very grand scale.

Anyway there was little for me to do so I thought that some action was required instead of sitting in the van and just waiting for something to happen. So locking the vehicle I strode across the road to towards the club. Having been to a branch of my Spanish bank that morning I now had money in my pocket and was not unduly concerned as to what I might find within.

Being a Monday night I had expected to find only a few clients in the place but it was quite busy. I then realised that most customers, naturally, preferred to park their cars out of sight to the rear of the building. Inside it was warm and friendly after the cold chill of the night air. I made my way over to the bar to the sound of Dusty Springfield singing about the son of a preacher man and could see shadowy figures on large sofas grappling in the corners. Immediately I was made very welcome by two scantily dressed, enthusiastic, girls behind the bar.

As these clubs, without exception, are all dimly lit, it is sometimes difficult to tell whether or not the staff were potential contenders for the Miss Spain title or aspiring actresses for a part in the 'X File'. Anyway I selected the one who to me looked the most attractive and ordered a drink for myself and one for her. Luckily, it turned out that, Carmen, for that was her name, happened to be the owner.

One other thing I have learnt in life is that you never rush into asking some unknown person for a favour until you have established some kind of initial rapport. Everyone has their own problems and for unknown people to impose themselves by immediately seeking a favour could be likened to an invasion of another person's privacy. So I chose to chat to Carmen, as best I could, on different things in general, until the question arose as to how I had arrived their. Explaining that my van had broken down I added that I was not sure as to what I was going to do. To my surprise, Carmen then placed her hand over mine and expressing some words of sympathy at my predicament, immediately took charge.

"Tomorrow morning," she said firmly, "I will telephone my cousin who has a service garage in Teruel and he will definitely help us."

At the moment she said, "Help us," I knew everything was going to be fine. So I thanked her very much and called for another round of drinks. She accepted and then asked where I was staying for the night. I laughed. "Where else? In the van I suppose."

Her large, dark eyes looked up at me as she responded with, "No. we definitely cannot have that, 'Un Inglés', sleeping in a truck. That is not correct."

I shrugged as if to say, "What alternative?"

Next, leaning across the bar and beckoning me placed her mouth close to my ear and said, "Why not use one of the rooms upstairs? They are very clean and for you it would only be two thousand five hundred Pesetas."

Naturally as far as I was concerned there was no alternative. I jumped at the chance. After another couple of drinks, I collected my overnight bag from the Austin and returned rapidly. Carmen herself conducted me upstairs and I was ushered into what can only be described as one of the most lavishly decorated bedrooms I have ever had the pleasure of seeing; let alone sleeping in.

It was stunning.

Spacious to almost the size of the bar downstairs, it had an enormous amount of pink and rose pastel shade drapes everywhere, even behind the bed and on the ceiling. One wall, which turned out to be a huge wardrobe, was completely covered with floor to ceiling mirrors and whoever had organised the discreet lighting had produced the effect of being on the inside some monstrous wedding cake. Immediately I detected a faint aroma of Madam Rochas eau de toilette which, in later years, was to remind me of the incident and at the same time bring added heartbreaks. Carmen, who must have been around forty years of age with a slim baby doll figure, appeared even more attractive in those surroundings than when I had first seen her. She instructed me to make myself at home, take a shower or whatever, and closing the door firmly behind her returned to her business downstairs. I took a long hot shower and as the water beat down on me, I revelled in the luxury of it all. Next, after towelling myself down, and feeling very much better, I fell naked into a very grand and more than comfortable Queen Size bed complete with silk sheets. Lying there comfortably I congratulated myself on my good fortune.

It must have been a while later when I was on the point of dropping off to sleep and at the same time wondering whether or not the Austin van had been sufficiently intelligent to have organised the whole episode, when I thought I heard the door opening. Being too tired to take any further notice I drifted off. Some minutes later I was disturbed by a rustling noise as the bedclothes were drawn gently back and someone slipped into bed next to me.

Now when I was a young child my mother used to tell me to hold out my hand and then with two fingers she would make steps around my palm at the same time reciting, "Walky round the garden like a teddy bear." And so Carmen's fingers began the same exercise on my chest, moving slowly down towards my stomach.

"What's going on?" I mumbled as her soft naked body, sending out signals of perfume, snuggled up to me.

"Nothing Englishman," she whispered, at the same time slipping her tongue into my ear." It's just that this is my personal bedroom and if you think I am going to sleep anywhere else you'd better forget it."

Her fingers took several more tentative steps as she added, "Of course, there is always your truck across the road."

I sighed contentedly.

"Hmmm! That feels nice."

Then turning towards her I made it just that much easier for teddy to go on walking.

Next morning after coffee and toast and very much refreshed, I found that Carmen had telephoned her cousin and he was on the way. Half an hour later the breakdown van appeared and hitched up the Austin. I expressed my gratitude to her as she was attending some mid morning customers who, even at that time, were drinking coffees and brandies in the bar and went off with her cousin to Teruel. He was somewhat older than Carmen and insisted on my relating all the details as to what had occurred. Needless to say he was wasting his time and only received vague answers. Later it transpired that the only thing wrong with that tough old vehicle was a dirty fuel filter. This was quickly replaced and the whole effort for towing and repairing, I remember, came to around only four pounds sterling.

*

Now the sun was really pushing out some warmth as I rolled happily along the windows down and singing at the top of my voice. At the village of

Barracas, where I stopped at two of the local cafeterias the day that the heat was melting the asphalt some years back, I drove into at would have been described in England, 'A good pull up for lorries'. There, after swaggering in with a couple of other drivers who had just climbed down from their juggernauts, I treated myself to a welcome break consisting of a 'bocadillo' filled with several different types of sausages and so large that I was not sure whether I was expected to eat it or play it. With this welcome feast went tumblers of wine mixed with lemonade and all followed by coffee and brandy. I sat happily smoking a 'Faria' cigar and felt that all was definitely right with the world.

Reluctantly I left and rattled on down towards the old historic town of Sagunto with its ancient Roman Theatre that would, in the next twenty years, be ruined by the socialist autonomic government who would insist on covering up all the old stones with, would you believe, white marble? Soon after Sagunto I was driving parallel to a sparkling blue Mediterranean sea along the coast road to Valencia. I was nearly home.

Arriving in Cullera late that afternoon I found Mary, together with Worthington, supervising the construction that was in progress on the premises we had contracted. Parked outside was a shaggy looking horse, obviously a tender for the local knackers yard in the not too distant future, together with an ancient cart full of sand, which I suspected had been removed from the beach. Mary greeted me with the good news that an English resident called John, a retired Dorset Thatcher, had offered to make a bamboo cane roof over the bar for us.

The policeman plumber was happily welding tubes together whilst his colleague, Vicente, was wielding a trowel in a professional manner. It was Samuel, owner of the shop next door that sold leather coats and accessories, who dropped by next and introduced himself. Being fluent in several languages he was to become very helpful to us in the coming months. I say months because at that time it actually was months before all the necessary paper work was completed in order for foreigners to open any type of business in Spain. The final opening permit, 'Permiso de Apertura', was always the last and without doubt, the most important to arrive.

*

So our days were spent chasing up items of interest to us for the business and providing continuing support for the local bar owners. We were quick to locate other foreign residents who were also bar owner's and one such person was an amiable Austrian, Horst Amon, who ran the most successful hamburger joint in town. Without tables, chairs or even bar stools and only six to eight people inside, it was packed.

A little shorter in stature than myself with watery eyes and weak chin his shortcomings were adequately compensated by the most enormous handlebar moustache. Continually brushing it first one way and the other with the back of his hand he tended this attribute as tenderly as would the wife which he never had. A jovial fellow Horst was always ready to invite anyone for a drink and in this respect there was never a lack of takers on this one.

Behind the bar, where he prepared and dispensed an incredible amount of hamburgers, Horst had a battered old freezer in which he stored a treasure trove of bottles of various well named schnapps. Most nights when the place was packed to overflowing outside, Horst would announce that he was taking a break. Then turning off the gas on the two burners over which he cooked his hamburgers in two large paella dishes, he would open the freezer, remove a bottle of Alborg, Jägermeister or such, pour a generous helping into a frosted glass then ease his way through the waiting customers to the street. There he would light a cigarette and take a well deserved rest for ten minutes or so. Everyone left inside the bar at that moment would either be ready to walk out or remain there to suffer the unbearable heat and smell of cooking oil, until he decided to continue serving.

After we had known him for sometime Horst, when in his cups and that was most days, would take out a letter of recommendation which he always carried with him. Through this the reader was informed that he had, at one time, been employed as Food and Beverages Manager at a large London Hotel. He was proud of this though I suspected that he had dedicated himself more to the latter than the former.

Another hand written paper fixed to the wall outside his bar announced that the official closing day was Tuesday, but most weeks he managed one or two other days as well. It was on these festive days that Horst and I would tour the other establishments in the immediate area. These included the Bar Frankfurt, frequented by some customers who, I found out later, were not really welcome in their own country.

Then there was Ross's bar, also small but with an excellent atmosphere, owned and run by a charming woman from Hamburg. Next door to this was the Tasca Tizona, just taken over by Joaquin, another good-humoured ex-seaman from Germany. The only one Spanish bar we really frequented on these tours was the Cafeteria Cristal, managed by a very happy family who were always ready to help in anyway they could, if called upon.

*

One fine day and most of them were, a trip to the police headquarters in Valencia resulted in the receiving of our work and resident permits along with the profuse thanks from the head of the foreign department for the express delivery of the gifts to his daughter in London. He was delighted and we even more as this was an addition to our limited, but never the less positive, list of contacts.

Another person we attempted to cultivate was the girl in charge of the tourist office at that time. On asking if there was anyway we could speed up the process of our opening the bar she explained that life was like that and sometimes the lake overflowed; .her reasoning which I never really understood. This was amply proved to us when she asked my assistance over translating the English language part of a brochure for publication to encourage the tourists to visit the Valencia region. I, naturally, obliged and returned the translation on completion. A few weeks later I came across a copy of the final brochure and was absolutely horrified at the vast amount of errors I found in the English translation. On seeing her in the street one day, I asked what had happened to my translation.

"Listen, Chris," she explained, "I am the official translator for English, French and German and if I submit any other person's work done by any of these nationalities and without any corrections on my part, my superiors will think that I am not doing my job correctly."

She then went on to point out to me that when I was eventually able to open the bar that I should, in what according to her was the 'traditional manner' in Spain, provide free drinks for everybody for one whole week. We had never heard of this one either. So if her name had been on the contact list at that moment it certainly was not the following day. After this I occasionally came across tourists carrying brochures and always had the urge to enquire as to how they were enjoying the comic strips in their native language.

On the subject of translations we were always amused by the menu at the Cuenca restaurant which was popular at that time. There were a few mistakes in the naming of the actual dishes but right at the very bottom it explained that, 'The management is always happy to conceive you'. From subsequent meetings with the owner I would not have been surprised if this had been an intentional error on his part.

*

A top floor apartment in Spain is known as an 'Atico' and our particular 'Atico' was on the tenth floor with a fine terrace of around thirty-five square metres. As the block itself was rather old the permanent residents, of which there were few, were always experiencing problems with electricity and water pipes. The next thing that happened, just after we moved in, was that the lift decided to stop functioning, fortunately without anyone actually being in it at the time. Now to walk up ten floors is a pain but not too much of a problem if time is taken. However for a Bassett-hound, not having the physical ability or the inclination, it is virtually impossible. So Worthington had to be carried up all ten flights at least twice a day. Luck was with him in that once he was safely at home the doors to the terrace were always open. So there were no real disasters to contend with. Lift failure was duly reported to the administration agency who confirmed it would be repaired but when, they did not know. After the first couple of weeks the problem of the dog, we decided, had to be resolved and this turned out to be fairly simple. Looking over the rather high wall onto the terrace next door I could see that the apartment to which it belonged was not in use. This apartment was part of another block that had its own lift. So climbing over the wall and onto the narrow ledge that ran around the whole of the building I edged my way along climbed over the next door's wall and onto their terrace. I was delighted to find that the apartment was open and the place completely bare. After that I would make this rather dangerous manoeuvre twice daily. Mary would pass Worthington over the wall to me and I would happily make use the other lift.

Some eight weeks later, just after the lift was repaired, we received the account for our part of the work undertaken. I judged it to be rather excessive at two thousand five hundred Pesetas, particularly as we had been such a time without the use of it. So I went along to the administration office where I was faced with a rather sour faced woman who was, apparently, in charge.

"I think that this account is incorrect," I said firmly but politely planting the paper on the counter where she could see it.

"You are quite right," she said after examining it. "The amount should be almost double that."

Somewhat taken aback I asked why.

"Well," she went on to explain, "There are a lot of people in your block of apartments who refuse to pay. So we have to increase the amount with those who will pay."

The way she said 'your block of apartments' sounded as though it was my own personal building and therefore I was totally responsible for everything. This annoyed me so I handed over the two thousand five hundred Pesetas and apologised saying that she was, at that particular moment, looking at another one who was not going pay for the other neighbours.

Chapter 10

One morning we took a drive up the mountain to the 'Santuario' or church, which dominated the small town of Cullera. From high up we had fine view of the whole of the bay, on down the coast towards Gandia, Denia and the Costa Blanca which lay in a blue haze in the distance. As we stood there gazing out at the sea a smart, grey, American Ford Mustang pulled up next to where we were parked and out climbed Samuel with another man. Introductions were made and that was the first time we met Pany the Greek. Thick set, about my own age, Pany was handsome with dark tight curly hair, twinkling, dark, mischievous eyes and a sincere smile which I could sense immediately would be attractive to most women. He spoke English and as it turned out, five other languages with equal perfection. After the initial introductions I asked Pany where he had studied.

"Leeds," he said, immediately. Then added, "You know the place where the birds don't sing. They cough!"

I knew then that we would get along fine and it was a little later, over a bottle of wine in the Cristal bar that we listened to Pany's story.

*

Pany had been married to a German girl whose father was a wealthy industrialist. He went on to explain that on the day after their wedding his father-in-law had driven the newly weds to Spain and at the Catalonian resort Las Rosas, on the Costa Brava, had presented the couple with the prestigious Las Rosas hotel, together several villas thrown in, as a wedding present. When I enquired as to what had gone wrong he explained that he had become annoyed with his wife commenting on the fact that if it were not for her father, Pany would, at that time, probably be picking olives in Greece. Together with her Germanic attitude towards the staff and Pany's tendency to invite the hired gardener into the hotel and out of the summer heat to share a bottle of wine it became impossible for the Greek. So one day he just packed his bag, walked out and headed towards Leeds. Why Leeds, I was never quite sure. Anyway, once there he studied English language, history and textiles. He also became very much acquainted with the British way of life, part of which included visits to the Mecca dance hall and having the opportunity of being asked by one of the local girls if he would like to escort her home. This he did and on arrival at the small terraced house the girl in question, very much to Pany's utter amazement, invited him in 'for a cup of tea'. Pany protested, thanked her very much and explained, to the equally surprised girl, that he was most sorry but did not wish to marry her. That being invited into ones home for the purpose of 'having a cup of tea, did not amount to a proposal of marriage in English culture ended with him accepting the invitation. This small but significant experience remained with Pany for the rest of is life. His description of entering the house via the back door after passing along what was know as the 'entry' and finding the girl's parents sitting comfortably either side of the bright coal fire with her father sucking the inevitable pipe only confirmed his mother's words during World War II that the British were coming and there was no need to worry as they had everything in perspective. Pany went on to say that he was now involved in the manufacturing and selling of ladies dresses and at the same time burying himself in his first love, Greek history.

I related our own particular story as to why I was in Spain at the same time complaining that things were taking a long time in respect of the opening licence. I also said that money was becoming a problem so some sort of action was required. However what, I had no idea.

"Well you came to Spain to open a barbecue," he said, after listening intently to my tale of woe. "What's stopping you from going ahead?"

"Money," I grumbled. "What else, apart from that and things like location, premises and a hundred others I could think of."

"Well. If you cannot have your own premises why don't we look for someone to cooperate with us?"

"What do you mean, 'we' and 'us'?"

"Look, Chris. My business is ticking over fairly well in Athens and I have some time on my hands. What do say we sort it between both of us? You just tell me exactly what you're looking for and let's see if we can do something about it, OK?"

"Fine by me," I said realising at that point that I was still thinking like someone from Britain and not taking into account different situations with potential business possibilities that were waiting around us. Especially when there were kind Spaniards who would be willing to consider certain gains in return for facilities placed at our disposal.

"Listen," continued Pany, "there are tourists here in Cullera even now and what has the place got to offer? Apart, that is, from the beach, bars and a couple of discotheques there is absolutely nothing else." He threw back his head and laughed; a deep happy, genuine sound that I got to know quickly. "So, Chris, let's go find somewhere where we can take these people out on a barbeque trip."

I readily agreed as just wandering around the bars while waiting for 'Permisos' of one sort or another was not proving at all positive. So, the next couple of weeks were spent travelling around within a radius of twenty kilometres looking for a suitable place. We soon discovered that this was not as easy as we had first thought. However, Pany agreed to press on convinced that it was only a matter of time.

Our own pub was now almost completed and looked, compared with the existing bars and restaurants in Cullera, somewhat more attractive and different. In fact what might be termed as more up market. A beautiful wooden topped counter made up of slatted strips of wood tightly joined together; it was around fifteen feet in length. Over this was John the Thatcher's bamboo roof and seeing this everyday reminded me that the fire risk factor in the UK would never have permitted such a thing. Going really rustic I had bought some large plant pots, drilled holes all over them, painted them red and made lamps. A German friend staggered in one day carrying a huge oar that he had found on the beach. I hung this behind the bar and painted on it, 'Don't let the bastards get you down'. This, we later, explained to our Spanish customers was a typical English toast. So in the coming months many a glass was raised and the words, 'Don't let the bastards get you down' echoed around the high ceiling bar.

Still lacking the final opening licence I could not charge people for drinks but with the door normally open an assortment of people wandered in. Most of them we knew due to their presence in our nightly activities of supporting the local bars with Horst.

"Sorry but I cannot sell your anything to drink," I would explain. "However, if you would like, I can invite you to whatever your wish."

Such an offer was readily accepted as most were dedicated to this delightful pastime. After a few days I found that these customers, especially the German tourists, would drink happily away for an hour or so. Then after they had left, I would discover money discreetly placed under the drip mats. One evening after a particularly busy day 'inviting' clients, there came a point in my thinking that this might be more profitable than opening as a normal bar.

*

On one particular night in staggered the policeman plumber dressed in full uniform, obviously on duty and pretty well the worse for drink. "What's that for?" he demanded pointing to the dart board after wandering around a while.

"Oh, that's an English pub game," I replied. "We throw these little arrows at the numbers on the board."

Here I produced a selection of dart sets from under the bar and laid them out for his inspection.

"Hu!" he scoffed. "Let's play the Spanish way!"

Then, without any warning, he pulled out his regulation pistol and before I could stop him, loosed off two shots at double twenty. Fortunately, his eyesight being somewhat impaired at the time, he hit the wall instead. Needless to say however the noise was horrendous and being very much concerned about the neighbours complaining, I quickly thrust a large glass of brandy into his hands and hustled him out of the place still muttering, "Little arrows. Bah!" I understand that after all these years the bullet holes are still there.

*

Pany came hurrying into the bar one morning and announced that he had at last found the ideal place for the barbeque project.

"Where?" I asked, equally excited at the news.

"Up on the side of a mountain," he explained. "About half an hour away from here through the orange groves. It's a tiny hamlet, just a few houses, called, 'Aldea-del-Señor' or as you say in English, 'Village of the Lord'."

"Sound fine," I said. "With a name like that we should not have many problems to contend with."

I presented him with a small glass of beer in celebration. "Does the owner agree to what we have in mind?"

"Not yet," said Pany shrugging, "But don't you worry about that side of the matter. He'll agree alright when we see him this afternoon."

At around four o'clock we piled into Pany's Mustang and drove out to the 'Aldea-del-Señor'. My friend was quite right, just a sad huddle of white washed cottages with unmade roads crouched half way up the side of a range of mountains called the 'Sierra de Los Pinos'. It was easy to park right outside of the bar as there was no other vehicle in sight. My first impression of the place, as we wandered in, was not at all positive, but there again I was not sure what to expect. A cheerless, scruffy place, with an assortment of tables and chairs scattered at random together with the usual stainless steel bar behind which were a couple of shelves displaying a very few bottles one of which I noticed had a label showing a huge bear with the name Black Bear Whiskey. Although it was quite warm outside the owner and his wife were sitting around a wood burning stove together with a pram in which it later turned out to be their newly-born daughter. Walking over to the bar we stood waiting.

Eventually the man stood up and came across. Immediately I was struck by the similarity of his appearance to William Bendix, the American film star who played tough guy roles in films, years back. Apart from his physical features, here the likeness ended. It was as Pany ordered two vino tintos that I notice, apart from the man's shirt which exhibited a wonderful selection of stains competing with the soiled apron around his thick waist, that his crowning glory were his finger nails. Chipped and absolutely filthy, they were so bad that I began wondering if he was working at some local mine where they were short of shovels. I mean, I know that a lot of people have black finger nails but José, for that is what turned out to be his name, had a monopoly on them.

His wife, a timid, frowsy, little mouse of a woman, refused to make eye contact with us and sat holding firmly onto the pram as if we might have been a couple of kidnappers. I felt like assuring her that everything was alright and William Bendix would protect her.

"You don't seriously think we should bring people out to this place dump?" I said quietly to Pany in English, as José wiped couple of rather grimy glasses with a paper serviette.

"No, Chris. It's just that they have a couple of terraces upstairs which would be ideal for what we have in mind."

"How the hell do you know that?"

"I walked up the mountain this morning and I could look down on the place."

My interest heightened and I nodded to Pany, "Right. Let's do it."

There were no subtle pleasantries where Pany was concerned. He beckoned José, who after serving the also black wine from a cracked terracotta jug, was about to return to his place by the stove.

"Listen my friend. The Englishman," he nodded towards myself, "and I are here to do you a favour."

José looked a little doubtful and I thought that if we were anywhere else, apart from here, this would be the moment we would receive our marching orders. But it was not to be so.

"You see," went on Pany, "The Englishman has a large and famous restaurant, in Cullera."

My heart sank at this lie but I saw a faint light of interest appear in José's eyes.

Pany then continued slowly and precisely. "As you probably know word has spread to Cullera about your famous 'Paellas'."

Pany paused to let this sink in and the other nodded as though he were not in the least surprised. "The Englishman has many customers who would like very much to travel out here to see for themselves what a culinary artist you are. You see he is not, being a foreigner, experienced in the art of making paellas."

José was nodding and fairly beaming now, opening his mouth and displaying what could only be described as a fine row of condemned houses. My attention would normally not have been draw to his dental condition if he had bothered to shave recently which he had not. I could now see that his mind was clocking up currency, a commodity much appreciated in most societies but guaranteed to instil a feeling of deep respect by most Valencianos.

Placing the wine jug a little nearer to us he said, enthusiastically, "No problem at all. Bring as many as you like, we have enough tables and chairs for many customers."   Here he indicated the bar with a casual wave of his hand. "And out at the back I have a 'Paellero' where I cook my famous paellas," he added expansively.

Pany turned from the bar and looked carefully about him, at the crates of Coca Cola, soft drinks and various beers stacked around the walls. His eyes also fell upon the cigarette ends and the screwed up paper serviettes on the floor all mixed up with the remains of shrimps and other small fish together with bits of sausage and bread. He then reeled in the line a little.

"Certainly not my friend. You cannot expect my distinguished companion here to bring his customers," here he looked meaningfully at me, "including the British Consul to... to... this!" Then in the grand style of Italy's dictator, Mussolini, he flung out both arms at the same time indicating the mess. "No! Definitely not."

José's expression changed rapidly to one of disappointment. "Well, it possibly does need a little cleaning up," he agreed, after a moment's silence.

"A little?" boomed Pany, now well animated. "A little? In any other country you would be locked up for such disgraceful premises."

Then he asked lowering his voice, "And what, may I ask are the toilets like?" He nodded to a door at the rear marked 'Servicios'. "Just a hole in the ground, I suppose?"

José shot out from behind the bar as though Pany was on the point of confirming this for himself. "Why not let us have a little more wine and talk about it?" he suggested.

But Pany was not to be side tracked on this one and in true Benito style he folded his arms, shook his head sadly turned his back on José and spoke to me. "No. I don't think that this place is suitable. What we really need is somewhere in the open air. If at all possible a place that has a large terrace with a nice view. Yes, that is what we want. A terrace with a nice view."

José caught the hook, grabbed Pany by the arm then swinging him round said excitedly, "Upstairs! I have two terraces. Come, I will show you!"

He was fairly pulling Pany who, still looking very doubtful, was staring pointedly over his shoulder in the direction of the toilets.

"Well we could just take a look upstairs," I said feeling a little sorry for José. "Being that we are now here."

José released Pany and caught me by the sleeve. "Yes!" he cried, "I will show you the finest terrace on all Levante!"

Pany looking suitably unimpressed, trailed after José who by this time was leading me out of the door.

There was a short, dingy, passageway next to the bar which led to a rather grubby patio with grapevines climbing everywhere as if intent on some form of escape. To one side there was a large plinth, around waist high, covered in cold ashes and bits of charred wood, over which was a crude chimney. This, I assumed, was where José cooked his paellas. This, I also decided, was well in keeping with the general air of the place.

"When did it last have a coat of paint?" Pany asked, looking around him.

That was a difficult one for the Spaniard as it was pretty obvious that it had never had a coat of paint ever. The bricks were as bare as the day they had been laid.

"I was thinking about doing it this week," said José looking rather surprised that someone would consider this a necessity.

"Really?" said Pany. "Well that's a start, anyway."

In one corner steep, narrow, steps led upwards and José ushered us towards them.   Once at the top the most amazing sight confronted us. There were, as Pany had said, two terraces. The one leading off to the right which lay over José's garage and the other, being the largest, was to the left. The spacious one was overlooking all the orange groves and rice fields with fine uninterrupted views towards Valencia. Absolutely ideal.

However what was surprising was that both terraces were completely full of chickens, ducks and turkeys, together with an assortment of wire cages in which rabbits hopped happily around. There was even a small pink pig that seemed intent on molesting everything in sight. It was exactly the impression I had of Old MacDonald's farm. The noise competed with the smell which was almost overwhelming. Pany placed his hands on his hips again and gazed majestically about him. José eyes never left the Greek's face, expectantly, waiting for some crumbs of comfort.

"Well, what do you think?" he asked, unable to contain himself any longer.

"Nothing that a bomb wouldn't put right," Pany answered dryly, continuing to stare about him with a calculating expression.

"All this would have to go," he announced finally.

"All what would have to go?" asked a puzzled José.

"This zoo. All these birds and animals." Pany waved his arms at the spectacle that was happening before our eyes.

"But couldn't you just use the big terrace?"

"What. The British Consul sitting over there, noshing paella, and over here all this going on?"

At that precise moment a mangy, scarecrow of a dog appeared from nowhere and was trying to mount the pig which in turn was squealing like crazy. I tried to hide my smile and had difficulty in not laughing out loud.

José, not really noticing anything unusual, said reluctantly, "Alright, both terraces."

Pany clapped him on the back, congratulating him on his wise decision. "We will make you the most famous restaurant for paellas in the entire region," he said grandly. "Here the people will eat," he went on waving his arm at the large terrace, "and here," turning to the smaller one, "they will drink at the beautiful bar and sing and dance."

"What beautiful bar?" asked a puzzled José, turning his eyes away from the scruffy mongrel which had given up on the pig and was happily chasing chickens.

"Why, the bar that you are going to build over there, of course."

"Am I?" asked an even more bewildered José.

Pany then placed a fatherly arm around the man's shoulders. "Where will people drink, my friend. Will not the Consul be thirsty after eating your paella?"

He then threw in some incentive for José. "Look, you build a beautiful rustic bar. My friend here will show you how," he nodded to me, "and we will stock it with all the drinks that we will buy directly from you. Isn't that a fair enough offer?"

Here he slapped José on the shoulder without waiting for the reply and the other nodded somewhat unenthusiastically, not really animated by the prospect of such an amount of work that seemed to be not of his making.

"Oh, and one other thing," said Pany. "The big terrace will have to have some sort of cane structure for shade when the people eat."

Again José nodded, resignedly. "De acuerdo," he muttered.

We retired downstairs leaving Old MacDonald's farm behind and the dog making amorous approaches to the pig again. Details were gone over with more red wine on hand. It turned out that there was a route along which we could manoeuvre a coach through the orange groves and stop at a large abandoned country house to break the journey. This, we agreed, would make it a real excursion. I drew up my ideas on the rustic bar which was inexpensive and simple to construct while Pany pressed José to start work immediately. Pany also dispelled any second thoughts that José might be considering by informing the bar owner that he, personally, would supervise the work, by bringing out his sleeping bag and camping outside the village. Then after even more wine we all shook hands and Pany and I set off for Cullera once more. José waved us goodbye shouting after us that we were invited for one of his famous paellas that coming week end.

"What's this about the English Consul?" I asked, once we were rattling our way over the cobbled main road.

"Oh that," Pany grinned. "One of my German friends who lives in Cullera will play the part of the Consul."

"German?" I asked, wondering if I had heard correctly.

"Yes, does it really matter?"

I considered this implication for a minute. "No. I suppose not."

The Greek was quiet for a while and I asked if anything was wrong.

"I was just thinking," he said seriously.

"What about?"

"It might have been a very good idea if we had kept on the pig and the dog. We could have made a bloody fortune!"

*

Waiting for us when we arrived in Cullera was Mary together with Vicente, the policeman brick layer who, looking smart in his uniform was lounging against the bar sipping at a monster glass of wine that Mary had served.

"Any problems?" I asked, still unused to seeing official dress without thinking that there might be something wrong.

"Nothing that cannot be sorted," said Vicente. "It's the van. The one you brought all your things in."

"What about it?"

"Well," he explained, "you're not allowed to be resident in Spain and have a foreign vehicle unless you pay import duties."

"So what do I have to do?"

He took a large swallow of the red plonk and smacked his lips. "A choice of three things. One you can take the thing out of the country...,"

Before he could continue I interrupted, "I only paid a hundred pounds for it. It's not worth going anywhere."

"Alright, Chris. Then you can drive it out into the rice fields, take the number plates off and let the gypsies take care of it. It will probably disappear in a few days."

"But there is also the possibility it might not," I said, carefully. "And the Guardia Civil?"

"Alright then," he went on patiently, "You arrange to have it stolen."

"I what? I arrange to have it stolen. What for? There is no insurance on that thing now."

"Who's talking about insurance, Chris? Forget about insurance. Just make sure it disappears. That's all."

With Vicente's words in mind, we all trooped over to the Cristal bar that afternoon and when I considered that there were enough people present, I stood up and called for attention. "Does anyone want to steal my van? The blue one parked outside the English bar," I asked as if it were the most natural thing in the world.

All eyes turned in that direction and although there were a few comments there did not appear to be any takers. Then a voice said, "Paco over at the bodega has one exactly like that. He might be interested."

Pany and I walked over to the bodega which was in fact a large shop selling all types of wines from huge black barrels, together with beers and spirits. We found Paco sitting at the back playing cards with three of the local cronies. I explained why we were there and he immediately agreed to steal the vehicle. It would, he explained, serve for spare parts for his own vehicle.

"I will have to help you," I said. "The battery is flat. Oh, yes and one other thing. When you get it to wherever you're taking it, make sure that you remove the English number plates. Alright?"

Paco agreed and that was that. Or so I thought. Later in the evening we watched as the old diesel van disappeared down the road. I felt a little sad but it had served its purpose.

*

Sunday arrived and armed with a camera we set out for the Aldea-del-Señor on a trial run. Just after the village of Favareta, we passed a tall, disreputable, looking tramp with extremely long hair and beard heading in the same direction. Pany gave him a couple of blasts on the horn and waved.

"Someone you know?" I asked rather taken aback.

"Not really, Chris. But, it could just be that he is walking home to his village where we are heading and we just can't be too careful."

A little further on Pany swung the Mustang off the main road and after only a couple of attempts, found a suitable small back road full of potholes but more or less negotiable for a coach. This led through the orange groves to the large abandoned house which lay resignedly at the end of an impressive tree lined driveway.

It was a lovely rambling old place surrounded by large fig and medlar trees. In front of the crumbling facade of the 'Finca' was a large man made lake which was obviously used for watering the groves. Swallows swooped dangerously low over the water and the 'grillos' chirped in the background. It was all very peaceful. We helped ourselves to the deep purple fruit on one of the fig trees.

"What a great place to stop," I said, and Pany agreed.

"The Germans will love it," he said.

My mind was working on customer satisfaction as I had recently come across a sparkling wine, rather like the Italian 'Asti Spumanti'. The bottle looked very attractive, just like a champagne bottle, with even a gold top. The decorative label read, 'Trival' and the cost, just twenty two pesetas a go. This was less than ten pence a bottle and even at that time, extremely cheap.

"Tell you what," I said, "We buy a couple of those portable ice boxes that people take to the beach, load them with ice and 'Trival'. Then when we arrive here we can mix the wine with fresh orange juice."

"And brandy," put in Pany, without any hesitation.

"Great!" I confirmed. "And brandy. Then when we arrive at the restaurant nobody will notice José's fingernails."

Both laughing we continued up to the village to be welcomed by several of the local residents who were gathered outside the bar.

"José must have spread the word that we are going to put the place on the map," I said as we parked the car.

Our first priority was to inspect the small patio where the paella was being prepared. It now looked very much tidier but still lacked a lick of paint.

"Mañana," said José, when he noticed Pany staring pointedly at the walls.

Next we climbed the steps to the terrace and I was most surprised to see that the only animal still in evidence was the mangy dog. Lying in the sun he eyed us with suspicion and I sensed that he knew we had something to do with the disappearance of his friend the pig.

"Don't turn your back on him," I warned Pany, "just in case."

The following couple of hours passed pleasantly with us and José eating paella seated around a table in the street and being served in true Spanish style by his wife. It was excellent.

"Under what name do you wish us to publicise your restaurant?" Pany asked José at one point.

The other, who had obviously given this some consideration, replied immediately, 'El Balcón de Levante'."

We congratulated him on his choice, raised our glasses to 'El Balcon de Levante'. And the wine flowed and the cracked terracotta jugs didn't seem that much out of place. The paella was followed by a large dish of local fruits including oranges, figs and nísperos. All this was rounded off by coffees, brandies and 'Faria' cigars.

Then, as the evening was drawing in we arranged to come out again in a few days to see how work on the terrace was progressing. Then thanking José drove very carefully back to Cullera.

The photographs were developed, printed and placed on a board with the title 'Excursion to the Balcón de Levante'. This was then hung in front of the bar. Next I went off to negotiate with the only existing coach company in Cullera. The owner was a kindly man by the name of Miguel. He took details and supplied me with a quote on the spot. Back at the bar we calculated the price of transport together with José's price for the food.

"Sorry," I said to Pany, "It doesn't look as though we will have enough clients to warrant the use of the coach initially."

"Don't worry, Chris. Many of these people have their own cars. We can all drive there. Then when trade picks up we hire the coach."

"How often do you think we can do the trip?" I asked.

He thought for a minute then said, "I don't know about you but I get very hungry these days. What so you say that we try two or three times a week?"

And so it was. We placed the publicity in all the bars, particularly Horst's hamburger joint and waited. Eventually people began trickling into the pub asking for details. In the meantime Pany, who was quite an able guitar player, had managed to acquire the loan of an instrument from one of the more attractive lady customers. So we had music to look forward to as well.

*

The first excursion involved around twelve clients and was a great success. Stopping at the friendly old house was really a pleasure for all of them and as for the cold 'Trival' type champagne mixed with fresh orange juice and brandy that was a complete hit. Pany had, prior to the trip, spent several days out at the village ensuring that José was ready to receive us and this time we ate on the large terrace. It was amazing how people of mixed nationalities, of all ages and different walks of life could set out to really enjoy themselves.

I was pleased to see that construction on the bar was going ahead fine. All in all we decided that if we were not going to be millionaires we were, at least, eating well. Next there came the first excursion using Miguel's coach. Thank goodness that in those days there were not the rigid laws that applied to vehicles as this particular one looked as though it might have been registered in the Doomsday book. I expressed my misgivings to Pany about this wreck that had probably been put to good use in the Spanish Civil war.

"You worry too much," he said, when we first saw it trundling down the road to where we were waiting outside the pub. "This is what people are here for. One of the modern super coaches would not be appreciated nearly as much."

And, of course, he was absolutely right. Everyone present firmly believed that we had organised this old rattler especially for the trip.

That day was something different. After stopping at the old house, dishing out the powerful 'Trival' mixture we all arrived in fine spirits at the village. There we found that José and the locals had decorated the main street with flags. They fluttered merrily in the slight breeze and we received an enthusiastic applause from all the neighbours present as we stepped down from the coach. Even the dog, apparently in a better frame of mind, came out wagging his tail.

I heard José asking Pany about something or other and Pany immediately pointed out one of our more distinguished looking customers, very tall and very slim with steel grey hair. Of German nationality, Rudi Urtinger was famous in all the bars in Cullera for his ability to drink non-stop around the clock.

"What was that about?" I asked Pany as José was enthusiastically shaking the surprised Rudi by the hand.

"Oh," said Pany, "José wanted to know who the British Consul was and I pointed him out."

The German, whose Spanish was virtually non existent, just kept nodding his head and smiling. This seemed to make José very happy. It was only after several locals came up to him and warmly grasped his hand that I noticed a puzzled expression appear on Rudi's face. Still never mind. We all climbed up to the terrace where a long trestle table had been set up so that we could not only enjoy the food but the magnificent view also.

There was only one minor upset and that was when Pany went over to the other terrace where the rustic bar was still under construction.

"José!" he yelled. "Come here!"

The other appeared to find Pany standing there with a trembling finger pointing.   "What the devil are those?" he asked.

José looking puzzled said, "Tables and chairs for the bar. Why?"

"And?" demanded Pany, folding his arms and drumming his fingers.

"And what?" asked José, even more confused.

"And what are those awful plastic tables and chairs doing in our rustic bar?"

"But, Pany. They are the latest tables and chairs that are easy to keep clean and to store," José protested.

Pany relented a little then placing a fatherly arm around the others shoulders, he said, "Listen, my friend. People do not come all the way from England and Germany to a nice typical Spanish bar and sit on plastic furniture."

José considered this for a minute then asked, "So what do they come all that way to sit on?"

Pany thought for a moment then said slowly, "Barrels."

"Barrels," repeated José unable to believe his ears.

"Yes barrels."

"Barrels that wine goes into?"

Pany slapped him on the back as though the man had gained twenty thousand points for his starter. "Quite correct amigo. I think that five or six large barrels for tables and around twenty-five smaller ones, to sit on. That should do it!"

Next taking a pace back Pany looked José squarely in the face and asked, "Is that not possible?"

Not fully convinced but not wishing to turn his back on any business at this late stage, José nodded his head even more so resignedly. "I suppose so," he said.

Later, animated by more wine, Pany played the guitar and we all sang with the German contingent happily out pacing the rest of us.

Then when it was time to leave the last thing I remember was José, together with some of the neighbours, standing there open mouthed as, after falling down the steps, we loaded one very drunk Rudi onto the coach.

The pleasure of this first real excursion was increased when, on arriving back in Cullera, I was informed by a smiling wife that the final opening licence for the pub had arrived. "Well," I thought, "That is something positive, anyway."

*

The first week in July was unbearably hot when we officially opened the doors. And what a disaster. For seven days Mary and I stood behind the bar serving the odd drink or two, mostly to people we already knew and watched as the rest of the holiday makers glanced into the place as they passed on the way to the beach doing the soft sand shuffle. Takings for that first week amounted to thirteen thousand Pesetas or in sterling a pathetic one hundred and twenty pounds. It seemed heartbreaking after all the effort we had put into the place.

Then after a few drinks and much thought one evening, we both of us concluded that the pub was possibly just that little too elegant for the type of customers that were accustomed to Spanish tapas bars and restaurants. With only one small hotel situated at the far end of the bay, all the rest of Cullera consisted of high rise apartments. Apart from many of them being owned by people from Madrid a lot were to let for the season. I had discovered that a family of four would rent a place for the month of July or August and as many as twelve or fifteen would arrive. The children would sleep on the balcony and granny would use the chair with the rest scattered about the place.

It was then that I read that Cullera had more people per square meter in August then anywhere else in Europe. So these potential customers of ours, foreign nationals apart, were families who dined mainly in the apartments and had the occasional meal out. Many times the meal in question consisted of one of Horst's famous hamburgers and chips.

"So what the hell are we going to do?" asked Mary, adjusting her sweat band.

I thought about it for a while then said, "Remember Betty and Gomar Davis that we met in Toledo? The nice American couple?"

She nodded still looking as though she was about to break into tears.

"Well," I went on, "if you remember they were telling us about a new fad in America called the 'Happy Hour'. That's when all the drinks are served at half price for one hour every evening."

She brightened a little, "Do you think it would work here in Spain? I mean, you know suspicious they are of anything foreign."

"Well, we'll soon find out," I said. "We have to do something. Any bloody thing."

A large board was found and I went to work. Profit margins on drinks were normally very good so there was plenty of leeway in calculating attractive prices just for one hour. A small beer from the barrel at 'Happy Hour' prices worked out at just seven pesetas or around five pence sterling and a 'Cubalibre', rum and Coca Cola, twelve pesetas. The words 'Happy Hour' were written in Spanish, German, French and English. The time we chose to do it was between seven and eight o'clock each evening.

The first day of this, new phase arrived, I placed the board outside the pub, and we waited. I remember clearly that just after seven, one of the town's teenagers strolled in looking rather nervous. "Excuse me," he said, "are those the real prices on the board outside?"

I confirmed that they were indeed and he ordered a Coca Cola which I served him with ice and lemon from a litre bottle. This he rapidly consumed, paid, and then glancing at his watch hurried out. Then little by little other customers began trickling in, all asking the same question about the prices. Next thing our very first customer returned breathlessly with several of his friends. Word was spreading like crazy and that was the beginning.

Now more than thirty years on I am still occasionally approached by strangers in Valencia who say, "Hey, I remember you. You're Mister 'Happy Hour' from Cullera!"

By the end of that week we had crowds waiting outside for us to open. Word had carried as far as Valencia, forty odd kilometres away, and youngsters travelled down arranging to meet each other, not at the English Pub, but the 'Happy Hour'.

Quickly we took on a young boy as a waiter and both he and I served while Mary, with her sweat band, slaved like mad in the pokey little kitchen preparing chips in the basket, jacket potatoes and portions of shepherd's pie. Promptly at eight o'clock each evening we rang the bell, turned everyone out and cleaned up the place, sweeping away all the debris including, many times, broken glass. We calculated that the profit on that one hour amounted to around seven or eight pounds sterling which at that time was adequate for our lease and lighting. A sigh of relief and a drink was called for.

Late one evening we had a formal visit by a group of other Spanish bar owners' and their spokesman informed us that the 'Happy Hour' was illegal and that I was not permitted to sell drinks at prices less than they themselves charged. Not really convinced, the next day I visited the administration man whose services we had used to organise our resident and work permits. He also confirmed that what I was doing was illegal. This was curious as everyone, depending on their category of establishment, had a list of maximum prices but certainly no minimum prices. It then occurred to me that this administrator was also representing the other bar and restaurant owner's.

Deciding that the matter required some thought I went along to the Cristal bar for a drink intending to figure out what to do. Gedo van der Weig was there. Tall, strikingly blond, and always elegantly turned out with collar and tie whatever the weather, this Dutchman was employed as sales promoter of apartments in Cullera for a local building constructor. .

"Ah," I thought as I entered the bar, "he'll know what to do."

So commandeering the stool next to him, I ordered a coffee and brandy.

"Hello my friend," he said, stretching out his hand towards me. "How are you?"

"Fine thanks, Gedo," I said, shaking it.

Then before I could mention the 'Happy Hour' dilemma he surprised me by asking, "Was that old van you drove from England, a blue coloured one?"

"Yes," I confirmed wondering why he asked. "It was blue."

"And it was, if I am not mistaken, a right hand drive?"

"Correct."

"Did it have English number plates?"

"Of course it did," I confirmed becoming irritated at all this. "But why all these questions, Gedo?"

He grinned and continued to stare over my shoulder. "Because, my friend, it is coming down the street right at this moment."

Quickly I turned and stared out of the window. And sure enough there it was in its entire glory rumbling up the road towards the bodega. "Good, Lord!" I said. "What the hell's going on?"

Then Gedo threw his head back and started laughing. "It looks as though Paco just changed the registration plates to Spanish ones."

"He can't do that," I protested. "How the hell is he going to explain how the steering wheel moved over to the other side if he gets stopped by the Civil Guard?"

"Don't worry about it, Chris. You gave it to him and it was up to him what he did with it."

"But I reported it as being stolen. Just to cover myself," I said, becoming nervous and thinking of possible complications.

"I still wouldn't worry. Until something happens, that is. Anyway, whatever he does can always be sorted out one way or another."

With that Gedo ordered us a brandy each and pushing the matter of the van to the back of my mind, I explained my 'Happy Hour' predicament.

"Don't worry about that either," he said with an air of someone who was well versed on Spanish law. "But if you want some legal advice call my lawyer in Valencia. His name is Antonio Bourgogne and he used to live in

England. Sunbury-on-Thames, I think it was. Anyway there would be no communication problems."

He then asked, "By the way, what are you doing for transport these days, now that the van has gone?"

"Nothing," I said, sipping my brandy. "Why?"

"Well you know I have a motor bike to get around on?"

I didn't, but I nodded anyway.

"I fell off the thing on some loose gravel up near the lighthouse and I want to get rid of the machine."

My ears pricked up as any form of transport to get me about would be more than useful. "If I like it, then how much?" I asked.

"For you I reckon, four thousand Pesetas."

"Fine," I agreed, "What sort is it?"

"A Moto Guzzi. Old, but it goes well."

"Great. When can I see it?"

"Actually it is parked outside right now."

So out we both went to take a look. My first impression was that it probably shared the same lineage as Miguel's coach but it certainly sounded alright when Gedo kicked it into life. I rode it down to the end of the road and back. It was simple to handle and apart from the occasional electric shock when I tried to operate the horn, it puttered along quite happily.

When I arrived back and had slowed to a stop, Gedo said, "I see you have the Dutch courage as you English say."

I heaved the bike onto its stand. "Dutch courage," I explained, "is when you have something to drink in order to do something difficult."

"Precisely," said Gedo. "That's just what I had before I fell off the thing."

"What Dutch courage?"

"No. A lot to drink!"

Back at the bar again I handed over the four thousand Pesetas, around thirty five pounds sterling at that time, and we shook hands.

"What about the papers?" I asked, suddenly realising that nothing had been mentioned about them.

"Oh, don't worry about those," Gedo said airily, at the same time carefully placing the money into his wallet.

"Don't worry. But what if I am stopped by the Civil Guard or something?"

"You won't be. Or at least I doubt very much that you will."

He sounded quite confident as he returned his wallet to his pocket.

"Why ever not, Gedo?"

Then indicating to the barman to refill our glasses, he said, "Because they all know that bike."

"They do?"

"Yes, Chris."

"How?"

Gedo nodded his thanks to the waiter and raised his glass towards his lips. "Because," he continued, looking thoughtfully at the glass. "That motorbike I bought from the Mayor of Cullera."

"So you bought it from the Mayor. So what?"

Then replacing his glass carefully onto the bar he slowly raised his hand and put an equally elegant index finger alongside his nose. "Well," he said, "the Mayor didn't have any papers either."

*

Next day I telephoned the lawyer as Gedo had suggested, and was told that if I wanted to give all the drinks away free I could do. There was no minimum price. So the 'Happy Hour' sailed on and I received yet another visit by the other bar owners. I repeated what the lawyer had said and offered to let them have his telephone number if they wanted to confirm it. They didn't and I was told that if we were stupid enough to work twice as hard for less profit that was our business. I said that possibly I was stupid but that it was my business and they left.

At times Spanish clients were difficult to understand in more ways than one. It was on one fairly quiet night that four well dressed customer came into the pub and ordered large Chivas Regal whiskies. This particular brand was, in those days, becoming very popular with much publicity and compared with other available whiskies, an expensive drink. The man who had ordered in the first place paid up happily when I said how much they cost and they all stood there talking.

Around twenty minutes later something was said and all four trooped towards the door not having even touched the glasses that were lined up on the bar exactly where I had placed them. Unable to resist I called out, "Excuse me gentlemen, but you haven't touched your drinks. Is there something wrong?"

The last one who was just about to pass through the door stopped and turned. "No. Nothing wrong with the drinks. We paid for them, didn't we?" I nodded and his parting shot was, "Well what are you complaining about?"

On another occasion in came another customer who, after the usual, 'Bueno dias', asked me which was the best whisky I had in the place. I pointed to the top shelf.   "From my personal point of view it is that single malt, 'Glenmorangie'."

He nodded indicating that I pour him a glass, which I did.

He then asked, "What about the ice?"

I explained that with a good malt whisky one did not normally ask for ice.

"Alright," he said. "Then I'll have a Coca Cola."

"Now just a minute," I said. "You're not thinking of mixing Coca Cola with my best whisky?"

"And why not? I'm the one who's paying," he came back angrily.

"Then you can take your business elsewhere," I said, removing the glass from in front of him and placing it behind the bar.

He stared at me for a moment then turned and stormed out of the door. I thought nothing more about it until two nights later when he reappeared with three friends.

"Four of those whiskies," he demanded pointing at the 'Glenmorangie' bottle.

Dutifully I poured the four whiskies and they watched me without as much as a comment.

"Now we want four Coca Colas," said the man.

"No way! Not in here," I responded, my temper rising.

Then one of the others said, "I will pay double the price if you put four Coca Colas."

"Fifty times the price and the answer would still be no!"

The first one then turned to the others and said, "I told you he was a crazy Englishman, didn't I?"

Anyway after more heated words they finally agreed to, at least, try the whisky with just a little cold spring water. After this they admitted that this was the way to drink good whisky, neat or with a little water on the side. I then invited them for a second round and from then on had four new appreciative customers.

*

A further two weeks went by then one evening into the bar came five men, three English and one Scottish. Immediately they started ordering pints of lager and put them to good use. It then transpired that they were part of a team of engineers that was installing machinery at the new Ford car plant in Almusafes about thirty-five kilometres distance. They said that at that moment they were living in an apartment in a tiny seaside place along the coast called Mareny Blau. Naturally Mary and I were pleased to have their business, particularly as they informed us that there would be many more British engineers coming along.

After inviting them for a round I asked as to why they had driven over to Cullera and was told that although there was a bar under the apartment block where they lived, the owner increased the prices for beer almost daily. In fact they had already made up their minds to move to Cullera at the end of the month. I, in turn, explained that in Spanish bars and restaurants there was, for tax reasons, a three price structure; one price at the bar, another at the tables and a third on the terrace. "However," I explained, "I charge the same price for all. Then there is no misunderstanding."

They seemed quite happy about this and stayed until closing time, returning the following evening. This continued and happily the pub now had some regular clients.

Then one night a short, dark and very angry Spaniard came in. Taking me to one side he asked me why I had stolen his best clients at the same time indicating Scots Ron and the others.

"Your clients," I said. "Your clients. I don't even consider them my clients. They are free to go anywhere they please. And anyway," I concluded, pointedly, "If you consider them as your clients why did you keep trying to screw them by putting up the prices of your drinks?"

Without saying another word he then turned on his heel and walked out.

That night the group drank more than usual and I was informed early next day that all four of them were in prison. Bit by bit the story was pieced together.

They had a SEAT car and on that fatal night, full of Skol lager, they had headed back to Mareny Blau along the narrow coast road that twisted and turned up by the lighthouse. Taking one particular bend too quickly they side swiped a vehicle coming in the opposite direction. This vehicle, it turned out, just happened to be driven by the local chief of the Civil Guard who seeing that they had no intentions of stopping, leapt out of his car and fired several shots in their direction at the same time memorising what details of the car he could.

It was early next morning their vehicle was traced to the apartment block where they were staying. One of the 'guardias' then opened the rear door and out fell Ron who had spent the night there. He was immediately hand cuffed and put under arrest. The others were quickly rounded up and all of them taken to Valencia. Then after appearing before the judge they were marched off to the 'Modelo' prison in Mislata where they spent a total of twenty-one days until the matter was sorted out.

Finally, an agreement was made between the judges, the police and the British Consul from Alicante and they were released, three to go free and the fourth, which had been driving at the time was taken directly to the airport and put on a flight out to the UK.

"What was it like in prison?" I asked when the remaining three trooped in again.

"Terrible," said Ron. "We were treated like animals."

"What did you have to eat?"

"Awful food. Rubbish and just a half a roll of bread."

"Half a bread roll?" I asked, surprised.

"Yes," said one of the others. "There was no toilet paper."

As an ex police officer myself, who had seen the inside of various prisons in England, it sounded very bad news to be in one of Spain's lockups. However, little did I realise at that very moment that I would remember their words some fifteen years later when I would also become acquainted with that very same prison.

*

Business grew with the arrival of more contractors for the Ford plant. There was a wide variation of nationalities and apart from the British included American, Dutch, French and many Germans. The latter group started to frequent the pub on Monday evenings, remaining there until closing time. They played darts and drank just about everything possible. We put out platefuls of sauerkraut with frankfurter sausages and this encouraged them even more so. One evening there were around seven or eight of them and I counted that they had consumed around sixty pints of larger apart from sixteen Bacardi and cokes, together with the odd whisky or two.

There was one particular client who came in every night and sat there drinking between ten and twelve Bacardi and cokes up until one o'clock. He would then stroll down to the beach, have a swim and return to finish off the night with several more.

As an encouragement for other clients we usually put out four or five litre jugs of lager placed along the bar so those who wished could serve themselves. On Sundays Mary laid on the traditional roast beef lunch and with little else to do the place was crowded all day. At that time chicken in the basket was popular and not having the time to cook the dish as it should be done, we made an arrangement with the 'Take Away' barbequed chicken place next door.

Some nights it was impossible to get more people in the bar, it was so packed. On several occasions Scots Ron and two others would take over serving the drinks and insisting that Mary and I have an evening off. Delighted at the opportunity we went out one night, returning at around one thirty a.m. Unable even to get through the door we crossed over to the Cristal bar where we found several glum faced English regulars.

"What are you doing here?" one of them asked.

"Couldn't get through the door over there," I replied, nodding towards the pub.

"Neither could we," came the reply.

*

Excursions to the Aldea-del-Señor continued two or three times a week and became even more popular. We had a fine mixture of nationalities joining us including some Japanese, Americans and even the odd Russian. In order to ensure that everything was in order for the paella, I would ride out on my Moto Guzzi, stop at the old house then continue on, supplying José with the final head count for the meal.

Once I waited in the orange groves for the appearance of the coach until I finally realised that there was something amiss. On returning to Cullera I found, much to the delight of all on board, the coach and a large Coca Cola delivery truck absolutely jammed together, side by side, on the narrow bridge over the river. Both had tried to pass at the same time. Everyone, apart from the two drivers, thought it was hilarious. Eventually the situation was resolved and they continued merrily on their way.

We had many characters now frequenting the pub, amongst them being 'Sleepy' Joe. Joe, who had spent some time in Belgium, was, in typical Belgium fashion, able to drink pint after pint, fall asleep at the bar then wake up and continue drinking. One Sunday afternoon after Mary had served all the lunches and the customers were settling down to some serious drinking, the door opened and came a Tunisian carpet seller. Joe, who loved to show off his knowledge of the French language, started talking to the man. Then turning to all those in the bar he explained to us that the man was offering him a carpet for four thousand pesetas.

"Now," said Joe to everyone present. "He has offered me that carpet for four thousand pesetas. But you must never accept the first offer. I am just going to offer him a thousand pesetas and we can start bartering."

Turning to the seller, Joe said in French, "One thousand pesetas."

"OK!" was the immediate reply. "It's yours."

After the laughter had died down Joe admitted that he had nowhere to put the thing so I came to agreement with him whereby he let me have it in return for so many pints and everyone was happy.

Mike McGowan was another very nice chap who worked as an engineer for a German company. An able guitar player he had just treated himself to a new instrument at around seventeen thousand pesetas, quite a lot in those days. Anyway, one day a crowd of us were sitting in the Cristal bar consuming metres of beer. This involved lining up beer bottles to the length of one metre, sixteen bottles in all. Suddenly Mike's wife, for no apparent reason that I could ever determine, appeared and broke a bottle of champagne over his head. She then ran out of the bar. Fortunately Mike's head must have been made of stern stuff as he suffered no apparent damage at the time.

On arrival home that night Mary and I found a coffee percolator, together with other electrical items outside our apartment door. It transpired that Mike's wife had gone to their apartment, thrown his precious guitar over the balcony (twelfth floor, I think it was), distributed a great deal of their personal things to friends and then disappeared in the direction of the airport.

Some weeks later I was driving up near the cliffs by the lighthouse when I saw Mike removing two suitcases from the boot of his car. Stopping, I asked what he was doing.

"I had a letter from the wife who's in England now."

"Oh, yes?"

"Yea, she asked me to send her things on to her."

"Did she now?"

"Certainly did," he said smiling. "So I'm obliging."

He then picked up the suitcases and walked towards the cliff.

"Yes," he said, over his shoulder, "I told her I was sending them on by sea."

And with that he flung the suitcases over the edge.

*

We had several American customers who owned apartments in Cullera and worked at the American base near Madrid. One was a retired bodyguard, of Mexican descent; to ex-President Lyndon B. Johnson, and the other a tough looking Texan who always brought us large jars of Jim Beam bourbon for our personal consumption.

This was the start of the Jim Beam Cub. Rather exclusive it consisted of only three members; myself, Joe Lucas and Ron Bartlett. This trio decided to dedicate themselves to the delights of this rather smooth bourbon and as long as the jars kept on coming, we continued consuming. On several occasions when supplies were really flowing, we thought that Jim Beam might be cited in a possible divorce case.

The pub also attracted numerous entertainment personalities that we had the pleasure to serve. These included Portuguese born Betty Massiego, contender for the European Song contest one year.

Another, Maribel Casanova, was a popular female Matador. With my attraction towards bull-fighting I remember asking Maribel as a fully fledged bullfighter what she did for excitement in her spare time. She looked at me seriously and said, "Quite honestly, Chris. I love diving into a really good novel."

Another customer, who arrived for the holiday season, was the well known Spanish television comedian, Manolo de Vega. Manolo had been married and divorced more than any other Spaniard I knew. He was a gentle personality who neither smoked nor drank alcohol but on screen was funny and provocative. Unfortunately Manolo fell from favour when he cracked a joke that involved Rey Juan Carlos, the Spanish King and this was not at all welcomed, particularly in the new democracy.

The end of that summer season saw the departure of most of the tourists but as we moved into autumn there was, thank goodness, no decline in the amount of Ford contractors.

It was towards the middle of November that Mary became moody and on several occasions locked herself in the toilet, usually with a bottle of wine, refusing to come out until it was finished. Eventually a visit to the local doctor confirmed that she was pregnant. It may sound silly but we had been trying for a family for years with all the tests showing that there was no reason why we should not have one.

Sometime before her pregnancy was confirmed, a regular customer by the name of Andy who was employed on an Arabian Gulf oilrig, being aware of our difficulty to start a family, came into the pub one evening and presented Mary with an African fertility mask. "Here," he said, "stick this on the wall in the bedroom. It never fails."

Not really believing it we complied however and then forgot about it. Whether or not it was due to that exceptionally ugly mask I do not know. However Andy drank free for a night next time he put in an appearance.

During those days towards Christmas we noticed that in the deserted beach area there were many stray dogs wandering about. Where they originated no one could really say. Sometimes they formed packs and presented an unnerving sight for the individual who found his or herself within their vicinity. At such times the local police would be informed and they would mount an operation to round them up. I did hear that they were then dispatched to Valencia zoo as food for the carnivorous animals there but never really knew if this was true of not.

Occasionally one of these dogs, in search of food, would hang around outside the pub. This turned out to be one of the very few lucky ones. A Belgian couple who were regular customers befriended the dog or the dog befriended them. I am not sure which. Anyway it was strange to see that at the moment they turned up the dog seemed to appear from nowhere. Then if they went to the beach the animal would wait patiently on the promenade until they returned. One day all three came in together, the dog looking extremely well groomed and jauntily walking along with a brand new collar and lead. They had taken him to the vet; he had received his injections and was now officially adopted. The following year the trio returned to Cullera and there must have been no happier dog in town as that one.

Moreover, talking of dogs reminds me of the strange, but true, story of Bungy.

Chapter 11

Tom Sullivan was married to Maria, a Spanish woman he had met in England. They had moved out seeking pastures new to Cullera several years before with their young son, Jimmy. Tom had worked in the building trade all his life and in Spain dedicated himself to taking on whatever jobs he could find. His apartment had a splendid terrace and whenever possible, and that was most mornings, Tom walked out and took in the view. Over to the right lay a sea of dark green orange groves leading across to the Sierra de los Pinos. Then if he turned just a little bit to the left he could see the fine broad sweep of the sandy bay.

The view from Tom's bedroom in England had consisted of nothing more than the dreary polluted waters of the Stoke-on-Trent canal, together with the black twisted iron skeleton and fading red bricks of Walton's abandoned brick works. So the tall peaks of the mountains, green in summer and ice cream tipped in the winter, suited him well. Even more so when he felt the warm Mediterranean sun on his back knowing that many of his friends were going about their business in the UK, conscious of the low temperatures and the high fuel bills.

However on the negative side life was not that easy for the family where Tom's work was concerned and for some time they had been considering on returning to England. Jimmy was now coming up to a critical age as regards schooling and neither parent was happy about the Spanish educational system which seemed to promote the local dialect more than the essential basic subjects. The boy himself was not, of course, pleased about his parent's decision to move, particularly as he had made many friends at school. And, of course, there was Bungy to consider.

*

Bungy had made his appearance the previous year, around November. One lunchtime, when Jimmy left school, he came across a group of boys energetically throwing stones at an ugly looking street dog that had, unfortunately, strayed into the area. Later when he thought about the incident Jimmy pondered on whether or not the dog had engineered the whole episode. Anyway, confronted with the situation at the time the boy had waded in scattering the louts and receiving several minor cuts and bruises for his efforts together with a mangy looking hound that happily insisted on following his savoir home. On arrival at the apartment block where he lived, Jimmy turned to the animal and explained apologetically that this was the parting of the ways, there being no possibility that his parents would welcome such an unsavoury visitor. The dog, seemingly unperturbed by this, wagged his tail, grinned at the boy and sat down.

Content that the animal at least had the good manners not to object, Jimmy went up stairs and thought no more about the incident until the following morning. Leaving for school he almost made it to the corner when a jubilant bark announced the dog's reappearance. Being an educated youngster Jimmy acknowledged the dog's presence but with reservation. He then continued on his way to school pretending that he was nothing to do with the underfed rangy canine that was trailing behind him. The dog seemingly to realise the social implications of being seen in the company of such a learned scholar maintained a respectful distance. Jimmy, admiring the dog's spirit slipped into school but not before tossing the animal half of what was to be his midmorning snack. The creature gratefully picked it up, nodded his thanks and made off into the nearby rice fields.

From then onwards this clandestine relationship between boy and dog lasted until such a time as Jimmy, having put sufficient pressure on his parents over some days, they finally condescended to allow the dog to take up residence in the apartment. Part of the reason that Jimmy used was that the animal bore a close similarity to the dogs they had seen some months before in the mountain village of Linares de Mora.

"After all," Jimmy had repeated several times to his reluctant parents, "those dogs in Linares were professionals."

*

This encounter with the 'Professionals' had taken place mainly due to his father's love of mountains. With over three hundred days a year sunshine Tom found that unlike England, here in Cullera it was difficult to tell where one season ended and another began. They just seemed to melt quietly into one another. It was inland towards Teruel and the high Maestrazgo peaks with deep lush valleys that you could observe and appreciate the climatic changes. So it was to there that Tom was drawn, whenever time and money permitted.

On one particular occasion they had stopped at an interesting looking village dominated by a huge crumbling grey church surrounded by a confusion of dwellings clinging to the side of a mountain. Going into a small, comfortable bar which also served as the village shop, they had ordered drinks and a plate of local cheese accompanied by hot homemade bread rolls. The only other customer in the place was and elderly man. Perched on a stool, rather like something out of Alice in Wonderland, this pixie figure with a face like beaten leather and the clearest blue eyes that seemed to be reflecting the very sky outside was enjoying a glass of wine. At his feet sprawled two of the ugliest dogs that the family had ever set eyes upon. To Tom's way of thinking the disorderly entanglement of spindly legs and bony bodies would have drawn the immediate attention of any British RSPCA inspector. There they reclined, more than lay, with the air of two labourers who, having completed their duties, were taking a well deserved rest. And if the old man's mudded boots with patches of moss still clinging to them were anything to go by, they had just returned from some sort of excursion into the surrounding woods.

A natural attraction to animals in general soon had Jimmy talking to the dogs.

"Nice to see the boy recognises a pair of professionals when he sees them," said the old fellow in near perfect English. He then laughed at their surprised expressions, a chuckling happy sound that one would expect from a pixie. "My mother was from Southampton," he explained. "I lived there for many years before returning here. My name is Luis."

Tom introduced himself and Maria, shaking hands and at the same time congratulating him on his English. He refrained from enquiring too deeply into Luis's reasoning for finishing up in that rather no-place spot. The man then nudged one of the dogs with his boot. "This one," he said, fondly, "I wouldn't accept a million pesetas for 'im."

"But that around four thousand pounds!" said Maria unable to restrain herself.

"As much as that?" asked Tom, equally surprised.

The leather features broke into an almost toothless grin. "'Course," he went on seriously, "'earned me more than eight 'undred thousand pesetas last year. And I reckon that this year'll be nearer a million. If weather 'olds," he added, draining his glass.

"Really?" said Tom, not quite certain how to respond.

"Really," repeated Luis, the blue eyes twinkled as looked at each one of them in turn.

"Don't believe me do you?"

Both Tom and Maria looked a little embarrassed, apart from Jimmy who was busily dedicating his attention to the two dogs. "Well," began Tom plucking up courage, "I cannot really think that they would be winning any prizes at the Kennel Club dog show in London."

The pixie chuckled again then slapping his hand on the bar top called, "Manolo! Traerme el saco!"

The bar owner dutifully appeared and from under the counter produced what looked like a very grubby potato sack.

"Whatever is in there cannot amount to much," thought Tom, "unless it's money."

"'Ere take a look at these beauties," cried the old one, tugging at the string and tipping onto the counter what appeared to be five mud caked potatoes. "What d'you think o' them?" Next, picking up the largest one, he began gently rubbing off the mud with his gnarled fingers. "This 'ere be going on for 'alf a kilo. Reckon it should fetch around four thousand pesetas at the auction tomorrow."

Tom at a loss for words asked, "For a potato?"

The fingers stopped rubbing and the blue eyes scrutinised Tom as though wondering whether or not the other was being serious. Then slowly he looked at each one in turn again. "You mean you don't know what these are? You really don't know?"

Tom shrugged, "Very sorry," he apologised, "but to me .... well, they look just like potatoes."

"Me too," put in Maria, feeling it was time for a little support for her husband.

Cocking his head to one side Luis studied the mud caked object in his hand. "I suppose you could say they look like potatoes," he said slowly. "To anyone who don't know, that is." Then seemingly to make up his mind, he said carefully. "These, what you think look like potatoes are, in fact, truffles."

"Truffles," repeated Tom.

The man held it out to Tom, who examined it, gently rubbing off the mud as he had seen the other do.

"You mean what they use in cooking," said Maria, peering over Tom's shoulder.

"Exactly!" cried the old man. "What they use in cooking. A tiny bit of fungus, 'course that's what it is will turn any dish into food fit for a king."

"Why are they so expensive?" asked Tom. "I mean if they were in so much demand they would grow more of them, wouldn't they?"

The blue eyes sparkled and the other laughed. "Not possible," he explained. "They grow wild. There isn't any way to cultivate truffles an' don't suppose there ever will be."

"I thought they only found them in France," put in Maria.

"They do, indeed, find them in France. But they just cannot get enough of them. So they come 'ere to buy. Conditions and climate are similar."

Maria nodded. "I saw a postcard with an old lady and a pig looking for truffles. It was somewhere in the middle of France."

"Exactly," said Luis, warming to his subject. "That's true. They use pigs. But 'ow do you think I would look with a couple of pigs trottin' after me on mi bike?"

They all laughed and the man called for drinks all round.

"So," said Tom, once he had a bottle of cold beer in his hand, "that's what the dogs do. Look for truffles?"

"Exactly. Trained to sniff them out they are. Both of these are professionals to the last 'airs on their tails."

"And where do they come from?" asked Tom, nodding towards the two animals which were now thoroughly enjoying Jimmy's attention.

"Oh, here and there," replied Luis vaguely. "Don't come easy and if you spot one 'e has to spend time with the likes of these for training. A bright dog would soon pick up the idea."

And so the afternoon passed agreeably with Luis the truffle hunter. Then, just before it was time to leave, he presented Maria with the smallest truffle. "You just try it, my dear," he said, wrapping it carefully in a paper serviette. "Just a little in one o' those Shepherd's pie you English like an' you'll see what a difference it makes."

Thanking him and bidding a special goodbye to the two dogs the family promised to return in the near future.

*

So Jimmy's persistent reasoning eventually resulted in his parents accepting their son's new friend. The plan of action had included a bucket of soapy water and a good washing on the terrace to which the dog consented gracefully. After this a visit was made to the local vet who examined the animal, administered various vaccinations and proclaimed the dog fit.

"Why do you want to call him Bungy?" Jimmy's father asked.

"No reason," said Jimmy, fondly scratching the dog's ear. "Just seems a Bungy sort of dog."

At school Jimmy was looked upon as being the 'extranjero' or 'foreign' boy, even after several years. Not that this was, in anyway, a disadvantage. Most Spaniards usually sympathise with anyone who has not been fortunate enough to have been born Spanish. However what it did do was place the boy somewhat apart from the rest and this in turn served to create and even closer relationship between him and Bungy. The dog, already having accepted Jimmy as his natural master, quickly grew to respond to the boy's commands no matter how silly they appeared to be. Tom constructed a serviceable kennel which was placed in a sheltered corner of the terrace. The day it was completed the family organised a special unveiling ceremony. Bungy, of course, did not disappoint them. After cautiously sniffing around the structure he went inside and to everyone's delight flopped down and smiled out at them.

Through his master's concentrated efforts Bungy's short haired coat took on a lustre of burnished gold and the animal, now on a normal diet, fairly exuded a healthy appearance. When walking his gait looked somewhat ungraceful but when running his movements were truly coordinated. And could Bungy run? Ears laid back, neck thrust forward, he fairly streaked along seemingly not to touch the very ground beneath him. Many was the time in the nearby rice fields that he took off after one of the big brown rats that made their home there, returning triumphal to Jimmy and dutifully placing the trophy at his feet.

So it was quite natural when the time came for Jimmy's parents to disclose their intention of returning to England that their son was upset and concerned for his companion.

"Sorry, lad," apologised his father. "But there is absolutely no way we can afford to put him in quarantine. We need every penny."

Eyes smarting, Jimmy protested, "But, Dad. Bungy is part of the family."

Placing an arm around his son's shoulders, Tom said, "I know he's part of the family but it is just not possible." Then drawing his son closer he said, "But don't worry, son. We will find him the best home possible and you will be able to visit him every time we come back here."

"But, Dad," insisted an almost tearful Jimmy, "·whose going to want Bungy? He's not even a good looking dog."

"Of course he is, Jimmy. You always said that he was a professional."

The boy's eyes suddenly lit up at his father's words. "That's it!" he cried. "The professionals."

Tom looked puzzled at his son's outburst.

"The man in the mountains," explained Jimmy, excitedly drawing away from his father. "You remember? That old man in the mountains, with the two dogs, that looked for those potato things."

"Truffles," said Tom automatically.

"Whatever they're called, Dad," Jimmy went on. "We can ask him to take Bungy. I know he would love it up there in the woods with his friends."

Tom was hesitant, calculating the implications. "I'm not sure. He's not really trained is he?"

There was no way Jimmy was not to be put off. "The man can train him. I know he can. You are always saying how intelligent Bungy is. Let's try. Please, Dad. Please….."

Well aware of his son's anguish, Tom finally agreed. After all it would not take too much trouble to find out. And apart from that he was also concerned for the dog's well-being. Much to his surprise Tom experienced little difficulty in contacting Manolo, the bar owner in Linares. Over the telephone he explained that they would be there on the following Sunday and would he be kind enough to let Luis know. He was told in return that as the old man came in most days there would be no problem.

"But, Dad. We won't have to leave Bungy there on Sunday, will we?" Jimmy asked anxiously.

"No of course not," his father reassured him. "We just see if Luis is in agreement and then we take him up there sometime before we leave."

*

Sunday arrived and the family piled enthusiastically into the car with Bungy looking his best after a good grooming by his master.

The main road swings inland towards Teruel some twenty kilometres north of Valencia. It is now projected that this highway will eventually pass through the Pyrenean mountains and link up with the French road network. Villages like Torres-Torres, Gilet and Estivella that in the past caused innumerable traffic jams for 'Los Domingueros', families that drove out on Sundays to make paellas in the surrounding countryside, are now by-passed. So in little more than one hour Tom was driving up to the high plateau beyond the orange groves and passing the small village of Barracas.

"This might be the place that Luis said where they hold the truffle auction," said Tom.

They all stared out of the window at an untidy straggle of houses, shops together with several large cafeterias that lay between the railway station and the main highway. Around fifteen minutes further on they turned off as before onto a minor road where the sign read Rubielos-de-Mora and the fascinating region of the Maestrazgo. On they went by scattered villages with high roofed wooden beamed dwellings clustered about the inevitable churches, several of which had high copper domes that reflected the autumnal sunshine. The road signs denoted village names that stirred the imagination; La Iglesuela, Mosquerela, Zucaina and Alcala-de-la-Selva, all having their roots firmly set as far back as eight hundred years of Moorish rule before they in turn were cast out by the legendary Rodriquez Diaz de Vivar, or as most people know him, El Cid.

Finally on cresting a hill Linares-de-Mora sprang into view and the small car seemed to heave a sigh of relief as they swung into the village square, pulling up in front of the fountain in the middle of which a rather drab, armour coated stone figure stood brandishing a sword.

"Look. Charlton Heston himself," said Tom as they climbed stiffly out of the car.

Pushing open the door and walking in to Manolo's bar they found that Luis, together with his canine truffle hunters spread-eagled around his feet, was already there perched on his stool.

"Amigos!" he cried, jumping up and embracing each one of them in turn, throwing his arms around Tom and in a Latin gesture thumping him on the back enthusiastically. Naturally Bungy made straight towards the two dogs that, in turn, treated the intruder with distain, raising their hackles in unison and stalking stiff legged around him.

"Quieto!" commanded he Luis and their duty completed the two animals lay down again and ignored Bungy who now moved closer to Jimmy.

Tom ordered drinks for everyone and after talking about generalities approached the reason for their visit. As he was speaking he could see Luis darting side long glances at Jimmy who was pretending not to listen.

Eventually Tom finished and they both sat quietly while the old man considered the matter.

"Of course," put in Tom, "we would pay for the dog's board and lodging until he masters the art of truffle hunting."

The other stiffened and the blue eyes turned towards Jimmy's father. "Ni hablar. Not likely. If I take 'im, I take 'im and that's that."

Tom raised his hands in an apology.

Then turning to Jimmy, Luis said, "What do you say that we take 'em for a walk, Jimmy?"

The boy stood quickly. "Yes, Sir, I'd love that."

Luis laughed and hopped down from the stool. "Come on then."

Then to Tom and Maria he said, "Won't be long. About an hour, I suppose. Alright?"

The couple nodded and watched as their son walked out with Luis affectionately draping an arm around the boy's shoulders and a trio of excited dogs prancing happily around them. Manolo, in between serving the odd customer that came in, proved an entertaining personality who related stories about the village and its inhabitants so the time passed quickly.

Eventually the group finally returned and Jimmy, with cheeks flushed, was first through the door with Bungy hot on his heels. With eyes shining he said, "Dad. Bungy helped find a truffle. It's going to be alright and I can come and see him when ever I want!"

And so it was a relieved family that drove back to Cullera that evening.

*

Life continued as before and the weeks turned into months as Tom and Maria prepared for their return to England. Finally spring arrived with the promise of a hot summer ahead and one day Tom announced that they would be leaving in around six to eight weeks and it was time to take Bungy to his new home. Apart from a few unhappy tears shed in private with his arms around the dog, Jimmy made ready for their parting. The dog, sensitive to its master's mood, began trailing after him wherever he went. Arrangements to finally take Bungy up to Linares were delayed for three days as the only two telephone lines to the village had succumbed to a freak storm. This was eventually rectified and Tom was able to speak to Manolo who in turn reassured him that they would be there as usual the following Sunday.

The day finally dawned and they set of in a sombre mood. Once passed Barracas they drove into a rain storm so forceful that the wipers struggled to keep the windscreen clear and Tom was compelled to pull over and wait until it abated. They then continued and up ahead the mountains came into view shrouded in mist. Finally the sun broke through just as they reached the summit and saw the village up ahead. Once inside the small bar their mood lightened as they found Luis, Manolo and the two dogs clustered around the wood burning iron stove. Bungy was readily accepted by his new companions and they all spent a pleasant two hours until it was time to slip quietly away.

On the return journey little was said, all them missing the presence of Bungy. Jimmy sat in the back of the car with is own private thoughts while his father drove, thinking that an unpleasant situation had been resolved.

However little did he realise at the time that it was not to be so.

Although that year the weather was particularly erratic, Jimmy was able to spend time on the beach with his friends which served to distract the boy from the loss of his companion. Then one morning, some five weeks after their trip to Linares, Jimmy's mother was distracted from her household chores by a frantic ringing of the door bell. On opening it she was confronted by a tear stained son clutching in his arms a very scruffy, sorrowful looking dog.

"Look, mum!" he wailed. "It's Bungy. He's come back."

As if in recognition the animal strained towards her feebly wagging its tail.

Maria was speechless and could only ask, "But how?" as Jimmy brushed past her carrying the dog out onto the terrace and gently placing it on the old blanket that had served as Bungy's bed. The dog lay their quite quietly seemingly to know that he was home at last.

"He was down in the street, Mum," Jimmy said through his tears, "just lying there outside the front entrance. Fetch dad. He'll know what to do."

When Maria found her husband in a local bar the news caused quite a sensation amongst the customers.

"But it has got to be over a hundred kilometres," somebody said. Then a second voice commented, "And those mountains as well."

Tom left them discussing the whole thing and returned home with his wife to find Jimmy cradling Bungy's head in his arms and feeding the dog scraps of food from the fridge. The dog looked up on Tom's and again wagged its tail in a pathetic welcome. His appearance was terrible, practically unrecognisable. Gone was the sleek glossy coat and in its place the hair was matted and filthy dirty. The ribs could clearly be seen showing that it had probably not eaten for days. On his back several bald patches bereft of hair indicated that he had possibly been attacked at sometime or other.

"What are we going to do, Dad?" asked a tearful Jimmy.

"Do?" repeated his father, appalled at the dog's condition. "Well, first I think is that he needs to be cleaned up. Don't you?"

Jimmy nodded. So together father and son set about carefully washing the animal and after which treating the wounds.

"Not a lot wrong with him," commented Tom. "Just a few minor cuts and bruises as far as I can see. That's all."

Bungy winced as Jimmy touched his paws and Tom thought about the hundred or more kilometres. "Poor, poor, Bungy," he said, gently stroking the dog's head.

That first night their pet just lay there quietly accepting the situation but the following morning he seemed much brighter and took to wandering around the apartment sniffing at the furniture as though renewing old acquaintances.

Next Tom gave his son some money and the boy slipped out to buy a new collar and lead to replace the one that dog had lost on its long cruel journey home.

"Is it true that your dog has returned?" asked the man in the pet shop.

"Yes, Sir. Over one hundred kilometres across the mountains," Jimmy replied proudly.

At that same moment Tom was attempting to contact the bar in Linares but received no reply. After several further attempts he managed to get through to one of the villagers whose house apparently served as the post office. He learned from the woman who answered his call that Manolo's bar was closed for a few days as he had gone to see his sister who had been admitted to hospital in Teruel. Tom then enquired whether or not the person at the other end of the crackling line was acquainted with Luis, the truffle hunter.

"Yes," responded the voice of the elderly woman. "He is my first cousin. He lives at the end of the village."

Tom, taking into consideration the amount of time left before they returned to England, saw no other choice than to return the dog to Linares.

That was, of course, if Luis would have him. So he said, "If you see your cousin please tell him that we will be up to see him next Sunday week."

"De acuerdo. I will do that," came the reply and the connection was terminated.

Jimmy had not received this news very well. "But, Dad, not again," he protested.

"Sorry son. But I cannot see any other solution. I'm sure that Luis can keep Bungy somewhere until he gets used to it. Then he won't want to come back."

Jimmy was not really convinced but some of the sadness was replaced with the pride when his dog received a great deal of publicity in the coming days. The news of Bungy's return spread and a local Valencia newspaper even published an article together with a map showing the dog's supposed route home. Jimmy enjoyed the limelight of his pet's achievement, particularly amongst his friends. Meanwhile his father continued to telephone Manolo in Linares but without any success.

Finally he said to Maria, "We'll go anyway."

*

The appointed day came and the family found themselves once again heading up to the Maestrazgo and Linares-de-Mora. The weather was fine and they made good time arriving at the village in just over an hour. Turning into the square, Tom parked the car by the fountain with the statue of El Cid. Then, just as he was climbing, to his delight, he saw the figure of Luis on his bicycle approaching from the opposite direction.

Waving to the advancing figure, Tom called out, "Surprise, surprise! Look who we have here."

The old man applied his brakes and skidded to a halt almost colliding with their car. He then looked in amazement from Tom to the back seat where the dog, paws on the window, was barking furiously. "But I can't .....," he began.

Then the rest of his words were suddenly drowned by the barking of three very excited dogs that came streaking around the corner at that precise moment.

Of course the one creating the most commotion, looking even fitter than the family remembered him and now obviously the leader of the pack, was non other than their very own Bungy.

Chapter 12

Gedo the Dutchman appeared in the pub one day with the news that as the construction of the apartment blocks was now completed he was without work. Not quite sure as to what he was going to do he said that he was thinking of opening a bar and asked my opinion. As money was short he was looking to organising something economical.

I thought for a few minutes then said, "Well most of the young bloods around here consider themselves John Waynes so why not open a Western Saloon? It wouldn't cost much. Just a wooden bar, bare boards and the like and that's it."

And so it was decided. As his 'Dutch Courage' had apparently, returned he borrowed my Moto Guzzi to ride around looking for suitable premises. This was fine by me as I had, by this time, bought a Citroen Dyane Six, second or third hand, white with the traditional duck transfer on the back. It was not at all fast but reliable and fun to drive. Some weeks after the purchase I came down one morning to find that a rear wheel was missing and someone had taken the trouble to raise the car up onto bricks while they removed it. Whoever did it obviously knew little about cars as at that time the unlocked bonnet just clicked open and the spare wheel just rested on top of the engine. The replacement wheel together with tyre cost me the equivalent of eleven pounds.

Anyway, Gedo eventually found his premises, not surprisingly, just down the road from the English Pub. I helped, much to the amazement of the other bar owners, to fit it out. It was simply called The Western Saloon. The Dutchman was in business.

*

Christmas came and went with Mary becoming steadily thicker around the waist. The Happy Hour continued to give animation to the bar and the Ford contractors their support. Weekends were particularly busy and apart from darts the clients organised drinking competitions.

One night Sleepy Joe collapsed after competing with Scots Ron and as they were carrying him out, the door opened and in came some new, rather well dressed, customers.

"Good, God!" said one of them, moving to one side as the inert body of Joe was carried out. "What happened to him?"

"The Sunday drinking competition," someone offered and then another voice piped up, "Yes. And he was the winner!" Looking horrified they immediately turned about and left.

Pany had returned to Greece but we still pressed on with the paella excursions. Reggie the fish and his wife, Carmen, had been out to the Aldea-del-Señor to look at a small cottage that was on the market.

"The price that the owner was asking," commented Reggie, "was way out of reality for such a small place."

"Why was that?" I asked him, out of curiosity.

He chuckled, reaching for his 'Peninsulares'. "It's your entire fault, Chris. The man said that due to the excursions that were arriving from Cullera, the place was now considered to be a major tourist attraction."

This might have been for a time but little by little it became noticeable that the portions of paella were diminishing in size as was the rest of the food. This created unwanted arguments between Jose and me. Unfortunately I lacked Pany's forceful character in dealing with this situation and was subjected to nothing but excuses and dirty fingernails. However we carried on with myself thinking how great it would be if we could actually set up one of our own barbeques somewhere. Sometimes we had as many as sixty clients eating; drinking and enjoying the flamenco show upstairs on the terrace which was fine. Then one night a small, but significant, incident occurred that was to make a further change in direction of my life in general. On that trip we were particularly lucky to have employed the services of a good guitar player and a Gypsy flamenco dancer. Everybody was having a great time and at one point I slipped away for a break leaving someone in charge.

In the bar downstairs José was attending to a few local village customers and while waiting to be served I stood next to an old man who lived in one of the cottages opposite. He was ordering a 'Faria' cigar, the brand manufactured by the Spanish government.

"That will be six pesetas," said Jose as he handed the man the cigar across the bar.

The man paid and Josè dropped the coins into the ever open till. He then turned to me and as the old fellow had lit up and wafted some of the smoke in my direction, I decided to order one.

José reached for a further cigar placed it on the bar and then smiled at me. "That will be seven pesetas to you," he said.

"Wait a minute," I protested. "But you only charged this man six pesetas." The one peseta being worth less than half a penny at the time

"Of course," replied José firmly pointing a grubby finger in the other's direction. "This man comes in every day and you only come two or three times a week."

I was more than upset, I was furious. "Listen here my friend," I said, leaning over the bar towards him. "I have brought you sixty clients today. They have eaten your measly paella and are at present drinking your lousy booze upstairs and you want to charge me an extra peseta on a bloody cigar. Well you know what you can do with it!" So saying I tossed it back across the counter and marched out. A few days later I wrote to Pany and explained the situation and he immediately replied saying that if I could find a suitable place then he knew a German friend who, after attending several of our excursions, realised the potential and was willing to invest in the project. I set about spreading the word around that I was in the market for something appropriate for a barbecue. Various offers came in and I checked the interesting ones but none of them really came up to expectations. Either they were too far in distance from Cullera or just not suitable.

Then I found the old water mill.

*

In the dim and distant past it had been a flourishing business situated within a couple of kilometres of Cullera. Until recently the present owner, Paco had used it to breed pigs. However the man was now in financial trouble and wished to sell the lease. Excitedly I wrote to Pany who immediately drove all the way over from Athens.

Together we examined the premises and apart from being frightened to death by the appearance of a very large snake at least two metres long, we decided that the mill was the place we were looking for.

"It stinks to high heaven in here," I complained as we explored the interior of the place, peering into musty rooms and filthy pens. "Those pigs really did a good job."

Pany nodded in agreement. "Yes. But we only need the use of the outside for a barbecue. What with the stream, plenty of space and these large fig trees for shade, it's ideal. No need for transport as people will drive their cars out here, or even walk."

When we asked Paco about the situation of the lease he smiled and came up with the famous phrase, "There will be no problem."

And so it was a few days later when Pany was on the point of contacting his German investor, Burkhart Krings, that Paco broke the news that there just might be a 'minor problem'.

"Here we go again, Chris," I thought. "Eyes down for a full house. There is a problem and it sure I going to be a big one!"

As an outsider and firm believer that most religions are one of the prime reasons for many of the disputes that exist in the world I suddenly found, much to my dismay, that we were actually negotiating with the Catholic Church. Apparently, many years before the owner of the property, possibly with a view to ensuring himself of an immediate place in heaven had willed everything to the church. The church now held the deeds.

It was around this time when all this came to light that I was presented with evidence that in the past, (the present I do not know), the church had sold land in heaven to many of the richer parishioners. The average wording on these deeds stated that on their passing, the late leaseholders would, on arrival in the great hereafter, be granted so many acres of land which would be situated so many kilometres from the sun, so many kilometres from the moon and blessed by adequate rainfall every year. This, to many churchgoing landowners, was indeed sufficient encouragement to part with the family business on a permanent basis.

Some years later in Valencia's Flea market, I came across a stall selling collectors items including old property deeds. On asking the dealer about deeds for land in heaven he said that the church kept them well secured in their archives. "Anyway," he added, with tongue in cheek, "if you are personally interested in buying any land in heaven, forget it. The church has sold just about every last square metre up there."

Ah, well!

On reviewing the situation Pany and I, together with Paco, enlisted the help of the local priest, whose powers and influence superseded that of everyone else in town, including the mayor and the police chief. Finally I was told that all was settled and that negotiations with the ecclesiastical powers would be concluded when Burkhart Krings presented the necessary money at a meeting to take place at the Archbishop's Palace, Valencia.

The date was set and Burkhart arrived some days before; an athletic, good looking blond, young man, around thirty-five years of age. His main interest lay in antiques but was on the lookout for some sort of enterprise in Spain. He was, of course, immediately welcomed by the regular clients in the pub who renamed him Bechenbauer after the famous footballer.

*

The fatal day of the meeting with the Archbishop's advisor took place on a wet, dreary Monday. The time eleven o'clock in the morning. The priest from Cullera, Paco, Pany and me together with Burkhart and his brief case bulging with money, set out for Valencia. On arrival at the Palace, we waited in a large hall sitting on bench seats and watching a steady stream of nuns passing money over the counter at the far end. With solid iron bars protecting the cashiers it looked like a modern church bank certainly not conducive to the religious image presented to the general public. Almost an hour passed before we were finally ushered into the presence of the Archbishop's chief personal adviser. I did not know what I was really expecting but certainly not, what I saw on entering that room.

With its high ornate ceiling, walls bereft of any form of decoration, it was gloomy and certainly to my mind, rather sinister. In the centre of the chamber, for it could not be described as otherwise, a gaunt, cadaverous figure, completely attired in a black cassock, was not sitting, but actually reclining on a chaise-longue. And there, placed meticulously in line at an obviously predetermined distance from him, were five upright, hard wooden chairs waiting for us. I was instantly reminded of a painting I had once seen of the Spanish Inquisition and for no reason felt a sudden chill envelop me. Without a single word of greeting and an almost casual, effete gesture with his long manicured fingers, the man indicated that we should sit.

We obliged and there we remained waiting while his cold expressionless, slightly malignant, eyes passed from one to the other of us seemingly, I imagined, to linger a little longer on myself who was seated at the end. I remember thinking that the chairs themselves must have also been employed for such interviews some five hundred years before, as they were the most uncomfortable ones that my rear end has ever encountered. Obviously designed thus they seemed to dig into the backs of my knees and there was no way in which to relive the pressure without wriggling.

Then for some unknown reason, possibly my wicked sense of humour, I felt the sudden urge to break the silence by prostrating myself at his feet and crying, "Alright, I plead guilty!" but thought better of it.

When the figure in black did eventually deign to speak it was in such a low voice that the others were obliged to lean forward in order to hear. I personally did not bother, as I knew that I would not understand most of it anyway. His gaze repeatedly turned towards me as though condemning me for not wishing to participate in the theatrics.

Here I would mention that in Spain the owner of any property that is re-leased normally receives twenty percent of the fee paid by the buyer. So this was definitely going to influence the matter somewhat. The church's cut was calculated at a figure of around two thousand pounds sterling. The price was made more interesting by Burkhart when the Bishop's adviser quietly expressed his opposition to a church property being used for such irreligious activities as a barbecue with music and dancing.

Paco, fearful that things were not going as planned said, "But the place has been full of pigs for years. So what is the difference?"

"Ah," came the reply after some considerable thought, "but the pig is a noble animal and possibly, unlike some of the people likely to frequent the place if it were allowed to be turned over to something that these... these... er, foreigners have in mind."

Here he looked pointedly at Burkhart, swarthy Pany and I complete, at that time, with a recently cultivated Pancho Villa moustache. More words were exchanged, and the offer increased, but obviously his mind was made up. There must have been some sort of secret signal somewhere because a door suddenly opened at the far end of the room and we were asked to leave by another cleric who appeared. The last I saw of the 'Adviser' he was gazing up at the ceiling as though attempting to evoke some comment from a higher being as to the way he had handled the matter. The words that occurred to me as we walked out were, "He can stuff it!"

*

Once outside the priest and a distraught Paco disappeared leaving me distressed and Pany somewhat embarrassed with Burkhart who finally just shrugged his shoulders saying that it was worth a try anyway.

"So what do we do now?" Pany, asked as the three of us stood looking up at the lead grey sky with scudding clouds and falling rain.

Then for some reason the answer occurred to me. "The Picanterra," I said without any hesitation. "It's lunchtime."

"Good thinking, boy wonder," returned Pany immediately following my train of thoughts exactly. "Let's go!"

Some five kilometres down the coast, south of the river Jucar near Cullera, there is a

lake called 'Estany' which is fed by the waters that find their way down from the `Sierra de los Pinos'. To one side of this lake lie two restaurants, the 'Salvador' and the 'Picanterra'. The former is what might be termed as 'up market' whilst the latter is where the fun is to be had.

Both places are renowned for 'All-i-Pebre' a Valencia dish composed of eels in a peppery sauce and 'Llisa a la Plancha' a grey mullet that feeds of the bottom of the lake and is prepared on the griddle. Then, of course, there is 'Paella'. Both of these dining venues have excellent terraces and one can eat whilst looking out over the lake to the mountains in the background.

At lunchtime each Monday a mixed crowd from Cullera descended on the 'Picanterra'. Consisting of local bar owners, club owners, prostitutes the gay community and anyone else who wished to eat well, drink well and be very happy at a modicum price, it was the place to be.

On that particular day as it was raining the terrace was out of the question so everyone piled into the dining room. There must have been thirty or forty of us all in the mood for a good time. Wine was liberally splashed out and dish after dish was consumed with everyone talking at once. The noise was deafening. I was sitting, much to my delight, with a girl on either side of me and opposite Burkhart and Pany were equally well accompanied. We had arrived at the coffee, brandy and cigar stage when I saw Burkhart say something to Pany who, in turn, doubled over with laughter, burying his head in the ample bosom of the blonde to his right. Coming up for air he peered across at me through the smoke-haze, tears coursing down his cheeks. "Burkhart just said that he preferred this to the Bishop's palace this morning," he shouted across to me. "He calls it 'cultural shock'!"

*

Around May, Pany returned to Greece and the following month I received a telephone call from my father with the sad news that my mother had died. I immediately flew over to England for the funeral, staying at my sister's house in Oadby, Leicester. I was there for a week and on confirming my return flight was startled to see that I was to check in at Gatwick airport at the unearthly hour of eight o' clock in the morning. Oadby being placed some one hundred and fifty miles away from Gatwick the operation required pretty good timing on my part. I was determined not to make a mess of it.

On the morning of my return, I leapt out of bed at four thirty, showered and was ready when the taxi arrived at five o'clock. The drive into Leicester was easy at that time of the day and I was already on the platform when the London train arrived at five thirty. After the Spanish trains this journey was swift and smooth and we pulled into St. Pancras, London, at a quarter to seven. There was a bit of a hassle with the morning commuters on the underground but I made Victoria station just in time to follow my suitcase rapidly onto the Gatwick express that was pulling out.

The clock at the airport showed ten minutes to eight when we arrived and I took great delight in casually wandering over to the checking-in desk exactly on time. The charming woman who took my passport and ticket listened patiently while I briefly explained how that I had left Oaby only three hours before. "That's really wonderful," she said, congratulating me. "However there is only one problem."

"Problem?" I asked. "Problem. What kind of problem?"

Appearing somewhat embarrassed she looked up at me, then placing the ticket where I could see it and with well-manicured fingers placed firmly on the flimsy paper she smiled. "It's just that your flight leaves tomorrow."

*

Within one month of my return my son was born. It goes without saying that there was a wild party organised. Just before the event Horst and I had decided to open another bar nearer to the beach in Cullera; it was called Los Cerezos (The Cherry Trees). We soon discovered that the employment of staff and leaving them to their own devices was not at all viable in respect of business. However we decided to play it out until the end of the season before closing down but not before my son's baptism celebration.

Pany had arrived again and after great deal of partying we put on some Greek music and began dancing. Then somebody tossed a plate into the middle of the tiled floor and it shattered impressively. Before long everyone was joining in until there was not piece crockery left to break. It was all certainly good fun but somewhat heavy on the pocket for replacements.

Next, my father, who had never been outside of the UK, came to visit us. His first evening there we were, as usual, extremely busy in the pub. Then around ten o'clock in came a new face. He was another short-term contractor from the Ford car plant. "And where do you come from?" he asked me when I had a moment to talk to him.

"Leicester," I said.

"Well I'm from Nottingham," he went on. "Just thirty miles up the road."

"Really," I replied attempting to appear interested.

"Yes," he continued, "and only once in my life have I been to Leicester." He thought for a minute then continued, "Must be going on for thirty years ago, or even more and even today I can remember meeting one really nice fellow. He was policeman by the name of Joe Wright."

The expression on is face changed to amazement when I said, "Well you're in luck. That's my father and he's standing at the end of the bar."

*

It was no joke expecting Mary to work in the bar and look after our son, so she contacted her cousin, Valerie, who lived in Morton-in-Marsh in the Cotswolds. At Mary's invitation, she immediately threw in her work at a local bank and came out to help run the pub. A mean darts player and could handle a pint better than a lot of our male customers, probably due to the training she had received at her parent's establishment, the Black Bear, in her home town. Some nights when we finished around two o'clock she and I would take the Moto Guzzi and ride the ten kilometres over to Sueca, the nearest major town, for a nightcap at the bar Llopis. Valerie was a great asset to have around and was loved by all the regulars.

October came and the excursions for the paella fizzled out through lack of tourists so we just had the pub to contend with. Not that there was any lack of something to do. There were always new faces appearing. Some nights when we closed I would wander across to the Cala Club one of the several discothèques in Cullera. This particular one was a favourite haunt for the night people, mainly transvestites.

*

It was one very quiet evening in the pub I was left talking to a new arrival from the Ford plant. Then, as I was closing, I asked if he fancied a nightcap at the Cala Club. He readily agreed.

It was still rather early when we walked in and there was nobody on the dance floor. However, around twenty minutes later two or three of the transvestites came in dressed to the nines and carrying handbags. The most attractive of the trio wore a trouser suit, make up and long flowing blonde-hair. I immediately recognised this one as being a bricklayer by trade. However, in the dim surrounds he looked for all like a beautiful young agile girl as he took to the floor swirling and gyrating to the music.

My companion stared and drew in a deep breath. "Wow! Just take a look at that!" he exclaimed.

I smiled, "Nice isn't she?"

"Wonderful. Absolutely wonderful!"

Then still ogling he nudged me with his elbow. "What I could do for that."

Inside I was laughing like crazy and encouraged him to add further comments. Then when I thought the right moment had arrived, I nudged him in return and said, "That my dear friend is actually a man."

He stood there almost drooling at the mouth and without taking his eyes of the dancer said, "I know! I know!"

*

One weekend we were extremely busy and one customer who was there until closing time was Ian. He too worked at the Ford factory and was married to a Spanish lady. As the Saturday evening wore on Ian became more and more legless with drink and at closing time it was obvious that he was not going to be able to drive the twenty miles home. So someone was going to have to make the journey and as usual, when it came to asking, everyone had suddenly disappeared.

Pouring Ian into my car we set off. Fortunately there were no mishaps and we arrived safely at his home around three a.m. Hauling him out of the car, I carried him across the pavement, propped him up against the wall and tentatively rang the bell. Nothing happened and I tried again, pressing my ear to the door to see if I could detect any movement within. The next moment it was flung open and there, brandishing an umbrella was this huge and very angry, woman.

Stepping a pace back I began to explain my presence but before I could utter a single word there was this horrible gurgling sound as Ian slowly slid down the wall, crumpled onto the pavement and began vomiting. I turned to look at him and next thing received an enormous whack on the side of my head and the woman began screaming. "Look what you have done to my husband! Who do you think you are bringing him home in this condition?" Then staring about her she began yelling, "Guardia! Guardia! Help!"

Again a further whack across the side of the face with the umbrella left my cheek stinging. There was nothing for it but make rapid departure so I covered my head and made for the car with her following, shouting for help while raining blows on my back and shoulders. As I was pulling away she continued hammering on the car and screaming for help. A visit and interview by Guardia Civil at that time of the morning was all I needed for my Good Samaritan act.

I was still nursing cuts and bruises when Ian appeared in the bar some days later. "What's up, Chris?" he asked. "Been in a bit of trouble?" He had no recollection of the incident at all but that was the last lift home he had from me.

Mac and Samantha during the preparation for the "Fiesta" in Siete Aguas.

Mary enjoying the rain.

CJ with the 3 kilo Radish that caused problems.

CJ with Jens the Dane

The celebrated "Dolfis" bar.

Samantha in "Fallas" dress with Adolfo owner of "Dolfis" bar.

Brian (Left) with Mike and Kathy just after the brothers realease from prison. Note the expression in their eyes.

Tony Strodder with Samantha (and a friend) outside "Dolfis" bar.

Chapter 13

Steve was another regular customer whose hobby was sailing. He wandered into the pub one morning and after a couple of beers suddenly, much to my surprise, asked if I would like to go with him to collect his yacht.

"Great, Steve. Where is it?"

"Cap d'Adge in France, not far from Bézier. That's heading towards Marseille."

He went on to explain that I would be away a week to ten days so needing little encouragement I immediately talked to Mary and she agreed. Together with Valerie, she would manage the bar.

And so began one of the strangest adventures of my life.

On the elected day Steve and I caught the coach from Valencia and made the journey to Bézier. Then, completing the trip by taxi, we arrived at the delightful harbour resort of Cap d'Adge.

Steve's yacht, Lively Lady, was around nine metres in length and looked as though she was ready to go whenever her owner decided. The small, tidy, cabin with its three bunks was quite comfortable and after installing ourselves we wandered off like two excited schoolboys in search of provisions. Later we took in some of the local colour at various night spots, ate in a restaurant with crowds of what seemed students' hell bent on enjoying themselves, and then returned to Lively Lady. Tired but happy, we tumbled into our bunks and prepared ourselves for sleep. It was my first night of actually sleeping on a small boat and I thought how pleasant it was being slowly lulled into a dreamless slumber as the yacht moved restlessly to and fro accompanied by the clinking of the rigging against the mast.

*

Next morning the weather was sharp, bright and breezy.

"A good day for great sail," commented Steve as we cast off and headed for the harbour mouth.

He was quite right. To me it was fantastic. Once outside in the open sea with full sail, Lively Lady went into her own and virtually danced over the waves. It was exhilarating and in what seemed no time at all we were around a mile off shore.

"There are charts in one of the drawers in the cabin," called Steve. "Would you like to check on our course?"

"Aye, aye, Captain!" I said as I slipped down into the cabin. The charts were in one of the drawers and I felt quite pleased with myself as I accustomed my balance to the constant movement of the yacht and quickly had them spread out on the cabin table. It was not difficult to assess our whereabouts however; the exercise only lasted for about two hours until it became clear that there were no more charts to be checked.

"Where are the rest of them?" I called up to Steve.

"There aren't any," came the reply. There was a minute's silence, then he called down to me, "There's the Michelin road map in one of the lockers; that should be helpful. You can calculate just about where we are by looking shoreward at the main road that runs along the coast."

I was doubtful about my capabilities to manage this form of navigation but found the map and climbed up to join Steve in the cockpit.

*

Taking stock of our surrounds, breathing deeply on the exhilarating sea air, I turned casually to look back the way we had come.

"Bloody hell! Whatever's that?" I said, staring over Steve's shoulder.

"What's what?" He twisted round to take a look. "Bloody hell!"

There, coming up cutting a furrow through the swell at one hell of a rate of knots, was a very large grey, sinister looking, boat.

"Don't know what it is," said Steve, "but it is sure making for us."

The growl of the powerful engines became more audible as it drew nearer. Then throttling back it slowed to the same speed as Lively Lady, keeping a parallel course some fifty yards from us.

"A motor torpedo boat," I said. "But what the hell are they up to?"

Two smartly dressed sailors had suddenly appeared on deck and begun manning the ugly, single, long barrelled anti-aircraft gun, swinging it menacingly in our direction.

"Christ!" I said, "That's an Oerlikon 20 mm antiaircraft gun."

I saw Steve's knuckles grow white as he steadfastly clung to the tiller. "Then why the hell are they pointing the thing at us then?"

Next a metallic voice boomed out through a loudspeaker in French. "Ahoy there! Will the yacht to our portside please identify herself, destination and reason for voyage?"

"A bit silly," I thought, as there was no other craft within sight.

"You speak some French," hissed Steve. "For heaven's sake say something. They are obviously customs or police and mean business."

Numbers and letters were emblazoned on the side of the MTB, and placing my hands to my mouth in true navel style I shouted in my best French, "Ahoy! Motor torpedo boat number....." Here I read out their registration details, "to our starboard side. We are the British registered yacht, Lively Lady, bound for Spain."

"And for what reason, Lively Lady?" persisted the voice.

As we had done nothing wrong to my knowledge I was beginning to enjoy this. "Lively Lady to motor torpedo boat," I yelled. "Tourist reasons. Vacations!"

"Where were you berthed last night, Lively Lady?"

"Cap d'Adge, motor torpedo boat."

I was now really getting into the swing of things. The two sailors manning the Oerlikon still had the muzzle trained on us and there was no doubt that on the captain's orders they would be delighted to use the thing. Next there was a lengthy silence as they probably confirmed details with the last night's port authorities. Then the hailer went again.

"Thank you Lively Lady. Bon voyage and good sailing!"

With that their throttle opened to the full and they heeled off turning back the way they had come, leaving us once again to the steady swish of the waves against the hull as we headed south.

"Wow!" said Steve, fiddling around and letting 'George' the automatic pilot take over. "I need a drink after that. Did you see the way those Frogs were handling that bloody gun?"

"I suppose they were just checking," I said, casually. "Pity they didn't board us. We could have had a party."

Steve glared at me. "Stop talking bloody nonsense and get me that beer."

"Aye, aye, mi Capitán." I called over my shoulder as I went below.

*

The day passed very pleasantly with 'George', doing most of the work. I, personally, did some sunbathing on the cabin roof, occasionally glancing across at the coast line not really having a clue where we were. "So much for road maps at sea," I thought.

That evening we found ourselves near to a small port.

"Where are we?" asked Steve.

"Take your choice," I replied, studying the Michelin with the aid of a flash light, "Port-la-Nouvelle, Port-Leucate or Port-Bacarès."

"Which is the furthest south?"

"Port-Bacarès."

"Then that's where we are."

Not really understanding this logic I just nodded and made the appropriate note in the log. As it was late and there was nobody around we just moored up off shore, climbed into our bunks, and fell asleep.

Early next day, after a quick brew of coffee, we set out once more with a following wind and made good progress. Lunch consisted of rather stale sandwiches with an excellent bottle of Corbière which compensated.

"And where do you reckon we will be tonight?" asked Steve, taking a large mouthful of wine.

As he had obviously gone into his 'Captain' mode and required a clear answer I quickly I tried to remember one of the names I had seen the last time I had looked at the road map. "Er... at this speed I think we should be around Port-Vendres near to the Spanish border," I said, attempting to sound confident.

Steve seemed satisfied and let me take over the tiller while he, together with the road map, did a little sunbathing. The sea became noticeably choppier as we neared the Pyrenean Mountains to our starboard side and the cliffs became gradually higher until soon they seemed to be towering over us.

Then late that afternoon I looked up and saw a small cemetery high up on the side of a mountain. "That looks very Spanish to me," I called out to my son.

"And?" he asked following my gaze.

"And according to the map it's a bloody long way to the next nearest port."

"What if we go about?"

"We can berth at Port-Vendres," I said, positively.

"OK let's go about."

Lively Lady responded and we tacked back the way we had come until an opening in the cliffs afforded us a glimpse of a couple of boats moored up in what looked like a very small, natural harbour.

"There we are, Captain. Port-Vendres," I called.

*

The sea was now becoming quite rough and after furling the sails, Steve started up the small diesel motor and we chugged in with the throbbing of the diesel bouncing off the lofty cliffs on either side.

"Look up there," I said, pointing upwards to a huge ominous slate grey mansion clinging to the edge of the precipice. Very much like some medieval fortress; it looked as though it had been constructed to guard the port as it squatted there smugly, defiant and distant.

"You wouldn't be likely to step out into your back garden too often if you lived in that place," said, Steve.

I nodded in agreement.

There were only two small, rather drab, sad looking yachts moored to the quayside and we tied up alongside them.

"Port-Vendres looked much larger on the map," I said, as we climbed ashore and automatically wandered over to what looked like the only bar in sight.

Once inside it was warm and cosy with the smell of wood smoke from the iron stove hanging in the air. We ordered a couple of hot coffees laced with Jamaican rum from the small pretty woman of around twenty-five odd years with green eyes and a mousy hair style that hung in ringlets down to her shoulders. She spoke a little English with an almost theatrical French accent which immediately encouraged Steve. Over in one corner of the bar a young boy of around eight or nine years was industrially doing what looked to be his homework.

"Eeeeze my son," said the woman when she saw me acknowledge the little chap.

Then I noticed one of those display stands holding picture postcards, so I wandered over to take a look at them while Steve chatted to the girl, who said that her name was Marie. The cards were all views of a small port called Cerbère. Turning, I asked, "Haven't you got any views of Port-Vendres?"

"No," replied Marie.

"Why not?" I asked, thinking it strange that there were not postcards of the place we were in.

"Because Port-Vendres eeze twenty kilometres down zee coast from 'ere."

Steve looked puzzled. "Where the bloody hell are we, then? You had the map last."

"Cerbère," I said, "right on the frontier. We must have passed Port-Vendres way back."

Steve shrugged and muttered something detrimental about the Michelin Company, while I sorted out a couple of postcards to send on to Mary and my son.

We then ordered a meal of steak and chips and were soon enjoying another bottle of Corbière. It was just when we had called for coffees that the door opened and accompanied by a wild gust of wind a man came in. The boy immediately jumped up and ran across to him, flinging his arms around him and talking away in rapid French. Marie came out from behind the bar and they exchanged kisses with him glancing in our direction and Marie saying something that I didn't quite catch.

He then came over and after the initial, "Bon appétit," stuck out his hand and said in Spanish, "Soy Juan Miguel. I am the customs agent in Cerbère." As he said this he winked as though sharing a joke with us.

We all shook hands and I found myself responding in Spanish.

"Pero Ustedes no son Españoles." he said, puzzled.

"No," I confirmed, smiling, "we're not Spanish. We're English."

"And where are you heading?"

"Valencia, if the road map permits us."

"Really? Valencia is my home town."

He then pulled up a chair and as the bottle of wine was now empty indicated to Marie that our glasses should be replenished. The boy, in the meantime, had returned to his studies.

Juan Miguel could have been around fifty years of age, somewhat overweight for his height, going prematurely bald and looking as though he was enjoying the good life. We talked about Valencia in general and a little later I mentioned the incident with the torpedo boat. He wasn't surprised in the least.

"They have a new customs chief," he explained, "and really have to knuckle under, what with Marseille being only up the coast; smuggling and all that. You were lucky as by law you should have informed the harbour master that you were leaving. Sometimes they make the boats return to harbour and settle the matter there."

We were now at the coffee stage together with our third glass of brandy when suddenly Juan said, "Your boat will be safe there. Why not come up to my house and have a drink?"

Steve and I looked at each other and both said, "Fine." He then gave instructions to Marie to get organised and close the bar. We paid and hung around while this was done.

Outside there was dampness in the air together with the smell of rain and the wind was rising. Juan Miguel's car was a large Citroen and all of us piled in with me and Juan Miguel noticing that Steve secured a place alongside Marie in the back.

*

The road out of the village twisted and turned up a steep incline and once at the top we swung left between two enormous iron gates.

"Good, Lord!" I said to Steve, "I think these lead to the place we saw at the top of the cliff as we came into port."

And so it was. The actual front entrance to this mansion was even more impressive than the part we had seen from the sea. Where the giant sized slabs of stone had originated from I had no idea. Pulling up we all climbed out and Juan Miguel opened the gigantic, solid, wooden carved doors with an absurdly small key. These led into a hallway completely lacking in any sort of furniture or decoration. Fiddling around he found the mains switch and flicked in on. However even the little light from the various bare bulbs did not seem to make a lot of difference. It was gloomy to say the least. Even taking into account my own active imagination I still could not shake off my original impression that this was, indeed, a 'grim' place.

"Straight on into the main room," said Juan Miguel, cheerfully as though reading my thoughts.

Through two more doors that looked as though they had been removed from some church entrance and we were standing in the main room that stretched the whole length of the house. It was immense. To the right was the longest dining room table that I had ever set eyes upon with seating for around thirty or more people but, without chairs. However what really did stop me in my tracks was that directly in front of us, with her back to an impressive bay window, stood the colossal figure of a woman. Constructed of wood and papier mâcher it was one of those gaudily painted mannequins that they bring out of churches for certain religious festivals. Arms straight down by her sides she stood there with that staring vacant expression on her mask-like features, her eyes fixed sightlessly on the wall opposite. She must have been around five metres in height as her clenched fists just came level with my face as I moved next to her.

"That's Loli," said, Juan Miguel, casually, but offered no explanation for her presence there.

Nearby, apart from the enormous dining table, was the only other piece of furniture in the place, a small table on which was a record player together with a selection of long playing records. Marie busied herself organising some music while Juan Miguel and the boy disappeared somewhere leaving myself, Steve and Loli staring at each other.

The frenzied wind outside was now battering at the leaded windows and taking in the scene I, for some reason, thought that this would be an ideal theme for playwright Harold Pinter. However the atmosphere lightened somewhat when Juan Miguel returned with a bottle of vintage French champagne and glasses. Soon the voice of Yves Montand filled the room and I felt easier. We then toasted each other and took turns to dance with Marie. The bottle was soon empty.

"Show Chris where the fridge is, Jean Pierre," Juan Miguel instructed the boy and I was led out through the hall and into the kitchen.

In contrast to the rest of the place it was quite small, the only furniture being a plain pine table, four chairs and a monster refrigerator in the corner. There was no evidence whatsoever of the usual kitchen utensils. Opening the double doors of the fridge I was amazed to see that it contained absolutely nothing but bottles and bottles of French champagne.

"Well at least the man has his priorities right," I thought, as I selected a bottle of Krug.

Back one again in the room we continued talking, dancing and drinking bottle after bottle of champagne. Then it was my turn to feel the warm embrace of Marie as we gyrated around the floor to the strains of Johnny Halliday. I was now beginning to think how pleasant this was with the music and Marie's perfume filling the air when suddenly the door swung open and there with a tremendous yell we were faced by the figure of Juan Miguel.

He had removed his trousers, socks and shoes and was dressed in a plastic false front, consisting of a bulging stomach together with a gross pair of breasts. Covering his face was a baby doll mask with rouge coloured cheeks and scarlet lips. All this would not have been so bad had he not been brandishing a long, ugly, very sharp looking, carving knife.

For me this scene was not so far from achieving the same effect as one of the sets from the film 'Psycho'. I was horrified. Then with another ear splitting shriek the man leapt onto the table and began charging backwards and forwards lunging to the left and right with the knife at nothing in particular. And if this wasn't enough another shout behind us announced the arrival of Jean Pierre complete in cowboy outfit and brandishing a very real looking pistol which he was waving in our direction. I just stared and prayed that it was not loaded. Marie must have been accustomed to these theatrics or possibly the worse for drink but she did not, in the least, seem perturbed.

The strains of Johnny Halliday gradually faded and an exhausted Juan Miguel fell more than jumped down from the table and collapsed on the floor near to Steve who stood staring down at him, unable to move. As I released Marie and moved over to them both I heard a muffled voice from behind the mask say, "Would you like some more champagne?" This was followed by hysterical giggles.

The boy in the meantime was pointing the gun at the tall mannequin and making shooting noises. "No thanks," I said, and as Steve seemed to be still quite speechless I added, "I think it's about time we were going anyway. Early start tomorrow morning."

Pulling himself up into a sitting position he dropped the knife and held out his hand which I took rather uncertainly. "Well, thanks for coming. It was fun wasn't it?"

"Great!" I said.

Then grabbing Steve's arm and jerking him into action we moved over to Marie who was examining the LP covers, still seemingly oblivious as to what was happening. Taking turns to kiss and thank her I then said to the boy, "Adios, Vaquero," and we headed for the door attempting to appear casual.

Outside it was a bitter blustery wind that greeted us. Little was said as we staggered down the hill to the port each of us with our own thoughts. I must say that my feelings were of relief when Lively Lady came into sight.

"Am I glad to see you?" I said climbing on board.

"Not as much as I am," muttered Steve following me.

*

Next morning dawned cloudy and grey. The wind had dropped and a light rain was falling when we surfaced at around seven thirty. Preparing the yacht for setting sail I turned and noticed that Marie and Jean Pierre were standing outside the bar watching us. Automatically I waved but there was no response from either one of them. Steve then tried starting the diesel but found that the propeller was enmeshed in one of the mooring ropes. Trying to release it with the boat hook was not successful, even though we could see it quite clearly in the clear water.

"Nothing else for it than to do it by hand," I said, going down into the cabin and pulling on my swimming trunks.

It was not too bad after the initial shock when I slipped over the side and into the sea and the job was soon accomplished. Steve helped me on board then started the motor while I went for a dry towel. We were just pulling away, heading for the port entrance and I looked shoreward to see that neither Marie nor Jean Pierre had moved. I tried waving once again but there was still no response.

"You know what I have just thought?" I said, looking at Steve who was huddled over the tiller in his waterproofs. "Did you notice that we never saw one other person all the time that we were there?"

"Not at all bloody surprised," he said.

We cleared the harbour, Steve cut the motor and we hoisted the mizzen-sail.

"It looks as though we are in for a blow. Make sure your life jacket's secure!" he shouted over the rising wind.

Until that day I had never experienced a storm in a small sailing boat, but what was waiting for us out there was certainly in keeping with what had passed in the last fourteen hours. To me it was frightening. The wind blew in savage gusts from the north and the sea seemed to be heaving in all directions at once. Turning south we rode before the mountainous white crested rollers that chased us, constantly breaking over our stern and soaking us to the skin. Both of us crouched there hanging on for dear life. I was terrified but at the same time exhilarated.

At one point I caught a glimpse of what looked like a small port as we were surfing along on the crest of a particularly giant roller. I shouted to Steve pointing out what I had seen.

"Shall we turn right?" he bawled at me.

"Turn right," I thought. "What sort of a sailor am I about to drown with?"

"Not bloody likely! Keep straight on. We'll ride it out."

The sensation was wild, just like being on some uncontrollable roller coaster with the ride seemingly going on forever. It was around an exhausting two hours later that we approached the bay of 'Rosas' that the sea began to change. Slowly the steep spume tipped waves became less and we were soon rising and falling with long dark green rollers. Neither of us spoke for quite a while.

Then Steve said, "I think a couple of beers might be welcome, don't you?"

"Aye, aye, Captain!" I saluted and went down to what had once been a neat and tidy cabin. Lockers had come open and there were things strewn everywhere. However with the thought that the worst had passed I pushed everything back in place and grabbed a couple of cans of beer from the fridge.

When I surfaced a pale insipid sun had made an appearance although there was still plenty of cloud about. From where we were flying along we could clearly see the coastline and the small white miniature buildings in the distance. The sun was now shining brightly over there and everything looked very normal. It was possible to pick out small toy-like figures sunbathing on then beach or sitting beneath colourful sunshades. I sat there in the still heaving vessel thinking that half an hour before I would have sincerely wished that I could have been part of that beach scene, but not now. It would not have been true to say that I felt almost reborn but looking back I could certainly say that I would not have missed the experience.

The sun's warmth gradually filtered through to us and as the wind died down to a gentle following breeze Steve decided to set full sail. Once completed there was little left for me to do so I decided to try my hand at fishing with a simple line and spinner that had taken my fancy in a shop in Cap d'Adge. Just letting it drop into the water over the stern I let the line run out. Nothing happened for about half an hour, then I felt the line jerk. Something had taken the bait. Having had a little experience as an amateur fisherman as a boy I took my time, playing whatever it was, until I thought it tired enough to be hauled in. Weighing in at around six to seven pounds the fish turned out to be a mackerel. I, personally, was delighted but Steve was not at all happy.

"Don't bring that bloody thing on board," he growled. "It'll stink the boat out."

If he thought I was going to let such a prize as that off the hook then he was very much mistaken. "Don't worry, I'll find something to wrap it in."

An old tee-shirt served its purpose and we continued to sail happily along without any more attempts on my part to add to the catch.

Not having any Spanish charts or road maps we continued navigating blind until late afternoon. The sea, very much calmer, looked very inviting and I would have loved to have taken a dip. However it seemed that just where we were, about half a mile off shore, we were following a trail of absolute rubbish. Plastic bottles and containers seemed more prominent than anything else but there were also bits of paper, cardboard boxes, wood and in fact anything that would float. It was very sad as from now on this ocean going dump was going to be part of the scene and even increase in size and variability in the next days as we neared Barcelona.

What wind there was suddenly dropped and we had to resort to the diesel. At one point we were sailing quite near the shoreline and I noticed that there were some sharp dangerous looking rocks quite nearby. Next I saw a large black fin moving lazily around in the water not far from the yacht. On pointing it out to Steve I intoned, "When the black fin shows, down she goes." He promptly responded with some very colourful swear words that indicated I should button my lip while he navigated.

A little later up ahead there appeared a fairly large port with a varied assortment of boats of all types moored up in neat lines. Steve swung the tiller and Lively Lady nosed slowly in. We were on the point of deciding where to tie up when a figure came hurrying along the quayside dressed in a blue jacket complete with gold rings on his sleeve.

"Must be the harbour master," I said, waving to the man who indicated a berth only a short distance from where we were. I stood ready to fend off while Steve expertly manoeuvred the yacht. As we were tying up the man started off back the way he had come, but turned when I called after him. "Is this any good to you?" I asked holding up the mackerel which was still showing signs of life.

He came back and stood staring down at us, then nodded. "Por supuesto!" he said. I passed it up to him. "Gracias, Capitán. Muchas gracias."

"He's not the Capitan," snarled Steve behind me. "I'm the Capitán!"

As this was the first port of call in Spain, we washed, changed and with the formalities completed, went out to explore what turned out to be the Costa Brava resort of Palamos.

*

I remember that numerous bars received our temporary support as usual and later we finished up at a night spot where there was a striptease show. The star was a young African girl who billed herself as 'Miss Rolls Royce'.

Although quite a delectable young woman I do not think the car makers would have considered her to be in competition to their product.

I phoned Mary and found that our business required my attention a.s.a.p., so arranged that she would drive up and meet me in Tarragona in a couple of days time, the new Michelin road map that Steve had bought, permitting.

At that point of the trip I had the feeling that Steve, for some reason, related all that had happened, including the storm, to my presence and was therefore quite happy to think that in two days time he, together with 'George', would continue their journey in comparative peace to Javea on the Costa Blanca where a permanent mooring awaited them. So the following two days we continued south with little happening except for trying to avoid all the refuse that continued to float around us. Pany kindly drove Mary up to meet us once we were in Tarragona and after a meal accompanied copious quantities of fine red wine from the region, we set out for the drive to Valencia.

*

Back once again in Cullera again my father said that it was about time he was returning home for the Christmas season. As Mary and I, together with our son, had received an invitation to spend the festivities in Le Sentier, Switzerland, at the house of Maurice and Marionette Bouchard, this fitted in well with our plans. With Valerie also deciding to return to England we arranged to leave the business open and in the capable hands of an English girl who was living in Cullera at that time.

Departure day arrived and Mary together with my son, my father and I, squeezed into the Dyane six. "Paris here we come," I said stirring the engine into life and moving slowly but surely in a northerly direction.

As usual, when travelling, my routes were still mainly governed by the whereabouts of favourite eating places and this time was no exception. Some twelve miles north of Valencia we turned inland towards Teruel and some three hours later we passed through my favourite city, Zaragoza.

It was great to be once again in Huesca, still comfortably pressed up against the background of the Pyrenean Mountains. Having stayed there in the past I was already acquainted with various restaurants and 'tapas' bars. Once installed in one of the smaller hotels we then made for one such place that produced a fine 'Chilindron'. This rather heavy dish is composed of chicken together with plenty of garlic, onions, red and green peppers, cooked in the oven. Being the winter season it guarantees the consumer one hundred percent fortification against the elements; especially when washed down with a litre or two of the Cariñeña wine.

Next morning, well rested, we set off again, hoping to cross over into France via the Col-du-Portalet and Formigal, some one hundred kilometres distance. The weather deteriorated as we left the village of Sabañanigo and up ahead we could see the impressive mountain peaks swathed in thick snow. I wanted to make Laruns that night as our first stop in France being as I knew of a good hotel with a nearby warm and very comfortable French bar Tabac. However it became obvious that the roads were becoming icier with snow gathering in the ditches on either side. It was going to be touch and go if we managed to cross the frontier at the point I had in mind.

We arrived at Biescas and filled up with petrol where, for some reason, the owners of the garage keep a wild boar caged up in the forecourt. The attendant who served us shook his head and said that the road was completely blocked a few kilometres further on. There was nothing for it but to turn around and drive back the way we had come and try for the frontier at the Col-du-Somport, via Jaca.

This time we were in luck and the little car trundled along quite happily over the main road recently cleared and gritted. As was expected the scenery was outstanding and quite in keeping with the season. Snow everywhere we looked and the forest pines weighed heavy with their winter coating. Much to everyone's delight we found a charming old hotel at Arundy about forty minutes after crossing the border. With dark polished, creaking, wooden floors and a welcoming log fire with flames flickering half way up the giant stone chimney. It was magic. We could not have been happier sitting there toasting our feet and breathing in the scent of wood smoke while dinner was being prepared. As the only guests that night everything was perfect, food, service together with the congeniality of the lady owner. At around eleven o'clock when the others, succumbing to the call of bed, I sat there agreeably drowsy, sipping a nightcap of coffee and calvados. Then having a pencil and paper serviette to hand I wrote down, *'Low slate roofs, chintz table cloths, Coq-au-vin and calvados. The scent of pine smoke, creaking stairs, blessed rest, a time to share'*.

And that summed it all up.

*

The following day, feeling very much refreshed, we set off once again after a breakfast of coffee, hot toast and a vast selection of homemade jams and marmalades. Driving out of the mountains we struck out across country towards the Périgord region, stopping the following night in Bergerac, specifically to introduce my father to the delights of various truffled pâtés and foie gras of the area. All in all it took us five days to reach Paris with the last night being passed in the Hotel du Perron just south of Orleans. One afternoon and evening was dedicated to Paris sightseeing, then assisting my father onto the boat train, we said our farewells and set out for Switzerland.

*

Maurice, Marionette and their lovely young daughter Dominique, were waiting for us when we arrived at Le Sentier a neat Swiss village crouching on the shores of Lac du Joux behind Geneva. Our friend Maurice, a man of impressive dimensions topped by an ever-ready smiling moustachioed countenance, was the epitome of the classical 'Bon Viveur'. When not teaching languages at the local college he was dedicating his pursuits to the niceties of life in the form of good wine and good food, together with anything else that might pass his way.

The first day there he insisted on showing me his personal wine cellar and I was absolutely in awe at the quantity of top class wines he had laid down.

"What do you do with these?" I asked, rather foolishly thinking that he might just be a collector of fine wines.

"Why drink 'em, of course. What do you think I do? Just look at them like my father did?"

He then said that as we would be having a special treat in the way of fresh water pike baked in the oven would I like to select the wines. I hesitated.

"Go on. Anything you like, something for an aperitif and something for the fish."

I just could not resist such an invitation and extravagantly selected my absolute favourite of all white wines, a bottle of Chateau d'Yquem. "I know it is normally for the desserts but I cannot resist this one."

Maurice beamed. "Rubbish," he said. "I make my own rules. Anyway, if Larousse Gastronomique says it can be drunk with the hors-d'oeuvres and the main course, then that is good enough for me. Moreover, you had better take another couple of bottles. We are going to need them."

He then went on to explain that the following day his wife would be preparing 'La Daube de Boeuf Provencale' and suggested that possibly a

Burgundy might be in keeping. I then chose a Clos Vouget and received a further appreciative nod.

Just as we were about to leave Maurice placed his hand on my arm and said, "I know you like cheese so I have had the local shop make up a mixed selection for us. What do you say we take a bottle of this as well?" Here he carefully removed from the rack a bottle of vintage Chateaux Margaux.

I protested but where Maurice was concerned his word was law when food and drink were involved. When we left with me carefully carrying the bag, I felt that I had won the lottery, which I probably would have to have done in order to buy those few bottles.

Our Christmas consisted of one glorious binge reinforced by our dining at some of the most delightful restaurants I have ever had the pleasure of visiting. There was one such place in Le Sentier that served succulent pig's trotters in Marsala wine and in true Swiss style portion after portion until we almost reached bursting point. Another time we drove up into the forest with the snow piled high on either side of the road to around six feet in height, to where we sat at scrubbed pine tables while they sent over plate after plate of toasted Raclette cheese together with the inevitable glasses of schnapps. At still another we were so high above the clouds that while we dipped into a cheese fondue we could look out at the mountain peaks like white capped islands all around us.

Then there was one of the finest meals I ever recall.

This took place at the 'Hostellerie du Moulin des Truite Bleues'. Just over the French border, near the small town of Champagnole, this old water mill restaurant serves exquisitely cooked crayfish fresh from the river and prepared slowly in vintage wine. Thoroughly and unforgivable indulging, especially accompanied by a fine Pol Roger.

Whilst staying with Maurice we took the opportunity to visit mutual friends who lived in Zug near Zurich. Ivo, head of the Leeman family, now lives with his charming wife, Francoise, in Paulliac near Bordeaux. Spending an unforgettable day with them we received, as a parting gift, several bottles of country farmhouse distilled Kirsch. It was potent firewater but what a wonderfully effective digestive after a hearty meal.

*

All too soon our stay in Switzerland came to an end and it was time to set out for Spain once again. Never will I forget our first night's stop, after leaving Le Sentier. It turned out to be a complete disaster.

We had booked in a large Michelin recommended hotel in Orange. Arriving in the evening our first priority was to feed our son, wait until he was slumbering peacefully, then going down to dine. Passing through the main reception area we were confronted by a large crowd of exquisitely dressed and very many bejewelled ladies together with their escorts in full evening dress. In the middle of this group was a short, snowy white haired gentleman who somehow reminded me of Leopold Stokowski. He was clutching a violin case. Someone then explained to us that it was a very special, very private, violin recital that was being held in the hotel for the city's dignitaries.

Moving through into the dining room we were ushered to our table where we ordered a couple of very dry martinis as an aperitif. This put us in fine form and as we had decided on fresh salmon this time I chose a suitable dry white wine. When the salmon appeared it looked most unappetising. Sad, thick dry red wedges of unappetising fish just lay there on the plate without even a sprig of parsley to make it a little more presentable to the eye. Without any hesitation I called the waiter over and asked to speak to the chef. If I had any glimpse of what I was embarking on at that moment I would have ignored the fish, drank the rest of the wine and retired to bed.

But no, I had to go ahead and make my point.

The chef duly appeared and on seeing that we were English introduced himself as being Canadian. Then, after listening to my complaint, he apologised profusely and returned to the kitchen and prepared us a first class dish of well presented succulent salmon. This was brought out together with an extra bottle of wine.

So far so good.

At that particular moment everything was fine. It was after the meal, when I was indulging in my passion for calvados that the chef appeared once again; this time carrying a bottle of the liqueur. "Prunier, from the Dordogne region," he explained, deftly opening the bottle and filling the small glasses he had brought along.

Related in someway to the pop star of that era, Cat Stevens, he turned out to be a most entertaining personality and together all three of us consumed the bottle of Prunier.

*

It was later that things became somewhat hazy and as our new friend had to return to the kitchen we decided to go to bed. We made the hotel room without too much attention being drawn to our erratic course and flopped down onto the bed. Mary, still fully dressed, was soon fast asleep. I then stripped off to my shorts and tried to sleep also but was prevented by two things. Piped music seemed to be on somewhere and the room just would not keep still sufficiently for me to find where to switch the thing off.

Eventually I realised that I was going to be sick and made the bathroom just in time. Burying my head into the toilet bowl I began vomiting noisily. Then I became aware of a strange phenomenon. When I came up for air the music had stopped. Then it began once more. As a further spasm noisily overtook me the music ceased again. It was most confusing. This happened several times with me retching, the music coming to an abrupt end and then beginning again after I withdrew my head from the depths of the toilet bowl.

Next thing I heard the telephone ringing in the bedroom. "Damn silly time to call anyone," I thought, not daring to leave the vicinity of the toilet. I let it ring.

Two or three more spasms occurred and next I heard a hammering on the bedroom door. Feeling somewhat better I made my way out of the bathroom and cautiously opened the door. Before me stood an extremely irate, red faced gentleman in full evening dress. He waved his arms gesticulated and shouting unintelligible French while I stood, glassy eyed clinging to the door and wondering what the hell was going on.

Then much to my relief our friend the chef came weaving along the corridor. "Wash th' matter?" he asked, steadying himself against the wall.

The Frenchman, now purple in the face was yelling even louder and pointing at me.

"Lishen, my fren'," said the chef forsaking the wall and placing a friendly arm around the other, "Jush tell me wash the' matter."

Purple face reached up and removed the offending limb but moderated his tirade to a more controlled tone. The chef listened moving back to the wall for more support.   Then turning to me said, "Your bashroom ish next to th' mushic room and yo're mashking noishes 'orribles. Totally dishturbing the conshert. This ish th' night manager. He ish a man very angry."

Needless to say at this point I sobered up very quickly, apologised and retired into the bedroom, leaving them outside still arguing.

Mary and son slept happily through all this and without relating to what had happened the night before I suggested next morning that we forsake breakfast and leave. I asked that Mary settle the bill while I brought the car around to the entrance.

On pulling away from the hotel Mary remarked, "I don't think we will bother staying there again. The man at the desk was most discourteous when I paid. Just went on muttering away about something or other. He didn't even have the courtesy to wish us 'Bon voyage' like they normally do."

*

So nursing the effects of the previous night's symphonic disaster, we continued towards Spain, crossing the frontier at Cerbère. I declined Mary's suggestion that we take a look at the port area where Steve and I had had that unforgettable night the previous year. However, driving up the steep incline and out of the village we did stop for a moment outside the chained and padlocked iron gates of Juan Miguel's mansion. At the far end of the drive, the massive grey stone building stood brooding and silent, looking for the entire world as though it had been abandoned. I stood there wondering if within those walls the Amazonian figure of 'Loli' was still keeping her mute vigil and the stocks of champagne lay resting within the large refrigerator awaiting the next unwitting guests.

Even though it was still January the sun was shining and everything was sharp and bright when we finally arrived in Cullera. A warm welcome was awaiting us at the pub. Everything was as we wished it to be and much to our surprise the accounts demonstrated that every one of our suppliers had been paid up to date and all the necessary costs of running the place had been settled. The icing on top of the cake was when Jane, the girl that we had left in charge, presented us with and envelope containing the profit of thirty-five thousand pesetas, no mean sum in those days. Another point worth taking into consideration was that the petrol cost for our whole journey had come to just seven thousand five hundred pesetas; a mere thirty pounds sterling.

Still extremely busy in the pub, we continued the 'Happy Hour' and the occasional excursion for paella. As my son was not yet one year old, we employed the services of an au-pair. Once she was established I enlisted extra help in the bar. This took place in the form of Mary Ostertaag. Originally, from Liverpool she was fondly known to everyone as 'Mary Fruitcake'. Married to Charles Ostertaag, a short sprightly man some good few years older than her, Mary was a popular figure in Cullera. Charlie, as we referred to her husband, had trained and worked with the famous chef de cuisine, Auguste Escoffier, at the Carlton Hotel, London. According to culinary history, Escoffier had been recognised as the 'King of Chefs and the Chef of Kings'.

Some of Charlie's magic had occasionally peeped through but as he was now well into his late seventies he tended to be rather senile. I still have to hand a mean recipe for an excellent 'potage' and simple, but delightful, vinaigrette sauce that he gave me.

One day Charlie skipped into the pub brandishing a magnificent pair of pruning shears that he had bought that very morning. Waving them under my nose, at the same time obliging me with a sly wink, he whispered, "Need some tomatoes? You know the ones just outside the village will make a lovely soup or 'sauce Provencal'. And with these," here Charlie waved the impressive looking instrument, "it'll be no problem."

Naturally I declined the offer, not because of the possibility of Charlie falling foul of the law, but the price of tomatoes at that particular time was absolutely rock bottom. Anyway, Charlie, unable to complete his negotiations, left the bar returning some hours later carrying a bag that must have contained around three or four kilos of ripe tomatoes. The value of this booty I put at around thirty pesetas or, at that time, twelve English pence.

"Want to buy these?" he asked, showing me the contents of the bag.

"No thanks, Charlie, You have them."

"They're the best you know."

"I can see that but we are well stocked at the moment, thanks."

Then just as he was about to leave a thought struck me. "Hey!" I called out after him. "Where are those shears you brought in this morning?"

Charlie stopped and turned a puzzled expression on his wrinkled features.   "Shears?" he said. "What shears?"

"The ones you came in here with."

He searched through all his pockets and peered into the bag as though they might be there; then exclaimed, "Bloody hell, I left 'em in the tomato fields!"

His wife, with her great sense if humour, helped me in the bar whilst Mary, together with the au-pair, dedicated herself to the apartment and our son. Things appeared to be going well but I felt that family relationships were failing somewhat. I began seeking excuses and blamed it onto all the hours I put in and the little time we spent together. And, of course, there were all the little incidents I had to contend with in the pub which did not help the situation. These incidents are always part of any business, but at times I thought that fate decreed that I, personally, would have the monopoly. This was, I think, due in part to the variation in nationalities and personalities that presented themselves at the place. I never really knew what to expect next. The three member 'Jim Beam' Club continued to thrive as always and one such notable confrontation occurred through the provocation of Joe Lucas and Ron Bartlett, my two companions.

*

Several times a week at around eleven o'clock at night Emilio, a waiter employed at a nearby cafe, would treat us to a visit. He would order a beer and place himself in a strategic position at the bar where he could ogle the female customers. I had noticed that each time any of them glanced at him Emilio he would make provocative facial expressions and if the occasion arose he would follow them to the toilets making silly comments in broken English. This, naturally, irritated me and I expressed my feelings to the 'Jim Beam' club members.

"Why don't you do something about it?" asked Joe Lucas lifting his glass and sipping his bourbon.

"What can I do? Nobody has ever complained and if I say anything the women customers would probably just say that they don't take any notice anyway."

"All the same something should be done," put in Ron Bartlett. "You don't need those sorts of problems."

I nodded in agreement. "Yes. I'll have to do something drastic to stop our Emilio."

"Like what?" asked Joe who was always quick off the mark.

"Dunno!" I said, and then stupidly came up with an idea.

"I know what. I'll tip a pint of beer over his bloody head if he starts that nonsense tonight."

Both of them laughed.

"Haven't got the balls," said Joe.

"Definitely not," agreed Ron.

This had now put me in a grave situation where the club was concerned. Disrespect for one of the Jim Beam team was definitely not to be tolerated. "How much?" I asked, regretting the words that seemed to be coming from someone else.

"Five hundred pesetas," said Joe reaching for his wallet.

"And another five hundred here," said Ron.

The money was duly placed in the cash register and we waited with me hoping that Emilio would not put in an appearance, just for once.

It goes without saying that at eleven on the dot in he walked, ordered a drink, placed himself on a stool and began staring at the most attractive female customers present. This was not too difficult as we were full. Within a few minutes he had embarked on his facial expressions involving puckering his lips up, blowing kisses and sticking his tongue out.

Of course the flack started coming in from my two friends. So choosing the right moment I pulled a pint glass of beer, walked over to Emilio and deposited the whole contents over his head.

To say that the exercise went flat would be an exaggeration. There was such a hush that you could have heard that pin drop as all eyes turned towards me. Naturally nobody, absolutely nobody, apart from my two friends, had any idea what had provoked me to do such a thing. Emilio was sitting there mouth open gaping at me, wet hair plastered all over his face and his shirt thoroughly soaked.

Eventually, after staring at me for a few seconds, he asked, "Why did you do that?"

"You know why. Now get out and don't come back," I said forcibly.

Of course it was impossible to explain to the rest of the customers what had impelled me to do it. It would have sounded ridiculous. Emilio left and after some minutes things returned to normal with my two friends congratulating me on my expertise in putting unwanted customers to flight.

I was feeling pleased with myself when suddenly the door opened and in came two, fully uniformed, very officious looking, Civil Guards. Beckoning me to the end of the bar the senior one of the two asked, "What have you done with Emilio? He's all wet."

This in itself sounded funny but I was too annoyed to laugh. "What do you mean he's all wet? Of course he's all wet. I tipped half a litre of beer all over him and if he shows his face in here again I will repeat the operation."

They both stared at me in amazement at my admission. Then one asked what had made me do such a thing. Quietly I explained precisely why I had acted in that way, leaving out none of the details, apart from the challenge from my friends. They remained silent for a while and I took the opportunity of offering them a drink. To my relief they accepted a brandy each.

"Will I have any problems?" I asked, pouring out the drinks.

The answer that came back demonstrated to me that there would always be people around that understand the meaning of 'logic'. "No. No problem at all," he said. "That is unless, of course, he wishes to make an official complaint, which I doubt."

They both removed their 'tricorns' before reaching for the glasses. "Anyway Emilio said that he spent quite a bit of money in here."

I nodded prudently although this was not entirely true.

"Well," continued the senior Civil Guard, "if you are prepared to tip beer over a good money spending client then kick him out, you must have a damn good reason for doing so."

*

As the days gradually grew longer and the Mediterranean sun became that much warmer each morning, business seemed to thrive at the same rate as my family life began to disintegrate. My wife had always had a tendency to suffer from the heat and had been working in the bar that was, unfortunately lacking in air conditioning. This had, naturally, taken its toll over the few years that we had been there. So having the services of the au-pair to look after our son she would be off around the town while I together with the staff struggled on with the pub. Arguments became rife, especially when I arrived home late and very tired. I felt that at the time I was actually prostituting my body in that I was riding on a wave of booze, hangovers, together with work and increasing family problems. How I managed at that time I will never know but I eventually came to the point where I had to do something and I decided that my marriage and family came first on the priority list.

So one day, leaving the bar in the hands of the competent staff, Mary, my son and I took a short holiday, driving up towards the wonderful 'Monestario de Piedra' or Monastery of Stone, near to Zaragoza. This enchanting old place, lying next to a natural park full of gardens, walks and a series of lovely waterfalls, would prove an ideal place for us to take stock, relax and gather up the remnants of our relationship.

And what a waste of time that was I decided after being there a few days.

Next we carried on up to historical town of Cuenca and browsed around the old town with its incredible 'Hanging Houses' that had been constructed precariously overhanging a cliff of several hundred feet. Even this was spoilt by the presence of an extremist modern art exhibition that was then a permanent fixture in the rickety old buildings. All in all, I calculated that the whole project was a complete disaster.

It was on the return journey that an argument arose that was of such unimportance that I cannot even remember what it was about. Anyway such was my frustration at the time that I almost ran the car off the road. Even today I still have cold shivers thinking about what could have resulted.

*

Once back in Cullera my spirits rose somewhat with the knowledge that Maurice and his family from Switzerland would be arriving for two weeks vacation. His first night's welcoming party was to be dinner prepared by Mary. Naturally it was important that the wine should fit the occasion, especially after what he had served us when we made the visit to his home.

The day of their arrival dawned and I went along to the local bodega to see what was available. After sometime considering their wide range I decided on a Rioja red, reserve wine. I was walking back towards the apartment when somebody called out my name. It was Gedo the Dutchman. He was waiting to have his haircut and the place to wait was, of course, in the bar next to the barber's shop.

"Chris!" he called, "Come over and have a drink."

Not requiring any further encouragement I crossed the road and joined him for a beer. After about a couple of minutes chatting about nothing in particular, he asked, "What have you there?" nodding towards my bag that had clinked interestingly when I put it down.

"Wine, Gedo. My Swiss friend and his family are coming for dinner tonight."

Bending down he peered into the bag and examined the bottles. "Mmmm..." he murmured. Not bad. Not bad at all."

"Thanks," I said, feeling pleased that my decision had warranted such praise.

"How much did you pay for them, Chris?"

"Four hundred pesetas."

"Mmmm...." he went again. "Not bad at all at four hundred pesetas for three bottles of good wine."

"Each," I corrected him.

"Each?" he said, staring at me in amazement. "What do you mean each?"

"Each bottle, Gedo."

"Chris! You tell me that you paid one thousand two hundred pesetas for these three bottles of Rioja wine"

"It's bloody good Rioja wine. In fact, 'Tondonia' reserve. One of the best."

But Gedo wasn't having any. "My friend you are crazy. You are silly."

"Am I?"

"Completely! Why do you not ask your friends first, before spending all that money?"

"Ask what friends what?"

He placed his hand over his heart. "Am I, Gedo van der Weij, not your friend?"

"Yes," I hesitated, "I suppose so. But what has that got to do with me buying wine for dinner tonight?"

He looked at me sadly, then said slowly, "Because, my dear friend, if you had asked me first I could have organised you a couple of bottle of the best wine in the entire world."

At that moment the barber appeared in the doorway and indicated to the Dutchman that it was his turn but Gedo, now in full flow, waved him away saying that he would be there in five minutes.

"The best wine in the whole world," I repeated, for something to say.

"Ah, yes….," he said, thoughtfully, seemingly deciding whether to confide in me some immense secret. Then making up his mind he said, "When I married Claire, her father gave to us five cases of this wonderful wine."

I nodded encouraging him to go on.

"And this very special wine I keep in the garage, for one important occasion. You see, her father made us promise that we would only drink one bottle on our wedding anniversary every year." Then he added, "It's an old Dutch custom. I think you English call it 'Going Dutch.'"

"I always thought that 'Going Dutch' signified you shared the costs of something with somebody, Gedo."

He hesitated, a trace of bitterness touching his voice. "Yes," he said, "her father shared the wine with me and she has been costing me ever since."

"Spanish wine?" I asked my curiosity aroused.

He looked aghast at such a suggestion. "No, certainly not. Ordinary Spanish wine is rubbish compared with this."

He sipped his beer, replaced the glass on the bar and went on. "No my friend, this particular wine is French wine from....from the Bordeaux region."

My interest quickened as he leaned towards me.

"This wine comes from an area where there is, how you say, a micro climate. The vines are sheltered by a range of hills that prevent the wet west winds from ruining them, at the same time keeping them above the dampness that frequents the area."

I was now beginning to be impressed by Gedo's knowledge of such things.

"Are you serious?" I asked.

He stood back his blue eyes searching mine for a sign of disbelief. "Yes, Chris. The wine is from an area near to where the great Clos de Vougeot and the Nuits Saint Georges' wines come from."

"Marvellous," I said wondering where all this was leading to.

He then reached over and laid his hand on my arm. "Don't you see? Five cases of this wine and Claire and I drink one bottle every wedding anniversary."

He seemed to be reminiscing and I could almost visualise the cosy candlelight and hear the soft music playing while they both sat hands clasped, savouring the wine.

"Her father said that we would have enough to see us through until our silver wedding anniversary."

"And a bit over, I commented, adding, "If your marriage lasts that long, that is."

"Exactly!" he cried, "Exactly! You are quite right. It probably won't. So that is where I can do you a favour."

"You can?" I pulled my arm away and reached for my glass.

"Yes, Chris. I am sure that my marriage will not be lasting much longer. Therefore I can let you have a case."

"You can?" I was certainly surprised at this sudden generosity.

"At a price, that is. Yes, a good price for a good friend."

"I wouldn't dream of taking your wine," I said mentally placing the words 'good price' against such a proposition. "And anyway are you sure it will be any good? I mean, most wines only have a certain time in which to drink them."

"That is why it is so special."

"How much?" I asked, more out of interest than commitment.

He thoughtfully ran his finger around the rim of his beer glass. "To you my friend I think we can say only five hundred pesetas a bottle. For a case of twelve, that is."

"You're totally out of your mind, Mr. Van der Weig,"

I finished my drink, placed the glass firmly on the bar top and made to pick up the bag.

"Alright, Chris, what do you say to two hundred pesetas a bottle? For a case of twelve?"

"Forget it Gedo!"

"Six bottles at two hundred and fifty pesetas each," he persisted.

"Six bottles at two hundred pesetas each," I offered, curious as to what this wine might be like.

He stared at me for a brief moment.

"Alright, done," he said, and we shook hands.

"Six o'clock I will have it waiting for you in my bar."

"I'll be there," I promised, picking up the bag then walking out into the sunshine, at the same time thinking that if this elixir was anywhere near to what Gedo had painted it would be worth observing Maurice's expression when he tried it. 'Rapture' I decided might just be the appropriate adjective in describing the look on his face.

*

The Swiss family arrived at around five o'clock that afternoon and after the usual greetings I suggested that Maurice went with me to pick up the wine, explaining what had taken place.

"Such friends are hard to come by," was his only comment. "You are most fortunate."

Elbowing our way through the swing doors of Gedo's Western Saloon, we found the place deserted save for Gedo's wife who was propping herself up at the bar. There was no sign of Gedo.

"Hello, Claire," I said and after the customary peck on each cheek I introduced her to Maurice. She almost fell into his arms.

"Ooops!" she giggled, "I think I'm a little bit drinky, drinky."

"Not important," I said gallantly. "Actually we are looking for Gedo."

At this she went into peels of laughter. "Gedo," she chuckled. "Gedo's not here."

"I can see that, Claire."

I watched as she buried her head in a glass of something or other.

"What's so funny, Claire?" I asked.

"Don't know if I should tell you;" she said, coyly.

"Come on. Don't tiddle around. Where is he?"

"It's so funny, Chrish. Wait till I tell you."

Then off she went again into more hysterics. Maurice was becoming irritated by this exchange and I wanted to finish it quickly.

"Alright, we'll come back later." I turned and made as if to move towards the door but she left the bar and clutched at my sleeve.

"No don't go, Chrish. Let's have a little drinkies first."

"Just tell me what's going on please Claire and then we will have the drinkies."

Taking a deep breath as though she was about to embark on a lengthy speech, she said simply, "Gedo has gone to Sueca."

"Why should he want to go there?"

"Because, Chrish. He has gone to buy six bottle of wine for twenty-five pesetas each and is selling them to shum idiot for two hundred pesetas a bottle." Again she went into convulsions, tears now streaming down her cheeks, while I stood there staring, the light dawning.

"Don't know who it ish," she said, pulling herself together.

"Well I bloody well do," I said, struggling to control myself.

"Who, Chrish?"

"The idiot you are talking about," I said through clenched teeth, "is standing right here in front of you!"

At that very moment the door swung open behind us and in staggered Gedo carrying a box with half a dozen bottles rattling around in it. Maurice, sensing something unpleasant was a bout to happen, quickly moved to one side as I stepped forward to confront the Dutchman, fists already raised.

"I'll bloody murder you. You conniving son of a bitch!"

Gedo stopped, rapidly taking in the scene before him. Then with a sickly grin appearing on his face said, "A joke, Chris. It was all just a joke."

He could sense that this was not stopping me in anyway and so raised the box to protect himself. "I'll give you joke!" I yelled and I went for the box. Next, before either of us could do anything, it slipped from his grasp and crashed to the floor. Bottles were breaking and an evil looking brown liquid spilling out everywhere. We both stopped and stared at the mess, then turning Gedo shot out of the bar with myself in hot on his heels.

"Come back here!" I bellowed, causing several people to stop, curious as to what was happening. But there was no chance. Gedo was in full flight towards the beach doing a fine imitation of marathon man.

Dinner that night was a success although Maurice's view was somewhat biased in that his friend should be set up for such a scam. However he did manage to smile as I recounted what had occurred to the others present. I never did find out what wine Gedo was on the point of selling to me but the stain on the wooden floor looked as though someone had spilt acid.

"Rapture," I thought, would probably not have been the expression on Maurice's face had he sampled it.

Chapter 14

When one is committed to working all hours and closing time does eventually come around at two or three o'clock in the morning, then one cannot, close up, just switch off, go home, climb into bed and sleep. Most nights, as many others in the business, I was so wound up it required an adjustment or time to relax a little before hitting the sack. Anyway, whatever I did at that time became a bone of contention where my wife was concerned. Whether I arrived home early or late, it disturbed her, woke the baby or whatever and this was beginning to tell.

Things were just not working out.

One of the after hours places I used to visit, after I closed the pub, was some five kilometres away at Favareta on the Alicante main road. This road house stayed open all night and did excellent business for people like myself who needed to wind down.

And it was there that I became friendly with three girls that were working at one of the drinks clubs near to the pub. Most nights I would see them there and we would talk about things in general before going our different ways home. One of them was an American. Attractive, slim and blond with a ready smile, green eyes and a husky mid-west voice. I cannot say that we hit it off immediately, but being a person whose facial expressions can reveal exactly what I am thinking, it soon became obvious to Kathy, for that was her name, that I had problems of one sort or another. Then one night over a drink I confided in her, explaining that there were business and personal pressures involved.

"It wouldn't be so bad," I complained, "if I could get on with running my bar, but going home to aggravation after working all hours, I just cannot handle it much more."

It was around a week later she saw that I was just about at the end of my tether. "You know, Chris," she said. If things become too bad you can always move in with us. No problem. There's plenty of room."

I thanked her and thought little more about it until the situation at home became even more impossible. There I was opening the pub at ten o'clock in the morning and most days working through to two and three the following morning. I was a wreck. In fact looking back I cannot for the life of me think how I managed. Anyway the moment came when Mary and I had an argument and at her own suggestion I was told that it would be better if I moved out of the apartment.

*

And so there I was one morning, with a suitcase containing mere necessities, accepting Kathy's offer and moving in with her and the two other girls.

What a change! I was reminded of a phrase that my mother had used every time for such situations. "It's just like hitting your head against a brick wall. When you stop it's marvellous." I immediately felt rejuvenated. They took to me and spoilt me; something to which I had not been accustomed to for a long time.

There was a further surprise in store when one morning I went to the pub to open up and found Mary waiting with a large brown parcel tied with string.

"Here," she said, thrusting it into my hands. "Here are some shirts and underwear, washed and ironed. I don't want those women to think that I don't look after you."

As for sometime I had even resorted to taking care of my own laundry this was, to say the least, most bewildering. However it did little to make me relent on the move I had made.

*

More than thirty years on I was reminded of this incident when I heard the story about the Spaniard walking along Valencia's beach at Malvarrosa. He suddenly tripped over the inevitable bottle with a cork in it. Then, as he had read various tales on the subject, he duly picked it up, removed the cork and rubbed it, releasing the Genie. Obviously being well prepared for such an event on being asked by the Genie what was his wish the man replied that as a monument to his memory he would like a bridge constructed connecting Valencia to Ibiza, some hundred miles distance. The Genie was horrified at the idea and said that the enormity of the project made it unreasonable and that as he was sure his benefactor was an understanding person would he please think again.

Eventually the man said, "Look, I have been married three times and on each occasion it has ended in disaster, through which I could see as being no fault of mine. What, I wondered, was would it be possible for you to bestow on me the gift of being able to understand women and how their minds function?"

The Genie thought for one moment then asked, "How many traffic lanes would you like on this bridge you were talking about?"

*

For a while things went along fairly well in my new residence and the girls took great care of my well-being. However the pressures still built up and together with the fact that the Ford factory was now practically completed and up and running, the majority of the customers were being transferred elsewhere. So I let it be known that I wanted out of the English Pub. At the same time I had become involved with Kathy. It was now nearing the end of the season and neither she nor I were happy about the situation, so we decided that the best thing was for her to return to the States. Things were organised and one sad day I drove her to Madrid airport and we said our tearful 'goodbyes'.

Within two days of my return to Cullera, Mary came by and said that if I wanted to sell my half of the business to another person then they both would take it over. Immediately I agreed and the sale was arranged. During the interim period before my final departure I had been speaking to Reggie the Fish and his wife Carmen about the possibility of setting up a similar pub, on a much larger scale, in the city of Valencia. My reasoning was pretty obvious in that this would ensure me of customers all the year round and I would still be within range of my son as regards visits.

*

The sale of the Cullera business was underway when, much to my surprise, one day, into the bar walked Gomer and Betty Ann Davis, the friends that Mary and I had met in Toledo some years before. It was a great reunion for me and on the first night this wonderful couple and I just talked until the early hours reminiscing about old times.

Finally, Gomar, who had been studying me thoughtfully, said, "Chris, you look absolutely knackered. If you don't slow down you will be having a heart attack or something." Here he draped a fatherly arm around my shoulder and continued. "When the sale is sorted out why not take a good holiday? Get away somewhere different."

Up until this point I had not really thought about doing any such thing. My idea was to continue as before, but in Valencia.

"Look," he persisted, "If you wish, as Betty Ann and myself are over here, why not take a trip over to my place in the States. You can stay for a few weeks and we will meet up when we return."

"Wow!" I thought. "Now that would really be something."

Not having been to America before I did not have to think twice before accepting. And, of course, there was always Kathy at the back of my mind, although I had no idea where she might be. The only lead I had was a Hayes, Kansas, telephone number.

Next Reggie and Carmen where consulted about the search for suitable premises for a pub in Valencia. They, in turn, immediately agreed and promised that when I returned all would be ready for the project. Under Gomar's guidance I bought a return ticket to New York and from there would catch a train to Philadelphia.

Then things started to happen.

*

The travel agency informed me that I would require an entry Visa for the USA. Naturally I was surprised that this should be so, but was not unduly concerned as the local acting American Consul, Dan Green, was a friend of mine and I felt certain that a visit to him would result in the matter being arranged.

I arrived at his office in Valencia one Wednesday morning and explained the situation

"Sorry, Chris," he said, "but visas can only be issued through the Embassy in Madrid."

"How long does this take?" I asked, obviously disappointed,

"Oh, a couple of weeks, at least I should think"

"But I am due to fly out next Tuesday," I protested. "Can't something be done?"

Dan Green always came up trumps and there are many English people who have found him 'tops' when it has come to sorting out their problems in Spain; even more so than the British Consul at that time.

"Tell you what to do, Chris." He removed the top from his gold fountain pen and began writing. "Phone the Embassy in Madrid, speak to this lady whose name I have written down, explain the situation and I know that if you go there personally one morning the visa can be issued in one day."

I thanked Dan for his help and phoned the lady in question. "No problem," she assured me. "Just arrive on Friday morning at eight o'clock, present your passport and you will have your visa ready in the afternoon."

"Wonderful!" I thought." What a relief."

*

Now I was more confident and late Thursday night drove the three hundred and forty odd kilometres to Madrid arriving in time to join the queue when the Embassy opened at eight. The charming lady to whom I had spoken on the telephone was at the reception desk and gave me a numbered ticket at the same time directing me past the Negro American Marine guard on the door to where I was to wait my turn.

We all sat in rows of chairs facing what looked to be several paying in windows at a local bank. Iron bars protected the personnel who attended us and I wondered who the hell would want to hold up an American Embassy.

Eventually my number was called and I approached one particular window and was formally greeted by a young, officious looking, Spanish gentleman who without any preamble asked bluntly, "What do you want?"

I explained that I was travelling to America for holiday purposes and would like the necessary visa.

"Certainly," he said, taking my proffered passport and writing down my details. "Come back next week and it just might be ready."

Not being totally unprepared for this response I explained the situation starting with Dan Green and mentioning my contact at the door.

"Well that is different," he conceded rather reluctantly, I thought. "Come back at four o'clock this afternoon and wait for me to call you over and you will have your visa."

Thanking him I left the Embassy with a spring in my step, did some sight-seeing around beautiful Madrid then, after an excellent lunch at one of the restaurants on the Gran Via, returned to the Embassy punctually at four o'clock. The man was still there behind the counter and he nodded to me indicating that I should wait. I sat down thinking that this was how things should be arranged and that I would soon be on the return journey to Valencia.

Half past four came and went. Then five o'clock came round and I began to become restless knowing that it was Friday afternoon and there was the general air of winding down that proceeds all week-ends, particularly in most governmental establishments. The hands of the clock on the wall slowly moved past the half hour mark and then, when I was just about to ask the man if there was a problem he beckoned me over.

It was just five minutes to six.

Glancing up from the papers he was shuffling around in his hands he acknowledged me with a brusque nod and said curtly, "Come back next week."

"I beg your pardon," I said, not quite sure that I had heard correctly. "What did you say?"

"I said come back next week and you will have your visa."

He then turned and made as to move off. I panicked. "Wait a minute!" I called out not quite certain how to handle the situation.

"Yes?" he said, stopping and looking at me most disdainfully through the bars. "And what is it now?"

I had to do something and quickly. Then an idea flashed into my head. "Oh, there's no problem. Monday will be fine," I said. "I'll just stay right here." And so saying I lay down full length on the carpet.

It took around two seconds for him to digest what had happened.

Obviously he had not received any training for this type of response. There was a fair size lip over the counter so he had difficulty in looking down at me. I could see his hands clutch at the bars and his face pressed against them as he strained to see what I was doing.

"You can't stay there," he eventually choked when he saw that I was quite serious and had no intentions of moving.

"I'm perfectly alright," I assured him waving. "It seems a new carpet. I'll be quite comfortable, thank you."

He might not have been warned that something like this might happen but he knew what to do if it did and hit some hidden button. Within seconds there suddenly appeared from nowhere the Marine soldier and what I assumed to be two plain clothed security men. All three skidded to a halt and looked down at me.

"What the hells going on here?" one of them demanded staring first at me and then at the man behind the bars.

"This man says he is staying there until Monday."

"He's what?" exclaimed one of the security men.

"To wait for his visa," explained my man now red in the face, possibly realising that now he was well implicated in this situation.

From my prone position I nodded a helpful confirmation.

"Get him out of here," hissed the clerk.

All three then moved forward as if to pick me up and immediately I raised my hands. They stopped.

"Listen," I said, speaking slowly and precisely, "I am asking, or if you like, demanding that you pick me up, manhandle me to the door and throw me out into the street."

They hesitated digesting the implications of this and I went into a very affected English tone of voice. "Because when you actually do forcibly remove me from these, how shall I say, unfriendly premises and this most disagreeable situation, I will be straight down to the newspaper offices of El Pais, ABC and will speak to the editors, both of whom I have the pleasure of being acquainted with personally. And when I do, believe me, relationships between America, Spain and the UK, will stink for at least a few hours when the news comes out tomorrow."

The three of them stood there staring down at me and nobody seemed to want to say anything. Then looking at each one in turn as might an angry schoolteacher I continued. "Why, you might ask? Because, sadly, you are nothing but a bunch of liars! I was told in Valencia that a visa could be issued within a day and this was confirmed by a telephone call to this Embassy. Nothing but lies. I was then informed by this person behind these, might I say very appropriate bars, to return at four o'clock and I would receive both passport and visa. More lies. I am then kept waiting for two hours only to be told to return next week. So, gentlemen I have decided to stay here. Alright? Now get on with it. Throw me out!"

The three of them looked from one to the other as if wondering which of them was going to make the first move and then at the speechless clerk whose face had now taken on a purple hue. Needless to say there was no lack of sightseers. A little crowd was gathering around me as if I were some sort of traffic accident. Nobody seemed to know quite what to do. Then one of the security men gestured the others to remain and disappeared in the direction of the offices.

All was quiet and I closed my eyes feigning a relaxed posture but inside my heart was thumping like a steam hammer. Eventually the man returned accompanied by another tall, white haired, gentleman who demanded to know what was happening.

Again with the affected accent I went through the whole story and finished by saying, "So you see it is all lies, isn't it? I really do not know why you feel the necessity to tell lies." Then I put in, just to add a little more food for thought, "Up until now I had always believed that Americans could be counted on and not feel the need to actually deceive people. But there again," here I shrugged my shoulders, "one lives and learns doesn't one? I suppose it comes from being deprived of what one might term as 'culture'."

The white haired man's expression changed to astonishment. He was speechless for a moment. "Nobody moves," he then instructed tightly after some deliberation. Next, turning he disappeared in the direction from which he had come.

Nobody seemed to want to move anyway and the little crowd grew larger. I heard a few whispered comments and one new arrival who asked, "Is he ill or something?"

Then a few bolder Spanish voices from persons who, I supposed, had received similar treatment were muttering, "Quite right," and "Bravo!" I kept my eyes closed and waited.

Next a deep bass voice asked, "And whaaat is the meaning of this, Sir?"

When I opened my eyes there was no way in which I was prepared for what was literally towering over me. This woman, whoever she was, was not just large but enormous. No, not fat in any way. Just huge all over and that included certainly considerably more than two metres in height.

My heart sank. "Ah, well," I thought, "in for a penny, in for a pound," and repeated the whole story for a third time beginning with an apology that as an Englishman I usually stood when addressing a lady and not, I gestured with my hands, from this rather embarrassing position into which I had been forced. She listened, stone faced, to my insinuations on the fact that telling lies were unnecessary, although I did see her eyes flicker when I mentioned the 'culture' bit.

After I had finished she stood staring down at me for about twenty seconds then turning to purple face who looked as though he was about to explode she thrust out a ham sized hand and demanded, "Passport!" The document was immediately thrust through the bars and taking it she handed it to another man who had appeared.

Next, without a word, she turned and sailed out together with her entourage jostling behind her like a fleet of small craft. Within three minutes the white haired man returned and handed me the passport. I checked it noticing that the visa stamp read for one year.

Slowly climbing to my feet I dusted myself down, nodded at him and said, "There, that didn't hurt did it?"

On the way to the door I was accompanied by the marine to whom I passed one of my visiting cards. "Well done," I said, "This will help to spell my name correctly when you make your report."

He took it without a word and as I walked out I had a feeling that he might just be throwing up a salute in my direction.

*

The flight across the Atlantic was comfortable and we landed in New York sometime in the afternoon. One of the customers at the pub in Cullera was Paul Parnes who appeared once or twice a year. We became quite friendly and he told me that he was a song writer who lived in Manhattan. So having his telephone number to hand I called him.

"Great to hear you, Chris," he said. "I will be in your pub tomorrow night."

"Sorry to disappoint you Paul but I'm in New York."

There was a minute's silence. Then his voice said, "What are you waiting for. Grab a cab and get over here to Riverside Drive."

"Right. See you soon."

I received a warm welcome there passing a very pleasant evening drinking martinis out of tin mugs on his penthouse terrace whilst watching the firework display in the distant Central Park.

Later I called Hayes, Kansas and was told by Kathy's mother that her daughter had gone on to Reno. Another call and Kathy was on the line. I just said, "Hi there! I'm here."

"Where?"

"In the States, of course. I'll be in Philadelphia tomorrow. Why not come over?"

"You're crazy. It will be several hours' flight and besides that I'm broke"

"Don't worry, honey," I said, feigning an American accent, "I'll wire you some cash through Western Union. You just get your flight organised, let me know your ETA and I will mosey on over and pick you up. OK?"

As Paul was not flying out of New York until the following afternoon he kindly drove me down to Central Station where I caught a train for Philadelphia. From there it was a twenty minute cab ride to Swarthmore and my friend's house was located. Once there I announced myself to the neighbours who immediately invited me to dinner that night.

They were wonderfully warm people and I immediately felt right at home. Kathy then phoned to say that she would be arriving the following afternoon. Next, after a good night's sleep, I lounged around the following morning, chose the sporting Ford Torino, from the two cars parked in the garage and headed for the airport.

*

Naturally, as I was not familiar with the directions, I arrived there sometime before the flight was due in, parked the car and automatically headed for the bar. The barman, a short stocky man with crew cut hair and eyes that seemed to be everywhere at once but in my direction, took his time in serving me and I felt that it might just have something to do with my being English. When I eventually was served the man standing next to me started talking to me and after the usual 'Are you English?' question, launched into explaining that he had been stationed in England just after the war.

"Where was that?" I asked politely, out of something to say.

"Chicksands," he replied. "Near to a town called Bedford. Do you know it?"

"I should do," I grinned, "after all I was stationed there for some six months. RAF on a combined operation with your USAF."

The barman who had his ear cocked in our direction suddenly burst out, "Jeeze. How 'bout dat! My brudder was based at Chicksands as well!"

Then with no more ado he set up three beers with bourbon chasers saying, "Dis calls fer a celebration. What d'ya say, English?"

I smiled and nodded. "If you insist."

"Hear dat," he came back, "if I insist. You becha I insist!"

With that we all shook hands and after that drink there followed several more with the bar tender, whose name, would you believe was Larry, saying, "On da house, fellas," each time.

Not having ever been invited for drinks in any other airport I had been in, I took serious advantage of the situation but was very glad when the announcement was made that the Reno flight had touched down.

Kathy was there as lovely as ever but minus her luggage which appeared to have vanished in the direction of the great unknown.

"Wonderful start," I said, "but never mind. We'll sort it."

At the enquiry desk the airline promised that hopefully the matter would be cleared up and with luck the cases should be delivered next day.

*

Feeling as though I had hit the jackpot we collected the long, sleek, Torino from the parking lot and headed towards the city which seemed to be shrouded in an early evening haze of pollution. Naturally I became hopelessly lost and after driving around for sometime decided to stop for a drink and ask directions. The area we were in at that particular moment looked exactly like something out of a film set. Aged Brownstone terraced houses like decayed teeth in the jaws of the city. Boarded up doors and windows together with signs saying, 'Condemned' and 'Dangerous' everywhere, all liberally plastered with an amazing assortment of inevitable graffiti.

"Where the hell can we get a drink around here?" I said becoming irritated.

"Chris," she replied, seriously, "There is no way we can stop around here. We're likely to have our throats cut."

At that moment, like a beacon in the dark, there appeared what looked like a bar. Actually it was more like an old wooden shack stuck in the middle of some waste ground.

"There," I said, "let's have one in here and ask for directions."

We parked and walked across to it along a little path through dry grass and shrubs. Pushing open the door we went inside. It was packed. The bar was typically American, circular and placed in the middle with customers crowding around it like sardines.

"Two beers, please," I called out to one of the three bartenders and up they came.

"How much?"

"Nothing, Buddy. The guy over there is invitin' the house for the night."

I could not believe it. My third day in the States, twice the drinks had been on the house and I was with Kathy. I was really beginning to enjoy myself.

The 'Guy over there' who was inviting looked a scruffy individual in a grey gabardine raincoat with a grey trilby hat stuck on the back of his head, rather Philip Marlowe style. "Quite honestly," I thought, "if he had walked into my place in Spain I would have asked to see the colour of his money before serving him with anything." However here it seemed to be quite normal. Kathy then asked a bar tender for directions to Swarthmore and he made it sound quite simple. When we left she drove and to my surprise, we arrived fairly quickly.

What I do remember most about the area in which we were staying was that it was completely alcohol free. You could drink all you wanted at home but there were no alcoholic drinks on sale at any of the shops or in the restaurants. Needless to say Gomar Davis had a well stocked bar in the basement of his house which included twelve bottles of Chivas Regal. This had me wondering whether or not with the amount of booze being splashed about there had been an offer by Chivas Regal that included a free liver transplant.

*

The next days Kathy and I visited her family and friends who lived within reasonable distances to Swarthmore. This first weekend was spent in New Jersey at such a friend's apartment that afforded a view of, according to our host, the woods through which George Washington marched when the English were routed.

It was from there that we all went up to New York in their new Cadillac and were amiably entertained at the Gaslight Club. There we dined on French cuisine and listened to our host while he explained how that in New York there still existed a 'Bounty' law that rewarded anyone reporting a person for tax evasion received a percentage of the money involved. This subject was brought about by the fact that our friend had employed a lady secretary who, for some reason, had alleged to the International Revenue Service authorities, that there was some financial fraud going on in the company. As this was totally incorrect nothing happened but for three whole months his company had been subject to a complete audit.

It was two weeks later that Gomar and Betty Ann returned and all four of us had a great time together. The days passed quickly and we had to come to grips with the decision to return to Spain. Quite honestly I felt that if there had been the slightest possibility of my remaining there and finding work I would have done so. However it would appear that with legal formalities this was impossible. I also had to contend with the fact that Kathy wished to return to Spain also. So arrangements were made and within a few days we were winging our way once again across the Atlantic towards Europe and a life that was seemingly to be filled with little else apart from problems.

*

Once again in Valencia we found an apartment and made contact with Reggie the Fish and Carmen who informed us that they had found suitable premises that were near to the city centre and would be ideal for what we were looking for. Four hundred metres in area that included a walled garden to the rear it was just the correct size.

It was going to take more finance than I had anticipated so I enlisted the help of Manolo and Conchin together with another friend and his wife, Alex. Alex's wife, Vicki, had been at one time, during the Second World War, a star dancer at the famous Windmill theatre, London. All of us were keen to get things moving, a builder was contracted and there was much animation in the place. My imagination was also active as regards a name for the bar. It was to be called the 'Great English Disaster', which I was sure would draw the curious Spaniards. We were to provide live music and entertainment and to create an even more original atmosphere I was to install swings, both doubles and single seats, instead of the normal bar stools. It was a time of much planning and excitement.

*

Then disaster really did strike. The owner of the premises who had rented the place to us was co-owner of the whole building together with his sister. It then turned out that he did not have the required permission of his sister in order to enact this transaction. This in itself was not surprising as they had not spoken for more than twenty years. The sister then encouraged by her son who had his eye on the property for another business, took legal action against her brother. Immediately the judge placed an embargo on the place and what was to be 'The Great English Disaster' became one in reality.

A meeting with the brother who had drawn up the contract with us terminated with his pointing out that as we were foreigners we were certainly not entitled to any sort of indemnity. Neither would we be allowed into the premises in order to remove all our things including kitchen equipment, coffee machine, cutlery as well as other furniture and fittings. A meeting with our lawyer confirmed that, as Reggie and Carmen were personal friends of several judges, it would be possible to go ahead with a civil action but this could mean up to several years waiting.

We decided that there was little alternative and I told him to start the ball rolling.

It was around that time that a visit to the doctor confirmed that Kathy was pregnant. Why, I do not know, but I greeted this news for some reason by saying that we would be having a daughter and that she would be born on the twenty-seventh of May the following year. However this did not serve to resolve our immediate problems. Fortunately Kathy was a qualified and very adept English teacher so we advertised in the local newspaper. The advertisement ran 'English in Twenty-four Hours'. Naturally there were many calls from students thinking that they would be able to dominate the language over night. It was explained that the course would be twenty-four one hour lessons over a period of time. Fortunately this was accepted by many and Kathy started her classes.

*

One evening the doorbell rang and who should be standing there but Gedo. The wine incident was long past so he was welcomed in. Apparently, as was expected, his marriage to Claire had ended and he had just returned from visiting a German girlfriend in Frankfurt. Apart from a few clothes his total possessions consisted of:

a tin of herrings,

a hard boiled egg,

and a one hundred peseta coin.

We offered him the spare bedroom and after a good night's sleep the next morning we talked about what he and I were going to do in order to survive.

The three of us happened to be sitting in Gedo's bedroom where there were several large boxes that held quantities of glass tumblers that fortunately had not as yet found their way into the disastrous embargoed pub. Anyway I think that it was Gedo who came up with the idea that his culinary knowledge was such that he was capable of producing large quantities of marmalade which we could then put into the tumblers, and together with our own labels sell the completed article.

"Then," he explained grandly, "the customer will not only be buying marmalade but will also be getting a free tumbler."

"Fine," I agreed, "but where do we sell it?"

"No problem," put in Kathy, enthusiastically, "Apparently on Tuesdays, near to the railway station, there is a street market and it is free to anyone who wants to sell whatever."

"Are you sure?" I asked, not really believing that it could be that easy.

"Quite sure," she confirmed.

So we set about organising things with Gedo in charge of the manufacturing side and myself writing out labels on which it claimed, '*Old English Home Made Marmalade*' together with a few other comments that referred to Grandma's very secret recipe. We already had a picnic table to hand and an imposing apron emblazoned with the Union Jack flag so considered ourselves in business.

The following Tuesday we loaded the car and drove down to the market. I was pleased that Kathy did not have any classes that morning as I felt that a woman's touch was necessary under these circumstances. It was bitterly cold and we set up the table then drew lots as to who should make the first stand whilst the others went for a coffee. Gedo lost and Kathy and I disappeared into a nearby bar leaving him offering samples of Old English Marmalade, spread on toast, to the passing shoppers. We were just finishing our coffee laced with brandy when Gedo appeared looking somewhat flustered.

"Better come quickly. There's someone out there wanting to see who's in charge."

"I don't suppose you told him it was you?" I said, as we followed him out.

Near to where we had set up the little picnic table in the small square, it was like something from a film set of the 'Hunchback of Notre Dame'. A crowd had gathered and this outlandish, Charles Laughton figure with an extremely ugly, twisted face, a pronounced hump on his back and an outsized tatty shoulder bag, was limping up and down at an amazing rate of knots shouting. But instead of,"The bells! The bells!" he was yelling, "Lissensia! Lissensia!"

All business had come to a halt at the nearby fruit and vegetable stalls and each time this theatrical figure vigorously waved his arms and shouted "Lissensia!" everyone joined in at the same time pointing accusing fingers in our direction.

"I think he wants to see our licence," said Gedo, quickly removing his apron and pushing it out of sight. Kathy, I noticed, had suddenly disappeared somewhere to the back of the crowd and I was left to deal with the situation.

"Er...Excuse me," I began, as the figure limped by our table. "But...er could you."

The man eventually paused and the grotesque face peered up at me. But before I could continue, off he went again with the entire crowd adding their support.

"Lissensia! Lissensia!"

It was incredible. Afterwards it seemed to me that he had been waiting for this particular moment all his life. Up and down he limped, arms going like windmills and bawling that one word over and over again. I tried to speak to him once more as he sailed by but he just would not listen so I moved over to the table and motioned to Gedo that we should start packing up.

Then a friendly voice in the crowd called out, "He's a little bit crazy but he checks the licences for the market and if you don't have a bit of paper with an official looking stamp, then it sets him off." The voice then added that such licences are issued at the town hall.

We dismantled our table quickly and with the angry shouts still echoing in our ears we made our escape. Later, armed with half a dozen tumblers of marmalade we did go to the town hall and found that the procedure for a sanitation license and all that went with it was not worth even thinking about. It was during the enquiries that we offered a very surprised clerk the marmalade samples and he almost wept.

"I've been here thirty-three years," he explained, "and nobody has ever given me anything. Gracias. Muchas gracias."

*

That same evening, while Kathy was teaching, Gedo and I visited Manolo and Conchin explaining our predicament. Manolo then kindly telephoned a colleague of his, who, apart from working at the same bank, ran a wine distributing business.

"That sounds more like it," we both agreed eagerly.

"Certainly more in your line, Gedo," I said, not without a little irony.

The following day we visited the warehouse and were shown enormous quantities of wine already prepared in attractive gift boxes. In each box there was a bottle of white, rosé and red. The wine was from the bodega 'Priorato' in the Tarragona area and each box was to be sold at two hundred and fifty pesetas for the three bottles. Out of this, our commission was twenty-five pesetas. Not much to start with but under the circumstances, not to be ignored. We were, of course, and much to our delight, given so many bottles as samples.

That particular evening we had a wine tasting party for the three of us. It was absolute nectar especially after what we had been buying at the local 'take away' bodega around the corner. Kathy, with her usual grasp of the situation and natural mistrust where wine and men were concerned, elected to take control of the accounts and both Gedo, possibly a little reluctantly, and I raised our glasses to this.

Now there has always has been a vast amount of wine in Spain, particularly in the Valencia region. In fact one year, in the early 1960's the village of Casinos, some forty kilometres from Valencia, had such an excess of wine that they had to use the local swimming pool as a storage space. There is a photograph to this effect at the Cooperative showing the pool with thousands of litres of red wine just lying there. So with this in mind it did not come as a surprise that it was not easy to sell large quantities of our Priorato, especially as it was from another region of Spain. However things did take a turn for the better with Christmas approaching and one of our best customers turned out to be the restaurant, Galbis, which later, as the Guinness Book of records shows, was to become world famous for their mammoth sized paellas, one of them for more than one hundred thousand portions.

*

Various visits to our lawyer were made in order to monitor the situation in respect of our law suit involving the 'Great English Disaster' and on several occasions it was arranged that I discreetly met with one or another of the judges involved in the case. At these meetings, usually in a local bar, I was advised on what action to take. Several times it was said that if such and such course was followed I would win initially but the following appeal would reverse things. Therefore on such occasions it would be more prudent that I request my lawyer to approach it from another angle. Anyway whatever we did it was going to take a long time and our third partner, Alex, was becoming nervous about the amount of money he had invested. This was around one thousand five hundred pounds, which even then was not going to see him bankrupt. That particular year we would have faced a very bleak Christmas if it had not been for our friend 'Priorato'. Then it was a couple of weeks into the New Year that there was some relief when Gedo's girlfriend arrived with sufficient finance for them to both rent their own apartment nearby.

It was around this time that I tried hand at teaching English. As regards conversation classes it went fairly well, as did the reading part but I was not competent on the grammatical side of things. However I persisted but when spring arrived decided to go down to Cullera and try my luck there. Fortunately I chanced on a friend who owned several bars and I arranged to take one over for the coming season. This indeed was a change and Kathy and I rejoiced in the fact that we would have an apartment by the sea and plenty of work. Kathy also felt that it would be just that much better to be amongst people she knew as May was rapidly approaching and the birth of our daughter was imminent. I personally, was wondering how things would work out with Mary and my son being just around the corner from us. Then the next thing I heard was that they had both left for England. At that time I was pleased, not in respect of any embarrassment as to their being in the vicinity, but that the UK would offer them the opportunity of getting them back on their feet.

*

Needless to say the work in the bar during the season was hard but it was pleasant not to have to worry too much about financial things for a while. We had retained our apartment in Valencia and I regularly sent off a cheque for the monthly rent. In Cullera we were told that although there was the private clinic where my son had been born it would be much less expensive if the facilities at the local hospital were used.

May the twenty-seventh arrived and true to form Kathy started to complain of labour pains so we drove down to the village hospital. There we were cordially welcomed by two very kindly nuns who ushered us into what they said was the delivery room. It was a cold bare place devoid of furniture with a marble plinth in the middle. Just the sight of this alone had Kathy trembling.

"What's that?" I asked, really knowing what the answer would be, but hoping that I just might be wrong.

"That's it," said one of the nuns. "We put the Señora on there and that's it."

"But there are no stirrups or anything," I was horrified, "and what about a doctor?"

"Sorry, Señor, no doctor," She smiled apologetically.

The implications were now becoming alarming. "And if anything really goes wrong?"

"La Señora will have to go to Valencia in the ambulance."

Poor Kathy could not stop shaking so I thanked them and we left. Half and hour later, without even thinking about costs involved, she was settled in the private clinic and ready.

"First things first," I thought to myself.

In Spain the mother-to-be is normally accompanied by her own mother who after the birth takes initial control of the baby's necessities. So when the doctor asked if I wished to be present at the birth I declined with the excuse that I was going to seek assistance in the form of someone who knew what to do after the birth. In the afternoon Kathy walked down to the delivery room with me carrying the drip feed (the lift had decided to break down) and I left, promising to return quickly.

Next it transpired that the father of Paul, who had taken over my old English Pub, had died suddenly and everyone had gone to the funeral. Fortunately, however, I did find a friend in the form of Olive Ryman, a mother of some experience, who heralded form Stratford-upon-Avon. She agreed readily to help and we both dashed back to the clinic just as they brought Kathy and our daughter back to the room.

As Kathy had never been acquainted with Olive she was a little surprised that when she recovered consciousness to see a stranger sitting their nursing our daughter. But all was fine and the following day Kathy came home with Samantha, accompanied by a small crowd of close friends together with Horst who had loaned us the total amount for the clinic costs. Samantha was a model baby and captured the hearts of all our friends and customers alike. It was a busy season and the heat was exceptional so we were both pleased when September arrived and we could return to Valencia.

*

It was two days before we left Cullera that on visiting the bank I discovered that none of the cheques I had mailed for the rent had been cashed. Then when we arrived in Valencia the first thing we found, pushed under the door, was a pile of official looking papers. Closer inspection revealed that they were court orders informing us that we were to leave the apartment for non-payment of the rent. The signature of the person who had acknowledged receipt of the documents was that of the Concierge or 'Portero' who looked after the building.

"What's the idea of signing these papers?" I asked him immediately, not without some antagonism surfing.

"Somebody had to sign them and as you weren't here, I did," he answered defensively.

"But you are not me, I pointed out."

"Doesn't matter," he replied belligerently.

"You've got to be joking." I could not believe it.

"Quite right," he went on. "If I hadn't signed they would have found a neighbour to do it."

His anger mellowed a little and he said patiently, "You see that is the way it is in Spain. If somebody, anybody signs they been received."

A phone call to my lawyer confirmed that this is the way it was, and still is, in Spain.

"And so what do I do now?" I asked.

"No problem, Chris. Just go down to the court that is numbered on the papers; pay the money you owe to the clerk and that will resolve the matter."

*

Next day I presented myself to the clerk of the court. A midget of a man who looked as though he might make five feet six inches with his umbrella extended. A deadpan face that you would associate more with a local undertaker than a court official he had that casual air of one who has held the job for many years, knew it all and was not to be messed around by anyone, particularly of foreign extraction.

I explained why I was there, produced the thirty-five thousand pesetas that was owed and I watched his tiny eyes light up. "An official receipt, please," I said placing the notes carefully on the desk. "And an official stamp as well."

He appeared somewhat hurt that I might doubt his sincerity but obliged, taking his time. Pocketing the paper I thanked him politely and walked out.

Back in the apartment things settled into a routine, Kathy with her classes and myself, apart from the odd class or two, taking care of Samantha. The rent was paid as before, by cheque and nothing was heard from the landlady. That was until the week before Christmas. On that particular morning there appeared at the door an official waving what turned out to be an eviction order for non-payment of rent for a period of some nine months. Quickly I produced the court receipt and check stubs.

"Better get in touch with your lawyer," was all the man said, and went away.

I did just that and was told, once again, to go down to the court with the receipt and speak to the same clerk.

Once there the unpleasant little man wanted to relieve me of the paper while he checked with the judge. "But you had the money. Here's the receipt."

He reached out his hand. "Here let me have it and I will speak to the judge."

"Not likely. Tell the judge to come here if he wants to see it."

Climbing to his feet and still with that bored expression he turned and disappeared through a door to the rear. Ten minutes later he was back.

"Sorry Señor," he apologised. "But the judge says that this receipt is not valid."

Again I could not believe it and just stared at him. "What do you mean? You wrote it out and now you tell it's not valid?"

He shrugged and indicated that there were other people waiting so I left.

A further phone call to the lawyer and again I was instructed to persist. However in no way was the man going to acknowledge my receipt. Then a final call to the lawyer resulted in his appearance some twenty minutes later and both of us confronting the clerk. Now it was somewhat different with legal representation being present.

"Is this valid or not?" demanded my lawyer towering over the obnoxious little man. "And if the money has been paid over. Where is it?"

For the first time the clerk had the decency to look somewhat sheepish. Next, bending down he opened the bottom draw of his desk and produced, much to my amazement, a bundle of peseta notes.

Passing them over to me he said, "Oh, dear. They must have been there all the time."

Turning to my lawyer, who in no way appeared surprised at this, I asked, "What happens now?"

He grinned and said, "Well if you want you can leave the money here, stay where you are or move apartments. It is entirely up to you."

I decided then to take it, cut my losses and move our home. Kathy was, as usual, magnificent and we quickly transferred to another apartment only some three hundred yards distant. Apart from the clerk's obvious intention to cheat me, what I could not understand was why the landlady wanted us out of there in the first place. The answer was not long in coming.

A few weeks later both the press and the television announced that three women who had rented our old place were, in fact, related to the

Basque terrorist group ETA. They had since been spirited off and the apartment temporarily sealed.

"Poetic justice," was Kathy's only remark.

*

It was just after we had moved that my old friend Horst Amon from the Cullera hamburger bar turned up one morning. He announced that he had sold his business and was returning to Vienna that very day, by train. Knowing that his business had always been one of the best in Cullera, I asked, "I suppose you got a good price, Horst?"

"Oh yes, I certainly did," he grinned rather ruefully. "But that was about a month ago."

"So what?"

He looked down at the floor as if expecting to see something there. "Nothing at all really. It's just that I spent all the bloody cash,"

So after around twenty five years he was retuning home with even less money than when he arrived. In fact apart from one small suitcase, his rail ticket and a few coins in his pocket, he had nothing else. He rattled the coins. "Enough for a drink on the train," he grinned, rather embarrassed by the situation.

On the way to the station both myself and Gedo, who had arrived after I telephoned him to say our friend was leaving, came up with enough money to buy Horst a bottle of 'Terry' brandy so that he would not have to spend what little he had on the journey.

As the Dutchman and I stood there silently watching the train pull away I had a small empty feeling that this also was the end of another chapter in my life. We had certainly had some laughs together, that was for sure.

*

Kathy, Samantha and I settled into the new apartment and the classes continued. Another quiet Christmas came and went but we were happy together. What I do remember about the actual Christmas day was that we made enough Christmas lunch for me to take what was left over to a relatively young man who was sleeping rough on some nearby waste land. He was sitting propped up against a wall and had frightened eyes like a dog that had been involved in an accident. "Gracias, Señor," he repeated several times as I handed over the hot soup and other goodies.

The New Year saw Kathy's classes increasing in students and I was dedicating my time mainly to Samantha.

*

Then one night somebody rang the bell outside of the apartment block and when I answered the intercom a voice balled, "You English?"

"Yes," I shouted back. "Me English."

"Door open. Come up please," the voice bellowed again.

I pressed the button to admit the man to the building and waited. As the lift was not working he arrived at the third floor puffing like a steam train. Red in the face he spluttered without any preliminaries, "English you right?"

"Yes, me English right," I confirmed wondering what it was all about.

Next taking a deep breath he wheezed, "In England you pay."

I nodded wondering what was coming next.

"In Spain pay you must," he went on.

I switched to Spanish and he face brightened as he had obviously assumed that I was incapable of doing so. "What's this all about?" I asked.

He then produced some official looking papers from a rather battered brief-case and waved them in my face. "You owe Mr. Alex Hamilton-Wright three hundred thousand pesetas."

This immediately upset me as Alex was well acquainted with the situation we were in as regards the English Disaster and here he was demanding his investment back right at that moment. "How much did you say I owed?"

Glancing at the papers again as if the amount might have increased in the last few seconds he then placed in front of my face so that I could see for myself.

"There! Three hundred thousand pesetas."

Taking a deep breath I then said in a loud voice, "Three million pesetas?"

Very startled he examined the papers again perhaps thinking that there might have been a mistake. "No. It says here three hundred thousand pesetas."

Again I repeated in a voice that echoed around the stairs, "Three million pesetas!"

"No!" he gasped looking bewildered, "Why do you say that?"

"Because," I replied quietly leaning towards him. "Because, my friend, in this block of apartments if anyone owes less than three million pesetas they are not considered to be anyone of importance."

Then while he was attempting to absorb this, I added, "You being Spanish should understand these things. And anyway I have no money so please tell Mr. Alex that he must wait until the matter is resolved through the courts."

He nodded, obviously relieved that he could report back that he had tried, and left hurrying down the stairs and shaking his head muttering, "Three million pesetas indeed."

*

That summer Kathy decided to stay in Valencia whilst I went to Cullera to seek work for the season. I was lucky to find employment as a barman at the popular Toyco restaurant on the sea front. Tony, the owner of the place, seemed quite pleased to have me as I still drew a fair amount of regular tourists to the place.

Having little or no money and nowhere to stay I spoke to Swiss Karl, who had taken over Horst's hamburger bar. He said that if I wished I could lodge at the village house he was renting. "But it is a bit basic," he warned me.

Basic was not the word. When I went along there it looked as though the place had been demolished at one time and a slum constructed in its place. There was no electricity and just one water tap in the corral. The toilet was also an outside, bucket of water, job.

There was a bed but no mattress or bed linen. It was unbelievable. But there again with no other alternative I was determined to make the best of it. I would manage and finances permitting tomorrow I would buy inexpensive bedding. Showering was not a problem as this could be done at the restaurant.

So that first night I finished around two o'clock after working through from eleven that morning and with painfully aching feet I started out for Karl's place about two kilometres distance.

The late night refuse collectors were much in evidence and making one hell of a noise emptying bins. As I drew level with them someone from one of the apartments above, obviously disturbed by the noise, decided to deposit a full bucket of water out of the window, hoping to cool down the council workers I suppose. Needless to say I caught the lot to the very last drop.

"Just don't let anyone tell you that things cannot get any worse," I thought as I dripped my way down the road leaving a snail like trail in my wake.

Once at my new residence I lit a candle that I had purloined from the restaurant, dried myself off and placing a blanket over the bed springs lay down in my shorts. I was absolutely exhausted. Then just before I managed to summon up enough energy to lean over and extinguish the candle I heard two very sharp clicks. Karl was in the adjoining room and I called out to him. "What the hell was that?"

"The mouse traps," a sleepy voice replied. "You can throw the bodies out in the morning."

"That," I thought, "will be the easy part," as I blew out the candle. The windows had never seen a pane of glass since the place was built. I lay there miserably waiting for blessed sleep and wondering how long it was going to be before the mosquitoes found me.

*

Again there was a lot of work that season and the heat seemed almost intolerable. This, together with my living conditions did not help a great deal. However I did manage to stay reasonably fit apart from contracting what is known as 'frozen shoulder'. This painful rheumatic condition which limited the movement of my right arm was nothing serious but just another item to irritate me, especially if I forgot I had it.

Towards the end of August things became quieter and the following month I returned to Valencia with, at least, something to contribute to the household expenses. Then it was classes once again up until Christmas when we had a nineteen month old daughter to consider.

With very little funds we decided to buy her just one good present and this took the form of a rocking horse. It was brought home and hidden away. Then on Christmas Eve we placed it behind the sofa in the lounge.

Next morning when Samantha wandered into our bedroom I asked her if Father Christmas had left anything. Shaking her head sadly and with eyes downcast, she said, "No, Papa. Nothing."

"Well I am sure that he must have left you something," I said. "Why not go and have a look around."

She disappeared. It was just a few minutes later that the bedroom door burst open and in she tumbled. Never, ever, will I ever forget the expression on her face. She was absolutely speechless. All she could manage was point towards the lounge. No words were possible. Just to see the happiness on her small face over that one gift made up for all I had gone through in those previous summer months seem more than worthwhile.

*

Again the New Year had little to offer and a further visit to our lawyer confirmed that things still looked positive but as to the actual sentence, that was anyone's guess. The meeting was short as he was in a great hurry. "I have to go to the prison," he explained. "I have a client to see."

Not being able to resist I enquired as to what had happened.

"Well," he volunteered. "There is a priest who lives on the Gran Via who has been organising divorces through some obscure African country and he has been charging one and a half million pesetas each person (at that time around six thousand pounds sterling) as usually there are two people involved."

He grinned. "Good money."

"Very good money," I thought detecting a slight note of envy in his voice.

"How did the authorities find out about it?" I asked.

Standing up from behind the huge desk he started shovelling papers into his brief case. "This idiot of a journalist printed an article in the newspaper."

"And they have put the priest in prison," I concluded.

"Good Lord, no!" he replied laughing, "It is the journalist who is in prison for writing the article."

He stopped for a moment when he saw the look of surprise on my face. Then he explained, "The judge said that if such things were made public then everyone would want a divorce which is not really in keeping with the church's image. Of course, as legal representative of the newspaper, I have to sort things out."

*

This reminded me of an incident that occurred some years before when I had been invited to a party at a chalet near Valencia. The host was a lecturer by profession at the university and that evening around ten o'clock there was a ring at the door. Apologising, he left his guests, retuning some thirty minutes later. The visitor had apparently taken their leave.

That night all of us had had more than enough to drink and before leaving I found me talking to him. Like many of his fellow countrymen he would never mention Spain's failings within the hearing of his fellow countrymen, but individually, well that was different. He then told me how the visitor that night had been his estranged wife. Apparently they had separated some years before which resulted in her returning to Madrid. There she had eventually met another man and this relationship had lasted up until then, both being unable to marry as neither one was divorced. Then inevitably one day she had found that she was pregnant.

At that time Spanish law dictated that it was not possible for a married woman to have a child other than by her own husband. For the single girl it was different. She could give birth to what was known as a 'natural' child. The church even made provisions for an unwanted newly born baby to be deposited with them in the secure knowledge that the mother's identity remained a secret. However for the married woman to conceive a child by a male other than her husband then that child could be removed from her care and she could face a serious term of imprisonment.

My host explained that his wife had presented herself at the chalet in order to ask him to sign the papers to the effect that the child was legally his. I did have the audacity to enquire as to whether or not he had signed the documents and he shrugged, "Of course, Chris. Of course I signed. It might just happen that she would be in problems. You never know, in this country. And anyway I would not like to see anyone in prison because of some stupid law."

Chapter 15

Around spring I received a call from Gedo. He had since married his girlfriend, Geisler, and moved to Moraira a coastal resort not far from Benidorm. I asked him what he was doing there and as nonchalantly as ever said airily, "I have a radio station, Chris."

"A radio station," I repeated very much surprised at this change of direction. "You actually broadcast and all that?"

"Yes, Chris. Great fun. If you want to come down here then perhaps we can work it together. It's called Radio Costa Blanca and we broadcast through radio España three times a week."

I needed no encouragement so packed my bags and leaving Kathy to her classes and Samantha to the infant school, I caught the coach the following day to Moraira.

It was a small but pleasant villa they had on a residential estate mainly for retired Dutch, English and Germans. Gedo and his wife, Geisler, now had a lovely daughter, just a little younger than Samantha. Her name was Sabina. It was all very nice.

The actual radio station had been built onto the side of the chalet and this is where we worked, when I was not out selling advertising space. As was expected I did most of the airtime selling and trundled around in an old diesel van visiting discotheques, hotels bars and restaurants. In fact anywhere that might yield a possible client. When a customer did show interest we recorded a couple of tapes along the lines the client suggested and I returned with them for their approval. Again nothing is easy but it was entertaining for me to visit these places and speak to different people. I was reasonably successful with many of the smaller businesses as most of them were English controlled.

As a confirmed admirer of that outstanding actor Peter Sellers, when working in the studio I used to love impersonating different characters.

Many were the times that Gedo said, "Right, Chris. Today we need an interview for the radio. Who will you be?"

We would then sit back and dream up something of interest. Many of the listeners were Dutch or German apart from a few English so this minor deceiving did not do anyone any harm and according to the correspondence we received made many people happy.

At one time I was the manager of a fictitious pop group called the 'Popcorns' who had successfully completed a tour of the UK, and were now resting in Benidorm. Another time I was Ranjit Patel a famous film star from India on his first visit to Europe. Then on yet another occasion I was Randy Rollings a country and western singer from the States who was a friend of many of the popular vocalists of that time including, of course, Elvis Presley. It was all harmless fun and most entertaining for both ourselves as well as the listeners.

Most of the work involved late nights and one particular curious phenomenon I remember whilst travelling around as late as two or three o'clock was that I would often come across people queuing up to use one of the public telephones. "What are those people doing making calls at this time of night?" I asked Gedo on one occasion.

"Oh, those," he laughed. "The public telephone has gone wrong again and they are all calling for free."

To me that was proof that lady luck can pass by in the most unexpected places.

We also used the van as a mobile discotheque and were contracted by several bars and restaurants in the area. Gedo delighted in playing disc jockey and we were well received by all. I enjoyed working with Radio Costa Blanca but was not sad when Gedo announced that he had received a good offer from a German friend to buy the business and was selling up. It signified that I was about to return to Kathy and Samantha.

*

Back in Valencia Manolo called me and asked if I might be interested in representing a jewellery manufacturer. I needed no encouragement and went along to meet the owner of the business.

Edmundo Gomez was a short, sparkling, man, slim in stature and a few years younger than me. I was to find out that he had a great sense of humour and was a hit with everyone he came into contact with. With his dark curly hair and eyes twinkling behind rimless gold spectacles he would have all of his clients eating out of his hand. He smiled most of the time but was most serious when it came to business. Kathy was enchanted by him and described him as being one of the sexiest men she had ever met. His English was perfect having studied in America.

So there I was, the agent for Leira Geminis, Spain, covering the UK.

Naturally it would involve me travelling to England which would certainly make a change after such a long absence. And anyway the idea of working around Hatton Garden, London, and the Birmingham jewellery quarter appealed to me. Kathy, apart from her private English classes, was also employed at a nearby academy which had quite a considerable amount of students who were looking to travel to England in the summer months in order to perfect their English. So we decided to it might be a good idea to set up a serious summer school and with this in mind we spoke to Manolo.

As usual he was quite ready to collaborate and whilst he organised the necessary pamphlets Kathy, Samantha and I, together with the jewellery collection, travelled to England to set the ball rolling. I was to make some visits with the samples and at the same time we would seek out somewhere suitable for the Summer School.

*

All three of us flew over and we stayed at my father's place in Leicester. Since my mother had died father had met up with and married Gwen. An old school sweetheart who was an ex-hospital matron, she had an egg-shaped figure similar to one of those dolls that if you pushed them over they would always pop right back up again. With unkempt, greying hair and ruddy cheeks she was continually pursing her lips and clasping her hands in front of her and obviously used to issuing commands in her forty-year-long profession. As a welcoming gesture she insisted on wearing her matron's cap and did not seemed amused when Samantha went into hysterics convulsed with laugher.

"A great start," I thought.

Gwen also assumed that we would be interested in various bits of hospital equipment that she had succeeded in retaining from her nursing days. By modern day standards these look like the sort of torture implements probably put to good use by the Gestapo in the Second World War. Apparently from what she said her pride had been somewhat dented when she took the lot down to the Red Cross offices in the city and wanted to present them to the organisation. The person in charge, (God Bless whoever it was), directed her to the nearest dustbin.

My sister, Josephine, who visited the pair on a regular basis, whispered to me one day that our stepmother was obsessed by administering enemas. Apparently my father would be sitting there happily watching the television when Gwen would suddenly say, "Right, Joe! There's nothing on the box worth seeing. Get upstairs and I'll give you an enema!" Various plastic tubes together with small taps and valves that were permanently festooned around the toilet were sufficient evidence that my sister was correct.

*

Beautiful Bath, in Somerset, we decided, was the ideal city in which to start our summer school. It had everything that the students could wish for. Neither too big nor too small in population and with plenty of history, particularly where the Roman baths were concerned. One statistic which appealed to those who would be signing on for the course was that Bath had been the home of Britain's youngest prime minister in the form of William Pitt the Younger. They were amazed that at twenty-three years of age this man could have been administering Britain's affairs whereas most of the world leaders in the nineteen eighties appeared to have one leg in the grave. The students, we decided, would love Bath. Next a visit to a car salesman friend resulted in us buying an old Audi 100 car for seven hundred and fifty pounds. Although I knew we would be running a risk with the Spanish authorities, by taking the car back to Spain, I decided to buy it anyway.

*

One clear sunny day we drove down the old Fosse Way to Bath making a calculated stop at the Black Bear pub, Moreton-in-Marsh, to visit Valerie and her parents. What a wonderful welcome was awaiting us and what a great atmosphere the pub had. It was not the sort of establishment that would fit into anywhere else in the world, except there. Promising to stop by on the return trip we continued on to Bath absorbing the autumnal colours of the lovely surrounding Cotswold countryside.

In Bath itself we found ideal accommodation for our students. The place consisted of several comfortable stone cottages knocked into one dwelling owned by a charming ex-RAF character that went out of his way to help us in contacting an agency that provided professional teachers for any subjects that one wanted. It all looked very promising.

*

Back in Leicester I went in search of my friend and ex-colleague, Mac, who ran a jewellery business that saw him visiting all the local markets in the area. I found him in one of his habitual pubs enjoying a pint of Marston's Pedigree. "Hello, CJ," he said shaking my hand vigorously. "How are we?"

I confirmed that all was well and over a few pints I explained my presence there and what I intended to do. Mac was never one for demonstrating anything, least of all enthusiasm. However when I mentioned the jewellery collection I was carrying he removed his habitual pipe and began to take things a little more seriously. "Well we'll certainly have to look at that tomorrow first thing, old chap," he said unable to disguise his curiosity.

I was pleased about this for the simple reason that, although I had seen how everything was manufactured on the jewellery side and had a reasonable attraction towards something eye-catching, I had had little or no experience in knowing what was and what was not of commercial interest.

In other words, important sales.

The next day was spent examining the collection and making plans to visit various possible outlets. We also talked about the formation of a company as there could well be other similar collections possibly involving gold jewellery. The name we decided on was the Valencia Fine Arts Company. As we sat there little did we know at that moment how in the not-too-distant future we would, together with a yet unknown person from Bradford, be considering the registering of a company called FU, Incorporated, based on the concept of the many disasters which would be forthcoming. Anyway in the following days Mac and I made some local visits with that first collection and although, due mainly to the Christmas buying being completed, we did achieve some sales.

*

The return journey to Spain was remembered for several reasons. Firstly, due to delays, we arrived at Calais late one night to be greeted by snow. Too late to find a hotel we decided to keep going. Fortunately with the Audi's front wheel drive we motored on for mile after mile following the two tracks down the centre of the highway. Then, as we arrived near Rouen, it was a relief to see the roads became clearer and in the city itself there was just a light drizzle falling.

"Don't worry," I said to Kathy. "We'll be alright now. First place we see in the morning we stop for breakfast."

So we did just that and then found to our horror that the banks were closed as it was Saturday. At that time we were not in possession of the 'hole in the wall' facilities available today for retrieving cash. There was only one thing to do and that was travel on with a watchful eye on what little money we had.

Finally with almost no petrol and around three hundred pesetas in cash we pulled up outside our apartment block in Valencia on the Sunday afternoon. All three of us were starving so we headed straight over to Dolfis our local bar and restaurant where I knew we had credit.

*

Having used the Dolfis bar on a regular basis for many years now it has always been a source of wonder to me that so many interesting, varied and fascinating, characters frequented it. With the same tradition of one accustomed to a pre-Sunday lunch drink in England I was usually to be found there most week ends. This one hundred odd square metres of tiled floor and stainless steel bar can be noisy, hot or draughty and on my occasions all at the same time. As for the regular customers Dolfis has claim to some outstanding ones. In fact I would say that he has a monopoly on some rather strange people which lend a theatrical atmosphere to the place.

Take for example the man called 'Horse'. He was a wild, unkempt, looking individual with a straggly beard and unruly hair that has not seen a pair of barber's scissors during the last decade or so. According to those who know him personally he had, at one time, been a successful engineer. That was until whatever happened, did.

The 'Horse' man will come into the bar, sit there quietly for a while then pull up his trouser legs to his knees and start neighing intermittently. To the regular customers his presence is no more than that of an unruly child but to strangers it can be a little unnerving. The bar staff who know him will castigate the 'Horse' man by saying, "Shut up and eat your hay!" This ensures some minutes of silence before the process repeats itself.

Then there is the 'X File' lady. A short middle aged, soul, who sells lottery tickets. Always to be seen in the same shawl, heavy skirt and woollen stockings, whatever the weather. Her lace up boots, which had gradually been disintegrating over the last ten years or so, are several sizes too large and her gait looks as though she had been coached by Charlie

Chaplin. Her greying hair is swept straight back on her head to form what looks like a portable birds nest.

Now 'X File' will sit at the bar and drink a small beer. No, there is nothing wrong with that. The only thing is that she has the habit of sticking her tongue out slightly from between her toothless gums. Nothing wrong with that either. I have seen many people stick their tongues out. The only problem with 'X File' is that she forgets to withdraw it. This could and still does lead to misunderstandings with new customers unaccustomed to her presence.

Another character who, unfortunately, has since left the land of the living and is now possibly roaming that great car park in the sky was 'Mad Max' Valero. This hard drinking, purple and crimson faced, truck driver began driving his father's vehicle at the age of thirteen years. With thick wooden blocks his father adapted the pedals of the lorry and taught Antonio how to drive. The situation, of course, at that time in respect of both roads and transport obviously cannot be compared with today so this arrangement proved most beneficial to the father for many of their trips, carrying animal foodstuffs, took them rattling over the cobbled stoned highway in the sturdy British Leyland truck from Valencia to Calamocha some hundred and twenty miles distance in Aragon.

One thing that Spain is not in short supply of and that is wine, and near to Calamocha lie the vineyards of Cariñena, one of the most heavy and earthy wines in all Spain. So it was quite natural that father and son would lunch at one of the few cafeterias and Antonio would drive back to Valencia whilst his father slept the 'siesta'.

Antonio was born in, Gestalgar, a small village some twenty-five kilometres from Valencia and over the years, his own personal claim to fame is that to drive along the narrow country highway to the city could be achieved in almost half the time using the truck as opposed to his car.

Antonio's village also lays claim to being the nearest habitation to where the twenty-first century 'Wolf Man' roams around at will but doing harm to no one. Some years ago he was surprised whilst sleeping in a melon patch near to the village and was taken into custody by the civil guard. His parents were somewhat embarrassed about having a 'Wolf Man' for a son and attempted to place a restraining order onto him. However, the court rejected this by saying that if their son, who was an adult, wished to be a 'Wolf Man', providing he did not cause any problems, then he could continue.

Another of Dolfis's characters is 'Harry el Sucio' or 'Dirty Harry', and is worth a mention. This two metre high, broken nosed, shaven headed man is a regular customer to the bar. One of his most memorable events began one night at around one o'clock. When leaving the cafeteria to drive home he stopped at a set of traffic lights. However the car behind did not. Harry in spite of his appearance is not normally given to violence but when set upon by three youths who piled out of the other car, he became annoyed.

Within a short space of time he had all three laid out groaning on the floor, then feeling someone grab his shoulder he had swung round and delivered another right hook to the jaw. However, the person on the receiving end happened to be a member of the local police force who had arrived unexpectedly.

Other officials were quickly on the scene and Harry was removed to the local police station where he spent a fairly comfortable night in one of the cells. On being released the following morning he enquired about his car and the fate of the three youths who had attacked him. The policeman on duty sheepishly informed him that they, together with their vehicle, had been allowed to leave the scene the previous night. It was only when the police had returned to the police headquarters that they found out there was an arrest order out on all three. And if that was not sufficient the car was stolen!

Yes, there are many characters that frequent Dolfis but, thankfully, interspersed by normal people. One Sunday I was at my usual place at the bar when the door opened and in came an obvious looking Englishman. Moving further down the bar he ordered his drink and stood reading the newspaper. This happened on several consecutive Sundays with neither of us speaking to each other. Then one particularly busy Sabbath we found ourselves standing next to each other and it was natural that we struck up a conversation.

"And where are you from, might I ask?" said the man who had introduced himself as Len.

"Leicester," I replied, and then added, "But I lived for many years in Surrey."

"Really," said Len. "My brother had a pub in Surrey."

I looked at him. "Well tell me the name of the pub and I just might know your brother."

"The Goldsworth Arms," said Len.

Now Surrey is a large county and there has to be thousands of pubs scattered around there, so imagine the surprise on Len's face when I said, "Then you must be Bill Mason's brother. The Goldsworth Arms is in Woking and it was my ex-in-laws that had the pub before your brother. Also, if it is of any interest, my ex-wife, Mary and I rented your brother's house from him for a couple of years!"

Well these things happen, I suppose but that incident was something extra special as Dolfis is not a place where you would expect to meet an Englishman and certainly not someone with whom you enjoyed common friends.

*

Another character I remember clearly also appeared one Sunday lunchtime. A large square woman who with arms outstretched finger tip to finger tip would probably add up to her overall height. I judged her age as being in her late sixties, grey hair going on white. Her round cheeks flushed red, were more in keeping with that of a farmer's wife than someone who lived in the city.

As with many Spanish women of her generation who had lost a member of the family, she wore traditional black. However, what did draw my attention to her more than anything else was that she clutched to her ample bosom, as though it contained all her possessions, a black handbag of enormous dimensions. Behind her and keeping very close was a sallow faced, rather sad figure, whom I correctly assumed to be her husband. Sparse grey hair going on bald he was reasonably well turned out in what was probably his Sunday best.

The place was crowded as usual and this always resulted in late customers having to wait for a table. The woman with the handbag was glancing nervously about her at the same time easing her weight from one foot to the other while her husband stood anxiously by looking at her like a faithful cocker-spaniel awaiting orders. It was then that I noticed her fleshy swollen legs and ankles.

"Muchas gracias, Señor," she said as I stood and offered her my seat.

The husband said nothing but nodded as I took her elbow and helped her up onto the stool. She perched there looking about her still clutching the huge handbag, waiting patiently for a table to become vacant.

And so began a ritual that was to last for sometime, at least when the pair had to wait for a table and I was in a position to offer a bar stool. After a few Sundays we began to exchange pleasantries, nothing serious, just comments on the weather, holidays and family. It did not take long for me to assess that they did have a family but were not in regular contact, if at all. After some months it became obvious that the woman's health was failing in that gradually it was becoming more and more difficult for her to walk. However I never ever saw her arrive at the Dolfis bar without her black handbag.

Then came a time when several Sundays passed and they failed to appear. This in itself was not traumatic for me as they were only really acquaintances. In fact I did not even know both of their names. Just that I heard her call him Emilio on one occasion. So I just assumed that with their non-appearance that that was to be the end of the story. But no.

It was some months later it was necessary for me to visit the Civil Governor's Palace in the city. Normally I would have gone on foot but the weather was so hot that crossing Valencia was like trying to transverse a giant sized oven with two feet of treacle around your legs. So I took a good air conditioned local bus. All the seats were taken so I stood holding on to the support bar and watched the city go perspiring about its business.

At the third stop I saw, to my surprise, the husband of the woman with the handbag climb slowly aboard the bus. He did not catch sight of me until he was quite close and I reached out and touched him on the shoulder. His grey suit was crumpled, his shoes carried a layer of dust and his shirt collar and cuffs were very much frayed. He turned and a pair of empty grey eyes looked up at me. For a second he was puzzled then recognition dawned and he clasped my outstretched hand smiling.

"Hello, Ingles," he said with a ghost of a smile. "It is you isn't it?"

"Yes, it is," I replied grasping his hand. "It is nice to see you after all this time. How are you?"

I looked into those expressionless eyes with their faint luminous rings around the irises and I knew what the answer was to be.

"My wife died," he said, flatly. And even as he spoke two very small tears formed.

"I am so very, very sorry," I said, the words sounding even more inadequate than they usually did. I then followed this with the expected courteous phrase used in Spain, "I am with your sentiments."

He nodded. "She was a good woman, Ingles"

"The very best," I agreed.

Then for a fleeting moment his eyes lit up as he remembered something. "She liked you, you know."

"I beg your pardon?" I said, not knowing how to respond to this but he didn't seem to hear me.

"Oh, yes. She really liked you. Talked about you a lot. Called you our 'Sunday Englishman'."

"That's nice."

"She certainly did," he went on. "Remember you made sure she always had somewhere to sit while we waited for a table?"

"'Course I remember," I smiled, adding something about it being the normal thing to do.

"And there was that time when you even made one of your friends give up his seat for her."

"Quite possible," I said, vaguely remembering.

"Oh yes you did! In fact I think you did it twice. We both laughed about it when we got home."

He was reliving those moments, reaching back in time to recapture a little of the happiness, no matter how faint, how obscure, that had once been his by right. His knuckles whitened on the rail as he looked at something in the distance and said, "Some Sundays her legs were so bad that I wanted her to stay at home. You know, have lunch there like we do, or rather did, during the week."

Again I nodded. He brightened again.

"But you know what? She would have none of that. 'Don't worry about my old legs,' she would say. 'You just get me to Dolfis and our 'Sunday Englishman' will take care of me'."

The bus had stopped and passengers were alighting while others climbed on board. I could see his eyes darting here and there, briefly searching their faces and I knew he was looking for her even though he was aware of the hopelessness.

The doors closed and the bus lurched into motion and his small impossible dream was once again denied him as it would always be denied until time would diminish the yearning.

He turned and looked up at me and his voice dropping to a whisper said, "Ingles. I know she was older than me. But I don't know why she had to die. Why she left me."

He was crying quite openly now and I reached out and placed my arm around his shoulder drawing him towards me. And there we both stood impervious of our fellow passengers he with his grief and myself with that impotency that comes at such moments.

"God, I am so lonely," he sobbed. "She said to me before she died. She said, 'Poor Emilio I don't want to leave you. I don't know what you will do without me'."

Reaching into his pocket he pulled out a grubby handkerchief and moved away, embarrassed, wiping his face. "I'm sorry about that, Ingles."

"It doesn't matter my friend. I really do understand. I possibly understand more than you think?"

"Really?" He was taking strength from my words. Pulling himself back.

"Yes," I said, "Because it has happened to me."

Then looking me straight in the eyes he asked, "Why does it have to be like this, amigo?"

He was now serious and seeking some sort of an answer that I could not give him; the one possible reply that would ease his torment. But, of course, there was no answer; no words. So I said inadequately, my voice sounding hollow to my ears, "I don't honestly know why it has to be this way, my friend. I am sorry but I do not have the answer."

The bus was stopping again and I took hold of his arm. "But what I do know Emilio is that your wife is waiting for you somewhere and she is relying on you, expecting you to keep things going as they were until you are together again."

He glanced at the passengers climbing aboard, eyes searching their faces.

"You honestly think so, Ingles?" He turned, studying my expression.

I reached out and squeezed his arm. "No, I don't think so, Emilio. I know so."

He digested my words for a moment, and then said slowly, "I live on my own now. No family. I have to wash and iron my shirts; try to keep myself and the place tidy, just as she did. The least I can do."

Again those hopeless eyes.

"You know, Ingles, I have been looking out for you?"

"For me? Well you know where to find me most every Sunday."

"Yes, I know." He glanced down at the floor as if studying his dust covered shoes. "But I don't really want to go there at the moment. Not yet anyway. You understand don't you?"

"I understand."

Then for no particular reason he laughed. Well not really a laugh; just a series of short breaths being expelled. With eyes still downcast, he said almost to himself, "I live in one of those old apartment blocks on the other side of town." A hesitation then, "On the sixth floor."

His voice became fainter and I had to stoop to hear the words.

"Sometimes like today, I get up in the morning and I just don't know what to do. Just walk out onto the little terrace and stand there, wondering whether it is worth it."

I remained silent staring out of the window at the busy city passing by, knowing that my answer, if there was to be one, must be important to both of us. I looked at him and suddenly he was smiling.

"Then I meet you. What a coincidence. I wonder why that should be."

I now had my response.

"Emilio, my friend. Before I could not give you an answer as to why we have been chosen to walk this path. But I can certainly give you an explanation as to why you should see me today."

I held onto his arm as the bus lurched. "Because this is the way it should be for without each other there is no hope." I then waited a moment before saying, "It is quite possible that you wife was saying to you this very morning, when she saw how unhappy you were, 'Don't worry, Emilio. Just find the Englishman and you will be alright. At least for today, that is'."

He was thinking, assessing my words.

"You know I never thought of that, Ingles. It could just be right."

The bus was slowing down again and I noticed that I had long gone past my stop.

"I get off here," he said, suddenly looking up and taking note of his surroundings.

We shook hands, his fingers frail in mine still seeking reassurance, Then moving towards the doors he suddenly stopped again, turned quickly and held out his hand once more. "I really am so very pleased to have met you today, Ingles. Perhaps I will come by Dolfis one Sunday."

I nodded and he moved away, pausing at the bottom of the steps he looked back. "We thought Sunday was a good day," he called. "Did you think Sunday was a good day, Ingles?"

I waved. "Emilio!" I shouted, ignoring the people around me, "Sunday was not just a good day for me. It was a great day!"

This time a wide bright smile lit up his face and he raised his hand and waved. I saw his lips move but only heard the hiss of the automatic doors closing. Then turning away once again he smoothed down his jacket and by the way his arms moved I knew that he was adjusting his tie.

The small voice within me was confirming that without doubt that one day however long it took he would find the lady with the enormous black handbag waiting for him in some place, somewhere. The bus pulled away and the last impression I had of him before being swallowed up by the lunchtime crowds, was that he suddenly appeared just that little bit taller than I thought he was.

*

After the exacting journey from England with little or nothing to eat en route Kathy, Samantha and I enjoyed a wonderful lunch at Dolfis. Then in the following days it was back to the old routine with classes for Kathy and me dedicating my time to the jewellery business.

Keeping contact with Mac in England did help and we were both optimistic as regards the future. During the coming months I also did several interpreting jobs, usually lasting a matter of days only, which helped economically but money still remained short. Neither did it help much when I came up with a dose of 'Shingles'. Fortunately our local chemist was able to help and I was able to recover from this irritating and painful condition. Recover, that is, in time to see Samantha catch measles. Whereas I recuperated without any visible effects, Samantha's condition affected one of her eyes causing it wander at will. A patch over the good eye was the standard treatment but it was obvious that at some stage in the future it would have to be corrected by surgery.

Our hopes for the future and the trip to England with the students remained strong. However on the twenty-first of February nineteen eighty-one there was an incident that made us wonder what the future really held.

*

The Spanish Government under the leadership of Adolfo Suarez nearly came to grief when a little man in civil guard's uniform complete with tricorn hat loosed off several shots during a parliamentary meeting and it was announced that the military was taking over the country. At the same time that this was happening in Madrid, in Valencia another military official, Millans del Bosch, ordered the tanks to be put out onto the streets of the city. The situation until that point appeared somewhat unreal but as the distinct clanking sound of the tank tracks drew nearer to our neighbourhood, the reality of it all became apparent.

Word had spread quickly that everyone had to be in their own homes by seven o'clock that evening; as a curfew was in force. This did not present any problem for our family but there were many people with obvious left wing tendencies who were forced to seek shelter in places other than their own homes.

With the onset of democracy, after the demise of General Franco, in order to physically express their socialistic or communistic leanings many such men had cultivated beards and for them that particular night was spent unhappily shaving off the evidence. It was quite amusing in the following days to come across people who you had seen before the actual date of the attempted Coup with fine bushy growths around their faces and were now totally clean-shaven.

Anyway on the particular night in question the Spanish television put on a film with Bob Hope and Virginia Mayo entitled 'The Princess and Pirate'. The showing of this old, but very amusing, comedy was regularly interrupted by various bulletins as to the general state of affairs concerning the Coup. During these bulletins, the newscaster kept glancing nervously off camera and we could see quite clearly the shadow of someone with a pistol on the backcloth. Most bizarre. Then it was back once again to Bob Hope wielding his cutlass in defence of the lovely Virginia Mayo. The following day, of course, things were back to almost normal with the culprits under lock and key although it did take sometime delving into the reasons for the incident.

*

That year July eventually came round and we were all set for our first group of students to go to Bath. Kathy and I, together with a young girl student who had offered to care for Samantha, drove over whilst the remaining students flew.

The three weeks there was an immense success and things looked set for such future trips.

The best laid plans of mice and men.

And so it was that the following year, Prime Minister Margaret Thatcher decided that in no way would the British people be blackmailed by the Argentinian General Galtieri and his motley group of friends in respect of the Falkland Islands.

Never before or since have had I experienced the general lack of geographical knowledge on the part of many Spaniards. All the parents of our possible students for Bath summer school that year firmly believed that the Argentinian air force was about to revise the system of carpet bombing on England that had been employed in the last world war. Bath, we were assured, was definitely not the place for their offspring, either then or at anytime in the future. Persistent attempts on our part to convince them otherwise came to nothing, particularly as their sympathies lay mainly with their Latin cousins.

*

Around this time I was approached by a Valencia jewellery manufacturer and asked if I would represent his company under similar conditions as I did for Edmundo Gomez at Leira Gemenis.

The jewellery collection in question was quite outstanding; exquisite designs and solid gold with precious stones. I immediately agreed and contacted Mac in England, telling him to stand by as I would be over. This was sooner said than done. Finance was such that at that time travelling by conventional methods was not possible and I left wondering how I would go.

Then someone mentioned 'Tilleys' and I knew what the answer was to be.

The village of El Puig, some fifteen kilometres outside Valencia is dominated by a huge monastery within whose shadow lies a small bar which could be termed as another 'Good pull-in for lorry drivers'. As the Valencia region excelled in fruit exports this small, homely establishment, was frequented by many British truck drivers who came bringing parts of machinery for the Ford Company and returning with their loads of oranges, lemons, melons, onions together every other imaginable fruit and vegetable.

The bar was named after its owner, a woman of immense proportions and warm character to match who seemed to thrive on Spanish 'bocadillos' washed down with copious draughts of Bacardi and coke.

So on a Sunday morning visit to 'Tilleys' with Kathy and Samantha I managed to arrange that I travel to England with my collection, worth around ten thousand pounds sterling, as a driver's mate on one of the huge fruit lorries that was to leave the following week.

Then the day before I was due to leave Valencia a local gardening enthusiast presented me with a gift of three radishes to take with me; one weighing a little over three kilos and the remaining two around two kilos each. I carefully wrapped them in tin foil and was ready to go.

Joe, the young man who had offered to take me was waiting at 'Tilleys' when I arrived so we set off immediately. The vehicle, a modern Ford Transcontinental, was a very comfortable truck in which to travel and from my privileged position, high up; I could admire the countryside as we passed. Joe with his Liverpudlian accent regaled me with stories on what it was like to be a long distance driver as we rolled northwards.

That first evening we stopped for a meal in some small French town and dined lavishly on Couscous. The bill when it came was quite considerable but we paid and left with Joe threatening to reverse his trailer into the restaurant. I calmed him down and we returned to the motorway. Everything was going fine.

It was when we came to the 'Péage' toll-gate that it was discovered that Joe did not have sufficient money to pay the toll fees. What little I had was all reserved for my trip. Now with quite a queue of vehicles behind us it was not just a case of reversing the sixteen-wheeled Ford truck and coming up with a solution to the problem afterwards. No, we were completely stuck with me, of course, being seated directly in the firing line of the passenger seat receiving most of the insults from the irate Frenchman in his little box-like cabin and behind us around twenty angry motorists wondering what the hell was happening.

It was then, fortunately, that I remembered that I was carrying, apart from the gold jewellery, quite a few sample sets of silver costume jewellery. Quickly I pulled out a selection and began bargaining with the man. Within a short time he had agreed to accept a pleasing combination, consisting of a necklace, bracelet and earrings with emerald stones. Behind us the queue had grown even longer and the voices rose to lynching pitch so I was very much relieved when the bar was lifted and we were once again on our way. Unfortunately this incident happened not too far from Cherbourg and the process was repeated one more time before we arrived at the port. I was rewarded for my efforts with a first class meal on the cross channel ferry and a comfortable bunk for the night. While the boat rose and fell lumbering its way over to Southampton and I lay there waiting for sleep to envelop me, my thoughts turned to Stanhope Perkins. Perhaps it was that I caught sight of a 'Brittany Ferries' boat just before we set sail for Newhaven that he came into my mind.

*

I had become acquainted with Stan since moving to Valencia. At that time many people who also knew Stan would say that he was bigoted, anti most things and consumes more alcohol than was good for him. Of course, they were quite right. However, it would not be correct in saying that he was bereaved of a polite and well-mannered exterior.

Medium height, short cropped hair, thickening a little around the waist, his stature is more compatible to sitting in the navigator's seat of the past president of the Congo's aircraft, where he was, than being desk bound in the pathology department of a local hospital, where he is now. Behind rimless spectacles his eyes change frequently, sometimes laughing at a new joke or muttering, "Son of a bitch!" which he does often. Complain? Of course he complains. Most people complain but I think that Stan has cornered the market where complaining is concerned. The weather, children, the noise, dogs; you name it and Stan will complain about it.

"Someday I'm gonna shoot that god damn dog next door," he would mutter in that mid Atlantic accent.

However it must be fair to say that of all things he might grouse about you would never hear Stan say even a single word against England. England to Stan is sacrosanct. Although he had spent on and off less than six months of his whole life in the country, he absolutely adores everything connected with that green and pleasant land. He loves the countryside, the towns, villages, high roads and by-roads, even the weather. And above all England signifies to Stan, quiet, comfortable, cosy, country pubs. All this is understandable for one who most days have to contend with the hot, dust laden and very humid atmosphere of Valencia.

Although Stan's grandfather was originally posted to Rhodesia whilst serving with the British army together with the fact that three of Stan's uncles were killed piloting bombers over Hamburg in World War two, he is not, according to UK authorities, eligible for British nationality. Stan was born in what is now Zimbabwe. Apparently English law does not respect bloodline as was told to me by a British consul. So Stan has been forced to take out Spanish nationality. This in itself was not a problem at the time of this incident but it saddened the man to think that there was no way that he could live in England on a more permanent basis.

Stan also likes his comforts, rarely leaving home even though invited to friends for meals or any other activity. However there is always a warm welcome to be had for anyone visiting his chalet near to Valencia.

"Sorry," he will normally apologise, "there isn't much on offer but I have some cold beers and a whisky chaser on the side. Is that's OK?"

Then his dear wife, Vicky, will find some Jacob's cream crackers together with a slab of Cheddar cheese and a feast would be had.

And so it was that I passed by one winter's day when the Levantine sun just held enough warmth that we were able to sit out on the front porch of the chalet. I knew that day was special as Stan, with the air of a magician producing a rabbit, appeared with two cans of Boddingtons's bitter. "Hey," he called, "This is really great stuff and I have you to thank for introducing me to it."

I mumbled something about it being a pleasure and reached out to stay the hand that was splashing out a liberal quantity of malt whisky to accompany the frothing pint.

So there we sat talking about nothing in particular when Stan said, reflectively, "You know what? I've been thinking."

I nodded encouragingly.

"I sometimes have the feeling that I'm on borrowed time, Chris."

"Borrowed what?" I asked, not hearing him correctly.

"Borrowed time, Chris. Past sixty. Not in good health and all that."

"And what actually do you mean by that?" I asked feeling that there was more to come.

"And," he went on, "I've been thinking that this Boddingtons's stuff is about the best beer I've ever tasted." Here he stroked the beer can as an antique dealer might caress some priceless Ming vase. Then taking a deep breath he said, "I reckon that when I go I would like my ashes to be put in into several Boddingtons's beer cans and thrown into the sea."

"Really," I said, not sure as to whether or not he was joking. "Not quite that simple, Stan."

He raised his hand and I just sat back and resigned myself for what was to come. "What I really would like is to find a close friend who would be prepared to catch the ferry from Santander to Plymouth."

"Then?" I interrupted my curiosity growing.

"Then," he continued, "before the boat docks at Plymouth to say 'God save the Queen, long live Francis Drake and long live Oliver Cromwell. Then, whoever it is has to toss the cans into the sea."

I nodded, trying not to smile at the image that appeared in my mind's eye. "Why the Queen, Drake and Cromwell?" I ask.

"Well," explained Stan patiently as if talking to one who has no sense of historic priorities. "The Queen always comes first." Here he raised his glass in a silent toast. "And as you know that I am a life long admirer of both Drake and Cromwell."

"Well, so what?" I wondered what was coming next.

He leaned across the table and stared directly into my eyes. "Will you do it, Chris?"

Suddenly realising which direction the conversation was taking I said, "Come on, Stan. You can't honestly be serious?"

"Of course, I'm serious."

I took a swallow of the beer without noticing that the glass was empty. "You're mad!"

"Perhaps."

He then stood up to retrieve another couple of cans from the kitchen but not before leaning over me and saying, "Perhaps I am mad, but that's the way I want it."

"You'll probably live another twenty years," I said, hedging.

"Possibly, but Boddingtons's will still be around."

And thus the conversation continued in this vein until it was time to take my leave. On the last note I said, "Alright. If you cannot find anyone else you can count on me."

I drove away thinking that no doubt things would possibly change in the not-too- distant future and wondering how many Boddingtons's cans Stan would fit into.

It was several weeks later that I had the occasion to telephone him about some translation or other and our previous conversation came to mind.

"By the way", I asked "have you spoken to anyone else about the Boddingtons's project?"

"Yes, I have actually. I spoke to our friend, Ken Martin."

I was curious. "And what did Ken say?"

"Well, Ken said that he would be prepared to carry out the mission, say God bless the Queen and long live Francis Drake but there was no way he was going to say long live Oliver Cromwell. In fact, when I mentioned it to Ken he went potty and refused to have anything to do with it."

"But why was that, Stan?"

"Well", he explained, "Ken converted to Catholicism and he puts the blame on Oliver Cromwell for killing Charles I, the last of the Catholic Kings. That's why."

"Then it's back to square one, Stan. Why don't we just forget about it?"

The earpiece crackled violently. "Not bloody likely. No way. So I've written to Brittany Ferries and asked them to do it."

I could not believe my ears. "What? You've actually written to Brittany Ferries about all this?"

"Sure have. So I'm hoping it is still on."

After discussing other items I finally replaced the phone wondering what Brittany Ferries thought of the whole matter and had a fleeting thought of a committee sitting around a boardroom table discussing the logistics of operation 'Stan's Ashes.' No, it was not possible. Or was it?

It was about a month later when I had occasion to phone him again and I bore in mind to ask if there had been any sort of reply from the ferry company. So after the main business was settled, I asked: "Any news from Brittany Ferries, Stan?"

His voice took on a disgruntled tone." Yes, they replied."

"Really, Stan?" I was amazed. "They actually replied?"

"And why shouldn't they have done?"

"No, nothing. I was just surprised that's all. Anyway, what did they say?"

I could tell by the hesitation that he was a little reluctant to talk about it. However out it came bit by bit.

"Well," he explained, "apparently there was no problem for one of the captain's of their ships to take care of the Boddingtons's cans, nor to say Gold bless the Queen, long live Francis Drake and long live Oliver Cromwell, but ......"

"But what?" I persisted.

"But ...," he continued irritably, "it was an environmental offence to dispose of refuse in the sea."

*

In Southampton, the custom's man diligently searched the cab of Joe's truck and pounced upon my package of radishes which had fallen down behind the seat.

"And what is this?" he asked, waving it in front of my face.

"You will never guess," I said rather stupidly.

"I'm not here to play guessing games," he snarled.

"Alright then if you insist. In that packet are three radishes."

His face darkened even more.

"I said, don't play games with me," he hissed. "Open it up!"

"I'm not playing games." I then unrolled the foil and displayed the radishes. His expression was a picture but he certainly was not going to lose face.

"Alright, on your way," he said, "before I really start losing my temper with you people."

And with that off he stalked without a backward glance.

Joe and I parted company near the Southampton bypass making arrangements to meet up in ten days time. I waved to him as he swung the truck in the direction of the sign that read 'Bristol' while I took up an optimistic stance next to the sign pointing to 'London and the Midlands'.

It was a miserable afternoon and heavy rain set in. Just nobody wanted to stop and I began to feel wet and despondent. Although I was possibly dressed too well for a hitch- hiker, with my neat well-fitted overcoat, smart holdall and the jewellery collection in a brand new leather briefcase, I just had to hang on in there. Eventually the people who did take pity on me were two local police officers in a squad car. My story must have sounded convincing or they wanted rid of me off their patch, as they drove me all the way along the bypass to the main London Road. Here my luck came into play as the driver of the next car that pulled up said he was going to Northampton. It was wonderful. The countryside simply flew by and we were soon well on the way. We even stopped in one of those lovely old world Oxfordshire pubs where I had an excellent pint of best bitter and managed to telephone Mac who agreed to pick me up in Northampton. After such a journey the bed at Mac's place was heaven when I fell into it.

*

Next day, after examining the gold collection we made out a plan of campaign and that evening adjourned to the Conservative Club in Blaby where I presented the steward with one of the giant radishes. Those members present were all astounded at the size of the thing and both Mac and I gleaned a little moment of notoriety as well as a couple of free pints of best bitter.

We sat in one of the deep comfortable settees enjoying the atmosphere and geniality of the club when suddenly a huge ham-like hand grabbed me by the shoulder from behind and almost yanked me out of the seat. "Oo the 'ell are you to come in 'ere tekin' the piss outa me?" boomed a voice in my ear. "Ah've bin growin' radishes fer nay on fifty years and yer can't tell me that's a bloody radish!"

He still held on to my shoulder in a vice like grip with one hand and with the other was waving the offending vegetable around his head in a very threatening manner. In fact I could almost visualise the headlines in the following day's 'Leicester Mercury', 'Ex-Leicester man brutally beaten to death with a radish at Blaby Conservative Club'. If the aggressor had not been so furious I would have laughed but he certainly seemed capable of using the thing. Instead, I cowered in my seat and covered my head until Mac, together with several other members came to my assistance and Bert was lead away shouting defiantly. "Never on yer bloody life a bloody radish. Ah'm tellin' yer! Fifty bleedin' years ah've bin growin' 'em. Tekin' the piss 'e is, ah tell yer!"

So that was the one and only time I visited the local Conservative Club. "Dangerous, very dangerous," I thought and decided that politics and radishes definitely do not mix.

*

The visits Mac and I made with the gold collection were received well but as it was a few weeks after the Christmas season only one or two minor orders were forthcoming.

"Pass by later on in the year," most buyers told us and some asked, "Will you be exhibiting at any of the jewellery fairs?"

It would seem from the exercise that the answer could well be to organise a stand at one of the fairs. I decided to enlist the help of Edmundo in this respect the moment I returned to Spain. Speaking to Edmundo was not going to prove difficult but the returning to Spain part was not going to be as easy as I thought, or rather hoped.

*

Joe and his lorry were there when I arrived at Southampton and after organising the necessary paperwork with the customs to say that the jewellery was once again leaving the country it was on board the ferry and outward bound.

All went well until we arrived near Lyon and it was there that Joe received instructions that instead of his destination being Spain it was now Marseille. This indicated he would be turning off towards the East further down the 'Auto route'. So we said our "Goodbyes" at Lyon and I waited hopefully by the side of a slip road connecting Lyon with the motorway. Eventually I was successful with a lift that was also going to Marseille, just to make matters simple. The kindly French driver dropped me off near where the road forked and I started walking south.

Of course, it wasn't long before a French police car pulled up and I was asked what I was doing hitch-hiking on a motorway. Documents were produced and when I opened the sample case and they saw the gold collection the word "Feu" was banded about quite liberally. Next after a lot of head shaking they eventually climbed into their car and hastily disappeared into the distance.

Night was coming on fast and the temperature was rapidly dropping to zero. I was freezing cold. Fortunately a petrol station came into sight and I turned off to spend the rest of the night sitting in a small cafeteria with those awful drink dispensing machines reading a book called 'Colossus' about the life story of the Spanish artist, Francisco Goya. Next morning at first light I was on my way again when after around half and hours walking a kindly Belgian couple taking pity on me, stopped and gave me a lift to the Spanish border at La Junquera. Knowing that the document registration with regards to the collection would probably take some time we parted ways and I was sad to see them go as they were heading towards Valencia.

Inside the Spanish customs office it was a very officious young woman who attended me. She busily completed the various forms. "Registration number of your car, please?" She suddenly asked, pen poised over the paper.

"Sorry, Señorita, I haven't got a car."

"Then which coach did you arrive on?"

"I didn't arrive on a coach either."

She looked up sharply, "Then how the hell did you get here?"

"Hitch-hiked," I explained. "Auto stop."

"Auto stop?" she repeated, looking from me to the jewellery articles. "You actually arrived here with more than two million pesetas worth of goods by Auto stop?"

"Yes," I confirmed sheepishly as the exercise was now beginning to appear rather stupid on my part.

Dropping the pen onto the counter she went away soon returning with another official who stared at me, held out his hand and said, "Your licence, please?"

I looked confused. "Licence? What licence?"

"Your gun licence, of course, what else?"

"But I don't have a gun."

He stared at me in disbelief. "You mean to tell me that you arrive here via Auto stop with two million pesetas in sample jewellery and you don't even have a gun?"

"Sorry," I said lamely. "No gun."

They spoke rapidly to one another and I caught the word "loco" several times. The official then quickly stamped my papers, signed and passing everything back over to me said, not without a little irony, "Adios and good luck!"

I walked out and headed towards the stream of cars again. However, it was not to be that simple. I had to pass a small wooden hut and inside sat an elderly Civil Guard customs man who shouted out that I was to present all my documents yet again. Into the hut, I went and when he saw the collection his eyes nearly popped out of his head. He took out each piece of jewellery and examined it carefully making complimentary noises. It did not take much for me to realise that he was after a couple of samples and when he waved one particularly expensive necklace and said that his wife would just love it, I shook my head. This seemed to irritate him and he kept me there for more than one hour, every now and again pointing at a bracelet or a ring and indicating that it would be a nice present for his wife. I kept shaking my head and saying that it was not mine to give and eventually he begrudgingly said that I could continue.

Lifts were definitely slow in coming and I was about eighty kilometres North of Valencia when I decided that it would be more prudent to complete the journey by train. Easier said than done. At Burriana I discovered that the last train had just left.

Walking along the main road, I noticed a crowd of people standing around near a bus stop so I joined them, wondering what it was all about. Then after about twenty minutes, the oldest and most decrepit coach I have ever seen pulled up and people started climbing on board. So as nonchalantly as was possible, I followed.

The driver, realising that I was somewhat different from the rest who were carrying wine skins, sausages, ham 'bocadillos', as well as their bulky luggage, asked me why I got onto his bus. I explained I wanted to go as far as Valencia and I would willingly pay something that was not too exorbitant. He agreed and told me that he was driving to Andalucía some eight-hundred kilometres distance. We rattled along at a snails pace and I had the feeling that it would be at least a couple of days before any of the passengers even came close to seeing Andalucía.

I was glad to alight in Valencia and made my way home to be greeted by an angry Kathy who wanted to know why I had not, at least, caught a train from Barcelona. The word that was liberally used this time was 'mad'!

Well, perhaps she was right.

*

Edmundo Gomez was in agreement that we should exhibit at the White House Hotel Jewellery Fair, Regents Park, London, later in the year. Some weeks went by and I was again approached by another silver jewellery manufacturer, David Garcia, whose extensive range of very inexpensive sets attracted my attention. I agreed to take on the collection.

It was around this time that a phone call from our lawyer informed us that we had won the lawsuit involving the English Disaster project. Now that really was the good news. The not so good part was that the judge decreed that each party should pay their own legal expenses. This, of course, made a sizable hole into the award. Never mind, even after the share out with the others involved we could now afford the operation for Samantha's eye to be corrected and things would be a little better financially. Also I could return to England with the new collection in style: by coach!

Arrangements were made once again and I set off. Naturally the same customs woman would have to be on duty when I presented the collection for examination together with the required documents at the frontier. She obviously remembered me from the previous time as when I walked in her expression changed. However, she brightened up somewhat when I explained that this time I had arrived there by coach.

"Things must be improving," she said, brightly. "What have you got this time, the crown jewels?"

In England, Mac and I did great business and sold a considerable amount of sets to various main buyers such as British Merchant Jewellers, Birmingham, and Ciro Pearls, London. It seemed, to my simple mind, that things were really on a positive move.

Oh fool that I was to become so complacent.

The coach journey back was only marred by one small point which was when I presented the samples at the Spanish frontier for re-entry into Spain. This time a sour- faced customs official took me into a back room, made me strip off and subject myself to a body search. This, in itself, certainly did not worry me but it upset all the passengers on the coach as we were delayed for almost an hour. After that incident, nobody would speak to me for the rest of the journey.

Back in Valencia the orders were handed over to David Garcia for processing.

Next Samantha was admitted to hospital where her eye was successfully corrected by a brilliant lady surgeon who was the absolute image of the American singer, Doris Day. Things were really looking up. Then Edmundo announced that he would like me to go with him to the Jewellery Fair in Basle, Switzerland. Needless to say with the thought of travelling anywhere at company cost I immediately agreed.

Then just two weeks before we were due to leave, I received a phone call from David who had dispatched the orders to England. Could I go over to the factory immediately as something terrible had occurred. Wondering what the problem was, I drove over there straight away.

"Just look at this, Chris," he said, pointing to eight little wooden boxes in which he had mailed the jewellery. "These have been returned."

Peering into each of them I saw crushed amounts of rings, necklaces and bracelets, all mixed up with semi-precious stones and realised immediately what had gone wrong.

"What did they do to my jewellery?" David asked, obviously very upset.

I tipped out a mess of pieces from one of the boxes onto the table. "I'll tell you what they did," I said angrily spreading the mishmash around with my fingers. "They put it under the hammer and smashed it all. That's what they did!"

He looked as though he was about to break into tears. "Who are 'they' and why should they want to do this?"

"They," I explained, slowly through gritted teeth, thinking about all the effort we had put into selling the items and at the same time realising why the prices had been so attractive. "They, my friend, are the custom officials in England. And 'they' would do that for one reason only."

He could not look me in the face. I think he realised what was coming, so I continued relentlessly. "The amount of silver content was just not up to UK standard. The figure you stamped on the items was false. That, Amigo mio, is precisely why."

He did not argue. His eyes just looked up onto row after row of shelves that held thousands of pieces they had manufactured and stored, possibly in anticipation of more UK sales. "Do you think 'they' would accept it as being 'almost' up to standard?" he asked miserably.

"No way," I said angrily. "Better forget it!"

And with that I walked out.

*

It was going to be a long fair in Switzerland, eleven days to be precise, but Basle was a really special place. I loved it. The atmosphere; the tremendous variation in restaurants with typical German eating houses, Italian ristorantes and a fair sprinkling of French bistros. The hotel into which we were booked was notable, old with echoing tiled floors and high ceilings. A huge iron bedstead that almost required a ladder to get into the thing dominated my room, in keeping with the place. Next to this was what I first took to be some sort of collection box one might come across in a church with the words 'Two Swiss Francs' written on the side. That first night, feeling in an expansive mood as I climbed into bed, I slipped the appropriate number of coins into it and had the shock of my life when the bed started shaking like crazy. This lasted for several minutes then as quickly as it had started the machine stopped. The next day I was told this was a massage machine designed to relax stressed-out guests before going to sleep. The only thing it did for me was make me wonder if there was any possible female company that might like to try it out with me.

The first weekend we were there the British Consul had organised a 'Tarts and Vicars' party. For the uninitiated, this involved those attending being obliged to dress up as either a vicar or a tart. An Irish customer and friend of Edmundo was staying at the same hotel so together we dressed Edmundo up in a skirt and high heeled shoes borrowed from an understanding receptionist and sweater complete with boobs in the form of balloons. A liberal amount of bright red lipstick and an also borrowed wig and we had the perfect tart. The Irish friend and I wore sober suits together with reversed shirts giving the impression of ecclesiastical collars. Of course from each of our rooms we took full use of the Gideon Bible.

All was fine until we walked onto the street in search of a taxi. In most other European countries, we might only have caused a few eyebrows to be raised but Switzerland, well that was different to say the least. Needless to say there was absolutely no taxi that would stop. Most slowed down but when they caught sight of Edmundo flanked on either side by the Irishman and myself, appearing to be serious members of the cloth, they rapidly drove away. So some thirty minutes later we had to return to the hotel and request the assistance of our receptionist friend. Even then as we walked out to the waiting taxi it was touch and go as to whether we made it to the vehicle before he took stock of what was happening and disappeared. Needless to say, the party was a real hit and everybody had a great time. Next day, of course, we were all rather hung over and were secretly pleased that there was not a lot of negotiating to be done at the Trade Fair.

One of the representatives of another jewellery manufacturer was Jean Michel from Belgium. According to the rest of those present, Jean was a wizard where women were concerned and it was with our full attention that he imparted to us that on that particular night he would be going along to the Red Rose Club where he had arranged to meet up with a very young and very attractive African striptease dancer.

"Of course," he said, with a rather superior air, "if you lot would like to see some real action then you should come along there at around eleven o'clock."

Naturally, we required no second invitation and all agreed that we would be there to see the 'action'. Edmundo and I rolled up at around eleven thirty so most of the performance was already happening with a beautiful, extremely well built, Dutch girl expertly disrobing on the small dance floor to a Joe Cocker number. We spotted our friends in one of the darker corners of the establishment went over and sat down.

As Edmundo, or possibly myself, had insisted that we stop by a couple of popular watering holes on the way it was not long before I felt the need for a visit to the toilet. This was, fortunately, situated at the far end of the club just past the bar itself and as I made my way there in the gloom I saw Jean Michel leaning nonchalantly on the bar talking to the African striptease dancer. And as far as I could determine in the dim light, she was certainly an extraordinarily attractive young woman of around some twenty odd years. As luck would have it, on the way past, I heard the girl speaking in English and in English blessed with a pure London accent. Out of habit and much training on the Costa Blanca radio station, as I eased my way by them I nodded to the girl at the same time saying, "Alo there mi ol' darlin'. Alroight then?" I continued on to the toilets. However, when I re-emerged and was on my way back to our group, she grabbed me by the arm pulling me towards and at the same time yelling out, "Oo the bleedin' 'ell are you then, John?"

I put on my best smile. "Mi name's Chris," I said and added, "that's if yer wanna know, darlin'."

She peered up at me, the whites of her eyes shining in the darkness. "An' where y' from, Chris, wiv an accent like that?"

"Lived in Wimbledon," I explained.

"Bloody 'ell," she exclaimed, "I'm a neighbour o' yours from Wands-facking-worth!"

Next turning to Jean Michel who appeared lost by all this exchange, she dug a well-aimed finger into his chest. "'ere you, mi mates turned up. Piss orf!"

Looking rather nonplussed Jean moved away.

She now turned her full attention to me. "So wot yer doin' in Switzer-facking-land then, Chris?"

"Well, yu know darlin'. Duckin' an' divin' like the rest o' them."

"'Ere you're a laugh, you are, Chris. Are you goin' to buy me a drink?"

"Sure will if it ain't gonna break the Bank of Switzer-facking-land," I said getting into the swing of things.

She giggled and ordered a small bottle of what just might have been champagne. I happily parted with what I considered a reasonable amount of Swiss Francs and placed my arm around her. Then after chatting some more, she admitted that she was hoping to get married to, as she put it, "Some rich old Swiss Geezer," thereby becoming a Swiss Citizen. Naturally I wished her, "Bleedin' good luck," and all was rosy at the Red Rose Club with myself sitting on a bar stool while she pressed herself against me.

When it came for her to do the striptease part she was really magic. All eyes in the place were on her as Joe Cocker yelled, "Leave your hat on!"

But the best part, from my point of view, was when she reappeared after changing and walked straight across to me and planted a kiss firmly on my cheek before once again cuddling up to me. Naturally, I wondered what sort of comments must have been passed around in our small group in the corner.

Towards the end of the night the girl asked, "Gonna take me 'ome then Chris?"

I had been preparing myself for this question and answered immediately. "Listen darlin'. Already I luv yer very much but there ain't no way I got bread enough to take yer 'ome. Sorry luv but that's the way it is."

She was quiet for a moment, sipping thoughtfully at her champagne. "Listen, Chris. I got to earn me bread ain't I?"

"Course yer 'ave," I agreed. "We all 'ave."

"Listen, I tell yer what I'll do, Chris. If I can't find no punters I'll be straight back and yer can come 'ome wiv me." Then as an after thought she added, "and I'll make yer breakfast in the mornin'"

I kept my fingers crossed as she disappeared and then some ten minutes later, complete with coat, she was back again. "OK, mate!" she said slipping her arm into mine. "Let's go 'ome."

I nodded to our group of friends who were also on the way out. "Hasta mañana!" I called. Needless to say breakfast the following morning was one of the most memorable ones but not as memorable as the hours that led up to it.

At the Trade Fair there was little comment to me personally but I could definitely feel the waves of envy floating around in the air. As for Jean Michel, he had passed a pleasant night with one of the receptionists at his hotel, according to his story.

It was during that afternoon that the telephone rang and Kathy was saying that she had received a visit from the customs police as regards our British registered car parked in the street. Apparently, there were two officials in plain clothes together with one, very vicious looking, dog. They demanded to know where I was. Kathy explained that at that particular moment I was in Switzerland. They then told her that the Audi was illegally in Spain and that it had to be removed from the street immediately. In the meantime, they demanded that she give them my British passport. According to Kathy, it took a little while for them to understand that my passport was actually with me in Switzerland. Anyway, she then explained that the friendly garage man in the same street had removed the car and placed it in his premises so, although temporary, all was now well. But that was only until I returned when I had to report to the customs department in Valencia.

Finally, the Swiss Jewellery Trade Fair ended and without any further visits to the Red Rose Club, we flew back to Valencia. On arrival, Kathy once again related as to what had occurred with the car and then said, "They will be waiting for you at the customs place tomorrow. Chris."

*

Next day I went along there and locating the office from the information desk climbed the stairs to the first floor. As the door was slightly open, I knocked and walked straight in. The place was a complete mess with files, desks and chairs scattered all over the place. In the middle of it all stood a tall, flustered looking, man of around sixty years of age. With his fresh features and white hair, he was not unlike my father in appearance. Extending my hands with wrists together, I approached him. "Well, here I am, officer."

He replaced the typewriter 'that he was holding onto a nearby desk and asked, "Who the hell are you and what do you want?"

"I'm the Englishman," I explained. "I'm here to be arrested."

"Arrested for what?" he looked genuinely puzzled.

"The British registered car parked in the Abastos neighbourhood. Aren't you going to put the handcuffs on?"

A moment's hesitation and the light dawned. "Oh, you're the one with the Mercedes."

"No, Audi," I corrected.

"Same difference," he replied. "It's now registered as a Mercedes."

Then looking down at my hands he said, "No, I'm not going to arrest you. In fact, I cannot do anything about it at the moment. You see we, or rather I, am moving offices to the Port area and look at all this." Here he waved his arm around indicating the chaos.

"How are you moving it?" I asked dropping my hands to my side.

"There's a van parked outside," he replied automatically.

I was quiet for a moment, then said, "Well, let's get on with it then."

He looked at me curiously. "You really mean that don't you?"

"Of course I do. At least it delays the nasty bit."

I picked up a couple of folding chairs. "Let's get you sorted out then we can get down to the matter concerning the Audi."

"Mercedes," he said, picking up the typewriter again and leading the way out of the office.

"Alright, Mercedes, if you say so."

It took us a good hour to load everything into the van then arranging to meet him around lunchtime where my car was now parked, he drove off and I wandered home.

"Any problem?" Kathy asked.

"Yes, my arms ache," I said and explained what had happened.

Vicente Montoya, for that was the official's name, turned out to be one of the kindest persons I have ever had the chance to meet. He arrived for our meeting armed with various documents and a roll of sticky tape and a sincere apology for being late.

"I'm sorry about this," he remarked as he stretched the tape across the windscreen of my car. "But as you are living and working in Spain you are not allowed to own a foreign registered car without importing it and paying the various taxes. So we have to 'embargo' it."

I smiled and nodded in agreement. "Actually I did know, so it is my fault entirely."

He stopped plastering tape, turned and looked me straight in the eyes. "You actually admit it?"

"Of course I admit it. Why shouldn't I admit it? It's true."

"And you are not at all angry?"

He stared at me closely not understanding, seeking an alternative motive for my admission.

"Good Lord no! Why should I be angry? I did it."

"And you are not at all angry with the person who reported you and for us doing our job?"

I smiled and shrugged. "Come on. I might be a little grieved by whoever did report me but why should I be angry at you for doing your job? In fact as an ex-policeman myself, if you didn't carry out your obligations, I would have little respect for you."

"Well," he said staring at me in disbelief, "most people call us Customs officials all the names they can think of and most of them refer to our parents."

"Possibly Sr. Montoya," I said, "but not this one."

He next produced a portable typewriter and inserting a form began banging away with two fingers. Then removing the page he turned and said, "Right, let's go and finish the rest over a couple of beers."

So over a couple of 'Aguila' beers in a nearby bar we completed the necessary forms that I dutifully signed at the same time asking what the results would be.

"Well, there will probably be a fine of around twenty-five thousand pesetas and if you pay that you can take the car out of the country."

"And if I don't pay?"

He looked a little embarrassed. "Well the customs people confiscate the car and it's auctioned."

"And that's it?"

"Yes, that's it."

"Well we had better have another couple of beers then," I said waving to the barman.

Around three weeks later I received the official fine and having decided to pay it and return the car to the UK I went down to the new Customs offices in the Port area.

The fine paid, I then had to face several flights of stairs to Montoya's office and present him with the receipt. Opening the door, I walked in and spotted him sitting at a large desk at the far end of the room, which was being actively run by around five or six other officials pounding away on typewriters and shuffling papers. When Montoya saw me he stood up, shook hands and seemed genuinely pleased to see me. More paperwork was completed and finalised by the use of an extraordinary amount of rubber stamps. Then at last, he handed me the papers liberating the car.

He next offered me his hand saying, "You know what? Apart from the Falklands and Gibraltar, you're not a bad sort for an Englishman."

Still holding his hand, I took a grip and gently pulled him from behind his desk. "Listen, everybody!" I called out to the rest of the office. There was an immediate silence as everything came to a halt. "Sr. Montoya here," I announced, looking around at the puzzled expressions before me, "has had my car. He has now had my money." I was silent for a moment then added, "And on top of all that he is complaining about the Falkland Islands and wants me, personally, to return Gibraltar!"

Of course everyone in the place fell about laughing and when the noise at last died down, I turned to Vicente and said, "For that, Mister Montoya, you can invite me to a whisky downstairs in the bar."

All present cheered and clapped shouting: "Go on Vicente. Buy him a whisky!" and "He has everything else now including Gibraltar. Why not celebrate?"

So down both of us went to the little bar situated by the gate where the customs control the traffic entering and leaving the port. It was during our conversation that I discovered that Vicente Montoya was the owner of an apartment in Siete Aguas where I was renting a small holiday apartment. So naturally, the next time were both visiting the village we met up and spent some happy hours together.

Vicente, who unfortunately is no longer with us, was wonderful company but had one failing in that he was forever apologising for what had occurred with my car. Apparently, he was certainly not accustomed to coming across people who committed misdemeanours and were not in the least angry at the law enforcers involved. That following weekend I told him that the Audi (or Mercedes) was being driven back to the UK in the next days and he thanked me for my cooperation.

*

Taking advantage of my journey to England I took along the silver collection that Edmundo, Mac and I were going to exhibit at the White House Hotel Jewellery Fair in London. At the La Junquera frontier post, I was disappointed to find that the young custom's girl was not, on this occasion, on duty. I had been looking forward to renewing our acquaintance and providing details of my car just to see the expression on her face. Completing the usual documents and then leaving the customs offices, I noticed that there was a little loose cable hanging down beneath the car. Moving round to the rear of the vehicle I placed the cases containing the jewellery samples onto the ground, walked back to the front of the car and opening the bonnet made a swift inspection. The cable did not appear to be attached to anything in particular so I closed the bonnet and I was once more on my way.

In those years, apart from in Spain, you could not buy oranges that still had their stems with a few leaves attached and I discovered that when travelling outside the country the most effective thing to use as tips in restaurants was, instead of money, mandarins or clementines, decorated with a bit of greenery. At the end of each meal, I would ask for a plate, go out to the car, remove a good quantity of fruit from the couple of sacks I carried, and return it for the service rendered. It always caused quite a stir and many were the times we were invited for an extra drink for this small detail.

It was only a couple of miles after leaving the customs post on that particular day that I was most surprised to detect the sound of fruit rolling around in the boot of the car.

"One of the sacks must have come open," I commented to myself.

Then I began to wonder why I had not noticed the noise on arrival at the frontier and it suddenly occurred to me that I just might not have replaced the jewellery cases after being distracted by the cable. I slammed on the brakes and sure enough when I opened the boot there were no cases.

"Bloody hell I must have left them outside the customs!"

Doing a swift illegal U-turn I hurtled back towards the frontier and skidding to a halt caused around four or five uniformed guards to rush out with their arms at the ready. I climbed out of the car with my hands half raised and walked over to them. Then looking beyond these nervous men to the custom's car park I could see the three cases exactly where I had left them. Nobody, in the last twenty minutes or so had taken any notice of them. I humbly apologised to the officials and explained what had happened expecting all sorts of complications in recovering the jewellery. But no, they were most sympathetic and I was allowed to walk over and collect them. The relief was such that I presented them with a selection of the mandarins and everyone was happy. After that all went well when I arrived in England and I disposed of the car, left the jewellery with Mac and returned on the coach which, to say the least, was an exacting journey. Leaving at 11:30 am from Victoria Coach Station, London, I arrived in Valencia sometime in the afternoon of the following day.

*

Edmundo and I flew over to London a few weeks later and met up with Mac for the Fair. We were exhibiting not only Edmundo's silver products but also the gold and precious stone collections from the other Valencia manufacturer. This latter collection drew the particular attention of a buyer from the Birmingham area that placed an order worth around eight thousand pounds sterling. Other orders were forthcoming but as the tendency in the UK, from that time onwards, was to manufacturer jewellery there or buy from the Far East, the event could not be termed as being a success. In fact, it turned into a disaster when the day after I arrived back Valencia I received a telephone call from Mac saying that he had stopped for a break on the way home to Leicester and on returning to his car found that it had been broken into and all the silver jewellery had been stolen. No, there was not any insurance as the premiums were not only extortionate but conditions which had to be installed like special locks and alarms etc. made it not worth the outlay. Mac went through the motions of reporting the theft and was told by the police that jewellery thieves usually waited at the end of such a Trade Fair and followed a likely target when they left for home, pouncing when the time was right.

*

Coming up to Christmas 1982 was not a happy event and was made even worse when just after this non-festive event, Mac telephoned again to announce that headlines on all the newspapers that particular day proclaimed the news that a certain Mr. Robert Clive Chatwin of Sutton Goldsmiths had visited all his shops, cleaned out all the stock and then just disappeared. Of course, amongst the items were the expensive gold sets, which we had sold him at the Trade Fair and mailed to him afterwards. Mac went on to say that, the estimated total value of the missing stock was around the three million pound mark and that the media reported, for some reason, that Chatwin was heading towards Spain, which at that time did not have any extradition agreement with the United Kingdom.

I reported the loss to our suppliers who were, naturally, not very happy with the situation. It was on the morning of the seventeenth of January that I received a telephone call to present myself immediately at the Police

Headquarters in Valencia. Chatwin had been arrested. He was recognised by one of the more observant employees at the Dimar Hotel, one of the cities better establishments.

Two charges were to be initiated against him. The first being that he had imported jewellery without paying the appropriate import duty and second, that of failing to pay the invoice for jewellery supplied by a Valencia manufacturer through Mac and myself. He had given his address as being in the Denia area, further south down the coast and was to be taken there in order to start the judicial proceedings.

Obviously it would be necessary for me, together with a representative of the jewellery manufacturer, to present ourselves at the police headquarters in Denia for the purpose of supplying a description of the gold pieces that had been sold to Chatwin in the UK. Things, I realised, were going to become very much worse, mainly as Kathy was taken ill at that time with what appeared to be pneumonia.

The day arrived for the trip to Denia and I, together with Alfonso the manufacturer's representative and samples of the gold collection, set off for this seaside resort about an hours drive away. On arrival, both British and Spanish reporters besieged us. Flash bulbs were popping cameras clicking left right and centre and I was subjected to an interview with the BBC television. We completed the formalities at the police station along with another man from Birmingham who was representing a company that had financed an exceedingly expensive motor caravan for Chatwin and was there to find out the possibilities of recuperating the finance or, at least, the vehicle. Also present were a police officer and a policewoman from Scotland Yard. Alfonso instructed me to invite these officials to lunch, which I did, and we went along to a superb fish restaurant overlooking the beach.

Before leaving the police station I asked where Chatwin was at that moment and was told that he was in one of the cells. Then, as an after thought, the official added, "He has company anyway. In the next cell is a Dutchman." I do not know what stimulated me to ask but I said, "And what is the Dutchman's name?"

"Gedo van der Weig," was the unexpected reply.

"My, God!" I thought. "I wonder what's happened to my friend."

The meal was excellent but as I was not driving began by ordering a large and very dry Martini as an aperitif. Plenty of wine was consumed and coffee afterwards with, of course, large brandies. Conversation flowed and I acted as interpreter and the two officers informed us that I would probably have to travel to Coventry, in the not-too- distant future, to identify our particular jewellery items that were mixed in with a large amount of goods that the UK police had recovered from Chatwin.

They would be in touch.

Leaving Denia for Valencia one normally travels up to the main Alicante to Valencia motorway along a straight road of around five kilometres. Alfonso was driving his old Citroen and I was crouched in the passenger seat. Feeling extremely depressed, possibly due to the amount of alcohol I had consumed, I began saying to Alfonso, "You know what? There has to be something wrong with me."

"What do you mean by that, Chris?" he asked, switching on the headlights as it was now becoming dark.

"Because everything and everyone I seem to come into contact with immediately has bad luck."

Alfonso thought a minute before replying. "Don't be silly, Chris. That's not possible."

"Bloody well is," I replied miserably thinking of what had been happening and poor suffering Kathy at home.

Then abruptly to my horror just up ahead I spotted a cyclist without any lights.   "Look out, on the right!" I shouted to Alfonso.

Alfonso swung the wheel over but not before just catching the cyclist who was propelled headlong into the ditch. Stopping the car we climbed out and went down into the ditch, which was fortunately dry, and extracted the elderly man together with his bicycle. Both, thank goodness, appeared to be undamaged. We dusted him down and the man agreed that it was his fault for not having lights displayed. We then shook hands and both of us climbed back into the car and drove on.

"There you are. I told you I was bad luck," I said after a few moments silence.

"Just a coincidence," Alfonso grunted obviously attempting to humour me.

"Bloody well wasn't," I replied belligerently, withdrawing into myself.

The flashing torchlight's of the Civil Guards waved us down as we approached the tollgate on the motorway just before Valencia.

"Let's see what happens now," I said.

My friend once again climbed out of the car and the official was soon writing out a ticket for a faulty headlight on the Citroen. It might just have been alright but Alfonso attempted to 'come to an arrangement' with the official who, in turn, became even more obstinate and increased the fine involved. My dejected companion resumed his seat behind the wheel and we drove on.

"Sorry about that," I said miserably.

Then as we accelerated away, he turned towards me. "Well for heavens sake, let's just see if we can do the last twenty kilometres without you creating another balls up. Just keep quiet!"

Kathy was not well at all and it was touch and go whether or not she be hospitalised. However, the next couple of days showed a good improvement and we all breathed a sigh of relief.

"What next?" I wondered.

It was not going to take many weeks until I found out. In the meantime two things happened. Mac telephoned me to tell me we had to present ourselves in Coventry for the identification of the jewellery we had sold to Chatwin and at the same time, I was approached by a manufacturer of small attractive barrel shaped purses made out of ostrich, crocodile and other skins. They were very presentable, I thought, and considered that there might be some sort of outlet for them in the UK.

*

So armed with samples I set off by coach once again to England. It was quite a memorable occasion for Mac and I when we visited the large hall where all the Chatwin goods were displayed. Of course, there was a strict control and most people were searched on leaving the premises. We recognised various pieces supplied by us and pointed them out to the police official who took notes.

I also noticed that there were quite a few elderly people searching, diligently, amongst all the bits and pieces on display and asked the official who they were. His reply was quite to the point. "They are customers who have taken watches, clocks, brooches, heirlooms and things to Chatwin's shops for repair and now hope that if they identify them they will be returned to them."

"What do you mean?" I asked, very much surprised. "Won't they be returned to them?"

"I very much doubt it. You see where the law is concerned a people cannot steal their own goods and if things go the way they look as though they are going, the 'Receivers' will get the lot. Then the people to whom this villain owes money will only be given so much in the pound."

"But that's terrible," I said. "So it looks as though all this, including my journey over here, could well be a waste of time?"

The man nodded in agreement. "Heartbreaking," he said.

And that is the way it was. I returned to Valencia and some two to three weeks later had a call from Mac saying that the 'Receivers' were, indeed, being awarded all that had been recovered.

To say that I felt cheated would be putting it mildly. Being deceived by a crook was one thing, but that the law should be a legal accomplice seemed to be too much. I could imagine what would be happening. There would be an auction and some well dressed, smiling, gentleman would be on the rostrum saying, "Ladies and gentleman next we have an ormolu clock that has been in the family of eighty year old Mrs. Jenkins for over a century. In all good faith she took it to a reputable jeweller to be repaired and it now rightfully belongs to us. Mrs. Jenkins was definitely the owner as we dragged her all the way over to Coventry from Wolverhampton in order to identify the article. Now do I hear a couple of pounds to start the bidding?" Of course, Mrs. Jenkins, if this valuable piece is included in your list of insured household items then you might just be able to claim through them and if not......, tough Mrs. Jenkins, you've been had!

As Mac and I were involved in this disaster, Mac thought it only reasonable that he show his face to our suppliers in Valencia. He arrived with a sample order for the small leather bags and purses that I had taken to Coventry. Apparently the company concerned sold through house-parties in the Birmingham area and was interested in handling these very attractive articles.

We had several meetings with the jewellery manufacturers about the situation and surprisingly found that they understood as to what had occurred. This animated us to seek a possible solution and one day Mac said, "Chatwin is in Alicante prison according to what you tell me." I nodded wondering what was coming. "Then what do you think about a trip down there, CJ to see what the state of play is where he is concerned?"

"Well it is only a couple of hours drive down the coast, Mac. We could try, I suppose."

As an avid reader of anything and everything, I have an enormous amount of books lying around and just before we set off, Mac was browsing through them. "Think we ought to take some reading material down there for Chatwin, CJ?"

"If you think so, Mac. What's caught your attention?"

"This one to start with," he said, sliding out a copy of Paul Brickhill's, 'Great Escapes'.

I nodded my approval. "There's also a copy of the 'Count of Monte Cristo' somewhere if you can find it. Oh, and don't forget that one called, 'They Have Their Exits' by Airey Neave, the Colditz fellow. That's really excellent. He might well be interested in that."

It was good to return to Benidorm, Spain's capital for British holidaymakers, with its ugly high-rise blocks of apartments, hotels, pubs and fun palaces. Being well out of season, we soon found an extremely comfortable hotel complete with many elderly retired British pensioners who find it less expensive to be there for three months on their pittance of a UK pension than to have to pay the high cost of living in Britain, especially where fuel expenses are involved. For a double room, without room service, (so what!), Mac and I paid around twelve English pounds for the two of us.

That evening we left most of the guests playing Bingo and hit the town visiting various places I had known during my time with the Costa Blanca radio station. Naturally, everywhere we went pop music, live and piped, was blasting out and one of the evergreens, Neil Diamond's 'Sweet Caroline', seemed to be winning in several places. To Mac who had heard about, but never seen, Benidorm, the place came well up to expectations, as he gazed around in wonder at all the activity. "Alright for a visit and a bit of a laugh CJ," he commented, "but I wouldn't fancy having to spend a holiday here."

*

The Alicante prison was a solemn, low lying, clinical looking place, with the expected high-coiled wire fences, all surrounded by a dry sun baked dustbowl. It was easy to find and I had little difficulty in organising an interview with Chatwin. We were ushered into a small cubicle similar to a telephone box with a thick glass partition containing limited facilities for conversation purposes. After only a few minutes wait, Chatwin appeared. Much shorter than I had expected, having only seen him from his photographs in the press, he was a slim, fair haired, rather nondescript individual and dressed rather shabbily. The way he peered about him he obviously had great difficulties with his eyesight.

He seemed pleased to see us. In fact,, I think from the way he spoke, he would have been happy to have seen anyone at that particular time as over the previous weeks his notoriety had diminished somewhat and he was not attracting the same limelight as before from the media. After the initial introductions and explanations as to who and why we were there we then asked if he had any ideas on how our particular problem might be resolved mutually.

"Listen," he said immediately, as one who had little to do but ponder on his predicament, "I have these two charges against me. One for the importation of goods without paying Spanish customs duty, which my lawyer assures me, can be resolved and secondly the fact that your particular invoice requires settling."

Both Mac and I nodded in agreement.

"What I cannot quite make clear," he continued, "is the fact that your payment for the goods received is not due until the beginning of February, a couple of weeks away."

Again we nodded understandingly. "Well it looks as though you are not going to be in any position to be able to pay anyway," I said.

Then glancing to the left and right of himself, although I was sure he could not see more than a few of feet at the most, he said urgently, "Listen, if you are prepared to withdraw the charges against me for non-payment of your invoice, I will tell you where, in the Pyrenean Mountains, I have buried a large quantity of precious stones."

Mac and I stared at each other in astonishment at this unexpected turn of events. For a moment we were both speechless. Then, just as I was about to question him for more information on the subject there was a hammering on the door and a young lanky haired man dressed in an expensive looking suit complete with white shirt and tie, came barging in. "Who the hell are you?" he demanded without any preamble.

I explained who we were and that we were there to help his client.

"Help my client!" he shouted almost choking on his words. "Help my client! But it is you who put him in here in the first place!"

I was about to offer further explanations when he stuck his head out and called "Guard! Guard! Come and remove these people."

The guard appeared and after some discussion, the man shrugged his shoulders and explained that it was the prisoner's choice as to whether or not he received visitors, no matter who they might be.

Both Mac and I realised then that we were wasting our time and thanking Chatwin we took our leave. Depositing the books with the man at the main gate we hung around waiting. After awhile the lawyer drove out in an immaculate new Mazda sports car. Skidding to a halt and leaving the engine running, he leapt out of the car and continued his tirade against both of us. I let him rattle on until he had run out of steam then, when he had quietened down somewhat, I deliberately yawned realising that it was obvious the man was a young state lawyer, representing a client who was not in any position to pay any fees. "I hope you know where the goods are buried because only an idiot with a thirsty beast like that you're driving would work for nothing." Then turning to Mac I said, "Come on let's get back to Benidorm, at least we can listen to 'Sweet Caroline'."

On the return journey, Mac was grumbling about the young lawyer's attitude until I commented, "Don't worry, Mac. Now he has been in contact with us he won't last long if things continue as they have been over the last few years."

And so it was. Only a couple of days after our visit it was reported in the Valencia newspapers that Chatwin had dismissed that particular legal representative. Mac returned to England and Kathy recuperated sufficiently to carry on teaching, at the same time managing to find a position as part-time English teacher at a local academy. I had some classes to help but was more than happy when for no particular reason I became involved in ceramics.

Chapter 16

It was the Moors first introduced the potter's wheel and the pottery industry into the Iberian Peninsula. Their base at that time was Malaga in Andalusia (originally Al-Andalus). Several centuries later they were eventually expelled by the Catholic Kings with Jaume I, liberating Valencia in the year 1238. Around that time two very enterprising men, El Conde de Carlet and Baron de Hervas, decided that the ceramic industry should be brought from its place of origin to the Valencia community and settled in the two small villages of Manises and Paterna. Their reasoning was based on the fact that this was where an abundance of natural resources provided ideal conditions for producing such sought after products.

And so it was in Manises that I came into contact with Grupexma, a company representing several ceramic and porcelain manufacturers for the purpose of exporting their products. The company secretary, a young and very dedicated Valencian, Pepe Esteve, had somehow got hold of our telephone number and called one evening to ask if he could be taught the English language in three weeks as he was off to a Trade Fair in Dallas, Texas, USA, in order to promote their products. He asked if I had ever heard of Dallas and I confirmed that my geographical knowledge did indeed stretch that far, even if it might have come about through a popular television series. I also mentioned that Kathy had relations living in Texas. Naturally, I went on to say that the amount of English he would learn in such a short period of time would not be of any value as regards negotiating at any Trade Fair.

"Then what do you advise me to do?" he asked.

"Look, Pepe," I explained, "you have a choice. One is that you use the services of an interpreter when you arrive and as they are professional people they are very expensive, or secondly you take somebody with you. But," I added, "that does not mean that I personally am looking for a trip to America." He was silent for a moment then said that he would consult with his employers and rang off.

Two days later he telephoned once more and asked that if Grupexma paid my fare would I be willing to stay with Kathy's family and help at the fair.

"No problem," I smiled to myself. "However I wouldn't like the one hour flight to and from Dallas each day."

"What are you talking about, Chris? You said that you had family in Texas."

"I do but their place is a one hour flight away from Dallas."

"Impossible! It's in the same state and can't be that far."

"Listen," I said patiently, "whether you believe it or not Texas is around the same size as Spain and possibly more so."

"Impossible!"

"Alright Pepe, just check it out and then call me back," I replied and hung up.

I learned later that they did find an English speaking Spaniard who was also visiting the Fair and came to an arrangement with him. It was several weeks later that I spoke to Pepe after had returned and although his geographical knowledge had improved his impression of America had deteriorated somewhat.

"I almost starved to death," he told me seriously. I could not believe my ears. Then he went on to say that there was no way he could find rice or a decent 'tortilla' anywhere. In fact he said that although he lived in Manises where Valencia's airport is located, when the plane landed on the return journey he went straight into the airport cafeteria and ordered some 'real' food.

"Ah, well," I thought "so it is not just the British holiday makers who long for their fish and chips and nice cups of tea!"

*

So with Mac's help I put out some faxes, posted catalogues and received a reply from a Birmingham based company who said that their representative a Mr.Tony Fabian would be travelling by car from Plymouth to Santander, arriving on such and such a day and would I be so kind as to meet him. I replied that it would be no problem and a little while afterwards received a telephone call from Tony Fabian himself, who had a distinct London accent and an obvious sense of humour. He reminded me of the time the ferry was to arrive and I promised I would be there. It was at that particular time I was just recovering from a bad dose of influenza, not feeling well and without transport.

"They said he was coming by car anyway," commented Kathy, "So if you feel up to it you can go by train or coach to meet him."

I confirmed that I would, hopefully, be in a reasonable healthy condition by then as it was to be the following week. Not exactly sure of what type of pottery he was looking for I checked the commercial directory containing all the Spanish manufactures' names and details and found that there was a very large manufacturer of terracotta pots not that far from San Sebastian in the same Northern region where Tony was arriving. I then booked a coach to Madrid and from there a train to Santander.

*

I will never forget the train journey from Madrid. There was still a lot of snow blanketing the countryside and sitting comfortably in a well heated carriage looked out onto enchanting Christmas-card-type scenery with mountains and small isolated farms scattered here and there. It seemed almost unreal, particularly as everything was bathed in bright sunshine with clear blue skies overhead.

I arrived at the Port in Santander as the ferry pulled in and immediately recognised Tony Fabian as he drove down the ramp in a huge shooting-brake.

"Hello, Tony!" I said walking up to the car as he climbed out. "I'm Chris."

He shook my hand, nodded then asked, "How the hell did you know it was me?"

Wearing an easy smile with a beaky nose and dressed in an ankle length leather overcoat, he looked puzzled.

"Easy," I replied, "You look like a bit of a 'Chancer'."

"What do you mean by that?" he asked.

"Nothing really," I explained, immediately regretting that I had referred to him in a somewhat detrimental term. "I mean anyone who is prepared to make this trip in the hope of sourcing something worthwhile must be taking some sort of chance." He nodded, not entirely convinced but let it drop.

That night we stayed in San Sebastian and the following day called at the terracotta factory I had found in the Rioja area. No, it was not what he was actually looking for. I breathed a sigh of relief because if it were ceramics he was after then Manises would be the ideal place. So on return to Valencia the following days were spent visiting various factories in that area and after almost a week of furious activity, Tony left with his car packed full of samples, mainly from the Grupexma Company. It was not long after that an order was placed for a container load and this time I felt that things might just be taking a turn for the better.

*

By way of celebrating this good news Kathy, Samantha and I visited several car dealers and elected to buy a small, second, third or fourth hand, red Seat 127. This was done by committing ourselves to signing 'Letras' or promissory notes.

We had the car for around three to four weeks, when one night at about four o'clock in the morning there was a ring at the door. I opened it to find a local policeman standing there.

"Yes?" I asked, still befuddled by sleep.

"Do you own a red Seat 127 car?"

I nodded.

"Where was it last parked?"

"Downstairs. Outside in the street. Why?"

"Well it's not there now," he explained. "It was stolen and the thief crashed it into a bridge just up the main road. We found your papers in the glove compartment. The boy is in a pretty bad way but the fire brigade has cut him out of the wreckage and he is now in hospital."

"So what do I do now?" I asked, not quite knowing how to react to this.

"Go down to the local police station immediately and fill in the forms reporting the car as stolen."

I nodded and for something else to say, asked, "Who is he, anyway?"

"Sorry Sir. Not allowed to divulge those details. After all he is the 'Presunto' or 'Presumed' thief."

"What do you mean? The man is trapped in the wreckage of my car, under a bridge, and it might not have been him who stole it?"

"Quite so," he smiled condescendingly as though explaining something to an idiot. "The judge will no doubt tell us whether he did or didn't do it. Anyway, it is not up to us."

I shook my head. It was unbelievable. Thanking him I made to close the door.

"Oh and by the way, Sir."

"Yes?"

"We have notified the tow truck company and the vehicle will be taken to the municipal breaker's yard."

"Breaker's yard?"

"Afraid so, Sir. It's a complete write off."

He moved to go then turned again.

"One other thing, the tow truck will cost around eight thousand pesetas and the payment is your responsibility."

"Naturally," I said, "it would be, wouldn't it?"

Resignedly I dressed and walked down to the 'Comiseria' to make a statement. On signing the document I asked once again why it was that I could not know any details of the person trapped in my car. Not that it was important, but I was still curious.

"Definitely not allowed, Sir," replied the official, emphasising his words by forcefully tapping the desk with his biro pen. "After all we have the responsibility of protecting him, don't we? I mean some people become very angry when they have their cars stolen and smashed up."

"Do they really?" I asked, sarcastically. "Absolutely amazing. I wonder why?"

The car was, as I had been warned, a complete write off and after paying the for the tow truck we continued honouring our promissory notes for the non-existent vehicle. The insurance on such an old car was not worth being fully comprehensive and the company was not interested in any type of action until the culprit was brought to justice; whoever this protected species he might be.

*

Some weeks afterwards, a telegram arrived to say that I was required to present myself at the courts on the following day for the trial. Kathy and I went along and were introduced to the very young, very fresh faced, state lawyer. His thick framed horn rimmed glasses, which I suspected were just for decoration, gave him an owlish, studious, appearance. He had been assigned to represent the 'Presumed' delinquent who, he informed me, making it sound as though I was the reason for his client's situation had apparently spent some time in intensive care after the accident.

"I really don't understand why you want to do this to my client," he said suddenly out of the blue. "Why don't you just withdraw the charges and let us all go home?"

"Not a bad idea at all," I replied, becoming irritated. "In fact, I think it is a very good idea. Tell you what, just pay me back the tow truck fee and take over the promissory notes on the car and we will do just that. Go home."

"But that's crazy!" he said as though discovering that he was talking to a complete moron.

"So are you if you think I am going to walk away from this," I replied, my temper rising. "Where is he anyway? We have been here around an hour or more and nothing has happened."

He turned and glanced towards the door as though expecting the offender to stroll in, then said, "I was told that he's in prison in Segovia and the Civil Guards are bringing him along."

And so we waited for nearly another hour when finally the lawyer disappeared into an inner office returning some minutes later to say, "They have postponed it. We can go now and they will notify us."

"You mean that whoever 'they' are could not even come out and tell us?" Another 'you poor idiot' look and, "Don't be silly. It is up to us to ask."

*

Several more weeks went by and again we received a further telegram instructing me to present myself the following day. Kathy and I arrived at the appointed hour and together with the young lawyer, joined a crowd of people who were milling around the small waiting area next to the courtroom. There were quite a few police officials present; probably there to testify as witnesses or to take advantage of the air conditioning as it was considerably more than just hot outside.

Every now and again from within the court an official would appear and shout out the names of the people who were required for the next hearing. Once he appeared and called out that all the police present were to take a note of what the judge had just issued. It was an order to seek and arrest a certain Juan Garcia Martinez. This was then followed by a description of the wanted man. The police officials present nodded seriously with some of them producing pens and scribbling furiously on pieces of paper. The man standing next to Kathy raised his hand.

The court official glanced across at him and said loudly, "If you have any questions talk to your lawyer."

"But!" insisted the man as all eyes turned towards him.

"But nothing," replied the official. "Just talk to your lawyer!"

He then turned and moved to go back into the court but not before our neighbour had shouted after him, "I haven't got a lawyer and anyway, I think it's me that you're looking for!"

Immediately we were pushed aside as three or four uniforms dived onto the individual possibly thinking that he just might change his mind and make a run for it. Kathy and I were in hysterics but most people around us seemed to treat it as being normal.

I turned to the lawyer and asked, "So, where is our man?"

"In prison in Segovia. The Civil Guards will be bringing him."

Nearly two hours later no one had appeared and yet again home we went. This very same situation occurred again several weeks later with exactly the same results. Then, when I was away from home towards the end of July, a further telegram arrived and Kathy went down to the court.

"Where is the complainant?" she was asked by the woman secretary.

"Complainant, not victim?" thought Kathy.

"That's really democratic justice," she said.

"He should be here!" insisted the woman ignoring the comment.

"Well he isn't," replied Kathy. "But I am. What is it you want?"

The woman pushed a form across the desk and explained. "We need his signature to say that he will attend court in October."

"But that is ridiculous!" Kathy was exasperated. "We keep coming down here on your instructions and absolutely nothing happens. Now you want a signature to make sure that we will be here so nothing can happen again. Right?"

"Well, it is not quite like that, really." The woman appeared a little upset that someone was actually criticising the system.

"I'll sign," said Kathy, taking the pen and scribbling her signature.

The woman became even more disorientated. "You can't do that!"

"I've already done it and if it takes as long as this to bring a thief to court, then it will be a lifetime before I'm convicted of signing for someone else."

She then marched out.

*

October arrived as, surprisingly, did the expected telegram and once again we go along to the court. It was becoming a complete farce. We now recognised many of the faces there and were on nodding terms with quite a few of them. I was beginning to feel as though we belonged to some sort of club for lost causes.

"Is whoever he is, here then?" I asked the lawyer who was not, in the least, perturbed by the situation.

"Coming from prison in Segovia …!"

"I just don't believe all this," I said cutting him short. Then pushing him aside I walked through into the inner office where I found a male secretary about to bite into a huge 'bocadillo'.

"Good day, Señor" I began politely.

He looked up obviously annoyed at my sudden appearance at this crucial point in his days work.

"It's about this delinquent who is supposed to be coming from Segovia prison," I explained.

"Oh, that one." The man was now smiling. "Well we have some news for you."

"Really? That's something." I was beginning to feel better already.

"Yes. We found out this morning that he is not in prison in Segovia. In fact he never was in prison in Segovia."

I was flabbergasted, almost at a loss for words. "Well, what gave you the idea he was?" I eventually managed to croak.

"His mother," said the man, cheerfully examining the contents of his 'bocadillo'.

"His mother?" I repeated realising I was very much losing the plot. "What has his mother got to do with all this?"

"Well," explained the secretary, slowly and precisely, so that there would be no misunderstanding on my part. "Some months ago we telephoned his mother."

"So?"

"Well," we asked her where her son was and she said that a postcard had arrived from him with a picture of Segovia on it."

I nodded wondering what was coming next.

"His mother then said that she supposed he was in prison there."

It was mind-boggling. "And you actually believed her?"

The man's expression changed and he glared up at me. "Of course we believed her," he said through a mouthful of tuna fish, as though I were a complete imbecile. "After all, if his own mother doesn't know where he is, who the hell does?"

Taking a very deep breath I said slowly," I wish to speak to the judge, please."

"You can't do that. Impossible!"

"Listen," I leaned towards him over the desk close enough to catch the smell of tuna fish emanating from his roll. "I am going to stand right here until I speak to the judge. Alright? And please don't talk about throwing me out because I've been through all this before."

He nodded reluctantly, stood up and then taking two steps towards another office door he suddenly stopped, returned quickly, removed his roll from the desktop and placed it in one of the drawers as though I might be tempted.

Eventually the judge, of no more than around thirty-five years, did appear and I reiterated all that had happened, finishing up by asking him what we were going to do about it. He was quiet for a moment, and then said, "We forget about the accused and hold the trial anyway. I'll tell the court secretary we will be in the courtroom next."

And so it was. Within twenty minutes all of us, minus the culprit, were seated in the small courtroom. I was then asked to take the stand.

"Will you mind explaining what happened?" the judge asked me.

Again I was at a loss for words. "It was a long time ago your Honour. I cannot even remember the registration number of the car." Then thinking quickly I said, "It is all in the statement I made at the time."

The judge then shuffled through the papers in front of him, selected one which might have been anything and said, "So you agree with this?"

"Yes your Honour, I agree."

Next he asked, "Have you any questions or comments?"

Looking around the court I said precisely, "Only that if the 'Presumed' could have known how to drive we might still have a car."

"Objection!"

The young lawyer leapt to his feet in true Perry Mason style. Then pausing until all eyes were on him he then said, "My client does know how to drive. Although my client, admittedly, has a record for driving away nineteen cars, he has never had an accident!

Also," he continued, pointing an accusing finger in my direction, "my client will no doubt be taking action against this man for owning a car with faulty brakes."

"Right," called the judge, banging his gavel enthusiastically, "sentence will be pronounced at a later date. We can all go."

I stepped down feeling more like Alice in Wonderland each minute. It was totally unreal.

*

The following day I was onto my lawyer explaining what had occurred. His comment was, "With this new democracy there is nothing to stop the man taking action against you for faulty brakes. If he wants to that is."

"But that is ridiculous and you know it!" I exploded. "The car was bought from an official dealer only three weeks before and everything had been checked."

His voice came back patiently over the phone, "I know, Chris. But he can still take action."

"And if he does what then?"

There was a brief silence then he replied, "Well these days anything could happen. If they found something it could be a fine and there again it might even be a prison sentence."

"A what?"

"A prison sentence."

This was becoming even more unreal and I conjured up a vision of the judge shouting, "Off with his head!"

A short silence then, "Could be, Chris."

"So what do we do?"

"Well you can talk to your car dealer and ask him for written confirmation that all was in order when he sold you the car. Then we go down to the court and make a statement, deposit the evidence there and that should stop anything else happening."

Then something occurred to me when he said, "We go down to the court," and I asked, "How much will all this cost?"

"Well you will need me with you at the court. So I reckon ….., around thirty thousand pesetas."

"Thirty thousand pesetas. But that is over one hundred pounds."

Then thinking quickly I said, "I'll do it myself!"

"You can't, Chris."

"I can't? What do you mean, I can't?"

"The court will not accept a statement without a lawyer being present: Spanish law."

I thought about that one for a moment, then making my mind up said, "OK, I will still go down there on my own and if there is any argument because you're not present then I will make my own statement saying that I would be happy to elect a prison sentence."

"You can't be serious, Chris?"

"Bloody well am. If they want to play games so can I. And if they do put me inside when I send a postcard to the judge he will know exactly where I am!"

The court offices were crowded when Kathy and I presented ourselves. It was stifling hot as the air conditioning had failed and all the windows were open.

"Look at that," said Kathy, pointing over to an unoccupied desk near one of the windows.

A sharp breeze had sprung up and official looking papers of all sorts and types had begun swirling around, eventually taking to the air with most of them flying out through the window. It was sometime before anyone decided to take action to stop it but nobody seemed worried that there could well be even more complications at a later date.

The lady secretary looked up as we came up to her desk. "Buenos dias. Can I help you?"

I explained what the situation was and presented her with my documents together with the written statement from the car dealer as to the care brakes.

"And where is your lawyer?" she asked glancing over my shoulder as if he might be hiding somewhere.

"Can't make it, Señora. And anyway all this happened to me, not my lawyer."

"But I can't accept this without your lawyer being present."

"Possibly," I said. "So if you cannot accept it then I would like to sign to the effect that in the event of anything else happening I would be quite happy to receive a prison sentence."

Her mouth opened but no sound came out. Then in a strangled voice she asked, "You what? You want to sign for a prison sentence?"

"That is correct," I confirmed adding, "If necessary, that is."

She continued to stare at me and then asked, "Who is your lawyer?"

I presented her with one of his cards and still in a daze she picked up the telephone and dialled. When she eventually replaced the receiver some minutes later, I asked, "Everything all right?"

She nodded, held out her hand and I passed the papers over. "Yes. He just told me you were mad and it was best that I accept the papers anyway!"

And so that was that. We never did find out who the 'Presumed' was. And neither were we notified by the court as to the sentence involved or even if the judge had decided that the person who the fire brigade had cut out from the wreckage of my car had actually been driving it at the time. Could be that the documents had flown out of the window the next time the air conditioning had broken down.

Chapter 17

It was Friday lunchtime and as usual everything was slowing down in anticipation of the coming weekend. I was looking forward to lazing around on the beach or a little adventurous visit to the mountains around an hours drive inland. Then Mac telephoned.

"Hello, CJ?" He greeted me formally. "Which do you want first? The good news or the bad news."

"Go ahead, Mac. Whatever it is I'm not in the least surprised."

"Well, CJ, the company that does the house parties wants to carry the whole line of purses, bags and some of the jewellery sets."

"That sounds pretty good news to me, Mac," I replied, feeling just that little bit better.

"Well, if you can get hold of a good cross-section of these, then they want to present them at the next meeting when all the female agents are present."

"Go on. No problem, Mac. Just tell me where and when this meeting is?"

"That's the bad news CJ. They say the things have got to be there by Monday afternoon in Coventry or, according to their MD, it is a case of we forget it."

I sighed, wondering how I was going to sort this one out. "OK, Mac. Just leave it with me and I will come back to you 'pronto'."

First I telephoned the purse and bag manufacturer to be told that he could have everything I wanted ready for the following day. "Well, that's one problem solved," I thought, breathing a sigh of relief.

Next I checked on flights only to find that there were no seats available for London that weekend and if there had been the prices were astronomical. Then I thought about the coach that ran from Valencia direct to London and took around twenty-four hours. So I telephoned the information office at the coach station only to be told that the weekend coach had already left that same Friday morning.

"What else is available?" Anything for tomorrow afternoon?"

"Nothing," came back the reply.

"Is there nothing at all heading that way?" I persisted, "There has to be something."

After a couple of minutes the voice said, "The only thing going in that direction is a coach to Lyon in France, but that is still well South of Paris."

"When and what time does it arrive in Lyon?"

"Midday on Sunday. That's the day after tomorrow."

"Book me a seat," I said immediately, not having the slightest idea what was going to happen when I arrived in Lyon but knowing damn well that something would. So   Saturday afternoon saw me at the coach station with a suitcase containing the purses and bags together with a fair selection of silver jewellery samples.

*

Midday on the Sabbath in Lyon there was little or nothing doing. In fact I likened it to what Edinburgh might look on a flag day. At the coach station enquiry desk I was politely informed that there were definitely no coaches to Paris until the following morning. I wandered off and not having any French francs found the nearest hotel and changed my pesetas. The next stop was the railway station which was not difficult to find. There they told me that there was, indeed, a train to Paris. The not so good news turned out to be that there were only first class seats available. However a quick calculation of my financial situation made it possible to book a ticket. Sigh of relief again.

The train was the high speed TGV. This, in itself, was a pleasing experience. Just to relax, stretch out my legs in a comfortable swivel chair that enabled me to watch the countryside fly by on whichever side took my fancy. It was non-stop to Paris and we arrived in around two hours.

*

Sometime in the not-so-distant past I remembered someone mentioning that there was a coach called the 'Magic Bus' or something similar that left 'Les Invalides' Paris for London once or twice a week. With this in mind I caught the metro over there and coming across a sign that read 'British

Airways' I assumed that this just might be the place where, at least, they had some information.

Female airline employees seem to come out of that 'something special' category and the tall slim, elegant, girl with swept back blonde hair and beautiful, deep green, eyes was certainly of no exception.

"Good afternoon, Sir." She smiled and gave me the benefit of a set of gleaming white teeth that would send any normal dentist climbing up the wall.

"Well ….," I began nervously and went on to ask about the possibility of a coach that might be leaving that neighbourhood for London. Her expression changed, but just a little.

"Coach?" she asked, obviously not accustomed to such enquiries. "This is a British Airways booking office. We have flights to the UK. In fact there is one tonight but nothing in the coach line, as far as I know, for London or anywhere else for that matter."

She smiled condescendingly, as if in compensation for the lack of such knowledge. I went weak at the knees. "Sorry, but I cannot afford the normal air fare. If there is no coach then perhaps you might be kind enough to help me find a train?"

"A train?"

"Yes, a train. There must be a train somewhere."

Before she could reply to that one the door opened and a second stunning girl appeared and went purposefully behind the counter at the same time saying, "Hi Josie! I'll take over now whenever you wish." And so saying she disappeared into an inner office. "Hi!" returned Josie and then turned to me again. "Look, I really am very sorry. I would love to help but …."

"It was," I thought, "time to bring out the big guns."

"I'm sure you would," I interrupted. "So please Josie, would you mind awfully telephoning the Gare Saint-Lazare, or wherever, to find out if there is a train? It's not a lot to ask."

Her expression hardened. "And what makes you think I will do that?"

"Because," I replied putting on my best smile and slowly producing several sample jewellery sets from my pocket as a magician might do, then laying them out in a neat row on top of the counter, "I have here matching earrings, necklaces and bracelet sets with genuine semi precious-stones. So Josie, when you make the phone call the choice is all yours," Here I raised my hand before she could answer, "and, if you are not in too much of a hurry, when your colleague takes over, I would just love to invite you for an after-work drink at the little bar across the road." Not that I had noticed any little bar across the road but I was sure there must be one somewhere near. There always is in Paris.

She hesitated and the semi precious stones responded helpfully seemingly to glisten encouragingly in the office lighting. Just a slight hesitation and she reached for the phone. A little later, after examining all of them, she selected a set with green emeralds.

"Just right to match your lovely eyes," I commented gallantly.

The train, she confirmed, would leave Paris at twelve o'clock that night and arrive in London next morning. I breathed a sigh of relief. I should be able to make Coventry around midday. So Josie and I spent a very pleasant hour chatting over drinks at that nearby bar.

"You know what?" she giggled after her second Martini. "I must be the first BA girl to organise a train booking!" Then for a brief moment she became serious. "Would you have given me the jewellery if I hadn't had any success with the phone call?"

Looking steadily into those eyes, I replied in all seriousness, "You know very well I would have done."

When we had exchanged addresses and said our "Goodbyes" I caught the metro over to the Gare Saint-Lazare and what a sight awaited me.

*

The previous day the annual Paris marathon had been held and there were a multitude of young people swarming around, about to catch the London boat train. I was thankful that Josie had, with her influence, reserved me a ticket. I climbed aboard and found that everybody in my coach had completed the twenty-five mile course and had received medals which they all proudly displayed.

There was a great festive atmosphere during the journey with considerable voices raised in song. Then one young man announced that he and his girlfriend were becoming officially engaged. It was time to delve into my pockets again and come up with an attractive engagement ring. Needless to say everyone was delighted and there was a great deal of applause as he slipped the ring onto her finger. Even today I sometimes wonder if that ring is still being worn as it was a rather special occasion.

Eventually we arrived in Calais and it did not occur to me that amongst all these casually dressed youths I, in my suit and overcoat, stood out like a sore thumb. I realised the error when I was quietly led to one side by the

French Customs officers and held back for a short time. However, after answering their questions and displaying the contents of my baggage, I was allowed to board the channel ferry and rejoin the party which was in full swing. The crossing was fine and I managed to find time to wash, shave and change, feeling very much better for the effort. The train arrived at London Victoria on time and I crossed over to the coach terminal for the last leg of my journey to where the meeting was to be held.

*

It was on boarding the coach I found myself assisting a young, rather pretty, nun with her baggage. I immediately took note that her expression and bearing exuded tranquillity as opposed to my dishevelled and harassed self. Now, extremely tired after travelling for nearly three days and feeling somewhat sorry for myself, I sank back into the seat next to her and thought about all that had occurred in the last few years. My fellow traveller appeared to be in the mood for conversation and explained that she was heading north to visit her family. After a few moments of generalities she enquired as to how I had arrived on that particular coach and I responded, as best as I could, not wishing to go into too much detail. Then suddenly for some reason she asked my name. It must have been at a moment when my thoughts were at their lowest ebb because I answered by saying, "Look, Sister. With all due respect we can talk and when we stop at one of the motorway service stations I would like to invite you for a coffee or whatever you wish. However please, please, do not ask my name because at this moment I am beginning to think that it must be Death."

I could see that she was a little more than disturbed by my reaction to a simple question so I added, "Sorry, Sister. I'm truly sorry. But that is just how I feel at present."

We did stop and we did have coffee and continued talking about nothing in particular. And so it was that on the last leg of the journey I felt, for some reason, that her just being there had helped me to unwind a little. However, she never did get to know my name and I have always thought that perhaps it was for the better.

The coach drew into the Coventry coach station at around one o'clock and I staggered off and across to the nearest pub where I ordered a pint of best bitter, relaxed even more before phoning the company.

"With all the best will in the world," I explained to Ron Jukes, the managing director, "I've got this far and I just cannot make it any further. Someone will have to collect me."

295

*

Twenty minutes later a car arrived and I was driven back to the company headquarters where I found, to my joy, Mac waiting for me. With around an hour to pass before the meeting was due to begin we discussed our presentation strategy.

Some twenty-five to thirty women were present at the actual meeting and I was aptly introduced as the 'Spanish Connection'. I said a few words about life in Valencia and what possibilities there were for the articles that I had brought along and all present seemed quite animated by this. Everything looked set for a promising future and together with Mac I had a celebration pint on the way back to his home where I was staying.

"Well what do you think, Mac?" I asked as he approved of the Marston's Pedigree pint in his hand.

"Looks alright, CJ, old chap, but if we don't soon have some luck I think we had better register FU Incorporated."

"What do you mean, Mac?"

"Well I reckon that everything we have touched so far has ended up a complete cock-up. We really have fucked up a few people, unintentionally, of course." He reached into his pocket for the usual pipe, withdrew it, and examined it fondly. "You know what CJ?"

"Yes, my fiend?"

He looked thoughtful. "We might even be able to turn this to our advantage. I mean there must be one hell of a lot of people out there that would love to see someone or other screwed up and legally. It wouldn't take much. All we would have to do is go along there and shake hands and that would be that. Instant disaster!"

"Great possibilities," I agreed, "and well worth considering, but just let's see how this operation goes, shall we? You never know, it just might work."

*

The return trip to Valencia was, surprisingly, without incident and a few days later I found myself standing outside the ceramics factory and watching this huge trailer being loaded with sixty cubic metres of ceramic flower pots together with some other attractive items from a nearby porcelain factory. As I stood there waving goodbye to the driver as he swung the vehicle north towards the UK and Birmingham I could not help believing that this part, at least, definitely looked positive.

Payment for the goods had been agreed on sixty days when the managing director of the UK. Company had flown out a week before and a meeting had taken place with the factory owners. It was all very amicable and as usual with myself translating on the part of the English director to the effect that this was to be the beginning of a long and fruitful relationship between both companies which would carry on into the future and bear fruit for all of them: all stirring stuff. Of course there was the usual wining and dining. Anyone who has acted as interpreter will appreciate that it takes considerable skill in being able to translate for several people whilst at the same time attempting to maintain pace with the consumption of the various dishes being placed before you.

It also amused me that the majority of the Valencia manufacturers who received visits from their clients always assumed that the customer would be in agreement with sampling the local dishes. Naturally in this part of Spain this would always be 'Paella' whether or not the client was in agreement. So after a morning dedicated to intensive negotiating two o'clock would come around and there would be much activity in preparing a visit to one of the local restaurants which, according to the manufacturer, made the best 'Paellas' in Valencia apart, that is, from his mother-in-law or some other member of the family.

*

It was two weeks later that Mac telephoned to say that the goods had arrived safely and apparently orders were already filtering in from B & Q and other such outlets. Good news indeed. Next I received a fax to say that a Mr. Ken Smith together with Tony Fabian would be visiting the ceramic trade fair in Valencia so accommodation was arranged and they duly arrived.

I must admit that I did enjoy acting as interpreter and Spanish agent as we visited the various stands at the exhibition. It was on the second day that we came upon a remarkable stand which was displaying a huge, eye-catching, range of ceramic money boxes and figures. They included all the Walt Disney characters, manufactured under licence, together with Popeye, Snoopy, Peter Pan, Snow White, Mickey Mouse and many others. They also had on show the exceedingly realistic busts of such famous stars as Marilyn Monroe, Clark Gable and Elvis Presley. Although none of the items were of immediate interest to my English buyers we did spend some time admiring these products. It was during the proceedings that the Spanish gentleman, who was obviously in charge of that particular stand, introduced himself as Fernando Contreras and presented me with his visiting card. Then while the others were examining the various products he went on to say that if ever I was interested in working for his company then I was to get in touch with him. The card named the company as 'Kramika'. Thanking him I carefully placed it in my wallet. Well, you never knew, did you?

*

It was around two weeks later, after my clients had departed, that I was to receive another call from Mac. "Hello, CJ. Have you shaken hands with anybody from Johnson Matthey, the merchant bankers?" he asked.

"Not that I can recall, Mac," I replied, somewhat confused. "Why, what has happened?"

"Are you sitting down? Because if not you had better do so right now."

"Come Mac give it to me straight. What's all this about Johnson Matthey?"

"Nothing much, CJ. Only that they have gone bankrupt. Down the tubes. Finished."

"So what the hell has that got to do with us?" I asked becoming a little irritated with the way the conversation was going.

"Only that the directors of our ceramic clients have all their money invested in Johnson Matthey Ltd. and as matters stand there is just no way it they can pay for that lorry load of ceramics and porcelain."

"You're joking, Mac! Tell me you're joking."

"Wish I was, CJ. But when I tell you that the receivers are in already, you'll understand the situation."

Was it possible? I just could not believe it. I groaned, "You mean there is no chance, Mac."

"Not from what they tell me. Just no chance."

"And what about the company that was interested in the purses, bags and jewellery?" I asked, thinking about my marathon journey.

"Sorry to say, CJ, but gone the same way. That company is related to this one."

My mind raced over the effort we had put in to all this and for a moment I was speechless. "I suppose they want me to break the news to the manufacturer as well, Mac?"

"It seems that way, CJ."

"Well let me think about it and I will get back to you as soon as I can."

I hung up the phone and sat down. I sure needed time to think and was certain that a stiff drink was called for. So closing the office I crossed over the road to Dolfis Bar and, ordering a large G & T, hid myself in a quiet corner and wondered what the hell I was going to do. I knew that on top of everything something like this was certainly not going to do me any good whatsoever amongst the ceramics suppliers. Also it was no good my telling our particular manufacturer that it was he who arranged payment terms. Sitting there quietly, I went over everything to do with this particular catastrophe. It was on the second or third drink that I suddenly thought of something. It was a comment that had been made to me by the MD of the company whilst he was over here in Spain. He had proudly mentioned, during one of the meetings, that he owned a villa further down the coast.

My idea might just work.

Returning to the office I composed a fax asking him if he wanted me to represent him at a possible judicial hearing in the near future. No explanations were given. I then faxed it off. The reply came back fairly quickly requesting that I clarify the matter. Off went another carefully worded reply saying that the supplier had been informed of the situation regarding the non payment of the seventeen thousand odd pounds and was considering requesting the authorities to place an 'Embargo' on his Spanish villa. What a relief when I received notification that payment had been made within two days! I could breathe again. But for how long, I wondered?

*

Collecting my commissions was not an easy matter either as most Spaniards at that time were in the firm belief that all Englishmen did not really need any money in the true sense of the word. They seemed to think that we always have quite sufficient anyway. This was aptly demonstrated some years previously when I did a translation for a Valencia Lift manufacturer.

It was a brochure and on the front page was the company name and behind this a beautiful modern looking building which gave the impression that this was the Head Office. In reality the Valencia office was situated in a block listed for condemning and located in one of the less desirable parts of the city. The building on the brochure, however, was in Germany and did not show the cars parked outside it as they were all

German registered Mercedes. Anyway, I duly translated the brochure, went along and presented it, together with my bill for around thirty pounds. As it was a Tuesday morning and the owner of the company was absent I was instructed by his secretary to telephone the following week and arrange to collect the money. I did so and was told once again that the owner was not available and would I leave it until the following week. So a further week passed and there were more excuses.

It was after almost a month that I went around to the office and marched in on the man concerned. He welcomed me and invited me to sit down. Then carefully he began. "Listen my friend. Every Tuesday I go along to the hairdressers at the Hotel Reina Victoria to have my hair cut and shampooed. I also have my nails manicured."

On saying this he placed both hands, palms down, on the desk so that I could see for myself. "This," he went on, "costs me one thousand Pesetas each visit and is, of course, very necessary to maintain my image. As an Englishman I am sure you understand that image is everything."

"What has all this to do with me?" I asked ignoring his hands.

"Well let's look at it logically, shall we?" He smiled displaying a mouth full of capped teeth. "I need the money and, well…., you don't."

I would not have minded but the man was quite sincere about it. He fully believed that I just did not need money. Well aware that I was about to blow a fuse, I just stood up and walked out.

Around seven o'clock in the morning one day the following week he was awakened by the bell ringing at his large expensive villa close to Valencia. Bleary eyed he opened the door wearing his silk monogrammed dressing gown and was immediately grabbed by the lapels and pushed up against the wall.

"Now you just listen to me, you bloody Spanish twit!" I hissed into his ear. "You might need the money for your bloody hair and poncy finger nails, but I need the money for simple things such as eating. Now are we going to settle this thing now or do I have to tell the German company that you are using their place on your publicity?"

He was struggling like a fish out of water.

"And," I added nastily, "perhaps you would like me to phone the tax office to tell them that you have paid me a sum of money without declaring it to them?"

It was the last bit that struck home. He stopped struggling and his eyes opened even wider. At that moment I heard a woman's voice calling from upstairs asking if everything was alright. I released him sufficiently for him to answer saying that all was fine and it was just a friend that had called around to collect something.

Following him into the villa I watched as he counted out the money. When it was all on the table I said, "I was thinking of having my hair done and a manicure this week. What day did you say, Tuesday? We could all have a fine chat there couldn't we; especially in the hotel bar afterwards with all your friends around."

Quickly, he added the equivalent of ten pounds and pocketing the money I patted him on a manicured hand and took my leave. "Now, that was pretty painless wasn't it?"

It was just a little while after that I decided to present myself at Kramika and see what Fernando had to offer. I thought that at least there I would have a regular salary for as long as mine and, of course, their luck lasted.

*

This factory was also near to Manises in a village called Quart de Poblet and compared to most of the surrounding places, a very modern building. Fernando welcomed me into his office and we talked with a lot of my attention wandering over to the enormous crocodile skin that stretched right across one wall, almost covering it completely. We discussed, then agreed on terms and I was escorted around the place and introduced to various people with whom I would be working. It was a pleasant, open-plan office, light and airy and my desk was situated close to the window where, although the view was not anything special, it suited me fine. I settled in happily as Export Manager and began making as many contacts as possible, including of course, Mac, to whom I shipped various samples that I knew would interest him. It was very pleasant working there and for the first time in a long while I was able to live a reasonably normal life.

*

One incident I recall with clarity whilst I was there was the story of Elena Valero. Still in those pre-Common Market days, I picked up the newspaper on morning to read that this young Valencia girl had contracted an eye disease which had left her with very little vision in one eye and was now threatening her other eye. This lovely, bright, eleven year old child, whose smile seemed to be directed straight at me from the pages of the 'Levante' newspaper, would soon be totally blind unless treatment was forthcoming.

From a poor background, her parents had taken her to a, supposedly, world famous eye surgeon in Barcelona. After paying an exorbitant fee for the examination and consultancy they were informed that an operation to save the one eye was possible. The cost, they were told, would be in the region of three thousand pounds. This was followed by the simple statement that no money added up to any operation. Just that.

So at that time in Valencia everything possible was being done in order to raise the finance for Elena and I, for my small part, wrote to the Moorfield's Eye Hospital in London explaining the situation and requesting their help. At the same time I pestered Fernando at Kramika into letting me have quantities of ceramic money boxes and figures that the quality control department had deemed as 'substandard' and therefore classed as 'seconds'. After this I visited all local bars and restaurants explaining the situation and asking them to help. Then, leaving them with quantities of these figures, I promised to call back and collect any resulting donations.

The Dolfis Bar was particularly enthusiastic and managed to raise quite an amount of money. Other sympathisers to the cause organised a pop concert with various local groups and singers participating. Moorfield's Hospital replied expressing their sincere sympathy and explained that they received such requests for help from all over the world, particularly from third world countries.

They went on to say that little could be done until Spain was fully integrated in the EEC. I, personally, was not unduly worried at this news as I could see myself and Elena, as a last resort, sitting in the reception area of this prestigious London Hospital with the British media present, refusing to move until some arrangement was reached. Fortunately this was not necessary and the ending was a happy one. With the publicity received by the surgeon, together with the money which had been raised, he had finally agreed to operate.

Now, somewhere today there is a woman of nearly thirty years who would never have seen what you and I take for granted on a daily basis. To me it was impossible to believe that anyone could take a decision to evaluate a child's eyesight on any monetary scale, particularly in a European country that was only fifteen years from the twenty-first Century.

*

Kramika's next trade fair held in Valencia was, apart from sales, to bring further adventures for me. The display on the exhibition stand looked attractive and there were very few visitors who could pass by without stopping to look or, at least, glance at the array of magical, brightly coloured figures on display. One such person strolled onto the stand and stood examining the realistic bust of Elvis Presley. Fernando nudged me and said quietly, "Looks English to me. You're department."

I wandered over and stood discreetly to one side while the man took in all angles of Elvis's features. A little taller than myself with tight wiry hair bunched back almost to the collar of his expensive looking suit, he moved quietly around with a rather puzzled expression on his youthful face. Eventually, he acknowledged my presence by turning and saying with a very English accent, "Buenos dias."

"Good day," I replied.

His face broke into a smile as he fully turned to face me. "You're English then?"

"Right, that is correct I am English. Chris Wright and originally from Leicester."

I stuck my hand out and received in return a strong, firm grip.

"Tony," he said, "Tony Strodder, from the Leeds, Bradford area."

"Well Tony, what do you think of Elvis's head?" I nodded towards the bust.

He was quiet for a minute. "Must have been in his earlier years," he said. "He looks quite slim."

I nodded in agreement and waited.

"Not really in my line, but might have a market. How much is he?"

I consulted the price list.

"Hmmm," said Tony. "Not very cheap is he?"

"I've never known a 'King' come cheap anywhere," I replied and we both laughed.

After that we went on to look at other articles whilst I answered questions as to how I had come to be in Valencia. Tony it, turned out, ran his own business which involved the supplying of Christmas stockings filled with gifts for the seasonal market. He also bought inexpensive plastic toys for the UK market from one of Spain's largest manufacturer's, Shambers, situated in Valencia. These toys were supplied on Tony's own cards with the words, 'Have a nice play!'

Yes, he was quite correct in that Elvis's head did not really fit into his line of business but we both later decided that Elvis did play a part in the establishing of a friendship and new member to FU Inc. that has now lasted over many years. Tony was staying at a hotel close to my apartment and one evening I was invited along for dinner. Afterwards we walked around my neighbourhood and he fell for the lively atmosphere in the bars with their tremendous variation of 'tapas'. Naturally, I introduced him to my friends and acquaintances and he felt quite at home.

Whilst we were drinking in one particular place, I was approached by an acquaintance that lived nearby. I had spoken to him on a few occasions and knew him as David. He had been employed at the Paris Opera House as a dressmaker for some years and was now living in Valencia. In fact, everyone in the area knew him. Actually it was impossible to miss him as he had distinct Chinese features and sported a perfectly groomed head of natural ginger coloured hair.

"Hello Chris," he said, as he came up to Tony and me. "May I speak to you for a moment?"

"Certainly," I said. "No problem. Is something the matter?"

Reaching into his pocket he produced a passport and handed it to me. I saw Tony's eyes widen as he took in the beautiful, slender, fingers with their pink varnished nails and the long eyelashes as he smiled at us. "Look," David explained, "as you see I am, in fact, Spanish."

Glancing at the document I saw that he was, by birth, a Spanish National.

"So what is the problem, David?"

"Well, it is like this. Everywhere I travel I come to the frontier control points and every single time they ask me, "And from where have you stolen this passport?"

"And?" I said smiling, as I could imagine any frontier control, apart from London, would be well surprised to the arrival of a Spanish Chinese with natural red hair.

"Well, Chris, tomorrow I'm flying to London and wondered whether or not you know if they have any Spanish speaking personnel at the airport there as I am sure to have problems?"

"Don't worry," I said, returning the document, "I'm sure that you won't have any problems. But if you do they are bound to have a Spanish speaking official on hand."

He thanked me and flashing a shy smile at Tony, left us.

Having seen the amount of unusual characters passing through immigration at London Heathrow I was certain that David, even with his unusual appearance, would not have too many difficulties. However, the next time I was to see him, he confirmed that he had been detained at the airport and that it was sometime before an interpreter had been found.

"They were very kind," he admitted, "but would insist on bring me cups of that awful tea."

The following day Tony appeared on the stand at the fair looking rather bleary eyed. He noticed me eyeing him rather oddly and said, "Nothing to do with last night's festivities. It's just that my room at the hotel faces that busy street and they are repairing the road."

"What at night?" I was amazed, knowing that council workers anywhere are just not inclined to take such extreme measures.

"No, of course not," he continued rubbing his eyes. "It's just that there is a bloody big hole there and as yesterday was Friday the workers simply covered it with a huge sheet of metal. Now every time a car, bus or whatever goes over it, there is this awful clanking noise and it is keeping me awake. I've tried moving rooms but the place is full."

"Don't worry, I'll fix the problem," I said wondering how I was going to arrange this one.

That day we visited other possible suppliers and after another pleasant evening out Tony returned to his hotel and I went home. It was around two o'clock in the morning that I visualised my new friend on the point of dropping off to sleep but each time being awakened by the noise of vehicles passing over the metal sheet covering the hole. So   picking up the phone I called the police headquarters and explained the situation saying that I was a neighbour and was being kept awake by the clanking noise.

"Sorry," was the reply that I had anticipated, "but today is Saturday and nothing can be done until Monday."

"I think it will be," I returned slowly but significantly.

"And just exactly what do you mean by that?" demanded the voice.

"Well," I explained, "it seems that several of the neighbours are just about to go down and move the thing away and underneath there is a bloody great hole around two metres deep."

A moment's silence as the man digested the implications and then the voice pleaded, "Please just tell them to hang on for thirty minutes. I'll get someone along immediately!"

"Don't know what happened," said Tony the following day, "but they came along and fixed that bloody noise last night. I'll never complain about Spanish inefficiency again."

I smiled to myself visualising the panic I must have caused.

Two days later Tony returned to England but not before asking me if I would be prepared to consider myself as his agent in Spain. I immediately agreed as I could see no confliction with the arrangement I had with Kramika.

*

One day I received another call from one of my friends at the Valencia Chamber of Commerce. He wanted to know if I was interested in helping an Englishman who was keen to buy textiles. Now this was definitely something different. So I agreed to meet the man concerned who was staying at one of Valencia's more reputable hotels.

Impeccably dressed in an immaculate pin striped suit with his greying curly hair cut to perfection, Ian looked how I would expect to see someone from one of the City banks in London. All that was missing was the bowler hat and rolled umbrella. I immediately noticed that he had little or no accent and was difficult to place regarding geographical whereabouts in the UK.

Over the customary drink he explained that he owned a retail furnishings company close to Birmingham and was interested in buying blankets. Having already checked out the suppliers, I told him that most of the factories were located some sixty kilometres from Valencia, in a town called Onteniente. After agreeing to the usual terms whereby he paid the general daily expenses and I received my usual commission from the supplier, all was set for the following day.

Surprisingly, everything went extremely well and in the one day, after visiting several manufacturers, we succeeded in putting together a whole container of, according to Ian, blankets that would sell easily through his warehouse. He stayed on for another two days and we made other visits of interest but little resulted regarding further purchases. An amiable person was Ian and going out with him was like going out with a bank manager or an accountant. He always wore a suit and tie, with just the correct amount of shirt cuff showing and was a hit in all the restaurants. We received the absolute best where service was concerned. The waiters bowed and scurried about appearing whenever Ian raised a finger. He spoke little of his private life but did mention at one point to owning a Rolls Royce. I told him how impressionable many Spaniards were and he said that the next time he visited Valencia he would drive over in the Rolls if I considered it worthwhile.

We said our "goodbyes" when I dropped him off at the airport and I was to let him know when the first shipment was ready and the payment transfer would be made.

306

Kramika, I was told by Fernando, was definitely closing down and I telephoned Mac, who greeted the news by saying that with us involved it had only been a matter of time, anyway. I was happy in the next days to receive a further call from the Chamber of Commerce to say they had another client for me wishing to buy ceramics and porcelain articles.

*

This was the moment 'Big Ted' arrived upon the scene. Not at all fat but big in every sense of the word. In reality a mountain of a man whose impressive appearance hid the fact that underneath he was, to me at any rate, a kind, hospitable, person; or one hoped. A car dealer, heralding from the North of England, he specialised at the top end of the market buying and selling expensive vehicles from firms that had the misfortune to go Bankrupt.

"You'll never sit yer arse in a better motor than a Mercedes," I was frequently told as we drove around in his shooting brake.

His wife, he explained, ran a gift shop and Ted had decided that a trip to Valencia, in order to source and buy direct from the manufacturers, would be worth while for the business. He then said that apart from ceramic articles, he was intent on negotiating a distributorship with the world famous, Valencia based, Lladro Company which produced the beautiful, intricately detailed and very expensive figures in porcelain.

Together we tried to organise this but were firmly told that apart from a small discount for quantities nothing else could be done as the UK was already tied up.

Close to the Lladro factory was a shop owned by the company themselves which supplied Lladro 'Seconds'. The figures on sale there were very near perfect and each carried a small red sticker to indicate where the imperfection was located. Even then, on many articles, it was difficult for the inexperienced eye to see where the fault lay. Naturally, the Lladro seal on the bottom had mostly been removed but one could still see that it was made by this legendary manufacturer.

So 'Big Ted' decided that if he could not sell the original figures they would have to make do with these 'seconds' which would be displayed in the shop for what they were. On that first trip he spent a fair amount of money both in Manises and at the Lladro shop. Every available space in Ted's Mercedes was used for the return journey to England. On the last day we enjoyed a good lunch together and just before he left he placed an envelope in my hand.

"'ere, count it. There's a grand there and what I'd like you t' do is buy a load more o' seconds and post 'em on t' me. Mek sure you've enough fer yer commission. Alright?"

"No problem, Ted. You can trust me."

Then just before he drove away, he took my hand in a vice like grip and said, "Just one thing, Chris. Ah don't want yer t' fuck me about, alright? 'Cos ah don't like being fucked about. Understand?"

I looked up at this very big man and said as levelly as my voice would permit, "Listen Ted, whatever happens there is just no way am I going to fuck you about. No way at all!"

Later, I placed 'Big Ted's' money in a safe place at home with the idea of making a trip to the Lladro seconds shop the following week.

*

It was on the Friday that I received a call from the blanket factory in Onteniente. They confirmed that they had been in contact with Ian in Birmingham and that the trailer would be ready for loading that afternoon. However, there was no way that shipment would be made unless the amount, or certainly something, was paid. I telephoned Ian, who said that all this had happened that particular morning and as the banks were closed nothing could be done until first thing on Monday. I explained that the factory was quite adamant in not shipping without seeing something up front.

"This is absolutely ridiculous," he said. "They should have given me at least a couple of days notice." The phone went silent for a minute then he spoke again. "Isn't there anyway you can help? It's only until Monday, for heavens sake. As soon as it arrives we can place a further order."

So in the end, this for Mr. Nice Guy read idiot, went to the post office with 'Big Ted's' thousand pounds and organised a giro. As I telephoned the factory to confirm that, indeed, there was something on the way and would they please ship the goods, I could feel that all would not be turning out as expected. The goods were duly shipped and arrived at the beginning of the following week.

There was, of course, no news from Birmingham, neither on Tuesday or Wednesday. A call to Mac enlisting his help was made but he too had little or no success. "What do you expect? It's the FU syndrome again!" was his only comment.

In the end I was panicking and visions of being on the receiving end of 'Big Ted's' fist started my legs trembling.

"You had better get over there and quickly," advised Kathy, not wishing to have the burden of a sudden death in the family. "It's the only way you will be able to sort it out."

So, together, we scraped enough money together for the air fare and I was off. Fortunately, the FU effect did not stretch to Iberia airways and I arrived at Mac's place without any mishap.

*

The following day I drove over to Birmingham in Mac's car and after a while, eventually found Ian's retail premises. It was a huge wooden constructed warehouse, crammed with furniture and furnishings which was open to the public. My first thought was that it must have been very difficult to organise fire insurance on such a place. I had deliberately not notified anyone of my arrival and walked in to find Ian, as suave as ever and looking like a contender for the best dressed man of the year award. He was sitting in his office and in front of him was a desk strewn with papers. I must admit his face did fall a little when he saw me but he soon recovered.

"My dear friend," he gushed, standing up and grasping my hand. "Do come in and make yourself comfortable."

Quickly he removed a pile of documents from one of the chairs so that I could sit down. "Well indeed what a surprise."

"I hope so," I replied without offering any formal greeting.

He sat down again and without any pleasantries began an impromptu speech. "You know something? My accountant and I were just talking about you this very morning."

"I hope that it was a positive conversation, Ian, I would hate to think I had come all this way for nothing."

"No, no, Chris. Of course not."

He began shuffling papers around and I folded my arms and waited.

"No," he continued, "but I must admit that the company does have problems at the moment. However it is nothing that cannot be sorted out."

He laughed but it came out more like a giggle.

"Now, let me see ….." He carried on searching through the papers then pounced, "Ah, yes. Here it is!"

From where I was sitting it did not look as though that particular document had any bearing on our business but I refrained from saying anything.

"Now let me see……. Yes, I believe the transfer to the factory was made this morning."

"No," I said firmly, not really knowing if it was true.

"No?" said Ian, looking up at me.

"No," I repeated, "definitely not."

"Dear me, I could have sworn the accountant organised it."

I then thought I would make it a little easier for him. "Listen Ian. I am not looking for problems but I want the deposit that I personally put on the goods. I would hate to see this company go, how would you say?" Here I looked around at all the furniture heaped around the place in what could only be described as utter chaos. "Up in smoke?"

The moment I had said that, by the way he looked at me I immediately knew. "Don't tell me you don't even have any insurance on the place?" I said now feeling more in control.

He ignored my question and stood up. "How much was it? One thousand pounds?"

"No. One thousand two hundred pounds," I confirmed.

"But I distinctly remember you saying one thousand pounds."

"Maybe, but that did not take into account my having to come over to collect and face the music from the factory."

He sighed and turned to a large wall safe which, when he opened, looked like Old Mother Hubbard's cupboard. However, after rooting around he turned and placed a bundle of notes in front of me. I sat there and counted each one carefully and found it was correct. Then I stood and we faced one another.

"Next time you are passing Valencia……just pass!" I said and turning, walked out.

Two weeks later 'Big Ted' telephoned to say that he had received the porcelain figures and was most relieved to find that there were no breakages.

"Not half as relieved as I am," I thought as I visualised the bunch of bananas that was holding the telephone receiver.

Several weeks passed and I was notified of the date of the bankruptcy hearing of Ian's company. I telephoned a friend, Mike Hayward, who lived in fairly close proximity to the court and asked if he would mind attending just to see what was happening. Later he called to say that he had been to the meeting.

"So what did smooth Ian have to say for himself?" I asked.

"Ian?" repeated Mike. "There was nobody there by that name."

"Then who was the Managing Director if he wasn't?" I asked, puzzled.

"A woman," said my friend.

"A woman?"

"Yes," Mike explained, "when she wasn't packing chocolates at the Bourneville factory, she was the Managing Director of the company that's gone bust."

"Amazing," I thought. "I had better not mention this to the supplier. They would never believe me."

I thanked Mike for his kind effort and replaced the phone thinking that the situation could have been very much worse where my health was concerned: especially as the thought of 'Big Ted's' image loomed into my mind once more.

Chapter 18

Some years before, whilst in Cullera, one of the many English customers that frequented the pub was Beryl. A charming lady with blonde hair and elegantly dressed which amply made up for the fact that she was on the comfortably plumpish side. With a wide captivating smile she had a fine, bubbly, sense of humour and was always a pleasure to serve. Her husband, whom I eventually met, owned a manufacturing company in the UK which produced articles for the maintenance of golf courses. As Spain was just beginning to blossom out where this sport was concerned, with the construction of new courses and the appearance of world class players such as Severiano Ballesteros, Beryl's husband was keen to exploit his products in Spain. At that time, little could be done with me being committed to the pub. However, once I was based in Valencia we were in contact. Not having the necessary licences for the importation of goods and at the same time, the space to store the merchandise, I spoke to three Spanish brothers, I knew, who produced fine classic furniture in a huge building with ample space. The senior of the trio was Vicente Damia, with whom I came into contact with through the Valencia Chamber of Commerce.

*

It had been at a time when, for some reason, I had been invited to speak at a Chamber of Commerce symposium to over forty Valencia company representatives. The subject was 'How to export to the United Kingdom'.

In the past I had received considerable experience on these presentations, having been employed by an American pharmaceutical company, so the presentation came quite naturally to me.

It was after the meeting that I was approached by a member of the British Embassy, commercial section, who congratulated me on my performance. "Why on earth are you not employed to do this sort of thing for the British companies wishing to export abroad?" he asked.

I was very much surprised by this and replied, "Quite honestly I thought there were qualified people doing this sort of thing anyway."

However, he then went on to say that as far as he knew this was not so. I then gave him my card and said that I was available anytime should he wish to carry the situation further. Of course, such was the apathy and complacency with the British companies then that, not surprisingly, nothing more came of it. This attitude was also confirmed later when looking through the list of exhibitors at the huge Valencia annual gift fair which I always attended I saw that the representation of British companies was sadly limited to just two with one having a Chinese name and based in Birmingham. On the other hand other countries were well into promoting their products with Germany very much in evidence.

Vicente Damia, of the furniture factory, confirmed that he and his brothers would be pleased to participate in the importation of golf course maintenance articles. So we began with low cost items such as flag pins, hole cups, bunker rakes, tee markers and other things. These I sold to local clubs with the help of another English friend, John Stepney.

The businesses was moving but very slowly as, at that time, import duties were extremely high and, as usual, cash was limited. However, we persisted knowing that golf was becoming more and more popular and that the possibilities were favourable.

The Kramika Company was now really flagging and I had the feeling that it would not be lasting much longer. Then, with the full consent of Fernando, I elected to go to the factory on a part-time basis. This now gave me time to dedicate to the golf business together with any work that Tony Strodder passed on to me or which I might come across. Visits to local golf clubs such as El Saler, (nominated at one time as being amongst the world's best golf courses), El Escorpion, Manises and El Bosque were not a problem but anything further a field was proving more difficult. However, John and I pressed on.

*

Around the same time there appeared in Valencia representatives from a Manchester, UK based company, called 'Freshpic'. They were in Spain to buy onions. A reputable supplier, whose premises lay quite close to Valencia, was found and when the 'Freshpic' buyers' viewed the mountains of Spanish onions on offer, they were in ecstasy. I learnt from one of the group, Robert by name, that it was not just necessarily the general appearance of the onions that denoted the quality but also the 'sound' of the vegetable. That is to say that when they were gathered in the palms of the hand, good onions always give off a distinct rustling noise.

Orders were placed and on the day the initial shipment was due to leave for Manchester, I went around to supervise the loading. Before Freshpic's truck could be organised, there was a huge German vehicle to be attended to.

I watched as the tailboard was let down so the sacks could be put on board and there, in the middle of the trailer, was the most beautiful, absolutely brand new, BMW motorcycle that I had ever set eyes upon.

"Move that bloody thing," said one of the workers to the well proportioned German driver, "We have to start loading."

"Not likely," he replied. "Just stick the sacks on top of it!"

Nobody wanted to argue and a while later off drove the truck with the BMW and onions.

Regular shipments to England followed and then, one day, the 'Freshpic' boys returned to Valencia together with another character in tow. A hotel owner from the North of England, he was thickset, little or no neck and gave the impression of being a middle aged, rather bucolic, Billy Bunter.

It was during one of the many evenings out together that I talked enthusiastically about the potential there was for the golf business in Spain. The new arrival listened to me attentively and then said that he had money to finance such a project. He then asked what our priorities were and I said that we really needed some sort of vehicle in which we could travel around Spain taking orders and making deliveries. The next thing I knew was that a deposit was placed on a brand new Ford Transit van. Meanwhile, it was decided that we needed stock which could be stored in the spacious furniture factory and as one of the investor's friends was willing to distribute quantities of ceramic flower pots, it would be ideal for me to drive the transit to the UK with the ceramics and return with the golf course articles. We visited a number of ceramic manufacturers and a large order was placed with one of them.

*

As it was holiday time, Kathy and Samantha decided to accompany me on this first trip to England. The journey was slow, due to the weight of the merchandise, but we eventually arrived after four days travelling and I was very tired to say the least. On the return journey, the van was loaded at the golf factory and the three of us set off for Valencia.

We had elected to cross the channel from Newhaven to Dieppe and the last night was spent in a quiet guest house similar to many others scattered along the South coast of England. The place was run by a pleasant couple who had opted out from the North somewhere.

We were sampling the great English breakfast next morning when the husband came over to the table and asked that he might speak to us on a rather confidential matter. Inviting him to sit down, in a lowered voice, he began. "Please do not laugh at what I am going to say."

"Of course not," said Kathy, politely.

Looking a little sheepish he said, "Well, my wife is not actually what you might call a fortune teller or anything like that but she does have certain powers."

"Does she really?" I said, encouraging him to go on at the same time wondering what the catch was. His voice dropped even more so that the other guests would not hear. "Yes," he continued. Then looking at Kathy said, "Well, this morning she told me that you had an aura around you, meaning that today you would be having problems."

Then appearing even more embarrassed, he said, "Wait a minute. It's better that she explains." Rising from the table he disappeared into the kitchen, immediately returning with his wife who sat down whilst he continued serving the other tables.

"Please don't misunderstand me," said the woman who had an open, honest, face and looked more suitable to be in the theatre or film industry than running a guest house in Newhaven.

"Of course not," said Kathy smiling.

"Well, it's just that I can see an aura around you that gives me the feeling that things are definitely not going to work out for you today."

"What sort of things?" I put in thinking that she might, at any moment, be going to tell me that she could see the letters FU over my own head.

"I've no idea. It could be anything but it is going to be a nuisance. Just keep your handbag near you. That's all I can say."

Later, as we drove towards the docks and embarkation point in Newhaven, we wondered whatever it might be that the landlady had implied by her premonition. It was only a few minutes later as we arrived at the control that we found out.

As we were carrying goods the customs official examined our documents and checked our passports. At that time both Kathy and Samantha travelled on their American passports and the official's expression changed when he saw them.

"Have you both got your visas?" he asked.

"What visas?" I said.

"The visas that you need for the lady and her daughter to enter France."

"Sorry," I apologised, "I really don't know what you are talking about."

"You obviously haven't been keeping up-to-date on the political scene."

We both shook our heads. He then went on to explain that there was tension between the United States of America and France. "Something to do with the French testing their nuclear weapons in the Pacific, I believe," he said and then went on to say that if we wished to continue with our journey it was up to us but he certainly could not guarantee that Kathy and Samantha, once on French soil, would not be sent straight back.

"Bloody marvellous!" I said as we parked to one side and climbed down. Handing them their overnight bags I said, "Ring Mike and Sara Hayward. They'll help you organise a flight." I then climbed back into the van and drove along the jetty towards the ferry. Looking back I could see Kathy waving and Samantha in tears.

*

My return journey was uneventful but I arrived home to face even more problems. FU Inc. was really coming into full swing. The new golf investor, together with several of his cronies had decided that he wanted to take complete control of the business with John and myself being ousted. He had begun by visiting the manufacturer in England and making some arrangement whereby he had the exclusive rights to receive their products and distribute them in Spain. Now he was trying to seek a similar agreement with the Damia brothers. A general meeting was convened where interested parties and their legal representatives would discuss the matter. Gedo, the Dutchman, had reappeared in Valencia and agreed to come along as his Spanish was still very much superior to mine and I did not wish to misunderstand anything that was said. He declined to say why he had spent two nights in the police cells next to Chatwin, the jewel thief, but apparently it was something to do with his wife from whom he was now separated.

We all gathered around one large table at the lawyers and the meeting began. The investor became very adamant that he wanted to view all the books and records concerning the company before even thinking about any transaction. Now this would have been fine if we had been in any country except Spain. However the asking price for the company being only around one thousand two hundred pounds made this look rather paltry to say the least.

An argument ensued which included threats from the investor mainly directed at John Stepney. These threats were emphasised to an extent where there was a great deal of shouting and bad language involved. The Spanish contingent did not, actually, understand what was being said but certainly from the tone of the raised voices captured the intended meaning. Eventually, the investor and his representatives stormed out and Vicente Damia turned to me and asked why I did not wish to buy the company. I explained that it was just not financially possible. He then suggested that I bought it by signing promissory notes on easy terms. I declined but Gedo said that he, personally, would take on the matter. We all shook hands and John went immediately to the police headquarters to report the threats that had been made against him. The police, in turn, arrested the investor and placed him in the cells for the night. Next day, he was released and told to stay away from John and myself at all costs.

*

Shortly after this confrontation Kathy and Samantha flew out from Valencia to the USA for a holiday. It was to be the first time Samantha had met her American relations who were numerous and scattered across that vast country.

Meanwhile, John Stepney and I loaded the transit van with golf course material and set off for the South of Spain while Gedo organised an office and the company which we had registered as Pargolf SL.

We were well received at such prestigious courses as La Manga, Sotogrande, Torremolinos, Las Brisas and many others. At night we found reasonable accommodation in the resorts of Fuengirola, Estapona and Marbella where it was immediately noticed that compared with the Valencia region, the people of Andalucía were far more receptive and hospitable to foreigners. One of the towns that I fell in love with was Linares. I knew of Linares only as being the place where Manolete, the greatest bull fighter of the twentieth century, met his untimely death in the local bullring.

John and I booked into a new hotel close to the town centre and after showering and changing decided to have a couple of beers and dinner somewhere.

Leaving the hotel we wandered around taking in the sights and sounds of this lovely old town and eventually opted to have a drink in what looked like a very typical Andalucía bar. Jostling our way through the evening crowd we ordered two beers. These were placed on the bar together with a fair size plate of cooked mushrooms in a garlic sauce.

"Sorry," I said to the barmaid, "but we didn't order these."

"I know," was the reply, "but this is the 'tapa' which is served with the drinks."

We thanked her and tucked in at the same time noticing that all the other customers were picking at different dishes placed in front of them as they ordered their drinks. More beers were requested and up came two miniature hamburgers. A further two beers resulted in the appearance of two delicious chicken croquettes. It was amazing. Naturally, by the third drink we were engaged in conversation with several of the local customers who were more than pleased to see that we were enjoying ourselves.

One man smiled and said, "Look, if you really want to try really excellent 'tapas' go down to the 'San Francisco' bar."

He then drew us a map on a paper serviette giving us instructions on how to get there. So paying for the six beers which came to six hundred pesetas or around two pounds fifty and with map in hand, we thanked our new acquaintances and left.

The 'San Francisco' was even busier and noisier. Ordering a couple of beers we wondered what sort of 'tapa' was going to accompany them. The expression on John's face when he saw the large plate placed in front of us was a sight worth seeing. It contained sausage, egg and chips. Admittedly the sausage was on the small size and the egg was probably a quail's but there was an abundance of chips. Later, deciding that there was no way we could face an evening meal, we decided to seek out a comfortable bar where we could have a couple of night caps and return to the hotel.

"There," said John, pointing across the road as we wandered around. "That looks like the place. There's nobody in there and not a sign of those 'tapas'."

Crossing over, in we went and ordered two beers. The man served us and busied himself under the bar.

"What's he doing?" asked John.

"Not really bothered," I returned taking a healthy mouthful of beer. "I'm more interested in those pretty girls that have just come in."

We had both turned to look at the girls when the barman said, "Here's your 'tapa'."

And there on the bar was this very large plate of small, freshly fried, fish!

My fond memory of Linares as being possibly the only place I have come across where it seemed impossible to become drunk. Come to think of it, with a few pesetas in your pocket it would be also very difficult to starve.

Eventually we returned to Valencia, if not with a full order pad, certainly with sufficient information to indicate that we were on the right course as regards golf. However, on the negative side it was clear that transport from the UK plus import duties, it was not conducive to good profit margins. Gedo then decided to search around and find Spanish manufacturers who could reproduce similar types of articles.

Chapter 19

Kathy and Samantha returned from their holiday and the day after their arrival all three of us went out for a celebration lunch at one of the local restaurants called 'El Horreo'.

'Horreo' in Spanish refers to a granary or barn in the Galician region. These are usually raised on pillars of stone in order to protect the crops from the damp earth and artistically can be very varied and attractive. Kathy, Samantha and I enjoyed a first class meal, accompanied by two bottles of wine from the Albacete area, followed by coffees and liquors.

"By the way, I forgot to tell you," said Kathy suddenly as the waiter delivered the second bottle of 'Castillo de Hinguera'. "Whilst you were out last night I had a visitor."

"Really? Who was it?"

"I don't know. He just rang the bell and when I opened the door asked if you lived there. Then when I confirmed that you did, he asked if I slept with you."

"He asked you what?" I said in surprise, almost choking on the wine.

"If I slept with you."

"Slept with me? Good Lord what a question. And what did you say?"

"Asked him who the hell he was and to show me his identification or get out!"

"Did he?"

"Did he hell. He just patted his pockets shrugged his shoulders and went away, fast."

We wondered who it could have been but did not let it distract us from enjoying ourselves.

It was later when we were walking back to the apartment that Kathy stopped and pointed towards the apartment block entrance. "Look! There he is again!"

I immediately felt that something was wrong, extremely wrong, and motioned her and Samantha to stay where they were while I crossed over and confronted him.

"And what the hell do you want?" I asked, not at all politely.

"Christopher Wright?" he asked without any preliminaries.

"Correct," I confirmed. "What's the problem?"

"Police," he said, fishing out an identification card. "We are waiting for you. You have to come with us."

"Not if you cannot explain what it's about," I replied not at all liking this little weasel- faced man who was head and shoulders shorter than me.

"Just stay here and don't try and go into the apartment."

This irritated me and thinking quickly I said, "Listen. There's a 'Comiseria' just around the corner. Let's both go along there and sort this out." I then turned and crossed the road to where Kathy and Samantha were standing.

"I told you to stay here!" snarled the little man close on my heels.

We had just made the other side when an unmarked saloon car came screaming around the corner and skidded to a halt. Out jumped three other men who, without any explanation, grabbed me. Automatically Kathy came towards me demanding to know what was happening.

"Stay out of it or you're inside as well!" snapped one of the men.

Samantha who was terrified at what was happening to her father came forward and was immediately pushed to the floor by the largest of the three; a tall, overweight, individual who looked as though he had received his training as the school bully. Next I was manhandled into the car and handcuffed with the manacles being purposefully snapped around my forearms which were very painful to say the least. Of course, I was furious and turning to the brute who had pushed Samantha I said a few choice words for which I received a not too lightly dig in the ribs. It was then that I remembered stories about people being wrapped in wet towels before being worked over so that the marks did not show. I quietened down a little and remained silent.

*

Torrente is a satellite town of around twenty-eight thousand inhabitants and lies around eight kilometres from Valencia. The driver of the car was obviously a Starsky and Hutch fan as he reached out and stuck the flashing blue light onto the roof of the vehicle. A few minutes later we careered into the town, coming to a halt outside the local police station.

An extremely old dilapidated building that looked as though it had served as the local Town Hall at one time with two huge wooden doors with a smaller door within one of them. I was frog marched through this small door by the four men and pushed towards some steps on the far side of an interior court yard. At the top of these was a rather austere office with the usual desks, typewriters and filing cabinets. Still handcuffed, I was told to sit down in one of the chairs facing a desk behind which weasel face made himself comfortable.

Then, much to my surprise, the other three officials began pacing up and down clutching at various parts of their bodies and moaning. The brute of a man who had knocked Samantha over was nursing one of his fingers and waving it in front of the others. "Just look at this!" he wailed.

"What on earth is the matter with them?" I asked turning to the Weasel.

"It's you," he said in all seriousness. "You have injured them."

"I've what?" I asked, amazed at this theatrical performance. "I've injured all of you?"

"Not me so much, just bruised my arm. Nothing really." He effected to rub the offended limb. "But all the others. Well ..."

He nodded towards them as they walked up and down making appropriate and very childish 'it hurts' noises. I was annoyed, to say the least, at this bizarre charade.

"Can I join the party?" I asked.

Then before he could answer I rose from the chair and joined them, parading about and moaning, "Oh! Oh! My arms hurt! Oh, look what they've done to me. Not one of these so called policemen knows how to put on a pair of handcuffs."

All three froze in their tracks in surprise and stood staring at me.

"My ribs!" I continued, "Oh, the pain!"

Next I added, just to emphasize the stupidity of all this, "But my feet are fine." And here I skipped from one foot to the other a couple of times.

"Sit down!" snarled the Weasel.

I did so at the same time shaking my head and commenting on how very sad it was that grown men should make a spectacle of themselves by such infantile actions.

"Documents," demanded the Weasel, pulling the battered old typewriter towards him.

I waved my handcuffs at him and producing the key from his pocket he reached over and released them. I ignored him for a moment rubbing the circulation back into my sore limbs. What documentation I carried in my wallet was produced and placed before him. He then began banging away at the machine with two fingers at the same time asking questions. The statement he wanted involved everything to do with the golfing project and I answered each one truthfully as I had nothing to hide. After some considerable time we eventually came to the end and passing over several sheets he said, "Sign there!" indicating my name at the foot of the pages.

Reaching across I moved to pick up the papers but his hand remained firmly holding them down on the desk top.

"Wait a minute I want to read them first?"

"No need to. Just sign."

I was astonished and drew back, thinking that I had misheard. "I beg your pardon?"

It was obvious that he was becoming angry now. "You heard me," he said through gritted teeth. "Just sign at the bottom of the pages."

It was so ridiculous in the fact I had never signed anything in my life without reading it through first and in these circumstances all the more reason that I should do. I just could not help myself and burst out laughing. "If I cannot read them you actors must think I'm a complete imbecile expecting me to sign. You would not dare to try and pull a trick like this in a civilised country. It's only third world countries that can try something like this. You must really be into dealing with idiots most of the time."

I folded my arms and sat back. "No thank you. I will wait and speak to my lawyer."

So there I sat and waited, listening to the silence that my little speech had provoked. These men, I was sure, were a breed of officials who had grown up under the Felipe Gonzalez government which at that time was the perpetrator of the GAL hit squad, sponsored by public money and took to eliminating suspected Basque terrorists. They were very much accustomed to making their own ground rules, especially when receiving orders from above. So if this influential person, who I later found out to be a woman lawyer of some prestige, said that I was guilty of whatever, then it was up to the police to make the case stick by whatever means were at hand.

"Sign," the Weasel insisted once again but with a little less enthusiasm. "Then you can speak to whoever you wish."

"Not likely. No way. I am aware of my rights."

He stared at me hard with little sharp eyes as though willing me to pick up the pen. "In Spain once you have signed, and not before, you are entitled to all your rights. You can even use this phone to call your lawyer." He nodded towards the antique instrument on his desk as though I might be tempted by the offer.

"No, definitely not," I said adamantly. "You must think I'm crazy. Forget it. I'm just not signing anything."

"Then you will be put into a cell until you do!" The pinched face glared across at me. "And that, amigo mio, could be for a very long time."

Shrugging my shoulders I then spoke very slowly so that all present could take note and there would be no misunderstanding. "You know something?" I began carefully, "This whole thing smells very much of being a complete set up. For the Torrente police to make an arrest within the jurisdiction of the city boundaries has to be motivated by someone." I then stood up and looked from one to the other. "So no matter how long it is going to take I am now your responsibility. But let it be known that I am not, repeat not, signing anything that people like you put in front of me, without consulting my lawyer. So where is this cell then?"

There was a few moments silence and the other three stared at the Weasel waiting for the next move.

"If that's the way you want it," he said, "fine. But you are certainly not going to like it. I promise you that."

The pen was again waved in my direction.

"No definitely not. To sign papers compiled by people who come to my door asking who sleeps with who and then knocking down a nine year old girl indicates to me that I would be more than a complete idiot to fix my signature to something cooked up by a bunch of gangsters. Now please, if it is not too much trouble, lead the way."

Together with the Weasel and one other official I went down the steps and across the court yard to where a young uniformed civil guard opened one of two heavy metal doors with a small grill in each one. I ducked inside.

*

One thing I must say in the Weasel's favour. He was quite correct. No way did I like it. In fact it was horrendous. Around three square metres with the only light coming in from the grill it took a few minutes for my eyes to accustom themselves to the gloom. However this was preceded by the incredible nauseating odour that wafted around my nostrils. The handkerchief I produced and pressed to my nose made little difference. It was appalling. When eventually I could take stock of my surroundings I saw in the dim light that there was hardly a single inch of the walls that was not smeared with excrement. Towards the back there was a stone plinth on which was a length of thin foam which I assumed served as a mattress and the dark hole in the corner from which the evil smell emanated did not warrant my investigation to know what it was.

Fortunately I was still under the effects of the luncheon and this encouraged me to hang onto my decision not to wait until I had a lawyer present. With my nose buried in my handkerchief, I sat on the plinth and waited. After an hour nothing had happened so I started hammering on the door until the young civil guard appeared.

"Get me someone in charge," I said and he disappeared returning within a few minutes led by a new personality who waved papers in front of the grill.

"Get my lawyer here first. Then I will sign."

"No," he replied turning away.

"Wait a moment!" I called after him. He stopped and came back. "What is it? So you will sign after all."

"No, I want a bucket of water and a cloth of some sort."

"What for?" He stared at me through thick lenses.

"What do you mean what for?" I looked back at him my face pressed against the bars. "To clean this filthy place, that's what for. Whoever permits this," here I waved my arm at the walls, "must be accustomed to living in filth. A bunch of gangsters is one thing but pigs as well….."

"Just sign," he growled ignoring the provocation.

Turning my back to the grill in answer, I waited and then heard him walking away muttering something to the guard.

Time went by and the hands of my watch showed that I had been there around three hours. Out of something to do I hammered on the door again and the same scene was repeated. Sign and I could phone whoever I wanted and be out of there straightaway. If not there would be no lawyer and certainly no bucket of water. Another hour passed and I wondered how long it would be before I actually did get out and if Kathy had found out my whereabouts.

Then I heard the key turning in the lock and the door opened to reveal the civil guard who presented me with a tin foil covered 'Bocadillo'. "Here is your meal," he said, "and some cigarettes."

"What about a drink?" I asked, very much surprised at this sudden generosity.

Moving to one side he pointed across the yard, "There's a tap over there."

"Thank you," I said, walking out of the hole and taking a deep breath. "You are very kind."

He followed me over to the tap where I drank and swilled my face with the cold, refreshing water. I then noticed that nearby stood a trestle table together with several folding chairs.

"Mind if I sit here and eat my roll?" I asked. "You know what it is like in there."

He glanced uncertainly up towards the office. "I suppose it's alright. There's nobody up there at the moment." So I sat down, unwrapped the 'bocadillo' and took a bite.

"Que aproveche," he said politely, "Good appetite!"

As was the custom, I offered some of the roll to him but he shook his head and said, "Gracias, pero no."

It was the traditional Spanish Omelette of potato and onion, hot, freshly made and must have come from one of the nearly bars. I munched on it slowly, allowing my taste buds to savour something pleasant and at the same time delaying the time when I would have to return to the stinking hole.

"Why is the place kept like that?" I asked between mouthfuls and nodding towards the cell.

"They just like it that way," he replied with another cautious glance towards the office as though he might be overheard. Then he added with a shrug, "It's inhuman. But what can I do?"

All too soon I was once again locked up and resigned myself to passing the night there. Sleep was impossible. I just sat, feet together, not daring to lean back for fear of coming into contact with the filthy wall. Just staring towards the dim yellow light that filtered through the grill from a nearby electric light bulb and occasionally mentally working out mathematical calculations using the six floor tiles. I knew that I was going to be alright as my captors had not resorted to the violence that they surely dealt out to other individuals. However, what did worry me at that particular moment was the amount of mosquitoes that seemed to float through the grill as if drawn towards me. There had been a lot of publicity and conjecture on the transmission of AIDS and it had even been suggested that mosquitoes could play a part. I whirled my handkerchief around quite a lot and occasionally hopped and skipped on the floor tiles. Next morning coffee was brought to me by another civil guard who was not inclined to let me sit outside at the trestle table.

*

It was a little more than nineteen hours after I had been first put into the 'pozo' that they came for me and I found myself once again sitting in front of the Weasel together with the lawyer that had been sent along by the Damia brothers. Quickly the lawyer explained that Kathy and Samantha were fine and that together with John Stepney I would be going before the judge that same evening.

"It might seem a silly question but what have we done?" I asked.

"Well," he began, "it would appear as though this Englishman who wanted to buy the business has reported you and John for theft of the Transit van."

So that was what this was all about.

It came home to me that at that particular time anyone so inclined could report whoever they wished for theft and without any firm evidence. It would be the judge who decided whether or not there would be cause for such an accusation.

"The Englishman did put a deposit on the Transit," I admitted, "but I have signed for and am responsible for a whole load of ceramics and other things which he has had at a considerable more cost than the deposit. Also your clients, the Damia brothers, have sold this golf business to the Dutchman."

"It's complicated," admitted the lawyer rummaging around in his brief case and coming up with what looked like a copy of Mao's little red book.

"What's that?" I asked as he began thumbing through the pages.

"Oh, this? It's a book on criminal law and I am not sure of the situation."

"Not sure?" I looked at him in amazement.

"Not really," he confessed. "You see I am qualified in company law and know little about criminal offences."

"I don't believe all this!" I groaned, burying my head in my hands then looking up to see the grinning face of the Weasel obviously enjoying the situation. "Anyway, what evidence is there?" I asked. "And where is the accuser?"

The lawyer gave up leafing through the book and turned to me. "The judge will decide if there is sufficient evidence for charges and as for the man who made the accusations, he left the country yesterday."

"Just great!" I said. "So what now?"

"Well, I've read through this statement that you made to this police official and there is no reason why you should not sign it."

The Weasel pushed a paper over and proffered a pen.

"Why didn't they let me telephone someone when I first arrived?"

The lawyer placed a hand on my arm. "Just sign," he said. "Don't let's go into that at the moment."

I took the pen read through the statement and was on the point of signing when I realised that there was only one sheet of paper. "Where are the others?" I asked.

"What others?" questioned the lawyer.

"The other papers he wanted me to sign," I explained. "There were at least two more pages."

"He's mistaken," the Weasel broke in all too quickly for the lawyer not to notice.

"No way! There were more pages and you wanted me to sign them without reading them."

Again the lawyer took hold of my arm. "Anyway, it doesn't matter now."

"Bloody sure it would have done if I had signed as they wanted me to," I stared back at the Weasel.

A short time afterwards I was back in the cell just sitting there and waiting. I was now extremely tired and certain that my whole body had taken on the fetid odour which clung to me like some foul smelling invisible cloak. I dozed fitfully just sitting on the plinth.

*

At last, around seven in the evening, they came for me and I was escorted out, through the main door to the street where a car was waiting together with a very quiet John standing by. Both of us were then handcuffed together and squashed into the back of the vehicle with another plain clothes police officer. As the car drove towards Valencia, nobody seemed concerned that John and I talked together in English. He had, apparently, fared better than myself and related how initially the police had come along to his office and asked where he had hidden the company Transit van.

"But you took the thing up to your place in Serra," I said.

"Yes, I told them it was parked right outside my house and wasn't hidden anywhere. But they didn't seem to believe me. Kept on and on saying that I was lying. Bloody ridiculous really."

"Have they got it now?" I asked.

"Suppose so. I gave them the keys."

He nodded out of the window at that moment. "Look where we are passing now."

I stared out at the Valencia prison, a huge gaunt grey building behind a high wall with unmanned watch towers. The slate roof came down over row after row of barred windows which looked like sightless eyes staring out at us.

"Hate to think that we might be heading there," said John.

"Hope not!" I agreed with him.

Our first stop was at the main Valencia police headquarters and with handcuffs removed we were hastened down a flight of steps and pushed into a large communal cell in the basement with what seemed to be a howling mob of delinquents. The noise was incredible. Drunks and drug addicts, most of them still under the influence, were shouting, arguing and occasionally fighting between themselves. Quite a few of them nursed open wounds but were in such a state that they paid little attention to the amount of blood that was being lost. Most were filthy dirty and I was thankful my nose had accustomed itself as the stench would have been overpowering.

John and I found a space near the wall, next to one youth whose jeans had been torn to reveal a long deep cut that was dripping blood onto the slimy floor. Glassy eyed, he sat with his back to the wall, muttering, oblivious to all that was going on around him. Both of us just stood there without speaking taking in the scene.

"You know something. The cinema and the TV don't come anywhere to the reality of this lot," said John eventually.

A while later our names were called out and thankful to hear the cage slam behind us we were hustled upstairs, handcuffed again and pushed into another car. The large communal cell at the courthouse was much cleaner with only very few people waiting to appear before the judge. Our smiling company lawyer was there and assured us that our respective partners were fine and that we should, hopefully, be released after seeing the judge.

"Don't forget to show the judge that," he said, nodding at the two nasty looking bruises that had appeared on my arms as a result of the handcuffs.

Eventually my name was called out and I was taken through into a rather sumptuous office where a grey haired, middle aged man, sat behind a large desk. To one side and sharing the same desk was a dry stick of a woman who was obviously the secretary.

The man shuffled through the papers on the desk in front of him, looked up eventually and said, "I see you are English."

"Yes, your honour. That is correct."

"Do you know London?"

"Not again," I thought. "Not another one who wants a smuggling job organised."

I nodded and confirmed that, indeed, I was well acquainted with London.

"In fact, your Honour," I added, "at one time I lived in Wimbledon."

His tired face suddenly lit up. "Really?" he beamed. "I go to the tennis championships there every year."

I then made what I considered a suitable comment on the wonders of the annual tennis championships although I possessed little knowledge on the subject or even knew the whereabouts of the courts.

He nodded, then once more his face changed again as he quickly returned to the matter in hand. On his instructions the secretary started hammering away vigorously at an ancient 'Imperial' typewriter as though reaping vengeance for the fact that she was on the late shift. Next the sheets of paper were ripped from the machine and the stamping and signing ceremony enthusiastically accomplished. My personal police official was presented with a copy and motioned to me that we were leaving.

"Just one minute," I said, rising to my feet and extending my bruised arms towards the judge. "Is this the way your policemen are trained to treat foreigners?"

Pushing back his chair the judge stood and came round the side of the desk with a now bored expression that seemed to intimate, "Go on and ask me something new." Then after a cursory glance at the damage he turned to my escort, who had in no way been responsible with the initial handcuffing, and proceeded to explain that handcuffs were meant to be placed on the wrists and not on the arms. The officer just nodded in return and said nothing. I was astonished as my escort must have seen at least twenty years service. The lesson over, the judge turned, waved his hand in dismissal and we were once again outside. John had been in before me and was waiting with the lawyer.

I was about to mention the Wimbledon incident which I thought was something positive, when the lawyer stuck out his hand and said, "Remove your watch and signet ring."

"I beg your pardon?" I was not sure that I had heard correctly.

Then seeing the expression on my face, he apologised, "Sorry, but you both have to go to prison for seventy-two hours while this is sorted out."

My stomach did a double somersault. "But I don't understand. We haven't been charged with anything. Or have we?"

"Doesn't matter. The judge, apparently, is sending everyone to prison for seventy-two hours at the moment and he can do just what he wishes."

"But why the watch and the signet ring?" I persisted.

"Very dangerous people where you are going. Likely to cut off your finger for a ring." He held out his hand and I passed the things over to him as John had done.

"Don't worry. I will see that your wives get these tomorrow and that some clean clothes are delivered to the prison."

My mind was in turmoil. Here I was at fifty years of age, absolutely stinking, worn out through lack of sleep, now being told I was to be put into prison without any charges against me. It was a double or even triple dose of FU.

"Don't worry," said the lawyer patting my arm as though reading my thoughts, "it will all be sorted out." But in no way did he sound convincing.

A while later John and I were again handcuffed but this time separately, then led out to a police van together with around six or seven other undesirable individuals. Amongst them was a young couple, in their late teens. The boy had been handcuffed with his hands behind his back and she, a slip of a girl, followed him closely trying to help him up the steps and into the vehicle. He tripped and fell flat on his face onto the filthy floor. Immediately she dropped to her knees by his side making strange sobbing noises. John and I were directly behind them and quickly we lifted them both and moved them onto the single bench seat that ran around the interior of the van. The door slammed behind us and we could hear several motor cycles being kicked into life.

"Christ!" said John. "We even have an escort."

The van lurched into movement and we were off to the sound of wailing sirens. Nobody spoke on the short journey. Most of us just sat and stared at the floor darting occasional glances at our fellow passengers whose faces appeared sallow and blotchy in the light of the single dim bulb in the ceiling that was protected by a wire mesh. We made one stop on the way to roughly remove the young girl who was still making those strange animal noises.

*

Shortly afterwards the van passed through the prison gates, shuddered to a halt and everyone was herded out. Once inside what I assumed to be the reception area we were lined up and the process began. Names were called out by an official who had the standard parade ground sergeant major's voice. Strangely enough, in my mind, it was at that very moment that I was transported back in time to some thirty odd years previously when, together with around forty other recruits, I had arrived for basic training at RAF Hednesford near Birmingham. Such was the power of that initial training all those years ago that when my name was called I responded by pulling myself to attention and shouting out, "Si, Señor!"

A sudden silence descended on the group and everyone turned to me in disbelief. I could see the guard staring at me, trying to detect some sign of insolence but then the roll call continued. Next we were ordered to strip and subject ourselves to a full body search which included hands against the wall and crouching whilst gloved fingers were inserted into our rectums. After this we were split into groups of three with John and me being accompanied by the boy who had taken the tumble in the van. We followed the guard who guided us to a cell on the top gallery of the nearest wing. Everywhere was deathly quiet as the other prisoners had been locked in for the night.

"Here," said the man, almost apologetically. "This is just for tonight. In the morning you will be moved to the other wing."

I made sure I was through the door first in order to grab what might be the best place. There was a barred window facing me some three metres high in the wall beneath which was a double bunk bed. To the left along the other wall was a single bed and to the right a small partitioned area that, as it smelt to high heaven, I assumed was the toilet area. I hauled myself onto the top bunk beneath the window thinking that I would, at least, have some fresh air to breath. John selected the single bunk and the boy made himself comfortable below me. Little was said and I lay watching the dark shadows of the trees moving restlessly against the orange light from a distant street lamps. Below me the boy tossed and turned obviously suffering from withdrawal symptoms. Every now and again he would cry out, calling the girl's name, at the same time complaining to no one in particular that all they were doing was 'shooting' a little heroin. I dosed fitfully and was pleased when the dim surroundings eventually took on recognisable shapes announcing another day.

Both John and I resisted visiting the foul smelling hole in the corner but the boy who had problems was now shaking visibly and could not hold out and urinated noisily. The door was opened and a guard indicated that we were to follow him. We did so moving down the precipitous iron steps with me steadying myself with the handrail for safety. There was now considerable movement of prisoners about us and I was suddenly shocked to hear a voice call out, "Hi Englishman! How are you my friend?"

I immediately recognised him as the homosexual bricklayer from my days in Cullera and nodded, calling back that I was fine. He gave me the thumbs up and carried on his way.

"Fine," I thought. "I said that I was fine. I must be out of my bloody mind."

We were taken through into the next wing and on the way were issued with a thin foam mattress each together with a set of grey sheets and what looked like an army blanket from the Crimean war.

All in all, everything had the appearance of being used God only knows how many times and I did not relish the thought of the next night. We then repeated our names to yet another guard who ticked them off on a clip board. At that point the boy, still visibly trembling and bemoaning his fate, was led away. The guard then called out to another prisoner, a tall blonde well built man of around forty years of age who, I later learnt, had killed a security guard in a hold up.

"Here Hans, take these two up to 216 on the top gallery."

Hans studied us for a moment then asked, "English?"

We both nodded and he said, "I'm Dutch. Follow me."

Up another set of steep iron steps we went, staring about us at the strangeness of it all. On one landing there were a couple of prisoners hard at work. One was balancing an iron bedstead while the other waved a hissing blow torch.

"What are they doing?" I asked our escort.

He followed my gaze. "Oh, them. They're killing off the lice inside the bed frame."

He opened the door of cell 216 and we went in. It was exactly the same layout as the previous one but devoid of any type of furniture.

"If you want a bed each you'll have to go along to the store and collect them," said Hans.

I looked at John who, after seeing what could be lurking in the bed frames said, "I don't think we'll bother. I don't think we will be here all that long anyway."

I nodded in agreement and the Dutchman laughed for some reason. "Well, make yourselves at home and when you're organised just come down stairs. The 'Economato' is open and you can use the yard." Then turning he walked out leaving the door ajar.

In one corner, separated from the rest of the cell by a wall, there was a toilet bowl which seemed to function and a sink over which dripped a single cold water tap.

"What's the 'Economato'?" I asked John, as I positioned my mattress on the floor and folded up the sheet and blanket, military style.

"It's a sort of store or shop. Somewhere you can buy things like food and drink."

He watched me arranging my bedding. "Why are you doing that?" he asked. "We might even be out today when things are sorted."

"Just don't bet on it, John," I smoothed off the blanket. "Better that we always think that we might be out tomorrow but never today and that way we won't be disappointed. You heard how that Dutchman laughed when you said what you did."

"I think that is going a bit far," John replied, but all the same followed my example of organising his bed.

I then washed as best as I could in the cold water, drying myself on my shirt with John following my example. We then decided to see what was happening below and walked out onto the gallery. Looking down over the rail it seemed that we were around twenty metres from the ground floor. Most of the cell doors were open and prisoners were coming and going as they pleased. The iron staircase appeared even more daunting as we now knew where our cell was. Stepping down I attempted to appear casual but kept fairly close to the hand rail. Once on the ground floor we walked over to the one open door against which lounged a guard reading a newspaper. He glanced at us casually but said nothing. The door led to the 'patio' or yard and we wandered through to join the other inmates taking their morning exercise.

In less than a few minutes we were approached by a short wiry youngster of around eighteen years of age, complete with what appeared to be a broken nose and a corner of the market on acne. Planting himself firmly in front of us he asked, "Want a Mozo?"

A 'Mozo' in Spanish refers, in one sense, to a young boy and in this case someone who is prepared to run errands or perform menial tasks.

"Tell us what you can do for us?" said John. Immediately taking control

The youth grinned and pushed back a grimy lock of hair that had fallen over his eyes.

"Stand in line to get your coffees, sandwiches or cigarettes. Organise all the beer you want and even something stronger if you like."

"Beer?" I queried, suddenly interested. "You can actually get us beer?"

"Sure. No problem! Only costs one hundred pesetas a can. Just tell me how many you want and they will be on the table at lunchtime."

"Right," I said, pulling some notes from wallet. "Two coffees right now, please. How much are they?"

"Five pesetas each."

"Well here's two hundred and twenty. That's for two coffees, two beers at lunchtime and of course, something for you."

He smiled again showing several gaps in his teeth, and then skipped off, disappearing past the guard, back into the building in the direction of the 'Economato'.

"Do you think that was wise?" asked John.

"Well he certainly isn't going to go very far is he?" I said, nodding at the tremendous height of the wall surrounding the yard. "Another thing is that if the coffee is good, at five pesetas a time and we have beer then I reckon we should manage alright."

Out in the yard the weather was fine and it was good to feel the sun on my back even with those walls all around us; especially after what I had been through in the past forty odd hours. We joined other inmates who seemed to be strolling or strutting up and down when suddenly the peace was broken by the thump, thumping of a low flying police patrol helicopter that appeared from nowhere and hovered directly overhead. Immediately everyone stopped what they were doing and began hurling abuse accompanied by equivalent arm and hand signals in the direction of the iron bird. Not wishing to appear any different both John and I joined in. Then after a few minutes the machine clattered off and everything returned to normal. We continued walking and at one point passed several groups of men squatting on plastic crates playing cards.

"Good Lord! Just take a look at that money over there," I said to John out of the corner of my mouth. "There must be thousands of pesetas; bundles of the stuff!"

He glanced over as we moved by avoiding eye contact and I heard an intake of breath. "Wonder how the hell they manage to get that lot in here?"

I smiled to myself thinking that as yet I had not witnessed any fingers being cut off and only the one guard for over a hundred inmates who did not seem to be particularly concerned. I cannot say I was beginning to enjoy the situation but I did feel a certain amount of relief that I could handle this even with my fifty years; for a while that was.

The coffee, when it arrived in paper cups, was possibly the best I had ever tasted. I sipped it, relishing each drop and looked forward to the caffeine kicking in.

"What's your name?" I asked the boy.

"Paquito, Señor."

"Well, Paquito it looks as though you're on the payroll!" I said, remembering some of the prison jargon I had read somewhere in the past. "You just come along anytime and check out if we want anything. By the way, what are you doing here?"

He thrust his hands into his jeans and shuffled his worn trainers. "Don't rightly know," he said.

"What do you mean, you don't know?"

"Well, they haven't actually told me yet. I was with some friends at a discotheque and a fight broke out, somebody got knifed and," he shrugged his shoulders, "here I am."

"You mean the judge sent you here on the seventy-two hour order?" put in John.

"That's right. That's what he said. A seventy-two hour order."

A sudden thought occurred to me. "Well, Paquito, how long have you been here?"

"Don't know really. Around three months I suppose."

"Three months?" put in John unable to suppress his surprise. "You are not sure but it could be three months. Haven't you got a lawyer?"

"Yea. They sent me one of the government lawyers for people with no money."

"And?"

"That was about a month ago. Haven't heard anything since."

"So what did the lawyer say?" I asked.

Paquito smiled to himself as though enjoying a private joke. "The lawyer said that he was having problems being paid by the government but he would try and do something."

Haven't you complained?"

"'Course I complain. I'm always complaining. But they say that if I signed the paper for the lawyer to act for me then that's what he's doing."

"Bloody marvellous!" said John, later when we had resumed walking.

Lunch was a fairly orderly affair and we were allowed one full bar, a quarter of a kilo, of bread each. We stood in line and received two plates onto one of which was ladled some type of meat in a rather suspicious sauce together with soggy looking vegetables. The other things available were a choice of yoghurts that had passed the expiry date and a variation of unripe fruit. It was noisy in the canteen and the moment we sat down Paquito plonked the two beers in from of us, whispering that it possibly would be better if we drink them later.

Then much to our astonishment we found ourselves joined at a table by what appeared to be three, most reasonably presentable, women. All had well kept hairstyles and wore liberal quantities of makeup together with false eyelashes. One even sported a low cut blouse beneath which I could detect a definite bulge of breasts.

"I just don't believe it," I whispered to John.

Then, before he could answer, the taller one of the trio with the auburn hair reached a rather large but well manicured hand across the table towards me. "Hola amigos," she said in a deep throaty voice, "I'm Mama Carla. I can see you boys are new here. So if you have any problems at all just come and see Mama Carla, OK?"

I smiled and introduced John and myself. "Fine by me, Carla. Thanks." There was little option but to return the handshake, and say "Hi" to the others.

"So what the hell?" I thought. "Live and let live."

The lunch was over quickly and on the way out John and I were instructed to call at the main office.

"There, I told you so," said John, convinced that we were on the way home.

"Wouldn't bank on it," I replied. "Don't think it is as easy as that; even more so after talking to Paquito."

This time I was correct and we were just handed two plastic bags each containing a change of clothes, washing articles and some books, before being returned to our cells and locked in for two hours 'siesta'. One thing I did learn immediately and that was where the terminology 'slammer' originated when referring to prison. There were two large bolts on each of the cell doors and every time we were locked in two inmates would be detailed to pass by and slam these into place as fast as was possible. If the timing was spot on the effects were quite impressionable with the echoes reverberating throughout the building and with my indestructible sense of imagination I wondered whether anyone, with a leaning towards composing music, had ever considered recording these effects. With modern-day pop I felt it would have had great potential.

The following morning we were horrified to find that during the night whatever insects were about had made a meal of us both with John faring worse. We possessed an ugly array of red bites and once again the fear of contracting AIDS returned but as nothing could be done about it I decided not to worry. There was no indication that we were obliged to attend breakfast, so we headed directly to the exercise yard.

It was then that I noticed that there appeared to be a pecking order in respect of the inmates. Whereas the petty thieves and delinquents would keep close to the walls huddled in groups, the criminals who had embarked on a higher level of crime would strut up and down the yard as though they owned the place. Not to be outdone we took to walking back and forth in a similar manner and I developed what I considered a style that was a mixture of the way John Wayne and Robert Mitchum moved around. Shoulders back, the left one slightly down, head inclined forward and arms bent at the elbows, I would pace up and down. Funnily enough as most of the others were similarly inclined this drew no attention whatsoever.

*

Later in the afternoon of the second day, the guard called us over and said there were two other English boys in the same wing. He explained that as they were employed in the workshop putting together light fittings they would not be back until that evening. We thanked him and spent a couple of hours discussing what they might be doing here. Somebody must have pointed us out to them because when eventually they did arrive they came straight over.

Mike and Brian Hill were brothers. Mike, the eldest, was fresh-faced with a well- tended moustache and quick watchful eyes that seemed to be everywhere at once. He did most of the talking while his younger, slightly taller and pale-faced, brother stood quietly by. Speaking with an irresistible, measured, Gloucestershire, burr Mike did the introductions and we shook hands all round.

Initially I detected a reluctance on their part to immediately disclose all their personal details, possibly due to the 'Best keep oneself to oneself surroundings'. However they were obviously most curious as to how John and I came to be there and after explaining what had, in fact, happened, Mike suggested that it would be more prudent that we invented something more impressive if we were to remain high on the 'pecking order'. Just being there on possible charges of stealing our own company effects would not really impress the other inmates.

Thinking of what might be more in keeping with the hierarchy around us, I said, "Just spread it around that we managed to get hold of the plans of Valencia Town Hall and got caught trying to sell the place to some rich American investment company. That should give us a few thousand points on the popularity scale."

We all laughed at this and they promised to comply.

Then John commented that we would hopefully be released the following day. Both brothers, I noticed, exchanged glances.

"Don't take it too seriously if you're not out tomorrow," said Mike quietly. "We have been here nearly three years now and have seen many coming in on seventy-two hour orders. Unfortunately some might well still be here." Then noticing the expression on John's face hurriedly added, "However, if there are no charges and you also have a good lawyer, it shouldn't be too long before you are out anyway."

I immediately started thinking of our present company lawyer, inexperienced in criminal law and made up my mind to mention it to Kathy when, or if, she were allowed to visit us.

"Bloody hell!" I thought half to myself as I glanced heavenwards at that moment and noticed, for the first time, that the roof of the place was shaped exactly like a coffin lid. "FU Inc. was really in action!"

Then Mike was offering some advice. "Whatever you do, do not eat the ends of the bread," he said seriously.

"Why ever not?" I queried, having always had an in-built tendency to bite off the crusty bits at the end of the roll.

"Because," he explained, "the bars of bread are delivered in those plastic fruit crates which have holes at the bottom. Then when the crates are scraped along the floor, the ends of the bread come into contact with everything that's lying there and as you've no doubt noticed, spitting is considered normal practice here by the majority of prisoners."

His advice sank in and I tried to forget that up until that moment I had enjoyed this activity over the last couple of days.

"Are there any problems amongst the other prisoners?" I asked, feeling the absence of my signet ring and watch.

"Not normally," confirmed Mike. "The prisoners here sort out any problems between themselves and everyone knows that persistent trouble-makers are transferred to another wing. That really is bad news as it's very rough in there."

"Sometimes there are accidents," put in Brian, nodding towards the steep iron stair case. "People sometimes …, shall we say, trip or fall down them."

"Right," said his brother, "we've also had a couple of 'flyers' in the last eighteen months."

"Flyers?" queried John.

"Yea. People, to whom the place has got to so much that they just cannot take anymore," he shrugged. "They take a dive off the top gallery."

"Bloody hell," I said again, imagining how anyone would look after travelling head first for sixty feet and connecting with the concrete floor.

"Actually, one just missed Brian here," said Mike, seriously. "By only a couple of feet," he added.

His brother nodded and grinned but I could see by his expression that he still thought what the consequences might have been. And at that moment I saw his eyes glance to a spot on the floor not that far away that seemed a little cleaner than the rest.

John changed the subject. "Why do they allow those transvestites to dress up like that?"

Both the brothers laughed but, although spontaneous, the hilarity did not reach their eyes.

Mike said, "Well, why shouldn't they dress up like that? They are no problem and provide a little diversion for the rest of the inmates."

"Yea, and when you've been in here long enough you find yourself peering down Carla's cleavage when she leans over," put in Brian.

We all laughed and it was then that the inevitable question arose and I asked, "Well, what are you two doing in here?"

"A long story," said Mike.

"A very long story," confirmed his brother. "A three years long story."

*

Then, with Mike doing most of the talking, we listened to what can only be described as a series of events that began on the sixteenth of July 1985 and has continued ever since. Even on into the new millennium.

That which occurred in this country of Spain, poised on the brink of being fully integrated into the European Economic Community, in the very same year and the very same month that I was, in my small way, endeavouring to help save Elena Valero's eyesight, can only be described as horrific.

A chronicle of events that included deliberate falsification of documents, crooked lawyers, manipulation of witnesses, downright theft (on the part of the authorities involved), misinterpretations by incompetent persons, torture (yes torture) and many more unbelievable happenings that culminated with a petition to the Committee of Human Rights at the United Nations in Geneva. The resulting sentence in 1997 (sixteen years after their initial detention) by this allegedly august assembly, ended in there being found a total of no less than eleven counts of abuse of human rights against Spain. There were, in fact, more but the Committee decided that eleven were sufficient to prove their point.

As very little notice has been taken of this by the Spanish authorities over the subsequent years, my heart goes out to, not only Mike and Brian Hill, but to the victims of non European countries in that their plight must be double-fold after any inadequate intervention by the UNO, my personal premise being that any law that has been passed and is not capable of being applied to the full is absolutely worse than useless.

Perhaps I am being too hard on the UNO, as I am sure that there are those amongst them, like Stephan Jakobi of the Fair Trials Abroad Trust, who was and probably still is genuinely dedicated to putting wrong to right. However, as has appeared in various world situations, their effectiveness does, unfortunately, leave a lot to be desired.

This is a true account of the Hill brother's story.

Mike and Brian had a thriving construction business in Cheltenham, England. Having worked hard for several years without a decent holiday, they decided to take a break before starting the fulfilment of several contracts for the local town council. With most of their friends, having visited Spain, the brothers felt a little left out in the cold when it came to holiday conversations so they decided that was where their destination lay.

Travelling in a brand new metallic grey camper van, fitted with all the necessary equipment that would eliminate hotel searching, they set out from their home town towards the middle of July 1985 with great expectations for an enjoyable holiday in the sun.

After the channel crossing they drove straight to Madrid and passing Spain's capital by way of the perimeter road turned onto the A3 route and headed south east towards, what they hoped would be, warm seas, sand and sunshine. Ignoring the traffic signs indicating the city centre of Valencia, they continued south following the coastal route at the same time enjoying the fine views of the blue slab of Mediterranean Sea to their left.

Fate, it seemed, had decreed that their first real stop was to be in the port area of Gandia. It was now late evening and feeling somewhat tired after their long haul they decided to have a drink before seeking out some Spanish food in one of the beach restaurants. Up until that moment everything had gone according to plan and they were both in a holiday mood, enjoying the novelty of a new country with its sights, sounds and smells. Parking the camper van they climbed down and stood looking about them. Their attention was then drawn to a nearby flashing neon sign indicating the 'Club JB'.

"Let's try that place," suggested Mike, the more adventurous of the two, not realising that with this almost insignificant suggestion they now had only a few hours left of freedom. After that it would be three extremely long years before they would be granted their liberty once more.

"Right, let's do it!" agreed Brian.

Once inside it took little imagination to realise that they had walked into what the Americans would call a 'Clip Joint'. However to the brothers this, of course, was no problem and they responded to the attractive girls serving the drinks. Time passed by quickly and it was very late when they paid and left. A meal was now out of the question so they decided to drive to Benidorm, the action holiday resort, some hundred kilometres distance.

*

It was around an hour later that they were pulled over by a civil guard vehicle and without any explanation dragged from their van, manhandled into the police car and driven straight back to Gandia. Here, both being frightened and confused by the events and having no idea why they were being detained, they requested that the police allow them to contact the British Consul or anyone for that matter who might clarify the situation..

Their request was categorically refused.

Next an unqualified student with some knowledge of school English was produced by the police under the guise of being an interpreter. They were then extensively interrogated but without the presence of any sort of lawyer or representation. Not surprisingly considerable misunderstanding arose. At no time were they informed of their rights, either at the time of their arrest, or during the interrogation.

Then after some seven to eight hours questioning that they eventually learned the reason for their detention that they had, supposedly, left the JB Club at three a.m., then returned one hour later and firebombed the premises by use of a home made Molotov cocktail.

For what reason nobody, either then, or until today, has come up with a sensible answer.

Next a witness was produced and what can only be described as a Marx Brothers' situation took place. This so called 'Identification parade' was an absolute charade. It consisted of just the two brothers handcuffed to two uniformed police officers. The elderly male witness who before the parade could not even come up with a description of the supposed authors of the crime now, surprisingly, had little difficulty in pointing them out.

They were to be held in police custody in Gandia for ten days, five of them without food and only warm water to drink. During this time they were to be humiliated, which by today standards would be terms as 'tortured'. Even some twenty years later they are still reluctant to talk about this particular episode, being convinced that nobody would believe them anyway. When I mentioned to Mike about the Guantanamo accusations he smiled ruefully and said that it was a pity that he and Brian had no photographic evidence of them both crawling around naked on the floor while being prodded in the testicles from behind with sticks in a so called 'Democratic' country.

Never again would they set eyes on their new camper van or their personal possessions which consisted of money, clothing and many other valuable items including Mike's Rolex watch. Nor would they ever be presented with any inventory, receipt or even informed as to where everything had been taken. Everything had just simply disappeared.

During that first long, hot, night in custody, another inmate intimated to them that the cell door was unlocked and suggested that they could attempt an escape. However, as they had done nothing wrong they sensibly realised that such an action would compound any guilt and thus ignored this advice.

On the eleventh day they were transferred to the prison in Valencia. From then on their ordeal took on even more terrifying proportions. They were eventually charged and it would be no less than sixteen months later that they would be brought to trial.

The first official court hearing, fixed for the 3rd November 198, was immediately suspended for two weeks as the court interpreter committed a crucial error. Having been asked what type of fuel their van functioned on, they answered 'Petrol' which was incorrectly translated as 'Petróleo'. This in Spanish signifies 'Diesel'.

A reserve can of normal petrol, conforming to UK regulations in that it was filled only to the stated safety line, was found in the van. The state prosecution then automatically assumed that as the van ran on diesel, then what was a container of petrol doing in the vehicle?

They decided that the two-week adjournment of the hearing would enable them to prepare their defence with a state lawyer who had been assigned to the case. This lawyer appeared, together with another unqualified interpreter, on the 1st November to spend around thirty minutes with them before promising to return later and leaving.

He never returned.

This same man approached the brothers' father, who was outside the prison, and through the interpreter asked for a sum of half a million pesetas (somewhat more than two thousand pounds) which, he explained, would be required for the 'Appeal'. Being somewhat confused and at the time not having this amount at that particular moment, their father refused and reported the matter to the Pro Consul in Alicante who, in turn, denied any knowledge of the conversation on a subsequent visit to the prison. However, at a later meeting, the Pro Consul did finally admit that this conversation had, in fact, taken place.

Amazing!

Next, an official complaint by the two brothers was lodged with the Spanish Law Society with yet again no response. Prior to the actual trial taking place on 17th November 1986, the State lawyer minus the interpreter and without any brief referring to their case, spent twenty-five minutes with the brothers. Fortunately they had two bilingual inmates who were able to assist them in making the relevant points.

Their own personally prepared dossier was presented in court but was never allowed to be referred to.

At the actual trial, Mike, being very much aware of what was happening and the possible grave consequences, requested that he be allowed to present his own defence. The judge refused his request and via the interpreter pointed out, "You will have the opportunity to do all these things by means of 'appeal'."

Naturally, this very statement insinuated that there was an obvious presumption of guilt even before the end of the trial, which only lasted some thirty-five minutes in all and totally prevented Mike from calling a witness on their behalf who was actually waiting outside the courtroom.

The one and only witness that had identified them at the 'Identification Parade' farce was eventually called by the prosecution. This elderly man said that the camper-van had been parked outside his house and at around 04:00 a.m. and he had seen two youths, who he could not identify, throwing a flaming bottle into the bar and leaving in the vehicle. He was then asked no less than three times by the judge to take a look at the accused and each time said that 'he could not remember the youths,' that 'he was an old man' and that, 'it had all happened sixteen months ago.'

On further cross examination he completely failed to give a clear description of the camper-van, saying that the vehicle had the letter 'A' affixed to the vehicle which could indicate that it was British, Austrian or even Japanese!

The sentence was eventually announced on the 20th November 1986, and dictated that a term of six years and one day was to be served by both brothers.

Again wonderful!

From 18th November 1986, Mike and Brian began writing letters of protest, not only to Britain but also to the Spanish authorities. Until 25th April 1990 they had written fifty letters to such officialdom at the British Embassy in Madrid, British Consul in Alicante, the Spanish Ombudsman, and the Ministry of Justice and even to King Juan Carlos of Spain.

The total replies received were just twenty five and of the letters to which no reply was forthcoming, eight were to British authorities who would, obviously, not even grant them the courtesy of an answer, even though it might possibly have been of a negative nature.

In all the brothers completed three years of the sentence and were released in July 1987. At my invitation they both came immediately to my apartment, the main reason being that under Spanish law they were committed to reporting on the first and fifteenth of each month for the remainder of their total sentence and needed somewhere to stay. So as to conform to this order they went to the authorities where they were told that there were no such records available so this obligation did not apply. It was then suggested that they could return home or wherever they wished. Sensing that possibly officialdom had an ulterior motive for this they continued to reside in my apartment and made several more attempts to clarify the situation. To no avail. It was after several weeks that they eventually decided to return to the UK being convinced that all would be fine. This was not to be so. Immediately they left Spain a 'Busca y Captura' (Find and Arrest) order was immediately issued for their not complying with the law and reporting as was obligatory.

So the saga continued with submission of the facts being made to the United Nations Organisation who, in April 1997, subsequently found Spain guilty of eleven acts of abuse against Human Rights. It is also worth a mention here that at the moment of writing, Spain has been condemned on twenty two such occasions by the UN and that there are a further one hundred and twenty two cases pending. It is beyond belief that a European country, being an integral part of the organisation refuses point blank to recognise it as such.

Two years later on December 1999 the local Valencia newspaper, Las Provincias, printed an article suggesting that Spain should respect the sentence of the UNO and indemnify the two brothers. However, it was pointed out, if they did return to accept any such payment then they would be immediately rearrested for not completing their obligations and reporting on a monthly basis after their release.

So having arrived at this point one would have thought a stalemate had been reached and that there was little else that the brothers could do apart from continuing their claim for compensation through lawyers.

*

Just eighteen years on from their date of release from the Valencia Modelo Prison the saga, almost certainly based on vindictiveness by the Spanish authorities, continues. Brian Hill now happily married and with a teenage daughter decided that the year 2005 would warrant a family holiday in the United States. On arrival they were informed at the airport that there still existed an order for the arrest of Brian and because of this they would therefore not be allowed into that country. After eighteen years!

Returning to England Brian was determined to have his holiday and following a telephone call to the UK Foreign Office accepted their word that a holiday in Portugal would not result in any problems; so they flew there. And quite rightly so there were no complications on entering that country. Nor were there any on leaving at the end of their break. However on landing at London's Heathrow Brian was immediately arrested and subsequently deported back to Portugal. Here he was held without any charges that were made known to him and later transferred to the 'Centro Penitenciario de Badajoz', Spain. There he remained for several months. Then it was only through the help of a kindly prison chaplain that he obtained his release. "Whatever you do," he was told, "don't attempt to return to the UK via any of the normal routes. You will only be rearrested." So with this in mind a car journey to Gibraltar was organised and from there he returned home.

At one point during the whole episode between the years 1988 and 1997 Mike Hill   paid a visit to the UNO headquarters in Geneva where he was made most welcome. It was there that a conducted tour of the building took him to an enormous room where aisle after aisle housed thousands of archives pertaining to human rights infringements throughout the world. The comment was made that it was pathetic that Spain should be placed alongside countries such as Chile whose despicable record was well known throughout the civilised world.

And so it was, whilst in the Valencia prison that John and I promised the two brothers that if and when we were released we would also contribute in anyway we could in obtaining their release and any subsequent efforts to obtain compensation. I also added that I would bring this to the attention of my own lawyer and suggested that they stay with Kathy and me upon being given their freedom, as no doubt they would be freed on parole.

The following day Kathy arrived to visit me and I immediately told her that in no way was I happy with the company lawyer who was handling my particular case. Thank goodness Kathy, being considerably brighter than me, had already spoken to our own lawyer who in turn agreed to sort the matter out immediately. Before our release did take place, we had spent a total of ten days in Valencia prison and were certainly pleased to be on the outside again. Our moment of leaving, as with every other prisoner, was quite an emotional affair, with congratulations on all sides and our surplus belongings, such as books, money and anything else of use being distributed freely to the others. I personally walked out with just a plastic bag of wet washing and a letter that the big Dutchman asked me to post for him.

It was great to be home but my mind repeatedly returned to the thought of Mike and Brian still being there. Our lawyer was duly informed of their plight and agreed to do whatever possible to help. As I was talking to him neither of us, or anyone else for that matter, even thought that in twenty years time, in the new millennium, Brian would be rearrested and held, first in a Portuguese prison then afterwards in a Spanish prison, without any formal charges for around eight months.

*

Much to the amusement of Samantha, it took several days after my release for me to lose the Wayne/Mitchum walk. Gedo, who had paid out the necessary advance fee to our lawyer, was working away happily with our new Pargolf Company. The transit van and goods were eventually returned to us and as it was obvious that our business was not sufficiently solvent to maintain the payments on the vehicle, it was suggested that I organise a sales trip around the golf courses before we had to relinquish it.

So one bright sunny day I set off alone, heading South to the Costa del Sol where I knew I would be well received everywhere I called. It was certainly great to be moving again and as I drove with the windows open, singing along to a Dolly Parton tape, I realised that my hair had grown much too long for comfort.

"I must do something about it," I thought to myself, "and at the first opportunity."

Now what else could be simpler than having one's haircut? In the past I had never experienced any problems and certainly never gave it any thought that this time would be any different. However, that was the way it would turn out to be ...well...different, to say the least!

Chapter 20

The region of Spain called Extremadura nudges onto the Portuguese border. Simply translated Extremadura signifies 'extremely hard' and not surprisingly so when referring to the climate there. In fact, some might consider this to be an understatement. The summers are guaranteed to literally take your breath away and scorch you unmercifully. The cruel winters, on the other hand, can be so harsh that earth sets rock solid. So much so that many of the cemeteries are obliged to prepare their graves the previous autumn, to await the newly departed. I was fortunate enough to arrive there before there were any significant signs of winter setting in and drove along in comfortable, bright, sunshine.

With my thoughts on having a haircut as soon as possible in order to appear presentable at a presentation to one of the more important golf courses in the region, I maintained a watchful eye as I rolled through the various villages between Huelva and Badajoz. The opportunity arrived when I came to a clean, tidy, 'pueblo' that displayed a sign claiming that it had been awarded the 1983 prize for the 'Best Kept Village in Spain'. It was getting close to lunchtime and to my right I noticed a striped barber's pole protruding over a small, discreet doorway. Then better still, as I passed, I saw that the place appeared to be empty. Parking was no problem and I left the van, much to my surprise, alongside an estate car displaying British registration plates. Then strolling back I crossed the road, pushed open the door of the shop and went in.

It was, as I expected, a small but orderly place with one well-used barber's chair, slightly tarnished mirror together with functional and spotless wash basin. Nearby were several comfortable looking wicker chairs around a coffee table on which were scattered the usual selection of outdated magazines. To the rear, along one wall, stood a fine old dresser with a variety of bottles alongside of which were several clean, sparkling glasses on a white lace cloth. The place felt, what I would term, instantly comfortable. As there was nobody in sight I stood there unsure as to what to do. Thinking back later, I realised that at that particular moment, as instinct had prompted me on previous occasions, I should have turned and rapidly got out of there. However, as life is not like that, it was not to be.

I waited.

Eventually a beaded curtain, in the far corner, was thrust to one side and there appeared a very young, very pretty girl of around seven or eight years of age, with large dark Andalucía almond eyes and black hair that was swept back into a long pigtail.

"Si Señor?" she smiled up at me.

I pointed to my lengthy locks, "A haircut, por favour."

She nodded then turning disappeared back through the curtain and I could hear her calling, "Abuelo! Grandfather!"

Two minutes later she was back leading her elderly 'Abuelo' by the hand. A slight, willowy figure of a man, who like so many others of the exacting region, had learned to bend with the winds of time. His skin was the colour of old leather and he had obviously been accustomed to working out-of-doors at one time. The unkempt hair was snow white as was his crisp, well ironed jacket. But what really drew my immediate attention were the thick pebble spectacles perched on his sharp nose. They were so thick it was difficult to see his eyes. All-in-all he reminded me of my old Physics master at college or the mad professor I used to read about in comics.

Peering in my direction, he said, "Welcome, Caballero. Welcome to my humble establishment!" I thought for a moment that someone else had entered the shop as the man was looking straight past my right shoulder.

Noticing my puzzled expression, the little girl explained, "My grandfather is blind in one eye," then added, almost as an after thought, "and he doesn't see too well out of the other one."

The barber laughed and I had to smile at this innocent betrayal.

"Don't worry, my friend," he said, thrusting his hand out somewhere to the left of me. "You will have the finest haircut in all of Extremadura."

Feeling obliged to grasp the waving limb, I nodded, "Nice to meet you." Then thinking quickly, I said, "Look, if it is any problem perhaps I can come back some other time?"

"No, no! Certainly not."

He came up to me now that he knew my whereabouts. "No problem, Caballero. No problem at all. Now let us have a little aperitif before we begin."

Then turning to the girl, "Carmen, bring the glasses and the very best wine!"

Carmen, obviously accustomed to the procedure, was already searching amongst the bottles on the dresser.

"Come, sit yourself down," instructed the barber. "You must be weary after your journey."

I was taken by the arm and propelled in the direction of the chairs and sat down. He managed to locate another chair nearby without incident and made himself comfortable.

"A little Manzanilla wine? The very best!" he cried, as the girl placed two brimming tumblers in front of us. Then leaning towards me he said, "My name is Alfonso Hidalgo. Pray, what might your good name be, Señor?"

"Christopher," I replied, "Christopher Wright."

"Ah, yes," he mused. "A fine Christian name Christopher." Then, "Would you be French, Señor?"

"No. British."

"Ah yes, British," he repeated thoughtfully, as a doctor might consider an unusual symptom. Then after a moment, "Your Duke of Wellington did a fine job of ridding us of the French."

I smiled inwardly as he made this matter of fact statement as one who might be commenting on a recent change of government. I murmured what I considered to be an appropriate agreement and reached for the two tumblers. Next, not fully confident on Alfonso's ability to locate them, I passed him one. Thanking me he then turned to the girl saying, "Gracias, my dear. Run along now and tell your mother I will be having lunch out today. Oh, yes. Also remind her that I will be back in time for the funeral."

The girl wandered off after giving her grandfather a customary peck on the cheek. .

"Funeral?" I enquired politely.

"Yes," he replied sadly, raising the glass in a silent toast, "First cousin on my wife's side. A fine figure of a man was Pepe; a very big man amongst lesser mortals. But it was his time." He sighed, "You understand?"

I nodded at the same time offering some condolences.

Steadily we drank the dry, golden, nectar and the conversation began to flow. By the first refill, at his request, we had discussed the demise of General Franco and the rapid return to Spain of the republicans such as Catalonia's, Taradellas and the communist figure, 'La Pasionaria'. As the Moorish wine was spilling into my glass for the third time, we were expounding on Spain's interpretation of the word 'democracy' and laughed together when I pointed out it had gone so far as to talk about 'democratic' refereeing at football matches. Then glancing at my watch I saw that it was well after one o'clock.

"Sorry." I apologised, "But do you think we might begin?"

"Of course, my dear friend." he cried, coming unsteadily to his feet. "To work!"

Once seated in the chair, Alfonso explained that as his right eye was the reasonable one, he would begin on the right side of my head, work his way around to the back and then on for the home straight, finishing up by my left eye. I nodded in agreement, drowsy from the effects of the wine. He appeared to be a methodical worker who maintained a constant flow of conversation as he snipped away. Sometime later I considered that this had possibly been a strategic move in order to distract me from what was actually happening to my hair. Anyway I closed my eyes ignoring the garlic breath that wafted freely about my head. The right side was soon shorn so Alfonso positioned himself to the rear. A while later a distinct change of temperature, affecting the back of my head, made me assume that his next move would be to the left hand side and, with luck, I would be on my way within fifteen minutes. Not so. At that very moment the Town Hall clock boomed out the hour.

"Dios mío!" Alfonso cried happily, "it's two o'clock."

The comb and scissors were tossed carelessly onto the shelf under the mirror.

"Here, what's going on?" I asked, rapidly coming out of my daydream.

"Nothing. Nothing at all, my dear friend," he explained, "it's lunchtime and I am taking the pleasure of inviting you for a meal at the Tasca across the road."

"But my hair?" I gasped, seeing my reflection in the mirror for the first time and rapidly coming to my feet. It was not just bad, it was ghastly. The right hand side and the back had been almost shaven. On the top were little tufts of hair sticking out at all angles. But if that were not sufficiently alarming, the left side still sported thick locks that fell over my ear. All in all, with the shroud like sheet around my neck, I looked as though I could easily qualify for a lead part in a remake of the film 'The Living Dead'.

"I cannot possibly go anywhere like this," I gestured helplessly at the reflection.

"Nonsense my friend. You will be perfectly alright with Alfonso Hidalgo. We will finish it later."

Again I started to object but it was hopeless. Next he deftly removed the sheet, and then with a professional flick of the clothes brush he located some invisible hairs on my jacket. After this he swiftly removed his own jacket, tossing it towards a nearby chair and missing. Then, grabbing me by the arm pushed me, still protesting, towards the door. Once outside I was to be given slight compensation as there did not appear to be many people about. He then launched us both across the road, gesticulating with his free arm in case any vehicles might be heading in our direction.

*

Now, if the street lacked people, it was the complete opposite once inside the 'Tasca'. It was packed. Waiters were trotting in all directions, while at the white marble bar customers were industrially munching their way through a great variety of 'tapas' washing everything down with the local, weighty, red wine served in the usual earthenware jugs. I groaned inwardly as the barber, refusing to let go of my arm, called out, "Buenos Dias everyone. This is my friend, the Englishman."

There was a distinct lull in the conversation as all eyes turned in our direction. Automatically I reached up and brushed back what remained of my hair, grinning stupidly as though it were some frightful joke. Several of the customers I noticed started nudging each other and others, obviously acquainted with my companion's coiffure abilities, looked on sympathetically.

"Come, my friend," said Alfonso, gently guiding me to the bar. "A glass of wine and perhaps a plate of 'Cinco Jotas' the finest ham in the entire world."

I grabbed a vacant stool in one corner and tried, desperately, to make myself inconspicuous. No such luck. The waiter who served us with a plate of ham and cheese had, without doubt, informed the kitchen staff as from then onwards I saw a series of faces grinning at me through the glass panel in the kitchen door. Alfonso then insisted on introducing me to various friends, some wearing black ties, which I presumed were in preparation for the funeral that evening. The wine flowed and after a while

I thought, "What the hell. Nobody knows me anyway so I might just as well enjoy myself." More appetising dishes appeared and I sampled them all, admitting to myself that Alfonso was right about the smoked ham. It was by far the best I had ever tasted.

Eventually, we moved over to the dining tables and prepared ourselves for the main meal with an even larger jug of wine being placed in front of us, prompting me to hope that I would find a suitable place to park up for a 'siesta' that afternoon. After ploughing through a main dish of 'Churrasco', barbequed steak, I was relieved when we eventually reached the coffee and brandy stage of the proceedings.

It was at that point that the door of the restaurant opened and people stood aside as in marched a short, round, very official looking man in police uniform. His cap was firmly set upon his head, signifying that he was there on duty. Clearly he was well-liked by the customers as there was a lot of handshaking and back slapping. Then he was speaking earnestly with one man in particular who later I was to discover was the mayor. Both of their heads turned in my direction.

"What now?" I thought as the police official made his way over to our table.

A momentarily look of surprise crossed his face when he noticed my hair. However, he quickly realised the situation when he saw my companion. Leaning over he whispered urgently into the barber's ear, then stood up waiting for some sort of reaction. Alfonso stared up at him then beckoned him to be seated and made the introductions.

"Don Christopher," he began formally, "I would like you to meet our Chief of Police, Don Juan Rincon."

I returned the handshake and the official removed his cap.

"Apparently he has a problem," explained Alfonso. "He would like you to help him."

"He has a problem," I thought and wondered, "What about me?" I smiled anyway. "But of course. What can I do for you?"

"Well," began the police chief, rather doubtfully, glancing at my hair, "we have arrested a man and we cannot understand him. He has a British passport and we are looking for someone to interpret for us. This man is also …," here he looked at me a little apologetically, "rather drunk."

I nodded and said that I would be most pleased to help in the matter.

"By the way, has this man done anything wrong, apart from being drunk that is?"

"Done?" repeated, the chief turning red in the face, "I should say that he has done something wrong. I will tell you what he has done, Sir. He has been arrested for impersonating a woman, Sir. That's what he has done!"

"A woman?" I echoed, rather foolishly, not believing my ears.

"Yes, Sir. A woman!"

*

The Town Hall also served as the police station and was structurally similar to the one where I had been held in Torrente, Valencia. However, here in this particular village, the two massive wooden doors appeared to be permanently open.

Together with Alfonso clinging to my arm, we were ushered inside where I found myself in a charming old courtyard. Here it was cool and would certainly be a first class refuge to seek when the summer heat descended on the area. Tables and chairs scattered about and I could see ridges made by cart wheels on the centuries old cobble stones. Overhead a roughly constructed rustic framework provided not only shade but a confusion of grapevines that must have produced an abundance of fruit in the previous month. Several doors led off the yard with the one nearest to the street displaying a sign that read 'INFORMACIÓN'. It was all very peaceful and not what one would expect as being a place for miscreants of law and order. "More like somewhere to hold a barbeque," I thought to myself.

The police chief signalled that we should follow him over to the far side where I could see two heavy, metal doors both with iron grills at head height. At the second grill a red bearded face with bloodshot eyes beneath shaggy brows peered out at us.

"There," said the chief, dramatically pointing at the face, "There he is!"

I just stood there staring. "But that's a man," I said, rather stupidly, immediately regretting having let the words pass my lips. "How could anyone with a beard like that impersonate a woman?"

"Open the door," he ordered a civil guard who had appeared. Then, "You, there, stand back," he said, gesturing towards the prisoner.

A monstrous key that seemed more in keeping with the Tower of London was fitted into the lock and the door swung open.

"There!" cried the chief dramatically pointing at a pair of the hairiest legs I had ever set eyes on, "He's wearing a skirt!"

The man himself was big. Another 'Big Ted' from the brogue shoes and tartan socks to the very top of his head, which if he had stood upright would be touching the roof of the cell. His beard hid most of his face but it was easy to see that he was certainly not smiling. I turned to the policeman.

"What he is wearing," I explained, indicating the offending garment "is not a skirt. It's a kilt."

At the word 'kilt' the giant took a step towards us. "An' hew the hell might yew be, laddie?" he growled.

I grinned up at him. "Don't worry I'm here to help you," I said, thinking quickly.

He stared hard at me and for the first time noticed my hair. We both remained staring at one another for a few seconds. Then clasping both his ham-sized hands to his face, the man wheeled round and staggered back into the cell. They've sent ma a bloody poofta!" he howled. "A bloody poofta!"

My companions stared at me in wonderment at the reaction my few words had produced. Alfonso, who had now moved forward to see for himself just what the problem was about, had to be restrained by the police chief. I grinned foolishly at them at the same time calling out to the man, "Sorry, but I'm not usually like this."

The lament grew even louder. "That's what they all say! A bloody poofta!"

"What's happening?" the police chief hissed in my ear.

"Look." I explained, "What he is wearing is a kilt. A Scottish kilt. From Scotland."

"Oh!" the chief said looking at me oddly.

"Scotland," I repeated.

He continued to stare at me, and then asked carefully, "And what is Scotland?"

I stared at him in amazement. "He doesn't even know where Scotland is," I thought. Then deciding that this wasn't exactly the time and place for a geography lesson, I replied, "It's a part of England where men wear the kilt."

"Still looks like a skirt to me," said another civil guard who had joined us. We all gazed down at the backs of the hairy legs as the man, leaning with his face to the wall continued muttering, "A poofta! A bloody poofta!"

"Look," I tried again, "It's a National costume, something like those white dresses and pointed hats that they wear in Malaga for the Fiestas. I'm sure this man doesn't know that it is not the thing to wear around here."

The chief's expression softened a little. Then I had an idea. "If he put on a pair of trousers could he leave?"

I waited while for him to digest this one and we stood staring at one another. Next, with considerable experience behind me as to what motivates Spanish authorities, I added, "You know something; it would save a lot of complications and an awful lot of paperwork."

I let this suggestion sink in and after a moment he replied, "Alright, but I'm not having him walking around my town like that."

"Fine," I said immediately turning and sticking my head through the cell door. "Look," I called out to the figure that seemed to be conversing with the wall, "Have you got any trousers?"

The muttering changed to an ominous rumbling noise that one might associate with a volcano about to blow its top. Turning he advanced menacingly towards me looking as though he would have no difficulty in tearing me from limb to limb. "Yew jus' listen ta me, Laddie!" he snarled, "I doon't know hoo tha' hell ye are but these are ma troosers!"

The group behind me, which appeared to have increased in numbers, retreated several paces.

Bloodshot eyes glowered down at me. "Wid it be ma kilt yer afta? 'Cause if it is ah'll brek yer back!"

Taking a pace to the rear I waved my hands. "No, no, certainly not," I tried reassuring him, "It's just that the problem seems to be your kilt. They've never seen one around here before and if you put on a pair of trousers they will let you out and we could all go ...go.... and have a drink."

The eyes widened and turned from me to the crowd behind. "Ah doont ha' ney troosers but.... a drink did ye say?"

"Yes, a drink. If not God knows how long you're going to be here."

"Who did that t' ye?" he gestured to my hair and instinctively my hand went to my head.

I considered explaining but it did not seem the appropriate moment.

"Di' they hol' ye doon?" he went on with a sudden change of mood, at the same time placing a sympathetic paw on my shoulder. Then giving the group a significant stare said forcefully, "Let ma ken hoo did it t'ya an' I'll mullock him right noo."

A shuffling of feet behind me confirmed that just by the sound of his voice and expression the support team was backing off even further.

"Look." I tried again ignoring the offer, "If we get hold of a pair of trousers will you put them on just to get out?"

He gazed thoughtfully eyeing the assembly at the back. "And a wee drink ye say?"

"And a wee drink," I replied breathing a sigh of relief.

Turning I walked over to the chief. "He says he is sorry for the problem he has caused and that he will put on a pair of trousers and leave."

"Has he got a pair of trousers?" somebody asked.

"No, but if we find a pair it will solve the dilemma," I said not having considered this one.

"That's all very well," someone else offered, "but where by all the Saints are we going to find a pair to fit him?"

We stared at the huge man who stood there swaying gently and gazing about him.

Then another voice said, "I might be able to help."

All eyes turned to the barber. "I'll need about half an hour and some to come with me. My eyesight is not too good these days."

The chief turned and spoke to one of the group who nodded in agreement and catching Alfonso by the arm they walked off.

"May we sit over there?" I suggested, pointing to one of the tables as no one seemed to know what to do next.

The police chief nodded and indicated the civil guard to relock the cell door on the Scotsman.

"Wait," I said quickly, "I don't think that will be necessary. He will be alright with me."

The chief then gave me a searching look as though there might be some collusion between the man and myself.

"Alright," he agreed, "but remember he is your responsibility."

I nodded and we all moved over to the table with the hairy giant following.

"And a wee drink," a voice prompted in my ear as we sat down at one of the trestle tables.

Turning to the chief I smiled, "Just a little wine perhaps? It's only to keep things on an agreeable level."

He nodded reluctantly and motioned to one of the civil guards who hurried away to reappear almost immediately with two one litre Coca-Cola bottles filled with Manzanilla wine and a quantity of plastic cups. We made ourselves comfortable and just to keep things moving along, I said conversationally to the hairy giant, "And what's your name?"

"Alex," he muttered, at the same time his eyes watching the guard pour the amber liquid into the cups.

"Well I'm Chris," I said intercepting the large hand that was already reaching out for a cup.

He shook it briefly, reached out and grabbed a cup, depositing almost all the contents down his throat in one gulp.

"Just please take it easy, Alex," I hissed, between clenched teeth. "There's plenty more."

A second cup followed immediately and you could see that everyone present was most impressed. One of the civil guards wriggled uneasily on the slatted chair possibly considering that it would not be too long before some restraint action was required.

"Take it easy, Alex," I pleaded again, "And let's get this over with."

The beard came to within inches of my face and the red eyes bored into me. "Jus' ye point him oot, laddie," he whispered threateningly, "An' I'll mullock 'im!"

For the lack of some sort of reply I foolishly raised my hand to my head and said, "No, it's alright really. It's just a joke."

"A joke?" he echoed in a voice that had everyone present waiting for the explosion, "is this wha' this shoower cal' a joke?"

He glared around at the company which now numbered around ten with the police chief placed strategically at the head of the table glancing nervously at us. I smiled back at him at the same time slipping Alex another cup of wine.

"So what are you doing here, Alex?" I asked, changing the subject rapidly.

He then explained that he had been to a wedding in Portugal and was, at that moment, "Awa' hame t' Scotland." Apparently he had stopped in the village and after a visit to several of the bars had staggered into the courtyard looking for a toilet. Some bright policeman had directed him to the cell and Alex falling for the trick found himself behind bars.

The two litre bottles of wine were soon emptied and I was wondering what was going to happen next when, thankfully, Alfonso and his companion returned. They came over to the table with the barber carrying a white plastic bag from which, with the air of a conjurer, he produced an enormous pair of black trousers. The whole party, apart from Alex who was examining the empty coke bottles, broke into spontaneous applause. There were cries of "Bien hecho, barbero! Well done, barber!"

The garment was handed to the chief who stood and walked round to Alex who, smiling for the first time also stood rather unsteadily. The Scotsman, with a slight bow, accepted the proffered article and automatically shook the chief's hand. A high school prize giving could not have produced as much formality as existed at that moment. I nodded towards the cell and Alex moved, rather erratically, towards it and disappeared inside. The company sat holding their breath in anticipation, nobody speaking and all eyes fixed on the cell door. When the Scotsman reappeared the applause was magnificent as a more perfect fit could not have been found in any top class tailors. There followed plenty of hand shaking and even some back pounding. Alfonso wandered about looking more like the happy professor who had just blown up the laboratory.

As soon as all this had quietened down, I took Alex's arm and as diplomatically as possible, expressed my concern about him driving after all the drink. Instead of the angry rebuff I expected, he just said, "Well ah dinna min' tellin' ye ah cuid do wi' a wee nap."

I squeezed his arm, "I would hate to see you back in that place again."

With that I explained to the chief that Alex would be taking a 'siesta' in the back of his car for a couple of hours. The policeman, pleased to see the situation being resolved, nodded and thanked me for my assistance. With that we all accompanied Alex to his car, which turned out to be the one parked next to my van. Then after more handshaking, the red beard and black trousers disappeared into the rear seat of the vehicle where an appropriate tartan blanket served as a pillow. The giant curled up and with a final wave dismissed us all.

"Even such a man of his dimensions was no match for the local wine," I concluded.

I then bid a last farewell to the police chief, Juan Rincon, who promised me that the next time I visited the town he personally would arrange a small 'fiesta' for me. Alfonso, clinging to my arm again, suggested we return immediately to his shop. It was, indeed, a relief to drop comfortably into the leather chair and just let Alfonso finalize the massacring of my hair.

"Well, I think that is about it," he said a short while later. I opened my eyes and saw that it did not look too bad, or maybe that was the effect of the local wine? "Anyway," I thought, "I can always buy one of those jaunty wide brimmed-hats that I have seen the locals wearing."

Payment for the haircut was offered but Alfonso claimed it would hurt his dignity to accept so I persuaded him to take a little something for his charming granddaughter and this pleased him. He then insisted that we take just one little glass of wine to toast our meeting and to the next time.

This completed, we shook hands and I made my way to the door. From where I was it was possible to see my van and much to my surprise I saw that next to it were a crowd of women. All dressed in black they were milling around Alex's car like a flock of angry crows. One, particularly large, woman was industriously banging on the roof of the vehicle with a fist which, from where I was standing, could possibly match that of Alex's in size.

"What is the matter?" asked a voice near my shoulder.

"I've no idea," I replied and went on to explain what was taking place across the road.

Alfonso listened then quickly thrusting me to one side he reached up and reversed the 'Abierto' sign on the door to read 'Cerrado' and turned the lock.

"I think it would be better if you leave by the back door, Amigo," he said urgently   tugging at my sleeve.

"Why? What the devil is the matter?" I asked, pulling my arm away.

Then, staring into the pebble spectacles, I said slowly, "That is my van next to the bearded man's car, so if there is anything wrong I ought to know about it. Tell me now before I leave."

He started wringing his hands and shaking his head.

"Well?" I demanded.

"Well," he began reluctantly, "That woman you can see; the big one."

"Yes, I see her."

"Well, she is Pepe's widow," he replied lamely, as if that explained everything.

"And so what?" I insisted.

Grabbing my arm his voice became insistent, "Don't you see someone must have told her."

"Told her? Told her what?" I was still puzzled.

He was now pulling me away from the door. "The trousers, of course," he groaned.

It was then, through the haze of wine, I began to see a tiny light at the end of the dark tunnel and was suddenly wide awake. "Wait a minute!" I said. "Just where did you get those trousers?"

"Come quickly, my friend; through the back door." He was now pleading, urging me towards the curtain to the rear of the shop.

"No!" I resisted. "Not until you tell me."

He looked up, "I did explain to you that Pepe was a big man?"

"Yes. And what has that got to do with it?"

"And it was you who wanted to help the bearded one. I did my best."

"Go on."

"Well, we didn't know that she would want to take a last look at her husband, did we?" He stared gloomily at the floor still wringing his hands. "They put a little window in the coffin and that is usually sufficient," he finished miserably.

His words fell on my ears a terrible image floated before me of the barber and his friend sneaking into the church, removing the coffin lid and then making off with the deceased man's trousers.

"Quick!" I cried out panic stricken at the same time hurrying towards the back of the shop. "Get me out of here. I'll be back later tonight for the van!"

Chapter 21

Once again in Valencia, two significant incidents occurred. One was the parting of the ways with the company vehicle which did not really affect me too much. Then there was the notification that I was to appear in court for 'Resisting Arrest' when the police came for me; which did.

I turned up on the appointed day of the hearing, dressed in my three-piece chalk striped suit, pristine white shirt, dark tie and my lawyer. The charges were read out inferring that I had not only resisted the four policemen but had actually attacked them. I denied the charges completely.

The young lady judge then asked me if I had any questions and I replied by asking where were the four policemen whom I was supposed to have resisted as I wished to question them concerning the incident and in particular the brutal assault on my nine- year-old daughter? To my surprise not one of the four officials was present. The judge then declared the case 'Archivado' or filed away. I still smarted over all that we had passed but felt that although justice had not been done completely it was a much fairer deal than Brian and Mike Hill received.

However, that particular hearing was not to be the end of the story for within two weeks I received a harsh letter from the Civil Governor's office indicating that the powers of darkness, that still tend to appear in Spain, were not just going to walk away and forget the incident. The contents of this letter more or less stated that although my case was dismissed, such behaviour could not be tolerated and I had just three weeks in which to leave the country. Another hurried visit to my lawyer resulted in his studying the order and then congratulating me.

"What do you mean by it being good news?" I asked, not really believing my ears.

"Look, Chris," he explained. "We will present an appeal against this which will take at least two to three years to come to court."

"So what is so good about that?" I insisted.

"Well, for one thing you will not be able to pay any taxes or such because to all intents and purposes you simply do not exist. Not until the final sentence, that is."

"What then?"

He smiled and I was reminded how very much he looked to the actor who had played Mike Hammer in the television detective series. "I doubt if anything will happen," he explained. "Spain is now part of the European Community and cannot afford any such minor problems. No. The case will be put in the archives, of that I am sure."

So that was that and he was quite correct in that around two-and-a-half-years later he telephoned to say that was exactly what had happened.

"Life is full of surprises," I thought.

With the transit van gone it was obvious that I required transport so Gedo decided on what a car dealing friend said was an old but 'reliable' diesel engine Chrysler. A tank of a car which we agreed would serve our purpose. I was to make one more trip in this, on my own, as John had left us and was now involved in other things.

A short while after buying the Chrysler, as old as it was, it must have appeared attractive to, at least, one other person as I came along one morning to find that some would be thief had tried to steal it but without success. However, in the attempt the ignition lock had been ruined and, as usual, FU Inc., being still in evidence, it occurred on a day when I had agreed to accompany Mavis Venables to a glass factory in the village of Olleria some eighty kilometres from Valencia.

*

Mavis is one of those extraordinary personalities that sometimes one is lucky enough to come across in life. No way would Mavis stand out in a crowd; you could well pass her in the street without even noticing her; however, if you wandered into a room full of people it would not take too long to realise that Mavis was present. When referring to her height and exterior appearance she would probably rate a comfortable 'average' but they would be the only features of Mavis to which one could safely say is 'average'. As for the rest of Mavis, well that is a different. Slightly angular facial features permanently blessed with fine rimmed spectacles behind which lurk dark, very much alert, eyes absorbing the minimum amount of detail of what might be happening in the immediate vicinity. A sense of humour, might you ask? Yes and no, Mavis does not laugh readily but when she does all about her feel compelled to join in, the jocularity touching her lips then rising to her eyes until she throws back her head and laughs, naturally and without inhibitions.

On the other hand, when serious, one is presented with a rather schoolmarm expression. Pursing her lips and returning your gaze, her eyes instinctively let you know that underneath lies an astute mind and if it is an excuse that you are about to make it had better be a damn good one.

This proud Staffordshire lass, with the accent to go with it, was at that time one of the very few women directors on the board of a UK Plc. I know that at the Lincolnshire market gardening establishment, where she was based, Mavis was well liked by her staff, preferring to go ten-pin bowling or to a football match with 'the girls' than to indulge in other more sedate activities becoming her position.

I must admit that when I came to know her I felt somewhat sympathetic towards her fellow executives as she did say that during many of the board meetings she would not stand any nonsense from them. "Lets cut the crap," she would remonstrate with her colleagues, "and get down to the nitty gritty!"

So when FU struck in the form of a would be car thief, in no way did Mavis mind my fiddling with the cables under the dash board of the Chrysler in order to start the vehicle. In fact, I think she rather enjoyed the theatrics as it fitted in with the image she had of Spain.

It was the Fabriglass Company in Olleria which we visited some sixty kilometres distance from Valencia. Kathy, for some time, had been giving English classes to the staff there so when Mavis and I rolled up we were made doubly welcome. After the conducted tour of the factory where we saw at first-hand how various articles are still 'blown' by the traditional methods Mavis was able to source the particular articles she was seeking.

It was natural that Samantha took a shine to Mavis and as the feeling was mutual, we all had some wonderful outings whenever she visited Valencia. One evening Mavis was talking about her company car. Nothing too ostentatious where she was concerned, just a comfortable top of the range Ford Escort which she loved to drive. Karl Bodie, a German friend who was employed at a local jewellery factory, was present and later gave me an exquisitely handmade, solid silver key ring; I decided to make a present of it to Mavis at Valencia airport on the day she returned to England.

*

A short while after Mavis had returned to the UK, and for no particular reason that I could think of, I suggested to Kathy that we get married. We discussed the matter in detail and the question arose as to where, when and above all what about Samantha, who was going on for eleven years of age. In the end we decided that we could combine a trip to England for the marriage and involve Samantha in the celebrations. The latter part was eventually arranged by the invitations reading that Samantha Eva requested the pleasure of such and such a person on the occasion of the marriage between Christopher Wright and Kathryn Leiker. A photograph of Samantha in full traditional Valencia costume also appeared on the invitation.

Mac was pleased to oblige with all the UK arrangements and the wedding was to be held at Market Harborough registry office followed by the reception at the Lutterworth Golf Club.

As the time drew nearer, the Chrysler, looking even older, its headlights more in the direction of the breakers yard than was normal, received a good service by the local mechanic who, smilingly, suggested we keep our fingers crossed. Then when we eventually set off, with no immediate problems, the powerful diesel engine propelled us through France and finally on to England.

It was a short while after we arrived and only a short distance from our destination that the beast finally presented us with a broken clutch; shades of FU once again. Determined that nothing was going to put paid to our particular day the arrangements went ahead whilst the repair was taking place.

*

What a wonderful time was had by one and all. According to the forecast, temperatures would exceed those in the Bahamas which I took as a good omen in that our decision to cement our relationship had been the correct one.

With the recovery of the now repaired Chrysler, all three of us set out for an improvised honeymoon in Devon the day after our wedding. We chose the village of Morton Hampstead as our headquarters and from there just pottered around visiting various places of interest which included Dartmoor; places that I had become acquainted with when living in Exeter many years before.

Of course the usual adventures happened including our becoming involved for two days with a mad, drunken, gypsy horse dealer who lived in a crumbling old farmhouse out on the moor miles away from anywhere. The building was falling so much into decay that vines were actually curling in through most of the pane-less windows. There was no electricity only oil lamp lighting and what water there was had to be drawn from an exterior well. The only saving grace was a corral in which he kept several fine looking horses. However even this was marred by the fact that within the enclosure was also several rolls of barbed wire which posed a threat to the animals.

His lady partner, a sadly lame, latter day debutante, who had opted out and sat for most of the time doing crossword puzzles in old editions of 'The Times' newspaper. Every now and then during our conversation she would refer to 'Daddy' who was, apparently, someone in the 'City'.

All too soon these few halcyon days were over and we set off for Leicester again, before returning to Spain. It was on the Exeter by-pass, whilst negotiating one of the traffic islands that the car, for some reason, decided to come to an abrupt halt. I swore, Kathy just shrugged her shoulders and searched for a cigarette while Samantha giggled, happily, on the back seat.

Several attempts to restart it failed and I climbed out, lifted the bonnet and swore at the engine. With the bonnet still raised I tried again to restart the thing. No such luck. Some minutes later, when I decided that I really must start looking for help, there suddenly appeared a police patrol car which pulled up and dispensed a burly uniformed officer who strolled casually across to us and enquired if there was anything wrong. I resisted the temptation to tell him that there was no problem and that we were addicted to parking on traffic islands with the bonnet up just so that people like him would stop and ask bloody silly questions. But instead I said, "Bloody thing won't start, officer. That is what the problem is."

He stared at me thoughtfully. Shall we give it another try, Sir?"

"If you insist," I grumbled, turning the key in the ignition. "But it won't make any difference. I've tried it a dozen times already."

Of course, the engine immediately roared into life and he stood gazing at me while I, in return, gave him a sickly grin.

"A dozen times, did you say, Sir?" was all he said, walking round and slamming the bonnet shut.

As we pulled away I glanced in the rear view mirror and saw him sauntering back to the patrol car, shaking his head.

We stayed at my sister Josephine's house where she lived with her husband, Alan, and the day before we were we were due to leave for Spain we did all our shopping, loading the car up with goodies such as tea bags, Bisto gravy and anything else that we could not find in Valencia.

The day of the departure dawned brightly with hope and around ten o'clock we set out. I really know very little about car mechanics, having only a very basic knowledge of what goes on under a bonnet. However, on that particular day I did learn something and that was when the main drive shaft which connects the engine to the rear wheels falls off it produces a great deal of clanking noise which attracts the attention of anyone within a radius of a few hundred metres.

This occurred less than one mile and only five minutes from our departure point.

"FU seems to be working well today, "I commented to Kathy who, as usual, shrugged her shoulders preferring to remained silent.

Resignedly, unloading all our luggage onto the pavement, we were watched by a small gathering of people who, by the excited hum of conversation and comments that involved the steering wheel being on the wrong side of the car, seemed to think that we might well be setting up a street market of sorts. I then wandered off found a telephone and called a local garage explaining what had happened. They eventually arrived with a tow-truck, removed the registration plates, handing them to me and then relieved us of the car together with fifty pounds sterling for the exercise. So there we all stood in funeral like silence and watched as they drove off. It was 'Adios' and 'Bye bye' to the Chrysler that had died hysterically on the London Road, Leicester.

A short while later a taxi deposited us once again at my sister's who opened the door with a bright smile. "We thought you might be back. The kettle is already on," she said.

*

Two days later all three of us sat comfortably on a charter flight to Alicante and some four hours after landing we were once again home in Valencia.

"We really must get hold of a car," said Kathy. "Brother Tom is coming over from the States for a holiday and I promised that we would show him something of Spain."

"Any ideas?" I asked, thinking that our general state of affairs was not at all good for receiving visitors, family or otherwise.

Looking thoughtfully for a moment Kathy then said, "I'll speak to one of my students. Her father owns a garage. Perhaps he can help."

So a few days later we took a local train out to Manises to where Andrés ran his Ford agency and vehicle repair business.

"You want a car then?" he asked.

"Yes. Just temporary like," I replied. "To rent. Doesn't matter what it looks like so long as it goes alright."

He turned to the wall behind him on which sets of keys hung on hooks. His hand moved over them hesitatingly, and then finally settled on a set which he removed and passed over to me. "Here," he said, "take the Simca. She's old but very tough and reliable."

So Betsy joined the family on a temporary basis. It felt marvellous to have wheels underneath us again and Samantha was elated. Andrés was correct. The car, I estimated, was around twelve to fourteen years old but went extremely well. Small things like not being able to open the door on the passenger's side and a general creaking noise on left hand bends were in evidence but it did not deter us in anyway.

"Well it is only for a short time," I commented with my inbuilt air of optimism.

*

A short while afterwards we drove out to the airport to meet my brother-in-law from Kansas. Kathy came from a background that included both Russian and Germanic blood lines, so Tom was exactly as his photographs had portrayed him. In his middle fifties, large and well built but not going to fat too quickly. Like most of the male members of the family Tom was losing most of his hair prematurely but it certainly did not seem to worry him.

Passing through the customs he appeared somewhat nervous, this being his first trip outside of the USA, but when he saw the waiting committee in the form of Samantha, Kathy and me he relaxed and walked over. Softly spoken with a mid-west accent he embraced Kathy, shook my hand warmly then turned all his attention on Samantha. He groaned a little as he gamely struggled across the driver's seat to the passenger's side of the car and Kathy whispered, "Suffers from back problems."

Sitting there with his knees drawn up (the seat mechanism would not function) he chatted away with Samantha and Kathy as I drove back to the city.

"How's the motorcycle going?" enquired Kathy, after she had sked after all the family at home.

"Yu referr'n to the BMW?" asked Tom.

"No the other one. The new one."

"Oh, yu mean the Honda Gold Wing. Yup that's going fine, Sis."

The car creaked more than ever as we turned into our road. "Yup," repeated Tom again adjusting his weight at the same time wincing audibly. "An' the Cadillac is also going fine too."

Kathy helped him unpack once in the apartment. Tom, apart from suffering with his back, was also a dedicated hypochondriac and carried with him an amazing assortment of medication. A little later Kathy confided to me, "I soon put a stop to any nonsense that might pop up with all that rubbish he has with him."

"How did you manage that?" I asked.

"Just told him that he had better not become ill while he is over here as he might become dead pretty quickly!"

That first evening we all trooped out to meet friends at a local bar with Tom assuring us that drinks would be on his account as he had 'big bucks' with him. Sitting on the pavement terrace of a local bar was a new experience for Kathy's brother. We ordered, I had my usual beer, Kathy her occasional gin and tonic and as was expected, Tom, a Coca Cola.

"What's that?" asked Tom, as Kathy poured her tonic over the lemon and ice cubes which clinked temptingly in the glass.

"Gin and tonic, Tom."

Tom watched fascinated as she lifted the glass to her lips and sipped. "Never touch alcohol," he said.

"Really is that so?" I put in, awestruck by this admission. "You mean you have never actually tasted a gin and tonic in your life?"

"Nope. Never had the occasion to, I guess."

"Well try this," suggested Kathy, offering her glass.

"Don't know ah rightly should, Sis," he said, reaching out for the glass anyway and taking a tentative sip.

Silent for a moment we all watched as he took a further swallow, letting the liquid slip down his throat closing his eyes in concentration. Then he nodded, "Nope. Must say t'aint at all bad. I jest reckon I might try one o' those in a minute."

And so he did. It was the following morning over coffee and croissants, Tom admitted that he had slept 'perty well' the previous night.

*

That day we set off for a trip up the coast and into the mountains around the Teruel region with myself insisting on us taking little luggage just in case we had to walk away from Betsy if she decided to follow in the steps of the Chrysler. Pointing the car in the direction of Peñiscola that small, one time island city, where Papa Luna the last Spanish pope resided and the place that was to become famous for the film 'El Cid' staring Charlton Heston and Sophia Loren. Forsaking that main coast road we took to meandering around the back roads eventually stopping at the village of San Mateo.

Electing to sit on the terrace of a small local bar we had the usual 'almuerzo' or mid- morning break. Unfortunately the place did not do hamburgers so Tom chose the 'bocadillo' of ham and cheese which suited him fine.

"What's that?" he asked as I sloshed out the wine from the inevitable chipped earthenware jug.

"What's what?" I asked, not really sure as to what he was referring.

"Wine," said Kathy, coming to the rescue.

"Now please don't tell me you never drink wine?" I said.

"Nope, guess not. If ah did ah can't quite remember."

Again Tom observed Kathy closely as she lifted her glass to her lips and sipped appreciatively.

"Here try some, Tom," she said, offering her glass.

Tom accepted, took a mouthful, again rolling the liquid around his taste buds before swallowing. Then after a minutes silence he smiled. "Nope, must say t'aint bad at all. Ah reckon a glass o' that wouldn't do me no harm."

This process was repeated again when a dish of mixed olives was placed on the table. "Don't suppose you've ever tried these either?" I said pushing the plate over to him.

"Wrong this time, boy," he grinned. "Those thangs are what they put in pizzas, ain't they?"

"Sure are, Tom," I said, unable to stop myself from emulating his accent.

"On their own," said Kathy, spearing one of the small black ones with a tooth pick, "they are an acquired taste. You might not like them."

"Sure as hell ah'm a goin' to give 'em a try, sis," he replied, also reaching over with a tooth pick and spiking one of the 'Sevillanas'.

Well from then on my brother-in-law quickly became, in his own way, an enthusiast for the Spanish niceties. He was determined not to miss out on anything and after that first day whenever we stopped for a break he would come out with such comments as, "Must say this here wine is a might better than the last place," as he swirled it around his glass or "No way are these olives like the last place. No, Sir!" At such times Kathy and I exchanged brief smiles and were both happy to see him enjoying himself.

Although back in the States, Tom had travelled a great deal on his motorcycles or in his Cadillac, it seemed to me that he had conformed, like so many of his patriots, to being all American and had not therefore sampled the delights of any other culture or life style. Rather like the old American publicity jingle 'Buy a Chevrolet and see the USA." In making his decision to visit Spain he had broken away, even though it be only for a brief period, from the conventional way of life to which he had been accustomed over the last half a century. His camera clicked and snapped at everything and anything. Not being used to physical exercise Tom was not in good shape. However he would puff and pant his way enthusiastically around castles and up and down steps while Samantha clung to his hand.

We arrived at Rubielos de Mora, which was celebrating its annual 'Fiestas'. Flag- bedecked streets with loudspeakers blaring out the traditional 'Jota' music welcomed us and we began searching for somewhere to stay for the night.

"I don't think we will be likely to find anywhere here," I said, avoiding the pedestrians who were ignoring the traffic and wandering at will all over the road.

Then Kathy spotted a sign that read, 'Fonda'.

Whereas Tom thought that it was something to do with an American film star we knew that it indicated the whereabouts of an inexpensive place to stay for the night. I pulled over and Kathy slipped out of the car and disappeared inside the small doorway in order to assess the situation. Ten minutes later she reappeared to say that the 'Fonda' was, as expected, almost full. However they did have one large room with two double beds.

"It's the only place in town," she explained, "and it's only one thousand pesetas for the night."

I glanced at Tom not quite sure how he would react. "Mind roughing it for one night?" I asked.

"Can't say ah've really tried ….," he replied.

"But you just think you might," I finished for him.

The room was, as Kathy had described it, spacious, very sparse, with a sink over which hung a cracked mirror and one single tap which set the plumbing groaning and rattling when turned on. The two large, rather sad looking double beds were bereft of linen.

"Where's Kathy?" Tom asked Samantha who at that moment had walked into the room.

"Mummy has gone down to the bottom of the garden to collect the sheets off the line."

"Well ah'll be...," Tom said half to himself and sat down on one of the beds.

I was swilling myself with cold water then drying myself on one of the towels which seemed to be made out of sandpaper when Tom called me.

"Hey, Chris! Mind jest taking a lookee over here?"

"Sure. What is it, Tom?" I said, wandering over to him.

"Here jest under ma mattress."

"What is it, Tom?" I asked again, puzzled.

"God dam it. Can't yu see?" he demanded, lifting up the rather flimsy foam mattress, all of three inches thick, "It's a door. That's what it is. A real door!"

"So it is," I said, attempting to be nonchalant and avoid any real problems that might terminate with us leaving again. "You can see where the handle was," I added taking a closer look.

"Yea!" said Tom. "But what in the name of sweet Jesus is that thar door doing on ma bed?"

It was obvious that the thing had been placed there to compensate for the worn sagging springs. So thinking quickly I said, "Well, Tom. Kathy explained to me that you suffered with your back and over here in Europe the doctors recommend that anyone with these problems should sleep with something solid under the mattress." I looked around the room. "You know what? I reckon that your sister has gone and found us some sort of health farm."

He followed my gaze around the cheerless chamber, his eyes becoming wider at my comments. "Health farm!" he then exploded, "Health farm! Whaaat! At three bucks a day for four people. Ya gotta be outa ya head!"

"Don't worry," I said, sympathetically, thankfully hearing Kathy arriving with the sheets. "After a couple of those gin and tonics you like, some wine, a good meal and being chased around by an unhappy bull, you'll sleep fine."

"Bull?" he asked, puzzled. "Bull. What unhappy bull?"

"Yew jest wait and see ol' Buddy boy," I replied, winking at him only too happy to have distracted his attention from the improvised facilities of the Fonda. "Tonight we are going to see 'El Toro Embolado'".

*

And so that evening we threw ourselves into the hectic throng of revellers, eventually finding ourselves a reasonably less crowded bar where we tucked into 'calmares a la romana', 'gambas a la plancha' and 'patatas bravas', all accompanied by the inescapable red wine.

Just outside the bar the usual barricades of farm carts had been manoeuvred into place around the village square and a liberal quantity of sand had been scattered over the cobblestones. In the centre a large post, slightly thicker than a telegraph pole and around two metres in height, stuck out of the ground like some giant finger pointing accusingly at the darkening sky as though daring it to rain.

It was around midnight that a good solid horsebox was driven into the now sealed off area and parked with the rear end towards the post. Immediately there was the usual furious activity with a dozen or more young men clustering around the vehicle all shouting advice and instructions to one another. One of the older youths carrying a heavy length of rope around ten metres in length which looked as though it had once helped to moor the Queen Mary was helped onto the roof of the vehicle. At the end of the hawser was a carefully made noose which he manipulated, dropping it through a hole in the top of the vehicle, and after several attempts succeeding in hooking it around the bull's horns.

It was then fed through an opening in the rear door and on through a hole in the pole, rather like a giant needle and thread. As the rope stretched out it was enthusiastically grasped by around fifteen youths who took up a stance that could be likened to a tug-of-war team.

Eventually all was in place and the rear door was carefully opened and the ramp dropped. There was the usual distinctive hush in the expectant crowd as everyone concentrated on the dark opening. Then slowly the ominous black mountain of muscle and sinew began to slide clumsily down the ramp. Someone shouted and the volunteers holding the rope heaved on it and little by little drew the reluctant animal to the pole until it was tightly fixed by the head to the wooden mast, nostrils flared and eyes staring.

Next to appear on the scene was another official carrying two coconut-shaped objects which were composed of layers of wax bound together with tape. These balls were firmly fixed by metal clamps to each of the bull's horns. Then, when all was in place, a prearranged signal resulted in these being lit. The rope holding the bull was quickly cut and the animal set free.

The effect was instantaneous.

With flaming wax dripping from its horns it was off like crazy, careering after its tormentors and followed by more howling youths. In the now darkened square, surrounded by ancient, crumbling, buildings with their high beamed roofs and the improvised barrier of old wooden carts, I felt part of some mysterious spectacle that was rooted way back in time. Amongst the participants I noticed several youths who, only one hour before, in the bar we had visited had been chatting away to each other and could have come from any middle to upper class families. Now they were transformed into screaming savages hot on the heels of the sinister black shadow with the flaming horns.

Tom, of course, was entranced by all this and his camera clicked and whizzed like mad. At one point, no doubt to his recent encounter with wine and several gin and tonics, he insisted on pushing his way from behind the barrier and into the square in order to take few 'close ups'. Fortunately with the help of several of the locals, I managed to restrain him but not without a struggle.

That night, totally exhausted, we all slept well oblivious to our surroundings and next morning Tom was just that much quieter than usual as he nursed one of his first real hangovers. The rest of this short but memorable holiday was spent in a more relaxed mode and we stayed with just sightseeing and picnicking.

When we finally took Tom to the Valencia airport, a few days, later he had with him more than just a few of the local 'goodies' packed into his suitcase. I expressed my doubts about the US customs letting him pass with olives, ham, sausages, not to mention brandy and wine. However he just shrugged and growled, "Ah guess ah jest feel lucky so don't you guys go worryin'. In fact if ah could 'ave gotten one o' them thar god damn long horns in ma bag ah reckon I could 'ave gotten that threw as well!"

The day after he flew out on, as he put it, the 'big bird', we received a telephone call from Chicago. By the sound of his voice and the riotous background noise, Tom's smuggling had been successful and he was celebrating with friends.

*

The month of September saw us back in the routine and I received a telephone call from Tony Strodder. "How are the 'Tapas' in Dolfis, Chris."

"Fine, Tony. Well at least they were last night. Why do your ask?"

"I am arriving tomorrow. Is that alright?"

"Fine, Tony. Your room is ready."

Still in possession of Betsy I telephoned Andrés and he confirmed that I could hang on to the car. This was good news as Tony wanted to visit the 'La Ilusion' factory in Zaragoza and that was an indication that we would be away for a few days. An unexpected trip would suit me just fine.

Samantha immediately transferred her allegiance to Tony when he stepped foot into the apartment, possibly the reason being that, being in the toy industry, every so often Tony would dispense toy samples to her like an out of season father Christmas.

*

So the day after his welcomed arrival Betsy creaked and groaned her way to Zaragoza. However, I felt happy that the passenger door had been fixed and there was not the usual, 'do you mind climbing in the driver's side and mind the gear-lever as you go. Ha! Ha!'

The first stop was made some two hours after setting out. A small rather dingy bar set at a crossroads to the north of Teruel and looking rather solitary, apart from a petrol station for company opposite. This was the midmorning break for Tony and me and with the taste buds in full flow our stomachs were blessed with a large plate of finely sliced Arragones ham accompanied by hot, freshly baked, thick crusty bread. Of course, once again not forgetting the powerful, because you're driving, heavy red wine from Cariñena some eighty kilometres further on.

Zaragoza was waiting for us as always at the end of a dry dusty carpet across the grey powdery plain. Just past the giant football stadium we dived headlong into the cool embrace of the wide, flower-bedecked, tree-lined 'Avenidas' with their sophisticated shops and department stores.

In this one city where one is never far from the shadow of the awe-inspiring cathedral, Pedro, owner of the toy factory, welcomed us with open arms while his retired father sat by in silent anticipation of 'doing business'. After twenty minutes general conversation followed by two hours of examining samples and discussing prices with myself interpreting, Pedro glanced at his watch and announced that it was lunchtime. With anticipation and an appetite to go with it we were hauled off to a nearby restaurant.

Here, in a smoky haze of barbecued lamb, Pedro introduced us to the owner who explained that he, personally, went twice a week to the local cattle market selecting the lambs for his kitchen whilst they wandered around on hoof, still very much alive. He was obviously well endowed with excellent eyesight as the meat that was placed before us would have fallen apart under the pressure of a postcard.

With lunch over Pedro insisted on giving us a sightseeing tour, as he put it, 'Mi ciudad' or my city. Apart from the cathedral and the Goya frescos this, to my delight, included an unexpected visit to the 'Plaza de Toros' or Bullring where we found the three 'Matadors' who would be appearing at the 'Corrida' the following day.

Standing quietly to one side we watched while they demonstrated their skills with the use of a bull's head mounted on two wheels and manoeuvred by an agile youth, to five aspiring young apprentices who were attending the 'Taurino School'. I estimated that the ages of these young 'Aficionados' ranged from not more than fourteen to sixteen years. My luck was in as one of the fully fledged matadors turned out to be a favourite of mine, Julio Robles.

I had always admired the style of this Valencia bullfighter. One of two brothers dedicated to the art, Julio was certainly inclined to be innovative during most of his fights, especially when animating a sluggish or cowardly bull that had received too much punishment under the 'pic'. He did not possess the rigidity of the present day Vicente Barrera who will stand tall, feet firmly planted together as though buried in concrete in the traditional 'Seville' style and pass the bull back and forth at chest height whilst occasionally staring arrogantly at the crowd. Nor did Julio have the suppleness of Spain's present day 'Numero Uno' bullfighter, Enrique Ponce. However Julio Robles had the fame of being one who would always give the public their monies worth.

Naturally I was thrilled when Pedro took us over and presented Tony and I as the group took a break. Even more excited when Julio insisted on handing me his magenta and yellow-coloured fighting cape then showing me the way to execute a simple half 'veronica', a full 'veronica' following on with a rather complicated 'chiculina' where one turns into the cape as the bull passes.

Having forsaken any inhibitions some good few years before I tried my best but all this only served to convince me that I would certainly not be up for grabs by any Spanish promoters.

Not six months after this incident I read that this charming, rather shy, 'torero' was badly gored whilst performing in France. The injury, sadly, committed him to a wheel chair for life and he died some years later. But those few moments I passed in the Zaragoza bullring still live on for me.

That night Tony and I dined at a Basque restaurant not a stone's throw from the cathedral with me ordering 'Lubina a la sal'. This sea bass is best cooked whole within a coating of rough sea salt on the griddle.

Served in its entirety, including the head, and then opened up, the delicate moist white flesh literally melts in your mouth. Everything was perfect in this pleasant restaurant with the only incident that introduced a little tension during the banquet being that a brusque manoeuvre with my knife inadvertently propelled the fish's, seemingly huge eye, directly onto Tony's entrecote steak. There it lay staring up at him as if daring him to continue eating. My comment that this would see us through the following day's meeting fell on stony ground.

*

With Tony's business completed, the return journey to Valencia was made via Alcañiz and Morella. For some forty kilometres the highway ran parallel to the erratic Ebro River which we could occasionally glimpse in the distance across a broad plain. Every now and then fields of pale peach and almond trees hoved into sight, their shimmering images becoming more distorted as the heat of the day increased. The rather sad town of Alcañiz came and went with the road writhing up and across a range of pine and beech covered hills occasionally opening up to offer startling vistas towards the Ebro's delta at Tortosa. It was after midday when we arrived at what I can honestly describe as the perfect example of the romantic spirit of Spain in its entirety.

The silhouette of Morella, at first sight, comes as a shock; totally unexpected. A long, wide, patchwork quilt, valley within the centre of which, rising to over one thousand meters above sea level, is what can only be defined as monstrous slab of rock crowned by the grey, rugged remains, of a castle. Around the base of this, cluster the red tiled roofs and white washed buildings, as though still seeking comfort and protection of the magnificent ramparts. It is understandable why this strategically placed capital of the 'Els Ports' region should have warranted the attention of both 'Templers' and 'Carlistas' some two hundred years ago with the latter group being led by the colourful figure of General Ramon Cervera, known as 'El Tigre del Maestrazgo' or the Tiger of the Maestrazgo.

On that particular day we dined in a quiet, cool and black beamed dining room of a small 'Casa de comidas' or eating place. It was one of those few establishments now remaining in Spain where once seated at your table whatever is available is placed before you. First to arrive is usually a litre jug of ice cold water together with a plate of mixed olives and a bar of bread, a simple green salad and, of course, a jug of the local wine. The main dish at that one exceptional restaurant was never disappointing and was nearly always deliciously tender lamb chops prepared on the griddle. The use of anything else but your fingers for eating these would have attracted attention and so you could chew and suck on the delicate bones as much as you liked in the accepted fashion.

There were only two other fellow diners present who appeared to be a clerical version of Laurel and Hardy. The obese one of the duo was persisting with some religious theory involving Saint Vicente Ferrer and Saint Vicente Marti, the latter being the patron Saint of Valencia, whose mummified arm can still be seen in the city's cathedral. Meanwhile his companion, who seemed no thicker than the toothpick he was applying to his teeth, was arguing his point in a shrill piping voice that grated on my ears. Finally, being unable to stand it any longer, I called across to the pair politely suggesting that perhaps it might be more Christian if we all could continue conversing in moderated tones as my friend, here I indicated Tony, being a committed Buddhist, was inclined to prayer during his meals. After that they fell silent, glancing suspiciously every now and then in our direction.

I explained to Tony what I had said and he gracefully complied by pausing between mouthfuls, raising his eyes heavenwards and mumbling to himself. In one of these murmuring moments I thought I detected something that sounded very much like, "I'll get you for that bloody fish's eye, you sod!"

It was as we were arriving back in Valencia that Tony mentioned that he was buying his wife a Rover car. So once home I telephoned my jeweller friend, Karl, who came around that evening and presented Tony with the appropriate, hand made, solid silver, Rover key ring. Tony responded by inviting all of us over to the Dolfis bar for some 'tapas' and drinks. The following day I drove him to the airport at Manises. It was sad, as it always was, to see Tony go, but I felt a little relieved in that I was now able to rest up for a couple of days.

Chapter 22

The calendar read September nineteen ninety when, metaphorically, Kathy and I struck oil, at the same time ignoring the fact that something good happening usually indicates that FU is not far behind. Nevertheless we enjoyed, at least, two days of euphoria.

Kathy was in contact with Loughborough College, England, for the purpose of organising Spanish students to travel there with the object of studying the English language. The college, situated in this pleasant old market town not far from my Leicester home, informed her that courses for European students wishing to go for a minimum of two weeks were subsidised by the European Government. Immediately I called the offices of 'Las Provincias' the Valencia regional newspaper which laid claim to having the largest circulation. This strategic move resulted in some kindly journalist writing a short article describing the courses and the costs involved. He also went so far as to mention our address and telephone number.

Immediately we were deluged by calls from students wishing to take advantage of the offer. As all this occurred at the beginning of September there were around twenty five young students asking for the opportunity to attend before they returned to their studies around the middle of October. Diligently Kathy and I took all the necessary details, at the same time imparting a glowing, but true, description of the college, Loughborough and the surrounding countryside. Happily, we then faxed the relevant information to the College. Within one day things had changed dramatically.

No way, we were informed, could the college accept such a large intake of Spanish students all at the same time. Wonderful! I was angry and Kathy was, naturally, upset. Further faxes and telephone calls failed to change the situation. They were adamant. Only one thing for it we agreed, and that was for me to make a trip over there and sort the matter out on the spot.

My flight was booked and I travelled with the rather absurd idea of contacting Esther Rantzsen, star at that time of the popular television program for justified complaints. However, eventually I found myself facing the Principal of the College in Loughborough, a most pleasant down to earth gentleman who completely took the wind out of my sails. He was most apologetic as to what had occurred but could do little about it as too many students of the same nationality would create a monopoly and this would not be good for the others attending. He then offered me full facilities of his office together with his charming secretary in order to help us relocate students to other similar centres in the United Kingdom.

In hindsight the incident, although extremely harassing at the time, did enable us to broaden our possibilities with other such colleges including Coventry, Cheltenham, Barry, Liverpool, Thurrock and many more. All the students who did actually attend the first trip to Loughborough enjoyed and benefited by the experience, returning to pass on the good news to friends. We were now firmly established in another fairly lucrative business.

*

The Loughborough incident also brought me in contact with Bob Cooper. A tanned, tall, good looking, tight athletic figure of a man he exuded, to me personally, a demoralising air of fitness. He taught engineering at the college which probably accounted for his speaking in clear precise tones with a North Midland's accent.

Together with his charming Spanish wife from the Catalonian region of Spain he welcomed me into their home and we became good friends. Bob confided in me over a couple of the best pints of beer I have ever come across, that he and his family would possibly be moving to San Carlos de la Rapita, Spain. There they were to set up an English academy under the Loughborough College flag. Their plans eventually came to fruition and Bob was appointed to the committee of the European government responsible for the organisation and distribution of funds relating to various educational programmes.

*

On returning to Valencia I found Kathy happily organising students for the UK study trips and then towards Christmas I received a message from

Andrés the car dealer. Through his daughter he asked that I go over to Manises with the equivalent of around three hundred pounds. It would be sad to see Betsy go but the cost of the rental for around four months seemed more than reasonable.

When I walked into his office Andrés was sitting behind his desk, telephone in hand and talking away to someone or other. Waving oil-stained fingers at me he indicated that I should sit down. I did so at the same time placing the car keys together with the money on the desk. Finishing the conversation, he then hung up and sat there looking at the desktop. "I think there has been some misunderstanding," he said after a couple of minute's silence.

"But there is the money and there are the keys," I pointed out. I reached over and tentatively moved the items across the desk towards him. "And," I added sincerely, "we are most grateful to you."

"No, no", he explained carefully, "you misunderstand me. I just want the money. The car is yours."

I could not wait to see Kathy and Samantha's faces when I rattled back to Valencia in dear old Betsy who seemed, at that moment, to be going better than ever.

It was after I had imparted the good news we received a call from Tony Strodder asking that I check on a delivery he was expecting from one of the Spanish suppliers. "Anyway, how are you, Tony?" I asked, after confirming the necessary information.

"I'm fine thanks, Chris," he replied. "It's my wife, Eileen, who is not too good."

"Why Tony? What happened?"

"An accident in the car. Nothing too serious but the car's a mess."

I expressed my regrets and asked if there was anyway in which I could help.

"Not really, Chris." There was a brief silence then, "But you could post me a Volvo key ring for my own car."

"Sure, Tony. No problem. I will speak to Karl."

This was soon done and the weeks went by and we settled in for the Christmas celebrations.

*

Yuletide in Spain starts on Christmas Eve and continues through until the sixth of January. A costly business for the parents but a child's delight in that they come to expect not only the gifts from Father Christmas but also from the Three Wise Kings who appear on the night of January fifth. In between, of course, are the New Year's Eve festivities as well. It is on this night that the majority of the Spaniards dine out. In fact, for the majority, it is a 'must' that they be seen out and enjoying themselves. That particular New Year's Eve we elected to go to Antonio's restaurant in Alacuas a small village just outside Valencia.

I had met Antonio some years before whilst in Cullera. We naturally became friends when I discovered that he had been working in Leicester, employed as hairdresser for Raymond, one of the top London houses. It was always fascinating for me to listen to him relate stories as to his sixteen-years of living in my home town.

One day as we shared a bottle of wine together, he said, "You know, Chris. I was in England for six months before I realised that you could have more than two pints in any one pub."

I grinned, thinking that this must be some kind of joke and said, "That is ridiculous, Antonio. You can drink as many pints as you like in any pub. What happened?"

He then went on to explain that when he first arrived in Leicester he had stayed with his brother-in-law and it was natural that they would visit the local pubs. "Well", he continued, "that first night when we went out we had already been celebrating before leaving the house. Then when we arrived at the pub and had a couple of pints each the landlord pipes up, 'Right that's enough you two. On your way!'".

After that the same scene had apparently been repeated on various occasions in different establishments.

"I don't understand it, Antonio," I said, somewhat confused by this.

"You wouldn't but I eventually did," he came back smiling. "Latin temperament and all that. You know how we are. Most of us Latinos cannot talk without waving our arms about. In fact most of us would be struck dumb if we lost the use of our arms. So you see all that it required was a couple of pints and we would start arguing away in Spanish at the tops of our voices. Then the landlord would eventually shout, 'Alright! Enough you two. On yer bikes!'"

So that particular New Year's Eve 'Fiesta' was great and as I drove carefully back home I thanked my lucky stars that the breathalyser had yet to arrive in Spain. It also would not have occurred to me that future such celebrations for our small family could be counted on one hand.

*

The New Year began with hope as always. The Valencia gift fair was held as usual and included a ceramic section. Kathy, apart from her teaching, had been appointed agent to a Scottish Company, Hudson's International. The owners, a Mr. and Mrs. Leslie Wallace, made frequent buying trips to Spain and Kathy helped source products, negotiate prices and organise transport. Hudson International was based in Glasgow and sold high quality gift packs under various trade names including Mrs. Bridges Pantry and Laird's Larder. The products included decorative ceramic jars containing jams, marmalades, pâtés and mincemeats.

The major supplier of the ceramic pots was Francisco Lerma of Manises. Paco, as we knew him, could easily have played a double for the American film star, Steve Martin, and was extremely helpful in all aspects as a manufacturer. So what with one thing and another the New Year started well. In order to maintain the momentum of the students wishing to travel to England for the English courses we placed the appropriate advertisements in the 'Las Provincias' and I also contributed with various articles which were of interest. These articles varied in content but generally covered what the Spanish student was to expect when arriving in England including information on the various centres together with what was available on the leisure side of life over there.

Then one day I received a telephone call from a woman who explained that she wished to be included on one of these trips. "How long do you want to go for?" I asked.

"Around two weeks," came back the reply.

"Sorry to disappoint you," I said, "but there is no way that you are going to learn English in two weeks."

"Well actually it is just for a visit," she explained, "and I thought this might be an economical way of doing it."

"Look," I suggested, "I might be able to help you with information on bed and breakfast accommodation, travel and things so call round to my office. No charge. That is if you wish."

So an appointment was made for the following day.

She arrived on time and we sat down in the office. Small of stature with blond hair swept back in a pony-tail and eyes that hid behind expensive designer, tinted spectacles. She had obviously gone to a great deal of effort to select her clothes and her overall appearance was of one elegantly dressed female on the fast track to middle- age. However, there still remained a suggestion that at sometime in the past she had been a woman who would have had little difficulty in attracting plenty of attention from most male species.

We sat there for a while discussing her journey to England with myself rummaging through files in search of practical leaflets and the usual travel details. Then, after around half an hour, when I was tactfully guiding the meeting to a close, she suddenly asked, "Where are you actually from in the UK?"

"Leicester," I replied, but went on to explain that I had spent many years in the Surrey area near London.

"Surrey," she said, savouring the word nostalgically and pronouncing it 'Soory'. "Well that is precisely where I want to go."

"Really?" I nodded politely.

"Oh yes. I want to visit some friends I knew a very long time ago."

Then delving into her large, also designer, handbag she searched around and then triumphantly pulled out an envelope. "Do you still think they will be there?" she asked, depositing it onto the desk in front of me.

"Rather a silly question," I thought, but picked up the envelope.

By this time in life I was not given to showing surprise and read the five lines over just twice without making any immediate comment. Like suddenly finding a lost key to the door of a previous life, I was transported back some thirty five years. The words staring back at me from the creased and rather grubby paper would not normally have had any great deal of impact had they not been in my own handwriting. What was written there was my own name, my ex-wife's name, our Surrey address and telephone number.

I sat there a moment while she studied my face expectantly from behind the dark glasses.

"Well I know one who certainly won't be there," I said, slowly.

"Really?" she leaned forward hopefully; removing her glasses I saw she had very dark, very Spanish eyes.

"Yes," I confirmed smiling. "That's me. I'm sitting here."

Her mouth dropped open and she sat staring at me, with me wondering who the hell she could be. Of course after the initial surprise and some mutual questioning that this mysterious woman, who had arrived, like a breath of wind from my past, was non other than Isabel, who together with Tony her husband had owned the club near Farnham.

Memories of my lounging in J.M. Barry's chair came rushing back to me and I could almost hear the urgent clicking as the ball ran around the roulette wheel. No, Isabel did not travel to England but she became good friends with Kathy and me. This was a blessing as at a later, not too distant time, she was to be there to help when things became really grim.

*

Samantha was now thirteen years old and a very capable young lady. So much so that just a few weeks after her fourteenth birthday she travelled to England as 'Monitor' to a group of young people who would be studying English at Luton College.

Before this was to happen I would receive another telephone call from Tony Strodder to the effect that his business had collapsed. On the upside he told me that he had found employment with another company who had supplied him with a new and very expensive car. And please would I mail him the appropriate key ring.

"No problem, Tony," I confirmed. "I'll organise that immediately."

I think that the new employment lasted around six months as he called to say that this company had also folded. I could not believe it. "You know what, Chris?" he said. "I'm beginning to believe it's those bloody key rings."

"Don't be silly, Tony. How can it be the key rings?"

He then reiterated on the series of incidents that had occurred since taking home a key ring for his wife's Rover car.

"But," I protested. "it's not possible. I mean look at Mavis Venables. She had one ages ago and she hasn't had any problems. Not that I know of, anyway."

"Beginning to believe anything is possible," Tony grumbled into the phone. Then, "Tell you what, Chris. Send one to this address I'll give you now. Let's check it out shall we?"

I objected to this but did what he asked.

*

One bright, hot summer's day that year, Kathy, Samantha and I set out for France on holiday. Betsy was as steadfast as ever although I had insisted as usual that we take just sufficient luggage so that we could just walk away from the old girl if she decided to expire on us, sentiments, of course, being a different matter.

We eventually arrived in the very pleasant town of Condom, which for some reason had attracted out attention. Situated in the Armagnac region, of ancient Gascony, the surrounding countryside was not too dissimilar from Leicestershire, having soft undulating green hills, valleys, woods and always distant spires.

We soon made ourselves at home in an inexpensive but exceptionally comfortable hotel a few paces from the languid, river Baise whose source originated in the high Pyrenees. The hotel owner, Pierre, was a 'Pied Noir' from Algeria, who seemed to have gathered as regular customers, some of the most gregarious and delightful mixture of Frenchmen I had ever had the pleasure to come across.

One morning, after a fairly heavy night in the company of my new friends, I found an envelope on the breakfast table which revealed a rather intricate, gilt edged and wedding invitation. "What's this then?" I asked Pierre as he poured out the coffee into what would have easily served as soup bowls.

"A wedding," he explained. "You are invited to a wedding."

"Really? Now that is nice." I was very much impressed.

"Yes," he went on a little more seriously, "the reception is being held here and as your bedroom is directly overhead I suggested to the bride's father that it might be better for everyone if you were invited along."

For a moment I wondered whether or not this strategic move could be considered a compliment or otherwise but thanked him anyway. Naturally a great time was had by all and that night, as we fell into bed in the early hours, it mattered not that below us voices were still raised in song.

When travelling I always insisted on taking along a picnic hamper but not just the normal hamper. I always made sure that ours was packed with our own cutlery, plates, wine glasses and table cloth. I also am a believer that sitting on grass strewn blankets was not really comfortable so we had a table and lightweight chairs as well. And we loved it.

*

On one particular day I turned off the main road and was searching for a suitable place to set up things for our picnic, taking into consideration that it was extremely hot and adequate shade was of prime importance. Eventually coming to a bend in the narrow ribbon of a road we spotted a beautiful green leaf-clad elm tree around twenty paces into the unfenced field.

"That's it!" I said, stopping the car.

All three of us piled out and were soon sitting down comfortably picking a pâtés, tasting tomatoes and tugging at chicken legs from the Leclerc supermarket. Suddenly a small car came by and stopped opposite us with the lady driver taking the trouble to lean across the passenger's seat and wind down the window. She then gave a friendly smile, waved and called out, "Bon appetite!" We waved back thanking her. Then as quickly as she had arrived she was gone, disappearing in the direction of the small village further down the valley.

It was at that moment Samantha noticed the abundance of butterflies that had begun fluttering around our table with the occasional one settling onto ourselves. Although not an expert it was easy for me to see that there were a great variety of species present and we were treated to a fascinating display of kaleidoscopic movement which lasted until late afternoon when they quickly seemed to vanish from sight.

Naturally, after that special day we referred to the place as the 'Butterfly Field'. In later years I searched but was never able to find my way back there. It felt rather like trying to get back to sleep and continue with that one pleasant dream which most of us have experienced at one time or another.

*

"It worked!" cried Tony, over the phone just two days after our return to Valencia.

"What worked, Tony?" I said, quite pleased that something had.

"The key ring of course. The bloody man's gone bust. Just like that!"

"But, Tony," I protested.

"No seriously, Chris," he continued enthusiastically, "the guy's gone bust!"

"Fine, Tony, but what do you want me to do about it?"

The line went quiet for a moment and I could almost hear him thinking. Then his voice said cheerfully, "Send me another one."

"But, Tony."

"No 'buts', Chris. Just post another one."

He then gave me the make of car. "Who is it for, Tony?"

"My bank manager, who do you bloody well think it's for?"

The key ring was duly mailed off to Tony and things returned to reasonable normality, if that were possible. Samantha's success with her monitoring the group to Luton was such that the following year she was to take other young students to Coventry College. In the meantime we were kept pretty busy with all the various other activities including the arranging, on my part, of the monthly Luncheon Club.

*

The English Speaking Businessmen's Luncheon Club, as it is so named, still meets almost every last Friday of the month during most of the year. Local Spanish and English businessmen, together with any guests they might wish to bring along, gather for lunch at different interesting venues in and around Valencia. Initially an all male group, usually hosted by one Geoffrey Dobson, it has been in existence for over thirty years. With no rules, regulations, dues, secretaries, steering committees, this successful circle moves happily along, as someone once put it, 'better than many governments'. Members taking turns to organise the meeting will seek out interesting places whose culinary expertise would appeal to the majority. Those who attended would then pay their share and everyone is happy. All-in-all it is something to look forward to for myself and I have come into contact with many interesting personalities. Geoffrey, who was referred to as the Club's President without portfolio, had in the past sold his interior decorating and furnishing business in Sloan Street, London and retired to live in Perello a small coastal village some fifteen kilometres south of Valencia.

*

On one occasion Geoffrey confided in me that he had back problems which were slowly becoming worse. Then after a considerable number of visits to the doctor, combined with the usual tests, he was advised that a surgical intervention was needed to resolve the problem. Under a private insurance he was to have this done at one of the local Valencia hospitals and requested that I accompanied him to meet the surgeon involved. This I did and a date was set for the operation.

Geoffrey eventually came out of the hospital with enough metal plates in his spinal column to set off all the alarm bells ringing through whichever airport he decided to pass. It was on one of my visits that he said, "You know, Chris. I am not going to come out of this business."

"And why not, Geoffrey?" I asked.

"I had a visitor last night." He looked worn out and I could see that he was wondering whether or not to continue.

"And what visitor was that, my friend?"

"Well, Chris it was a sort of what might be called an apparition, spectre or whatever. Anyway it came through the window and perched at the end of the bed looking down on me."

"Come on, Geoffrey, are being serious?" I said, not quite knowing how to respond to this.

"No seriously," he went on. "My partner saw the same thing and he passed on soon afterwards." Then seeing my expression he continued in a lighter vein, "Not to worry Chris. I've had a pretty good innings anyway."

Naturally I animated him as much as was possible but he appeared convinced as to what he referred to as being the 'inevitable'.

*

It was one Friday that they discharged Geoffrey and he was taken home to his duplex in Perello, where he was received by two friends who ran the local nursing home. These capable young men had agreed to attend to his needs until he was up and about again. The second night after his homecoming I received a telephone call at around one o'clock in the morning. "Geoffrey has died and we are not sure what to do," said a voice.

This in itself was not too much of a surprise as I was almost prepared for it by what Geoffrey had said. However, out of curiosity I asked, "Why me?"

"Well your name came out of the hat on the third try," the voice said.

"Right, I will be there in around thirty minutes."

I arrived and it was obvious that some sort of immediate action was required. I cannot remember why but I telephoned a funeral parlour in Sueca a nearby town. The first question they asked me was whether or not the deceased had any type of insurance. As the woman at the other end of the line sounded a very kind person I told the truth by saying that I did not think so but not to worry as something would be arranged.

Within an hour Consuelo arrived with her team and took total control. When all was completed she asked me to sign as being responsible for everything. I did so thinking that as a last resort I could seek help through the Luncheon Club if necessary. Then after Geoffrey was taken away I found the telephone number of his family in England and immediately called them. Following the normal condolences and general information, much to my relief they assured me that there would be no problem as all funeral expenses would be met by themselves. The actual event the next day went as well as funerals go, being mostly attended by members of the club.

*

Afterwards I was placed in charge of the ashes and immediately contracted the help of another member, Tony Patterson, who was on the managerial side of one of the large Valencia hotels.

"What are we going to do with them?" asked Tony.

I thought for a moment then it came to me what I had heard somewhere in the past. "Well, I did hear that he wanted them scattering between the eighteenth hole and the clubhouse at the El Saler Golf Club."

We stood there looking at the black urn on the back seat of my car.

"Right, Chris. Let's do it!"

So the following day found Tony and me arriving at the Golf Club only a short distance from the village where Geoffrey had lived. Pepine Cabo, the club's professional, who I knew from the time that Gedo the Dutchman and I had been supplying the club with golf course material, was located.

On seeing me he gave me the usual bear-like hug and quickly expressed his sympathy over the Club's loss in Geoffrey. He went on to say that Geoffrey had been much respected by his fellow members and all the staff. I thanked him at the same time saying how much Geoffrey had enjoyed his years as a member of this prestigious Club. Then I explained that that was precisely why we had brought him along there.

Taking a pace back Pepine stared at us both. "You brought Geoffrey here? Here to the Club?"

I nodded, "That's correct."

"How did you bring him here?"

"In the car," I said. "You don't think he walked here, do you?"

The golf professional's face turned ashen. "How is he?"

I shrugged. "Pretty quiet, I suppose." Then turning to Tony for confirmation I said,. "That right, Tony?"

Tony nodded, "Yes very quiet. He's in the back of the car."

"Dios mio, Chris." Pepine's face was a picture. "What are you going to do with him, Chris?"

I managed a serious expression. "Well his last wishes were that he be scattered between the eighteenth hole and the Club House."

Pepine was aghast. "Scatter him? What do you mean scatter him?"

Then not wishing to continue in this vein I explained that our friend had been cremated, at that particular time it was still a relatively unknown form of burial and to see Pepine face return to its normal happy expression at this news was a joy to behold.

"Sure, Chris," he said very much relieved. "Scatter him wherever you want to."

As we returned to the car I could feel Pepine's eyes following us. Then removing the urn Tony and I walked the short distance to the appropriate spot which appeared at that moment free of players. Next, for some reason, the instant I began to release the ashes a sharp breeze sprang up and from behind me Tony's voice shouted, "For heaven's sake watch what you're doing. Geoffrey is going all over me!"

*

Several weeks passed and I began to receive the occasional call from Consuelo at the funeral parlour. No, she had not received any communication from Geoffrey's family and could I help resolve the matter. The woman was so extremely nice about the whole thing that I began to feel concerned for her. I personally felt that I had discharged my duties and it was now up to the family to respond. Several telephone calls resulted in them promising to settle the matter. Then on the final call I was told that once Geoffrey's duplex had been sold the account would be settled. This was very much easier said than done. The duplex consisting of two apartments knocked into one was bought by Geoffrey on two different sets of deeds which, after many years, had still not been processed. One deed belonged to someone locally and the second to someone in the north of Spain. To me this smelt of nothing but problems which could go on for years even if Geoffrey had been still alive.

I pondered on the matter and remembered the non-payment of the ceramics some years before. Keeping this in mind I still gave the family time to come up with the solution. Then after several more apologetic telephone calls from Consuelo I decided some action was required. I let the family know that the funeral company was considering an 'embargo' on Geoffrey's duplex.

At around the same time I also received a call from a local car repair shop that had fixed Geoffrey's car before he died. They asked me about possible payment. So feeling somewhat peeved about being placed in this position I included them in the 'embargo' threat as well. Within ten days all was resolved, the parties receiving their payments. Everyone this side of the channel was now happy again and I sure that included Geoffrey wherever he might have been.

"Where are you going for your holidays this year?" someone in Dolfis asked me one day.

"Oh, I don't know. We might just drive to Paris or somewhere."

"What in that old car of yours?" someone else put in and there was laughter all round.

"And what is wrong with my old car?" I asked, irritated that Betsy should be referred to in such a manner.

"You would be extremely lucky to arrive at the frontier," another voice said.

More laughter.

I was now genuinely angry. "Right you lot. A couple of beers from each of you if we make it."

So it was settled and arrangements were made. Kathy was pleased that she would be seeing Paris again and Samantha was excited. The journey took several days to complete but was, as always, very pleasant and we eventually arrived one sunny afternoon.

*

Our hotel appeared to be on the edge of a very unsavoury neighbourhood with what looked like a monopoly of down-and-outs and strange looking individuals from North Africa. Kathy was not unreasonably nervous and this conveyed itself to Samantha so that I decided that something must be done.

"Look," I explained to them both as we set out to see the city, "all that you have to do is give them the impression that you are actually worse than they are."

"How, Papa?" Samantha asked.

"Just watch and I will show you. Stay a reasonable distance behind me when I walk down the street."

I then went on ahead and what was to be known as the 'Paris Walk' was created. This consisted of my weaving my way along the pavement and each time anyone came anywhere near me I would wave my arms about like a windmill at the same time screwing up my face and snarling.

This had an immediate effect of causing the most malevolent looking individuals to quickly cross over the road to the other side and leave us a clear passage. However this hilarity that my behaviour caused my family was short lived.

On the first night Kathy became ill. Doubled up with pain she had me thinking that this could well be appendicitis so I took her immediately to the renowned American hospital in Paris. Here she was given a series of tests after which the doctor in charge said that it could well be a hernia and so that it would be better if we returned immediately to Spain by air; the journey by road might well be too exacting. Arrangements were made and a telephone call to Gedo confirmed that he would be there to meet Kathy at the airport when she arrived and take her directly to the hospital. Samantha and I saw her safely off at the airport then turned Betsy's bonnet south again.

*

On arriving in Valencia we found that Kathy, after more tests, had been released but that an operation was necessary. So that was to be the beginning of what was to be heart-wrenching times with treatment, tests, hospitalisation and all that went with it. The very few close friends that we had rallied around us and helped where they could. However it was mostly up to Samantha and me.

In Valencia there are what is known as good hospitals but bad hotels and good hotels which are bad hospitals. Kathy, on our private insurance, was admitted to hospital which had the reputation of being a good hotel so was, at least, comfortable. Patients are allowed to carry their own medical files where tests and X-rays are concerned and from the beginning I knew what was probably to be the inevitable. However, having said that, hope springs eternal and ignoring this possibility we struggled on in the belief that everything might just turn out for the better. Sadly it was not to be.

Chapter 23

To the south of France amongst the gentle hills and valleys of Gers which eventually give way to the tall peaks and sharp pinnacles of the Pyrenees, lies the small placid village of Chantilly. With around two hundred inhabitants it is to be found snuggling in the fold of a hill that affords protection from the chilly winds that come scurrying down from northern Europe in the winter and at the same time providing a soil that produces mediocre claret, appreciated mainly by the local people.

Chantilly can only be reached by a slim road that seems to be anxious to be away from the main highway, between Marciac and Bassoues. Even this peters out on the far side of the village as there does not appears to be any particular reason why it should wish to go further. A brisk walk from the bus stop on the main road takes about twenty minutes and the asphalt covered country lane winds along by unfenced fields. At one point there is a bend and set back from this is a large solitary elm tree. There is nothing special about this road, the tree, nor indeed the sleepy village of Chantilly. However those villagers who live in the area and walk, cycle or drive along this road know that when they are approaching the elm tree they are passing the 'Butterfly Field'.

It is named as such for the simple reason that on this very spot, during the warmer weather of late spring and the long hot summer days, there appears an amazing amount of butterflies. Fluttering, shimmering and weaving their intricate dance from flower to thistle they present a spectacle that never ceases to enchant passers-by. Seemingly to disappear when the greenery becomes too high they then reappear after the harvest time.

One late autumn afternoon, when a weak sun was bidding farewell to a rather damp dreary day, the village priest was returning home after visiting a neighbouring parish when, in order to save a few paces, he cut across the bend in the road by the old elm which stood proud but somewhat unhappily deprived of most of its leaves. Hesitating for a moment the priest dug into his pocket and produced his favourite pipe already charged with tobacco. The other pocket revealed a box of matches and the old man lit one, ignited his pipe and tossed the match away. As it spiralled downwards his eye automatically followed it to its final resting place amongst the roots of the elm. It was there that he noticed a smudge of colours lying on the dank green moss. Moving nearer he looked down and saw what were the remains of a butterfly. Dark purple coloured wings tinged with red and a most unusual shade of almost emerald green, lay there spread out as if waiting for the very breath of life to revive it and allow it to once again rise and flutter away. About to withdraw the priest then caught sight of a slight movement not far from the insect and there, to his surprise, lay another butterfly of similar appearance. It was at that same moment that he thought he saw the creature move. Move, that is, in the direction of the first butterfly. Then dismissing it as a trick of the fading light or a possible current of air, he walked over and gently touched the remains with the toe of his shoe. Nothing. It was totally lifeless.

A slight breeze tugged at the priest's coat tails as if reminding him of the cheery fire awaiting him at home. So restoring the now unlit pipe to his pocket he turned up the collar of his coat and clutching it to his throat directed his footsteps towards the village. As his pace quickened his mind dwelt on what he had seen. His conclusion was that it had been something unusual, but as to its significance he could not determine.

*

That particular morning she woke abruptly which was certainly not normal as the medication usually made the transition between blessed sleep and wakening more difficult. In fact most days now were met with a curtain of misty haze through which she had to struggle before realisation of her surroundings came to her. The early Levantine sun filtered through the slatted blinds and blotches of yellow sunlight appeared on the dark polished surface of the wardrobe. Then as the sun rose these tiny pools of light became more and more numerous and she began to count their appearance silently to herself. By the time she had reached seven she was suddenly aware that the pain had gone. Holding her breath for what seemed an eternity she lay still, not daring to move, in case she was mistaken and the relief only momentarily. But no. Releasing her breath in a long drawn-out sigh from her aching lungs she now knew that it had really gone. For a moment or two she just laid there within the warm covers, savouring this moment of bliss, this miracle. Then reaching over to the bedside table her pale fingers sought the ever-ready teaspoon and she tapped the empty glass that lay next to it. Almost immediately a muffled voice called out, "Coming, darling!"

Smiling she lay back on the pillow feeling more relaxed than she had in weeks, even months. He hurried into the bedroom wrapping his dressing gown around his thickening waist and looking rather like a worried Father Christmas with his disarray of unkempt white hair. Passing straight way to the side of the bed, he bent down and kissed her forehead at the same time gently brushing back her hair. "How's my Sunday girl today then?" he asked, smiling down at her.

She attempted to speak, to call out the glad tidings. But it would only come out in a whisper. "It's gone," she said.

He leaned closer to her, reaching for those hands. "What's gone, darling?"

Smiling up at him she said, "The pain, of course, silly."

"Really, darling? You're not kidding me are you?"

"No, I'm not kidding. It really has gone."

He returned the wan smile and felt that prickling sensation at the back of his eyes.   "Why that's wonderful, darling. Marvellous."

She nodded happily. Well, then Sunday girl. You just lie there, take it easy and I will make us both a nice cup of tea. Even better than they make in Benidorm." He, grinned, stood up moving away, then turning again said, "Oh, and by the way. If you really do feel up to it perhaps we can ...er, go today." His tone had become serious, almost apologetic and he stood there silently waiting as she absorbed his words. Not wanting to hasten the matter.

"Yes, why not?" she mouthed.

"Fine. That's settled then."

He returned to the bedside and once again leaned over to kiss her and then standing gave the thumbs up sign and went out to the kitchen.

"How about going to the bathroom?" he asked later after he had plumped up the pillows so that she was able to sit up hold her cup and enjoy the tea together. "Now the pain has gone, perhaps we can manage to walk?"

From the comfort of her bed she listened, remembering and reliving the distressing moments of the last time she had attempted those few paces. The very thought of that excruciating pain that seemed to engulf her whole being.

Seeing her hesitate, he said, "Don't worry love. Just let's try and if it is too much then we forget it. Alright?"

She nodded her tired consent. Next slowly pulling back the blankets he reached down and gently moved her legs to the edge of the bed. "Ready?" he breathed.

"Yes, darling. Ready."

Gently he eased her into a sitting position the knelt down in order to put her slippers as best as he could. His heart ached and he wept inwardly at the sight of the swollen ankles with the ugly puffy swelling that was beginning to extend upwards. "How are we doing?" he asked, straining to keep his voice normal, not wanting to betray his anguish.

Again she nodded, "Fine. I'm just fine."

"Then off we go."

Placing both his arms under hers he gradually straightened up feeling her tense, waiting for the agony to consume her. To her immense joy it just did not happen.

"Well?" he ventured almost dreading the answer.

"Still fine," she repeated. "I'm just fine."

Holding her as close to him as was possible without hurting her he could feel the wasting body within his arms and silently prayed that in some way it were possible to for him to absorb her suffering. "Then it really is time to go," he said, quietly, almost as though acknowledging the last words, the final full stop of his very own existence.

Step by step they moved out of the bedroom.

"Help me wash?" she whispered. "I still feel weak and want to look nice for the journey."

"Yes darling off course."

She glanced in the bathroom mirror and caught a slight glistening of tears in his eyes. Happiness that all was going well? Perhaps. She truly hoped so.

Some while alter after he had helped her bathe and dress with her choosing something comfortable in which to travel, she sat in one of the large comfortable arm chairs in the lounge, admiring the flowers about the room that friends, neighbours and students had recently sent. He had gone to bring the car around to the front of the building so that it would be reasonably close for her faltering steps.

Letting her hand fall by the side of the chair she brushed her fingers along the new red leather overnight case she had bought sometime previously for the trip that never materialised because of her illness.

Lovingly she gazed around the apartment, her tired eyes resting on the familiar porcelain figures, the sketches and the water colours gracing the walls, the favourite miniature crystal glass swans and butterflies. She smiled as she remembered him saying, "Well, if we cannot buy any paintings then we will just have to paint some." And he had done just that, taking his time and reproducing some enchanting views of places that they had visited at one time or another. And each time they had a little extra money he would have them framed, returning from the shop and saying, "All dedicated to my Sunday girl." Yes it was all here in this very room. Fifteen years of happiness, of arguments, reconciliations, laughter, tears and generous feelings.

And above all things that inseparable togetherness.

Two people with turbulent disordered lives had finally met. Two lonely drifters steering their boat of dreams round the bend of Moon River searching for the end of the rainbow but safe in the knowledge that if they never found it, then it would not matter as they had their own pot of gold in each other.

"Alright off we go." He came into the room. "Betsy is downstairs waiting."

She reached up stretching her arms towards him. "I'm ready, darling."

Helping her to her feet he held her close again, savouring the moment but afraid, very much afraid. "Don't forget your case, love," he said steadying her with one hand whilst leaning down and picking it up. "Right, come on then. Off we go."

Slowly they made their way down the narrow hallway and out of the apartment.

"I've put extra cushions in the car," he said, "so you'll be quite comfortable."

*

Once outside she felt the warmth of the Mediterranean sun give her a little more strength and she raised her eyes to the clear blue cloudless sky above, ignoring the hum of the city noises and wondering. Betsy, like the faithful old girl that she was, roared into life and they pulled away into the stream of traffic.

Once clear of the city the car settled down, producing a relaxed but sure rumble from the aged engine. The highway ran parallel to the sea and she reached for her glasses as the sunlight, reflecting off the waves, threw up sharp points of hard light hurting her eyes. They passed Portsaplaya the small new coastal development that had the air of a miniature Venice about it. A small neat harbour consisting of a mass of moorings, right alongside the pastel coloured houses with their plant filled gardens. She glimpsed little brightly painted boats bobbing up and down, straining at their moorings, almost as though they too wished to be set free and travel with her on this journey of no return. She smiled to herself feeling somehow alive again; somehow just as she used to feel when teaching her students. Seeing their young faces anxious to learn in the knowledge that today the English language was a necessary element to most careers. Remembering how they in turn had confided in her trusted her and were all that better prepared because of her.

Some two kilometres before the old Roman city of Sagunto he turned inland and the road twisted and turned through quiet grey stoned villages surrounded by acres of orange and lemon groves. It was late spring, a time when the last crop of oranges was still on the trees, their bright ripe colours contrasting to the fluffy white blossom that announced the beginning of the new harvest. She wound down the window and immediately the inside of the car was invaded by an exquisite fragrance. Breathing deeply she filled her lungs, slightly dizzy from the heavy perfume.

"Alright, darling?" he glanced across at her.

"Mmmm," she said. "That blossom is marvellous."

"Wonderful," he replied, guessing more at what she had said than actually hearing.

The road continued upwards gradually the orange groves giving way to almond trees that thrived more on the stony dry soil. In no time they had breasted the pass and were travelling along the high land mass that precedes Teruel.

This old town is where the tourists arrive in the summer, followed by below zero temperatures in the winter. It was as they were passing the parador hotel that she awoke not realising that she had fallen asleep earlier. Carefully and so very gently she stretched out her legs rejoicing that the torment had actually gone.

"Fancy stopping for a cuppa?" he asked, glancing sideways at her, at the same time leaning a little in her direction in order to catch her reply.

"No. Not yet. Let's get on please," she whispered.

So on they went. On past the heavy red soil that served the vineyards of Cariñena. On, until the charcoal hills before Zaragoza came into sight preparing them for a view of the cathedral with its tall spires pointing the very way to heaven. Betsy competed with the lunchtime traffic confidently negotiating the wide bridge spanning the river Ebro.

Her head rested on his shoulder and she slept again with him driving carefully so as not to disturb her. After another half an hour a long low dark smear appeared on the horizon, a smoky grey smudge reaching across the skyline as far as the eye could see. "Hey," he called softly, briefly brushing her hair with his lips, "look what's up ahead."

She opened her eyes and watched as the indefinable outline gradually took shape to form the Pyrenean Mountains. Little by little the hard granite peaks came into view and way up she could see the little white caps of snow gracing their giant heads. And it was then that the same old feeling began to return as it always returned when they passed along this particular stretch of road. A delicious sense of homecoming enveloped her. Like the traveller whose steps become lighter, quicker and whose weariness becomes less at the thought that they are about to be reunited with their cherished old home.

In no time Betsy breasted the summit of the Col-du-Portalet and the frontier post to be waved on by a solitary uniformed figure in a tricorn hat who smiled, she thought, just for her.

'When you stand just don't forget that from the Col du Pourtalet over streams and mountain heather you can see for almost ever'.

The road with its copious quantity of potholes, souvenirs from the previous winter's snow, tumbled down into France with Betsy taking everything in her stride. Past steep green mossy banks choked with spring flowers including the dominant presence of wild Irises. On by sudden outlets of cascading ice cold, crystal clear water sparkling in the sunshine. Over narrow, grey, stone bridges below which gushed glacial torrents fed from the melting snows above, bounding over boulders almost the size of small houses. Pure air flowed into the car like an elixir and again she breathed, inhaling deeply. Neat, tidy, picture postcard villages with slate roofs and shuttered windows came and went as the landscape changed to flourishing green fields with sloe eyed cows chewing contentedly, watching them curiously as the sped by.

The sun had begun to sink when they turned off the main Marciac road and she felt a quickening of her pulse as the inevitable feeling of expectancy embraced her. Betsy slowed to a crawl, gently following the narrow road to where the solitary elm stood. The tree was now showing signs of a new leafy coat as the life within completed the eternal circle.

*

The car stopped and they just sat there silently holding hands neither of them speaking. Then, momentarily afraid that all was not as it should be, her grip tightened.

"I'll get the chair out and put it under the tree," he said, his lips close to her ear.

She nodded still staring out of the window reluctantly releasing his hand, as he climbed out of the car.

Once the chair was set under the elm he returned and gently helped her out. As her feet touched the ground she expressed an unbelievable sensation of weightlessness and seemed to float over the grass as, with his strong arms about her they made their way to the tree. Tenderly he lowered her onto the chair and she sat there anxiously for several minutes waiting, her eyes searching about her. It was then, as if to dispel her fears and confirm that all was as it had been before, and be as it ever would be in the future, she saw gossamer wings begin to appear. Imperceptibly, almost magically, the frail creatures began to arrive. Within moments they were weaving, dancing all in one spectacular rhapsody of colour. She gazed about her enraptured as to what was happening. Butterflies, butterflies and even more butterflies. All in all a virtual rainbow of colours. Bright red hues, sharp yellows, blues and greens all joined in a shimmering ballet of light such as she had never witnessed before. A hand rested gently on her shoulder and she turned to look up at him.

"Darling, you know that I have to leave you."

There were many things he wanted to say; things that should have been said in the past. Things she deserved to hear. But his voice failed him and he did not trust himself to go on. The words just would not come. She nodded seeing the tears form in his blue eyes. Then reaching up she gently rested her caring hand against his cheek. "I know, darling. I know," she said quietly. "But don't worry I will be waiting."

"Will you? Will you really?"

He was crying openly now, tears coursing down his cheeks as he looked deeply into those green eyes, pleading confirmation as though the destiny of his very soul depended on the answer. Raising her other hand she cupped his tear stained face and looked at him, smiling. "You know I'll be waiting for you. Don't worry. Time is of no importance to us. Do not think that because you cannot see me that I am not near. I will always be by your side. Remember that, darling. Always remember that."

He leaned over and kissed her, again wishing that the wings around them would form a carpet on which the two of them would be carried away to eternity. Then straightening up he placed his hand on her forehead as though in silent benediction, turned and moved away.

She watched as with hunched shoulders and hands thrust into his pockets, he walked back to the car. Opening the door he stood for some moments looking back at her and she had the sensation that he was calling to her. His lips were moving but there was no sound. Then his image blurred and the next time she looked he was already in the car with the engine spluttering into life. Then he was driving slowly away and she momentarily glimpsed his tear-stained features as he took one long last look in her direction, leaving her in the company of the butterflies whose numbers seemed to be increasing by the minute.

Contentedly she sat as they fluttered and encircled her about her. Then without warning directly in front of her appeared a magnificent creature. Large dark wings, each set with a golden eye in the centre that pulsated hypnotically. She watched fascinated as the eyes split into two then four. The process repeated itself and then there were eight. She began counting and this beautiful butterfly floated slowly towards her. A cry came from her lips as it alighted on her outstretched palm and a feeling of warmth and happiness such as she had never thought possible embraced her at last.

*

Something had disturbed him more than was normal and he awoke from a shallow sleep. Slipping out of bed he draped his dressing gown around him and hurried into her room. The pallid face lay against the white pillows and her outstretched hand rested on the covers. Sightless eyes stared fixedly at the golden blotches of sunlight that slipped through the shutters and onto the dark polished wardrobe. Slowly moving over to her he sank to his knees and reached out smoothing her hair, kissing the warm lips for the last time and then closing those beautiful emerald green eyes forever.

He knew not how long he stayed thus but when he did eventually climb unsteadily to his feet he was attracted by a slight sound behind him. Turning he saw a butterfly vainly battering its wings against the window pane. Automatically he walked over released the catch and opened the shutters. The small delicate creature fluttered out and he stood watching as it flew away on some mission known only to itself, becoming smaller and smaller until it became a speck in the distance. His vision blurred and it was at that moment he realised that the true mourning was yet to come.

*

It was New Year's Eve when Kathy left us and I telephoned Consuelo who told me not to worry as she and her assistants would be over immediately. In keeping with Spain's tradition the kindly neighbours crowded in and sat quietly together in the lounge saying little but by their very presence helping to ease our distress.

The following day at around eleven o'clock in the morning the telephone rang and I picked it up to hear dear Mavis Venables wishing Samantha and myself a happy new year and at the same time asking after Kathy. Sadly I related what had happened and straightway without any hesitation whatsoever she said, "Don't worry, Chris. I'll be on the next plane out."

"But, Mavis, it's New Year's Day. Samantha and I can manage," I protested.

Her voice resounding with her no nonsense tones said, "That is precisely why I am coming. For Samantha!"

There was no more argument and Mavis arrived that very evening. In the meantime Samantha and I were cleaning and tidying the apartment in preparation to receive any visitors.

At one point Samantha, who was removing the dust from the multitude of ornaments scattered around the apartment called out, "Papa, one of the glass swans has gone."

I happened to be in the room and said, "Don't be silly, darling. It has got to be there with the others."

"No, Papa," she persisted. "It is just not there."

I moved to her side and followed her pointing finger.

"Look, Papa. It's gone."

Sure enough there were only two swans where there were normally three of them placed in a prominent position on the sideboard. My mind was too full of other matters and I just patted my daughter's shoulder. "Don't worry, dear. It has to be somewhere."

Then as I left the room her voice followed me. "It's the mummy swan that's gone, Papa."

It was a relief to see Mavis again and I immediately knew that her very being there was also going to be a cornerstone for the next days. Everything went reasonably well. Friends from the luncheon club were in the majority at the funeral and Paul Bennett conducted the improvised service with the solemnity that it deserved.

At the time I had no real thoughts about the future and just took one day at a time hoping that my 'Lassez faire' attitude would not prove too negative. Reluctantly we saw Mavis off at the airport with me almost in tears with gratitude that she should have reacted so spontaneously to the situation.

*

Karl, the jeweller friend, was now without employment due to the closure of the factory so he joined me in my office and we went about organising the students who still wished to attend colleges in England. We advertised more in the Las Provincias newspaper and I continued writing articles which proved an excellent form of publicity.

Tony Strodder phoned me one day to say that the last key ring I had mailed to him had worked but not to the extent of the previous ones. "And why not, Tony?" I asked. "Well the bank manager didn't get the sack," he explained.

"Sorry about that," I said, rather tongue in cheek.

"Oh, no," he came back. "He didn't get the sack. They just moved him out to a small branch. Miles away from anywhere, somewhere in the Yorkshire dales, I believe."

Almost three weeks to the day after that sad New Year's Day, Samantha was again cleaning the apartment when she called out to me. "Look, Papa. The swan has come back."

"It must have been there all the time," I said, "or at least, somewhere."

"No," she insisted with that childish innocence, "it was definitely not here and nobody has been in here."

"Alright, darling, if you say so."

So I just left it at that, returning to the office knowing that she was telling the truth but not wanting to dwell too much on the significance.

*

Apart from organising students for the UK, I also had the family home to run now which, naturally, included cleaning, washing, cooking and a fair amount of sewing. The apartment block in which we lived only had fourteen apartments so it was natural that we all were acquainted with each other and I began to wonder why all the husbands did not seem so friendly

409

as when we were a complete family. Then one day I was hanging out the washing when I heard an upstairs neighbour shout to her husband, "Look at the Englishman. Everyone knows he does everything there is to do and you, you lazy donkey; don't even know where your trousers are!" On the economic side Samantha helped a great deal at week ends by teaching English to groups of young children. Although being my daughter must influence my point of view, she was a first class teacher, obviously having inherited this from her mother.

*

One day I was in the Dolfis bar when a friend asked if I were interested in opening a pub in the neighbourhood. Apparently my fame, or whatever, still followed me from my Cullera days.

"Sorry," I said. "Firstly I don't have any finance for such a project and secondly it would have to be something a little different than just a pub."

"What do you mean, Chris?" he looked puzzled.

"I mean that a combination of a pub and English centre would be more likely to succeed as things are today." I took a swallow of the San Miguel beer. "You see at the moment there are many students who spend a great deal of money in learning the English language but have absolutely nowhere handy where they can practice speaking it. Somewhere where, for a minimum fee and a pleasant atmosphere, they could practice what they have learnt would be ideal."

So my friend spoke to another friend and the London Tavern came into being.

*

It was also around about this time that Bob Cooper called me to ask if I was short of a car.

"Why, Bob?" I asked, surprised that this came at a time when I was thinking that dear Betsy was near enough to retiring at around twenty years.

"Well, Chris," he explained, "I have treated myself a new Rover and the Ford Granada is just standing there near my place in San Carlos de la Rapita doing nothing."

He went on to say that it was a large estate vehicle, fully automatic with every imaginable extra.

"How much, Bob?"

"Who's talking about money? You can have it."

Sad as it was to see Betsy returned to Andrés in Manises, I accepted Bob's generous offer and went with Karl to collect the Granada. So Betsy II had arrived to join us. It was joy to drive and with all the space served well for collecting things for the construction of the London Tavern which was going ahead rapidly. When finally complete the place looked great. Not only did we have the bar but kitchen and lots of space for tables and chairs. Naturally we also provided typical English dishes together with the usual 'Happy Hour'.

On the opening night television cameras arrived and we received considerable publicity. So much so that another local television asked that I do a cookery program. Naturally I agreed and prepared traditional dishes such as shepherd's pie, steak and kidney pie, crown of lamb and even Christmas pudding.

*

A regular customer to the pub was Irish Tony a tall, heavy built, man with fair hair, a magnificent nose and pale eyes that appeared to change colour depending on his frame of mind. He was married to Lola a short, dark, capable woman he had met whilst on holiday some years before.

We were discussing the television program.

"Do you think that your Spanish is up to being on television?" Tony asked, looking at me over the brim of a pint of John Smith's bitter one day.

"Hope so, Tony. Anyway with all the different ingredients and what have you they won't notice it too much."

"Just as long as you don't say anything that possibly might get you into trouble."

"What the hell do you mean by that? What could I say that might get me into trouble, Tony?"

"Oh, I don't know. But if you become flustered lose your cool or get angry with the interviewer, you just might let something slip."

"Well I could always say something in English and nobody would notice." Then a thought occurred to me. "You know what, Tony. I could always come up with something like, 'Kiss my arse'. Go down well that would."

"Come on. You wouldn't dare, Chris!"

"Try me. How much, Tony?"

"A couple of pints of this." He waved the near empty glass of John Smith's special.

"You're on."

"In English?"

I thought for a moment. "No not in English. How about Irish?"

"You mean Gaelic?"

"Gaelic or garlic, it's all the same to me."

"Very funny! Just make sure you say it. I'll be watching."

All went well and there I was in front of studio audience that would have fitted into any WI meeting place anywhere in England. I described the preparation of the various dishes and eventually arrived at a dish which was a favourite of mine; sausage and bean stew. This is prepared in the usual casserole with red beans and cider for flavour.

"So can we explain to the audience what this is?" asked the interviewer.

Going into detail I described the dish, preparation and contents, adding that the sauce had a special name.

"Really?" he said. "That is interesting for our viewers."

"Yes," I smiled. "Actually it is of Irish origin and is called, 'Poc ma thome'."

Next moment things became slightly embarrassing as he insisted that I repeat the name so that the viewers could take note if they wished. I did so but fortunately was not asked to spell it out.

Next day I came across Tony in the street not far from my apartment. "What about the bet then, Tony?"

"Fine by me," he said. "Didn't get you banned then?"

I shook my head. "They wouldn't dare. Where do you suggest we have those pints?"

At that particular moment we were standing outside a new bar that was supposed to be on the point of being opened any day.

"Let's have a look in here and give the place the once over. You never know they might have the beer already."

So in we went.

It was obviously nowhere near ready to open either on that particular day or during the next week. The workers were going at it full steam, finishing off the very expensive-looking decor. We both stood there taking in the scene when next thing we were approached by an angry looking man dressed to look as though he were in charge. "And what the hell are you doing here?" he asked, as though we might be there to rob the place.

"Sorry," I apologised, "but we just wandered in here and as I live nearby wondered what the place looked like." He drew himself up to his full height of around five feet two inches.

"Well you've seen it. Now leave!"

"What sort of beer will you be serving?" asked Tony, eyeing the word 'Pub' which was liberally plastered everywhere.

"What's that to do with you?"

He was now becoming really angry.

"Nothing I suppose," said Tony. "Just interested that's all."

"Then get the hell out of here!" the man stormed.

I saw Tony's eyes begin to change colour and take on that 'look' so I grabbed his arm and pushed him towards the door.

"Now you just listen here," said, Tony resisting. "You wouldn't be threatening my friend and me, would you?"

"Just get out!" shouted the man beside himself with rage.

Tony took a step towards him with myself still clinging to him and the man suddenly realised what was about to happen. Turning he looked around for the back-up team in the form of the workers but clearly they were keeping their heads down and did not want to know.

"Come on, Tony," I pleaded. "It's not worth it."

Finally he relented and I managed to get him outside pointing him in the direction of Dolfis. "That was a near thing," I breathed.

Tony glanced over his shoulder and softening somewhat said, "Well I must admit that's the first pub I've ever been thrown out of when the bloody place wasn't even open!"

*

So the London Tavern was off to a good start and still being in contact with Mary I telephoned and suggested that my son, who was now twenty years of age, came over and joined us, if he wished. Within a week my son had arrived and took up duties in the kitchen.

Students began to arrive at the pub in the early evenings, the attraction being 'Happy Hour' and the capable English teachers such as Ken Martin we had on hand. Things looked too good and the phrase, 'The best laid plans of mice and men', came to mind making me think that FU was not far behind.

The two partners who had financed the venture were so overawed by the layout of the place that I had designed, so much so that they were completely opposed to my original idea of bar plus language centre. It was a two-to-one situation and they decide that the place should be orientated towards being an up market restaurant.

Disagreements began and I found that it was impossible to argue with one partner dedicated to drink and the other, José Luis, to more potent substances. Things were not going at all well and with the other two taking so much time off because of their addictions it was obvious that my son and I had to manage most of the work and with little reward.

*

After around six weeks my son announced that he would be returning to England and not having received any wages for the previous week, stopped coming in to work. Then just before he left for England he appeared one morning and asked José for the money that was due to him.

"No," said the man adamantly. "There is no money."

"But you promised it to me and you owe it to me," insisted my son.

"Well forget it," said, José Luis.

My son who was head and shoulders over the other said, "Well if you won't give it to me I will just have to take it." And so saying he walked behind the bar, opened the cash- register and removed some notes, then headed towards the door.

"What are you doing?" shouted my partner.

"Taking what's mine," said my son.

The other stood there dancing from one foot to the other. Then suddenly he said, "What about the money for those photographs you owe?"

My son stopped, turned, laid two notes on the bar and said calmly, "There it is," and walked out.

"We've been robbed!" howled José Luis, now crimson in the face. "Call the police!"

Thinking quickly I said, "Right. You call the police and in the meantime I'll get all these customers to give me their names and addresses and they can come down to the police station and make statements."

At the time there were no more than six or seven people in the bar and the moment I uttered those words the place could not have emptied quicker than if I had shouted, "Fire!"

They simply ran for the door.

Eventually the police did arrive and asked what had happened. José Luis explained that this young Englishman had come in, walked behind the bar, removed money from the cash register and had run for the door.

"Wait a minute," I put in quickly but firmly. "Be more explicit, José. He did not actually run to the door, he walked. And remember he also left payment for the photographs."

The police officials looked at us in amazement. "You're telling us that someone comes in here, robs the cash-register and before he leaves pays for some photographs?"

I nodded, "Quite correct, officer. That is exactly what happened."

Then looking carefully at me for a moment one of them said in all seriousness, "Is this something from your English Coronation Street?"

So saying they both left and that was the end of the incident.

*

Samantha's educational pension from the American government had ceased and she also decided to go to England. There she hoped to obtain a degree in marketing. It was also most fortuitous, for all of us, that Mary had very kindly offered to accommodate her. This wonderful gesture on her part was to ease my mind considerably. In the meantime whilst trying to run the London Tavern I left Karl to organise the student trips to the UK. It was not long before Karl too decided to branch out on his own with this business and set up an office only a stone's throw from mine.

The general situation of organising the pub became intolerable and finally I decided to walk out and leave it to the other two bright partners. Great! Now I was on my own and little, if anything, coming in economically.

My social life had come almost to a standstill so it was with anticipation that I accepted an invitation to a party to be held on the outskirts of Valencia on one Saturday night. It was being given by, Inmaculada, a young woman who I had met at one of the local bars in my neighbourhood. A charming person with a competence in the English language that was close to perfection. I had been so impressed by her knowledge and spiritual love of life in general that one evening I said to her that if ever I had a Spanish daughter I would hope that she would be exactly like her.

Not wishing to attend the 'Fiesta' unaccompanied I contacted a friend of many years, Jacky. A willowy blonde, English lady, always elegantly dressed who had been married to Rafael one of the most great-to-be-with Spaniard's I had ever come across. Unfortunately Rafael had died just after Kathy and so Jacky now had the problem of living as widow in a Spanish society. It was not easy for her so the possibility of a joint evening out was eagerly accepted.

*

When we eventually arrived the party seemed to be in full swing. Initially, as the eldest there, I felt a little uncomfortable. However, things brightened somewhat when the female half of a duo that was singing country and western songs started paying attention to me. Who I took to be her husband was the guitar player. Rather none- descript and reminiscent of the hippy young men, he wore a goatee beard and long hair in the style that was reminiscent of the Bob Dillon era in the sixties.

Now his wife, partner or whatever, well she was different. She appeared to have been modelled on the Barbie Doll. However, instead of flowing golden locks she had a head of dark shoulder length hair. To say that she was gorgeous would be an understatement. A peaches and cream complexion and all that went with it, she was easily the most attractive girl there.

I feasted my eyes on her at the same time feeling rather guilty that Kathy was not present. So the party progressed and I made a small contribution to the singing and guitar playing which was made all the more pleasant when I sensed that Barbie was paying me just that more attention than was normal. It even crossed my mind that to wonder why it was me when there were so many other eligible young men there. Anyway, finally the party came to an end and we all said our 'Goodbyes' to each other with myself receiving an unexpected hug and kiss from Barbie.

It was around three months later that I had another call from Inmaculada to attend another such 'Fiesta'. Naturally, I accepted with anticipation. This was heightened with Inmaculada saying that certain persons there had requested that I was to be invited.

So once again Jacky and I arrived at the appointed time and found the party in full swing. On joining the other guests I was knocked completely off balance when Barbie appeared, flung her arms around me, pressed her lips close to my ear and repeated several times, "I'm so glad that you could make it!"

My ego took a quantum leap and I mentally chalked up another twenty thousand points. Glancing around the room in search of Barbie's Ken with his guitar I turned to her. "Where's your husband tonight?"

Barbie smiled rather slyly. "Oh, he had to go away for a couple of weeks. So he's not here." She then said, "Why does it matter?"

"No, I suppose not really."

I do not remember a great deal about the party only that I was dancing and circulating most of the time with Barbie on my arm. Time flew by and

I only became just a little bit nervous when she whispered, "My husband told me to pay all my attention to you."

I could not believe my ears and my heart missed at least two beats. However on reflection some minutes later, from what I had read, this was almost the accepted form of behaviour from the younger generation. It was quite late and we were dancing comfortably close with her breasts pressing against me, when she suddenly said, "Listen, Chris, I have to leave now and get home to the children. Thanks for a wonderful evening." Then manoeuvring herself to an even closer embrace she whispered in my ear, "Here, take this and we will talk later."

Into my hand was pressed a piece of paper which I quickly slipped into my pocket. As the music finally faded there was one last hug and lingering kiss and she was gone. My hot fingers fondled the slip of paper and I delayed the moment before I sought the privacy of somewhere to read it. After around ten minutes I could not contain myself any longer and slipping into the bathroom locked the door and drew out the folded paper. Carefully I straightened it out and feasted my hungry eyes on the lettering at the same time visualising what delights were soon to be within my grasp.

It read, 'Jesus Christ loves you. If you want to know more, telephone 'The Family' at this number in Geneva, Switzerland'.

Ah, well!

The next time I saw Irish Tony I related what had happened and he sympathetically placed his arm around my shoulder. "Never mind, Chris," he said. "It must have been someone from that 'Bonk for Jesus' campaign I read about."

Then I thought my luck had changed when Tony suggested that I might help him in his painting and decorating business. Prepared to do anything on a survival basis I readily accepted. Initially things moved along smoothly and I quite liked the physical effort involved. However, as usual, FU was not far behind, at least on one occasion.

*

Although Leicester was my home, I do remember hearing a northern expression for describing a 'braggart' as being someone who is 'All mouth and no trousers'. There was another saying I vaguely remember, and that was 'Be careful or they will have the trousers off you'.

And so it was on one particular occasion when I went to work for Tony. The place we had been contracted to decorate happened to be, as one might expect from and Anglo-Irish joint effort, an Irish pub in Valencia. It was called for no particular reason, The Black Sheep. Being summer the weather was, of course, hot and thus called for a working dress code, in the form of shorts and tee-shirts. These we changed into before starting work, leaving our normal clothes at the far end of the bar on some chairs.

It was around lunchtime that I discovered that some opportunist had slipped in through the unlocked door and removed my trousers together with my wallet, documentation, money and keys to my apartment. The first thing I did on discovering the theft was to take a deep breath and calculate that the sum total of the incident was a financial loss and a lot of aggravation in the replacement of papers. So if the apartment had not been robbed already I reckoned that I could just about live with that and was not going to become upset by the matter.

Our first priority was to pack up and hurry over to my apartment in order to confirm that the thief or thieves had not beaten me to it and used the keys. My relief was immediate as the door appeared firmly closed and according to the neighbours nothing suspicious had occurred. Then I enlisted the help of Tony. With little effort of persuasion on my part I placed a large beer in his hand and sat him on the terrace outside Dolfis so that he could observe the entrance to the apartment block.

Next I presented myself at local Police Station in order to report the theft. There I was informed by the officer on the door that as it was holiday time there was a lack of staff and things would be a little slow. With only four people in front of me he calculated that waiting period would only be around half an hour, I thanked him and sat for the next two-and-a-half hours wondering why I had done so. Anyway, eventually my turn came and I was ushered into the inner sanctum by a charming young policewoman who, during the writing down of the events under the heading 'Robbery due to inattention', smiled at my bad luck and expressed the hope that I had further pairs of trousers at home. After much signing and stamping of forms I finally left and returned to find that Irish Tony was in a mellow mood. No, he had not seen anyone of doubtful appearance enter the apartment block which was a further relief. The relief was not for me, particularly, but for anyone who might have been apprehended by Tony.

Now it was time to contact the company that handled my house insurance and explain what had occurred and that I required the services of a locksmith in order to enter my apartment.

"No problem," said the man at the end of the line. "Go home and wait by the phone and we will call you when the locksmith is due to arrive. By the way what is your home telephone number?"

Without thinking I began reeling off my home number then stopped when I realised that if I could answer my phone then I would not be requiring the services of a locksmith. I quickly pointed this out and the man seemed quite impressed at my reasoning. Then in that case he said that he would arrange for the locksmith to call me on my mobile and added that if the key to the main entrance had been stolen then I would be responsible for the cost of changing the lock and the re-issuing of keys to all the neighbours. "However," he added, "if you had just lost the keys somewhere, then the insurance company will pay all this." When I asked why this should be so he could not answer and muttered something about company policy.

"Anyway get the locksmith here first and we will talk later," I said.

Another hour had passed with Tony and me increasing the profits at the Dolfis bar when I received a call from the locksmith himself.

"Please give me the numbers on the keys that you've lost," he said, "and I will buy you some new ones."

My sharp reply that if I did have the numbers of the keys that I too was capable of buying some new ones and would not require his services anyway, was received without animosity. He then added that he would be there within an hour.

*

To our surprise he appeared within the allotted time. I was certain that he must have stopped off on the way over because his behaviour could only be described as hovering somewhere between drunk and legless. This became even more apparent when, on arriving at my apartment, he asked that I open it up and plug in the electric drill he was carrying. "Oh, and by the way," he added. "Would you mind bringing out any screwdrivers that you might have lying around? Mine are not very good."

His glassy eyes peered up at me whilst I patiently explained that this was not possible. Tony in the meantime had rung the neighbour's bell and within moment we had the drill working. With much noise and cursing the locksmith finally had the door open and my relief was instant when I saw that all was intact.

The three of us celebrated with cold beers, which was a mistake on my part, as the locksmith sat on the stairs and watched as I screwed on the new locks that he had produced. When all was finally completed we trooped down to the street again with me receiving a spontaneous lecture, from the fellow, that I was never to carry both my keys and wallet around together. One or the other he explained should be left at home. As if this crazy idea were not sufficient he went on to say that he thought that losing ones trousers could only be termed as rather 'indecent'.

At that moment it was Irish Tony's turn to grab my arm and propel me across the street to Dolfis whilst the plumber staggered off in the direction of his car. Happily settled in the bar once more we had drunk only a couple of beers before my mobile rang. It was a minute before I realised that it was the locksmith and a further minute passed before I could understand that he wanted me to go over to where he had parked his car. So leaving Tony I walked out, crossed the street and found him sitting on his tool box surrounded by all kinds of instruments and gadgets. In the car, parked nearby, a large German shepherd dog was leaping around barking like mad.

"What's wrong now?" I asked, staring down at him.

The bloodshot eyes looked up at me. "I've lost my keys," he lamented.

I just could not believe my ears. "Lost your keys? How could you have lost your keys?"

He shrugged looking around him dejectedly and then rummaging through the array of objects as though they might suddenly leap out at him.

"Perhaps they are in the car," I suggested.

"That's the ones I lost."

"And the keys to your house? What about those?"

"Those as well."

I was sorely tempted to say, "Then your wallet must be safe at home," but thought better of it.

"Look, you obviously had them when you arrived here. Where did you go after you parked and before you telephoned me?"

He thought for a moment then said slowly, "Well, it being hot weather I went into a couple of bars and also to the shop to buy your locks."

"Right. I'll stay here and pray that your brute of a dog, that seems to think that it is all my fault, will not break out of the car and you go find your keys."

And so off he went, weaving from one side of the pavement to the other and taking twice the distance than if he had walked in a straight line.

After what seemed a very long time he eventually reappeared but not before the dog had given up attempting to get out at me and was now lying almost comatose with the heat inside the car.

"Look," he said, triumphantly waving a set of keys at me, "they were in the shop."

I just nodded and watched as he collected his bits and pieces together, carelessly tossing them into the car boot. Next, with that certain diligent concentration that only drunks can command, he opened the door and fell into the diver's seat. I moved back in case the villainous looking beast within should decide to make one last attempt at savaging me. Fortunately it just lay there gasping and I felt somewhat better for the animal's discomfort. The last I saw of the pair was as they drove away, with more skill than I thought possible.

It was two days later that I received a telephone call. It was the sober, rather sheepish voice of the locksmith enquiring as to whether or not he had changed the locks to my apartment.

"No," I said emphatically, "It was me that changed the locks. You just happened to be there at the time sitting on the floor."

"Sorry," he said, apologetically, "just don't remember anything."

"Do you remember losing your keys?" I asked.

His voice took on a defensive tone. "Lose my keys?" he said. "Don't talk rubbish. I'm a locksmith and locksmiths never lose their keys!"

*

The painting and decorating business was spasmodic and I was constantly keeping my eye open for something on a more permanent basis to assist me financially and keep my head above the economic waterline. I was also a little depressed and this was not helped by my receiving a letter from Mavis, which after hoping that I was in good health, included the news that she had recently resigned from her directorship. Apparently this was due to some internal problems on which understandingly she declined to relate.

"The key ring," I thought immediately. "No. It was not possible after all this time. Or was it?" I had now reached the point of believing that anything was possible.

Chapter 24

I always found that the Dolfis bar was as good a place as any to sit and ponder from which direction a new set of problems would arriving. And I was doing just that one day when in came my friend, Jens Svensen.

Just seeing his smiling face and I felt just that much better. Always well turned out in a suit and tie no matter what the season or weather and with what remained of his sparse fair hair at all angles, Jens was the image of the classic blue eyed, fresh faced, Nordic gentleman. Around the same age as me he was just a little shorter in stature but this was adequately compensated by Jens's tough muscular constitution. Normally most affable to the extreme I had, over a period of time, learnt to respect that beneath his congenial exterior lay a smouldering volcano of a temper ready to flare up at any moment. A resident in Valencia for some years, his love of Spain was marred only by one thing; the noise. This was the downside for Jens as where we lived, according to the statistics; it was possibly the noisiest city in the world; or certainly one of them. And so it was that unlike myself, who ignored the continuing assault on my eardrums, Jens would hurl vile abuse at any of the young tearaways on their ear splitting, exhaust- manipulated scooters, who came anywhere near him.

One day one of these riders, obviously angered by Jens referring to his parentage in public, pulled up to exchange words calling Jens an 'Old fool'. Beside himself with rage Jens was on his feet immediately and heading towards the youth who had prudently stopped some five metres away. The young teenager, seeing my friend's face a mask of hate, went to ride away, panicked, and in his nervousness stalled the bike. Next thing Jens had him by the throat and would have strangled him if I had not acted quickly and dragged him off. No you didn't mess with Jens.

"Expecting anyone?" I asked him as I placed a cold glass of Aguila beer into his hand the moment he arrived.

"No, Chris. Why do ask?"

"You keep looking out of the window, Jens. That's why."

"Just looking at that very nice car of yours, actually," he explained.

I too stared across at Betsy II who was parked there looking extremely grand compared to the average smaller cars. "Yea, it's a fine car alright. Extremely comfortable to drive together with one hell of a lot of room."

"That is just what I was thinking, Chris. There's a lot of room in a car like that."

He continued to stare out of the window. "Goes alright does it?"

I laughed. "Should think so with a two-point-eight engine, six cylinders and automatic transmission; even electrically operated seat that warms your arse when it's cold. In fact the lot. The only thing wrong is that she's a thirsty beast and consumes at lot of juice."

He turned to me and smiled, although I could see by his eyes that he was being serious. "Juice eh? That's just what I was thinking about. You know you might be able to earn some real money with a car like that."

"Really Jens? Is that so?" I put down my glass and was all ears at the mention of the magic word.

"Yes, Chris. Let's talk shall we?"

Moving over to a quiet part of the bar, which is normally difficult anywhere in the area, we sat down and I listened. Jens ran his finger around the top of his glass and began. "Well you know that one of my, how do you say interests, is in the liquor trade?"

I nodded conjuring up a serious expression.

"Well," he went on, "I reckon you might just do yourself a bit of good transporting some 'special' white wine for me."

He emphasised the word 'special', so I said, "What's so special about it, Jens?"

The blue eyes twinkled. "So special, Chris, that it is nearly around one hundred percent proof."

"That's not wine. That's pure alcohol, Jens."

He grinned, "You said it. Not me."

Turning he looked out of the window again across the road to where Betsy II was sitting quite peacefully. "I reckon that you could get at least three hundred and fifty to four hundred litres in that car. Possibly more," he said, almost to himself.

"But isn't carrying a ….," here I hesitated, "a 'special' white wine, kind of illegal?"

"Quite. Of course it's illegal. But that should not be too much of a problem."

So we just sat and discussed the logistics of setting up my new employment, that of professional 'Bootlegger'. I confess that the little excitement stirring within me was not entirely undue to a film that I had seen many years before. It had starred Robert Mitchum who was running illegal 'Moonshine' whisky along Thunder Road, somewhere in the state of Kentucky, USA. The only thing that I was a little nervous about was that Mitchum had eventually finished up being fried to a crisp as he crashed into a local power station. Anyway I was certainly not going to be silly enough to try and outrun the civil guards in Betsy II.

*

We arranged to meet the following day and over lunch, Jens pointed out on the map where I was to collect the 'special' white wine and I was a little more relaxed when I noticed the absence of power stations along the route.

He then went on to say that to buy 'legal' pure alcohol was actually less expensive than 'illegal' alcohol. However all production of it was strictly limited and the duty payable was extortionate.

As Jens subtly put it, "You see, Chris. It is only the government we are deceiving. And where does their money come from? I'll tell you where, my friend." Here he spiked a juicy piece of entrecote with his fork and thrust it towards me to emphasize his words. "It comes from us. That's where it comes from!"

He chewed thoughtfully then reached for his glass of Enterizo wine before continuing. "So, my friend, who are we really cheating? Ourselves, Chris. That's who."

Put that way it didn't seem so bad, although I was doubtful that a defence lawyer could sell the court this one.

"Here," he stabbed a finger at the map. "That's the pick up point to the north west of Valencia. Some three hundred kilometres distance, I reckon."

And so it was that the first run was planned for the following week.

"I'll tell my contact that you will be up there to collect on Saturday morning," said Jens. "Best time really. There will be less people around the place, not many trucks on the main road and with a little luck, less police as well."

During the next days I went about checking the car. Mechanically it was fine so there was no problem there. Tyres had to be looked at and inflated correctly which I did, noticing that they would soon need changing. Never mind it would be a fine investment for my new business. The tank, of course, must be full at all times. To run out of petrol could mean big problems and would justify my being committed to an institution for the mentally retarded.

"What happens if I'm stopped?" I asked, Jens.

He thought for a moment then said, "Well tell 'em that you're carrying water."

"Water?" I said. "I'm carrying three or four hundred odd litres of water?"

"Well tell 'em that it's special water. Holy water direct from Lourdes or somewhere. They've got to be Catholics so you just might pull it off."

He grinned. "And by the way."

"What, Jens?"

"Have a good lunch or whatever but no alcohol. Remember."

"OK, Jens."

"And something else, Chris."

"What's that?"

"For Christ's sake don't smoke in the car!"

*

The appointed day arrived and I set off driving happily along admiring the variation in scenery as I headed North West from Valencia. My arrival was anticipated and I was warmly welcomed by the supplier. Immediate action was the order of the day and Betsy II received her cargo of fourteen thick plastic containers each containing twenty five litres of 'special' white wine. This was all covered over with a large blanket I had thoughtfully brought along.

Then I was on my way back again keeping a watchful eye out for the one police check point that I had passed on the way there. The civil guard, I had noticed on the way up, seemed to have only been inspecting heavy goods vehicles. However, just in case they were still active, I slipped in behind the largest truck I could find when I neared the place; the theory being that either we both would sail straight by or that in the event of the truck being pulled over there would be less chance of it happening to myself.

For lunch I chose a restaurant where I could observe the car. It must have been the only meal that I had eaten in the last thirty years that had not been accompanied by a bottle of wine followed by coffee and brandy. So everything went well; possibly too well. But the thought of any interference by FU did not really enter my head.

The following trips which occurred every two to three weeks also went fine. I was able to acquaint myself with the whereabouts of the law and at times slip off the motorway and carry out small detours on the minor roads which were usually devoid of traffic and civil guards.

*

I was now carrying seventeen containers of almost pure alcohol on each run, a total of four hundred and twenty-five litres, and had begun to suffer the worst sin of all in the 'Bootlegger' manual.

That of complacency!

Whether or not this had contributed to the downfall of Robert Mitchum in the film, I could not remember. However, it certainly happened to me. Fortunately, I must add, not with the disastrous results that might have been comparable to Mr. Mitchum's demise. It was like this.

On the final return trip I had stopped for petrol at a reasonably deserted filling station and replenished Betsy II's tank to capacity. Then shoving into the cassette player a copy of the 'Best of Frankie Lane' I pulled back onto the motorway and wound the old girl up to the stated limit of one hundred and twenty kilometres and hour.

There was a fair amount of traffic about and Frankie Lane and I were giving out with 'Mule Train' at the tops of our voices when without any warning there was this almighty explosion and for one split second I thought that the whole car had disintegrated. Next thing Betsy II started to career from one side of the motorway to the other. Fortunately what traffic was in the vicinity at that moment underwent rapid avoidance manoeuvres. I remember shouting out repeatedly, "I just don't believe this. It is just not happening!" I fought to control the wheel, realising immediately that if the blow out caused the car to summersault then it was 'Good bye, adios, Chris' and 'Hello, Mr. Mitchum.'

I was terrified.

Afterwards I likened it to attempting to steer an out of control swimming pool travelling at speed. Certainly not to be taken lightly. Surprisingly enough this one time I did get lucky, extremely lucky, and managed to pull over and stop on the hard shoulder, killing the engine.

Frankie Lane was now warbling 'I Believe' and had just arrived at the part where he reminds the listener that, 'For everyone who goes astray someone will come to show the way.' With shaking fingers I stopped him in mid-sentence by switching off, not concurring with Frankie's sentiments. That someone would be along to show me the way was the last thing I wanted; especially if they arrived on motor bikes in official green uniforms. Still very much in shock I took several deep breaths, at the same time offering my thanks to that big 'Bootlegger' in the sky.

"Now, Chris, don't panic. Not yet anyway. Just take it easy, fella. Don't rush. Get out of the car and simply change the wheel. Bloody hell! I'll have to remove God knows how many of those bloody containers just to get at the spare wheel. What did Jens say? Tell them its holy water. He must have been out of his bloody mind."

Anyway, believe it or not, I did it.

Just keeping my head down and not even looking up to see if there were any unwanted visitors arriving. In seconds flat I was surrounded by plastic containers while I hauled out the spare and jacked up the car. What did very much surprise me was the fact that in the past whenever I changed a wheel there had always been one wheelnut that had refused to budge. This time no such thing. They all came off perfectly and with rapid 'pit stop' precision I had the spare fitted, the 'holy water' back in place and was on my way again, still shaking but moving.

At the next turn off I found a small bar in one of the villages and consumed, much to the barman's astonishment, three cups of 'camomile' tea before driving on. No, Jens was not unduly surprised that I wanted to give the business a rest after what had happened, so we left it at that. The only real downside was that I have never really been able to listen to Frankie Lane again.

*

Things in general did not seem to improve and I considered joining the 'Foreign Legion' (I was now over sixty but intended to lie about my age!), or rob a bank. The latter was postponed as someone advised to wait until I was seventy. Apparently Spanish law gives consideration to robbers over seventy years making it extremely difficult to come up with a prison sentence. Perhaps the instigators of this sympathetically orientated legislation had suffered something similar.

*

Anyway I felt that much better when one Friday morning the telephone rang and I found it was Spanish friend, Juan Noguera, asking me if I were interested in another week end in Madrid with himself and his delightful partner, Eva. This to me was marvellous as it indicated that I would be spending another couple of hours wandering around the world- famous Prado museum. Apart from being able to feast my eyes on the works of my favourite artist, Goya, I knew that when I visited the museum's cafeteria I would be drinking one of the best prepared gin and tonics in all Madrid. And what is more it would be free!

This had come about on one of my first visits there some years before. Deciding that it was 'Drinkies' time I had wandered into the cafeteria and together with Russians, Chinese, Japanese, Germans, Americans and English had fought my way to the bar for refreshments only to be almost totally ignored by the harassed barman who, it appeared, either did not understand my order or did not want to understand.

Eventually I was served and found myself with one of the worst gin and tonics that had ever been placed before me. The gin, a Larios, was fine but the tonic had come out of one of those dispensers and totally ruined the drink. Trying to make the best of it I stood there sipping the mixture when, quite unexpectedly, the crowd around seemed to disperse, leaving just myself together with the barman. Knowing that now he could not very well ignore me I called him over.

"Excuse me," I said. "Is it something I've done?"

He looked puzzled and I continued. "First of all, awhile back you seemed to be happy to serve everyone else except myself. Then when you did get around to it you presented me with this lousy gin and tonic. I mean I can see that you don't really need my business with this entire overflow from the United Nations crowd. But let's be reasonable."

He then laughed, apologised and taking my glass said, "Go into the corner of the bar over there."

So I moved to the place indicated and stood observing him as he expertly prepared a real G & T in a large bowl shaped glass with plenty of ice and lemon, the final touch being a slither of lemon being passed meticulously around the rim of the glass. This was then placed in front of me together with; thank goodness, a bottle of 'Schweppes' tonic.

"Here," he said, "All on the house from now on."

And so it had been for several visits there, possibly two or three times a year.

*

Naturally when Juan telephoned with the invitation of a further trip there was no way I was going to turn down the offer. The Prado museum always had something of interest to offer and on those Sunday afternoons the entrance fee was waived. That particular day I discovered that there was an almost private exhibition in the museum's basement. It was billed as 'Delfines' or Dolphins and it was fascinating to stroll around the glass show cases and stare at the entrancing objects covering the centuries dedicated to this loveable sea creature.

After some time my personal, inbuilt, clock reminded me that it was time for refreshment, so I wandered along to the cafeteria. It was not too crowded and I was pleased to see that my now accustomed place in the corner of the bar was unoccupied. As usual my friend the barman was on duty and immediately acknowledged my presence with a wave of his hand. Then leaving several surprised customers, who were obviously there before me, he began to prepare my particular beverage. We had grown quite friendly during my previous visits and this time was no exception. The appearance of another young assistant barman enabled us to chat a little. It was after finishing my second G & T with myself going through the motions of offering payment, just in case the situation had changed, that he said, "No. It's on the house as usual. You should know that by now."

I nodded and thanked him.

He then said, "By the way. I've never asked before. But what is your name?"

"Chris," I said. "Chris Wright. Why is it you ask? Is it important?"

He smiled, "No, not really that important. It's just to keep the records straight."

I looked puzzled. "What records?"

"Well you see, Chris. There are just three people who are never charged for drinks in the Prado cafeteria."

I nodded and he continued seriously.

"Yes. One is King Juan Carlos. The other is the Director of the museum and the third is you."

I was smiling as I left, certain that it was not at all true. "But," I thought, "what a fine sense of proportion the man has.

Chapter 25

The so called 'Swinging Sixties' evokes all kinds of memories for me, both good and not so good. However, one thing I do remember is that I carried over from the 'Forgotten Fifties' a grotty guitar, on which I could strum a fair selection of popular songs, together with the ability to remember the lyrics. The strumming bit, at which I would rate a minus something on the amateur scale, was adequately compensated for by my raucous voice and even today I can still attract some spasmodic and possibly sympathetic applause over at the Dolfis bar in exchange for singing blues numbers and 'Golden Oldies'.

It was during one of these spontaneous sessions, after the Madrid trip, that I was called upon to sing 'Dream'; one of the Everley Brothers songs. As this was one of the very few ballads to which I knew all the correct chords it was received extremely well; in fact, so much so, that I was asked for a repeat. A possible combination of wistful words and the consumption of the potent local plonk only served to bring home to me my continuing existence in life as widower and thus being very much on my own. So on that particular night I fell into bed feeling a little more than just sorry for myself.

And it was on that one night I had a dream which a can still remember to this day.

In this dream I was, for some reason, presented to a woman who suddenly appeared from nowhere. Straw coloured hair, dark hazel eyes, flawless skin and a smile that would light up a whole room. In no way could I class the reverie as being erotic; it was just the warmth of her personality though her smile that induced in me a kind of tranquillity and contentment that I not encountered in a long time. The following morning I awoke with a sense of expectancy that something pleasant was about to happen for a change. Then the previous night's reverie could have been likened to a re-run of the incident for when I walked into the Dolfis bar around lunchtime, there she was.

"Hi, Chris," Jacky called out as I walked through the door into the general hubbub of the place. "Let me introduce you to my sister, Vicki."

I took the proffered hand and looking into those hazel eyes was unable to prevent myself from saying, "Hello, Vicki. I believe we met last night."

For a moment she looked somewhat taken aback but responded with that sparkling smile with which I was already acquainted. "Hello, Chris. It really is nice to meet you."

It was a magic moment for me.

The three of us chattered about things in general with Vicki taking the lead and asking pertinent questions about the array of 'tapas' Dofis bar had on display. I described each dish to her at the same time explaining that the Spaniard's love of food dictates that they each have their own personal list of preferred places that specialise in their favourite dishes. I pointed out that I, over the years, had mentally built up my own selection of bars that could cater to my own particular tastes.

"Dolfis, for example," I said, "has always been noted for 'patatas bravas' and the place next door for 'gambas al ajillo' (prawns in a hot garlic sauce). While there was yet another bar in the area that served nothing but 'glochinas al vapor' (steamed mussels from the Valencia region)."

Vicki looked at me carefully. "Then you will know where I can find the best anchovies?"

"Easy," I smiled. "Tonight I will show you."

So around nine o'clock that evening we met and went along to a local, Guimera bar, that serves hand prepared anchovies, marianated in the finest virgin olive oil from Jaen and placed on small rounds of toasted bread with just a little shredded fresh tomato and a touch of garlic.

I ordered six and Vicki loved them. Next we moved on to the Dolfis and there we sat contentedly picking at 'patatas bravas', sampling spicy snails, enjoying 'esgarat' and sipping Spanish 'Cava'. It was all very splendid and for once I felt my real self once again. Even more so when I asked for the bill and Amando, son of the owner grinned and said, "Everything on the house tonight, Chris. It's just great to see you enjoying yourselves."

After that I showed Vicki around Valencia, stopping at various other 'in' places and then finishing up at the colourful Casa Blanca dance hall by the Malvarosa beach where we watched a wonderful display of traditional Argentinian tango dancers. It was around two o'clock when I dropped her off at her sister's apartment but not before achieving the promise that we meet the following day.

*

The summer sun was high in the sky when we drove out to the 'Puerto de Cataroja', a small inland port, where the boats used for fishing the Albufera Lake are moored.

There at the Casa Baina restaurant where the local fishermen gather, we lunched on 'allí pebre', eels prepared in that succulent hot sauce, drank dry Viña Sol wine and were thoroughly spoilt by Marcial, the owner. Afterwards, armed with large Gordon's and tonics we stepped out into the late afternoon and strolled along the riverside.

Vicki stopped without warning and pointed ahead. "Do you think anyone would mind if we sat on that boat over there, Chris?"

That 'boat over there' was a rather dejected, faded blue, vessel not much bigger than a dingy, moving restlessly between two larger fishing boats moored nearby.

"No, of course not," I replied. "Today has been especially made for sitting on boats."

Carefully we climbed on board, she tentatively taking the initiative, with myself following, after passing the gin and tonics, the ice cubes chuckling merrily in the clear liquid. The movement disturbed the water and there were little plops and splashes as the multitude of small creatures that made their homes along the river bank became unsettled.

It was springtime with the promise of a long hot Spanish summer and we sat on the wooden seat facing what remained of the warm sun. Across the river the fields of spiky dry stalks of last year's rice crop stretched out before us towards the indistinct blue smudge of the 'Sierra de los Pinos' mountain range in the distance. A family of long tailed egrets with curved yellow beaks picked and pecked fussily about on the opposite bank, like fluffy white balls of cotton wool on spindly legs. A large grey, lazy winged heron, deciding that our presence interfered with his fishing, launched itself ungainly into the still afternoon air and leisurely winged his way in the direction of the wild Albufera Lake.

We sat quietly for some minutes, not needing the sound of words.

Then without warning Vicki asked, "Would you like to kiss me?"

I was not sure that I had heard correctly; thought my ears were deceiving me. A glance told me that she was not even looking at me. Just sat there staring straight ahead, her eyes fixed on something in the hazy far off horizon. Her perfume came to me like a sensual will-o'-the-wisp.

"I'm sorry," I ventured.

Now she turned towards me and the fragrance became even stronger. Deep hazel eyes looked straight into mine. "I said would you like to kiss me, Chris?"

The sun's rays touched the straw coloured hair fragmenting the light into a thousand bright points. I momentarily closed my eyes. Then breathing deeply I heard my voice from a long way off. "You know I would."

A brief hesitation, then carefully placing her glass on the seat next to her, she moved towards me. "Then kiss me, Chris."

Warm touching warm with soft touching soft. Falling, falling and in one single moment those sad, miserable days and interminable long, lonely nights, all fading away.

Oh, those nights.

My arms instinctively embraced her even more so and she responded; just holding on tight.

"Dear, Lord," I thought. "If there is ever a moment in which I could chose to die, let it be now. And the only wish I would crave would be a little window in heaven where I could look down onto this small boat and remember."

We moved apart but not before, unable to help myself, I murmured, "I already love you so much."

Almost before the words fell from my lips I regretted having said them. She withdrew, turned away and stared into the distance again.

"No, please don't, Chris. I cannot accept the responsibility at the moment."

"I'm truly sorry."

I then moved to reach out to her in a brief show of contriteness but held back for fear of further rejection. The hazel eyes turned towards me again and she placed a hand softly on my arm. "You do understand, Chris, don't you?"

I averted my eyes.

"Yes, of course I understand," I answered miserably, not understanding nor wanting ever to understand.

"What on earth is that noise?"

She moved away, breaking the spell. A high drawn out lamenting cry came from an almost derelict building behind us on the river bank.

"A cat," I replied, automatically. "It sounds as though it is trapped."

A brief shadow crossed her face. "Can we break in and rescue it, Chris?"

"I wouldn't really recommend it. Not here in Spain, anyway. They probably wouldn't understand."

"But being trapped must be awful."

"Aren't we all trapped? In our own way, that is."

"I suppose we are."

She retrieved her glass and raised it to her lips. I followed suit, the now tepid drink tasteless to my mouth. "How can we escape?" she asked, catching on to my mood.

"Escape? Escape to what?" I closed my eyes feeling the warmth of the sun's last rays on my face. "Freedoms just another word for nothing left to lose. Janis Joplin."

"Janis who?"

"Janis Joplin," I explained. "She was an American rock singer."

She persisted. "But if you had everything, wouldn't you be free?"

Again I smiled, more to myself. "No not really. The Tao philosophy says that to have absolutely everything would mean that you would finally finish up with nothing."

There was a moments silence as she digested this. Then she laughed; a happy infectious sound that lightened my spirit a little. "I understand what you are trying to say. But it sounds silly all the same."

"No definitely not because the contrary is true."

I turned to look at her. "You see. A person who has nothing whatsoever is in a position to have everything."

"So nothing is important," she said, making it sound more like a statement than a question.

"Oh, yes. Nothing is very important. 'Nothing' is the essence of life, of everything. We use it all the time."

"We do. How?"

"Well this boat for example." I ran my hand over the dry, flaking paintwork. "It might just be the most beautiful boat in the world. But without the space where we are sitting, it would not be very serviceable." I then pointed to her glass. "That glass which you are holding might be a most wonderful work of art ever invented. But again, without the space inside or if you like the nothing inside that you are making use of, it would be totally impracticable."

Then warming to the subject I continued. "It is the same with a house. We live inside the space and we look out of the windows. Nothingness again. Even a wheel without the hole in the middle would be less than useless."

The pitiful, heartfelt, cry came once more.

"We really must do something about that cat," she said, seriously. The sound distracted her; worried her.

"Perhaps it is the space inside it's tummy that is making it unhappy," I offered.

She laughed. "We could rescue it and feed it anchovies," she said, brightly. Then, as an afterthought, "Are you taking me to the anchovy bar tonight?"

I looked at her again and said quietly, "I would take you to the moon, if you wish."

"Don't be silly."

"Alright then, I won't take you anywhere and the 'nothingness' would prove my point."

Again that laugh and again that closeness; feeling that I had not experienced in a long time.

"Of course I will take you to the anchovy bar."

Her tone unexpectedly became serious. "How long has it been, Chris?"

The question was sincere, not curious, but sincere. Without seeking her eyes, I automatically answered. "How do you want it? Years, months, days or hours?"

"That close?"

"Well, yes. I suppose we were," I agreed, begrudgingly as though it was exposing the cross I was to bear for always.

"You really do miss her, even now."

An observation. I moved the insipid liquid around in my glass. "When there are no more words left, only then can you cry," I murmured, quoting Hamilton. Then, shrugging I added, "I suppose the crying also has to stop sometime."

Even then as those hollow words came out I could feel the bleak days and the terrible isolation of those wretched nights reaching out to me. And her very nearness, for a brief moment, only served to make me feel lonelier.

"What do you miss about her?" Her soft voice came from a long way off.

"I don't really know," I lied. And even as I spoke I knew that she was aware of the untruth. So I continued, "Her laugh, I suppose. Her way of speaking in that warm, mid- west American, tone of voice." I wanted to add, "Her very nearness in the night and above all her just being there when I needed her most."

Instead I said, "And a shoulder to cry on occasionally."

Those hazel eyes turned towards me once again. "And did you?"

"Did I what?"

"Occasionally cry."

A slight anger touched me at this inquisition; this prying into my innermost feelings. These were things I had never discussed with anyone since Kathy had died. These were deep personal feelings that I had harboured now for what seemed an eternity. Had cultivated within myself and which in turn had grown into a tree of bitterness, the fruit of which would eventually destroy me.

"Cry occasionally? I suppose I must have done."

Not wanting to remember. Not wishing to continue along this theme that I knew would inevitably lead to my fostering further resentments. Feeling exposed, feeling vulnerable.

Over the river the sun, now a pale orange sphere floating in a sea of lemony greens and blues, was gradually descending behind the distant, dark secret, mountains. A sudden splash and a black, sleek coated, water rat launched itself into the river and swam purposefully away.

Again placing the now empty glass onto the seat beside her, she reached over laying her velvet soft hands over mine and pressed gently as though trying to relieve the terrible hurt that she also had been subjected to, many years before.

"Chris, look at me."

I obeyed and sort the depths of those eyes.

"Chris, are you crying?"

I attempted to say, "No. I'm damn well not crying." But it wasn't there, just wouldn't come out.

Then again she spoke, only this time the voice that came to my ears was not that of her voice. It was a voice I had heard before. Coming like a call from the distant past it was the voice I had lived with all my life. The small voice that we all have within each and every one of us stretching out across time and space. And it was then in that very moment of my existence that, for one brief instant, I glimpsed through the windows of my mind at the intricate pattern of tragic circumstances that had brought us together, placing us both together on this old boat. In a port that was not really a port, just a still, silent, river that really led to nowhere. The voice within that had answered me when I needed it most; had come to me, just the way that she also had come into my life. It was all here. I remembered hearing the same voice in another place, in another age, saying that 'time was of no importance'. Time, no. But togetherness, yes. If this closeness, this intimacy ended in the same breath as those seven simple words that she was about to utter or when we left the boat to whatever the future held in store, it would be of no significance. This singular precious moment was etched in time and would, by this, remain eternal. There was a 'before' to this moment and an 'afterwards'. But above all there was a 'now'.

And it was that which counted for everything that really matters.

"Here," she said, quietly embracing me, "use my shoulder, if you wish."

EPILOGUE.

One of Spain's last, carefully guarded, secrets is to be discovered in a geographical box. This box can be found by imagining a line drawn from the town of Castellon to Vinarós along the Costa del Azahar, then inland to ancient and irresistible Morella, across in a north westerly direction to Teruel and then back to Castellon. The area which it embraces is known as 'El Maestrazgo'.

*

I was comfortably settled at the bar of 'El Pichón' in the small town of Rubielos de Mora, lying on the edge of this region when, much to my surprise, the door opened and in trooped a crowd of what I knew as British senior citizens. Glancing out of the window I saw the words 'Saga Tours' emblazoned on the side of a large coach. The last person to descend, I rightly assumed, was the driver who when he appeared elected to stand next to me. After he had been served his 'Café con leche' I turned to him, "You certainly don't see many tourists in this particular area of Spain," I said.

He looked up at me with the expression of someone who is not surprised at anything, least of all in finding a fellow countryman in an out of the way part of the world. His answer came with that no nonsense, glorious, cockney twang. "No, mate," he said. "Yer not bleedin' likely to either."

"Really and why is that?" I asked, conversationally.

"'Course not. 'Ow can yer expect people to visit a place they 'aint capable of pronouncin'?" He stirred his coffee after carefully emptying in the two sachets of sugar and said thoughtfully, "Na, I mean how d' yer tell yer mates where yer goin', or where yer bin fer that matter, if yer can't speak it?"

He inclined his head towards his passengers who were wandering around the bar, examining the owner's fine display of huge fossils, collected over many years, busily visiting the toilets or asking questions of the charming blonde lady who was obviously their guide.

"I'm jest passin' frew with this lot from Peñíscola to Teruel. Now thems places, same as Benidorm, Malaga or Marbella, which yer can speak. But Mystrago. No way!"

And, of course, he was quite right. What travel agency would be inclined to include classes on the pronunciation of their tourist destinations? Very few, if any.

*

'Maestrazgo' pronounced 'My-strath-go' signifies 'Territory under the jurisdiction of a master' and this particular region has been under rule during the times of the Templar Knights until the beginning of the XIV century. Later during the 'Carlista' wars it passed into the hands of the rebel general, Ramon Cabrera, or 'El Tigre del Maestrazgo' as he was known, and from then on the fifty seven municipal boundaries have remained very much as they are today.

Since those far off times there have, of course, been many changes; some say for the better, others are not so sure. One indisputable improvement, however, can be seen in the construction of the highways. This has come about mainly during the twentieth century. Prior to that the roads were little more than dirt tracks, accustomed to carrying mule and donkey carts. These tracks were then eventually covered over with cobble stones with the arrival of the motor car.

To drive around that region in the early nineteen sixties was not for the faint hearted as there were two main dangers to be on the look out for. The first was the existence of 'barrancos' or dykes that unexpectedly crossed the roads at irregular intervals. Fed by the melting winter snows and sudden summer storms from the gaunt grey peaks rising up to a two thousand or more metres, these gullies were natural water courses often as much as one or two metres deep. If your car was blessed with a good, firm, suspension it was possible to drive carefully down into them, keeping a wary eye open for large boulders at the bottom, then up and out on the far side. Of course, that was when they were dry.

And when it was raining? Well that was another story.

What was curious was that you could be driving along in bright sunshine enjoying the scenery when, unbeknown to you, high up above in those sullen pinnacles a storm might be raging. Then gushing torrents of muddy water would come hurtling down at racing car speed, filling those channels in seconds. Swirling waters carrying logs, huge boulders half the size of your car and the occasional dead sheep or goat that had had the misfortune of not being sufficiently agile to get out of the way. When this happened the only solution was to wait patiently until the waters subsided and then continue.

As if this were not sufficient to dissuade the motorist, there existed a second difficulty; that of large stones. Confined always, thank goodness, to hills and unusually long inclines, these stones were deliberately placed there. The carrier with his mule and cart, transporting feed, wood or whatever, would grant his beast a deserved break on these hills by seeking out a large stone at the side of the road and placing it behind one of the cart wheels. This would then take the weight and the animal could rest. Then after a while the drover would climb aboard once more and with a cry of, "Ooooo Pah!" stir the animal into action, leaving the obstacle still in place. These stones, often the size of footballs, would then lie in wait for the unwary motorist. It is on more than one occasion that I have seen oil sumps ripped out due to this inconsideration. Nowadays, thank goodness, things are different. The major roads in the region are blessed with fine asphalt surfaces and there are, of course, less carts.

*

All over Spain the traveller can occasionally come across small chapels in the most out of the way places. For most of them there is logic as to why they have been positioned where they are. However, nobody really knows why the church elders should have elected to build one plain little worshipping place high up on the slopes of the Maestrazgo.

One theory suggests that there had been a stray drop of wine spilt onto the plans of some ecclesiastical architect who liked his drink. On being asked, by the unexpected arrival of a visiting bishop, the significance of the blot, the enterprising man replied that it marked the whereabouts of a new chapel.

"And to whom is this place of worship dedicated?" asked the suspecting bishop.

"Why, St. Bartholomew," answered the architect convincingly; 'Bartholomew', of course, being the bishop's name.

Constructed of grey slate the chapel stands to the north of San Vicente de Pedrita, facing down the valley towards the Mediterranean, some hundred kilometres as a bird might fly. Having finally been abandoned by the church authorities it is now a popular youth hostel. The Spanish love of picnics has resulted in the construction, in the grounds, of stone fireplaces, tables and benches. Ample water is available and it is a very pleasant place to be.

A few paces away from the picnic area twenty seven steps, hewn out of logs, lead down to an old rickety bridge under which a reed-choked stream flows. To the left of this bridge, under a mossy bank, a natural fountain with ice cold crystal clear water tumbles out onto dark green moss covered rocks.

I stood on the bridge and listened to the wind in the silver birch trees. The sharp brittle sound was that of little old ladies chattering away at some tea party and very much different from the dismal, mournful, sighs of the wind in the pines further up the mountain.

Perhaps it had been there all the time. I did not know. I suddenly spotted it clinging to the rough bark of a tree some ten metres distance. By any means of my imagination I could see that it was not an outstanding butterfly, in appearance that is. But it was large. A rather drab off-white colour with dull green edging to its large wings which it was flexing occasionally as though taking advantage as to what remained of the afternoon sunshine filtering through the trees. I watched it for some three to four minutes before it took to the air and flew straight past me towards the spring where it alighted on the damp moss, presumably to drink.

As I continued to observe it my thoughts to the wonderful butterfly field that Kathy, Samantha and I had discovered in France those many years before. I know not why but my mind next turned to the thought that it was sad there being little or no communication between us and whatever hereafter existed.

Then, as if responding to my thoughts, the creature took to the air once more and without any hesitation whatsoever, flew directly towards me. Twice it circled around my head and then gently alighted on my left shoulder. Next it moved slowly down until it was in the region of my heart. There turning it appeared to be looking straight up into my eyes. Thus we remained for what seemed an eternity but what was in reality, must have been a few fleeting moments. Then flexing its gossamer wings once again it took unfalteringly to the air, disappearing into the reeds down by the stream.

Slowly I climbed back up the steps to where Betsy II was waiting patiently. Once in the car I sat quietly together with my ghosts. They were all there. I could hear Pany remonstrating with José about his fingernails and wondered if the paella maker had ever blessed the cooking area with a coat of paint. Mac was there, removing his pipe and asking, "Well, CJ, would you like the good news or the bad news?" Jens, I could hear saying,

"Tell 'em it's four hundred litres of holy water, you're carrying." FU was sure to be lying in wait somewhere in the background, ready to make its presence felt. However, at that special moment, it did not seem to matter so much as those few minutes spent on that bridge had given me a most profound sense of peace, of well being, and at the same time a renewed faith in butterflies.

It was then, as I was pulling away, that I noticed at the side of the road a pair of off white, shabby looking training shoes, one with the remains of a lace and one without. Now, how on earth did they arrive there? Yes, I had my camera with me and for one brief second my foot hovered over the brake pedal but, somehow on this one occasion, I drove on resisting the temptation to look skywards and say, "Hey, Mr. Mercer. What fine mess are you going to get me into now?"

Christopher John Wright

CJ with Vicki. Happy Times.

About the Author

Born in Leicester prior to the second World War and the only son of a typical English «Bobby» Chris Wright attended a local grammar school until sixteen years of age. Before compulsory service in the RAF he has various jobs, and in his spare time played «Boogie Woogie» piano for American and Canadian servicemen in some of the less desirable city pubs. After the RAF he decided to settle down by joining the Exeter City police force. Good intentions were rapidly brought to an end when one night he was instructed to stop a smash and grab gateway car. Expertly accomplished by a well-aimed truncheon at the vehicle's windscreen Chris was to discover, after the car had embedded itself in the front of a local cafeteria, that he had stopped the following police car. Next came a period of trainee management for a national chain store followed by some years of pharmaeutical representation in the Surrey and Midlands areas. A desire to try self employment found him and his wife running a Northamptonshire country pub accompanied by a depressed Bassett hound, a donkey and an over-sexed cockerel, together with a delinquent goat that seemed bent on destroying his livelihood. It was the offer of a partnership, and the reasoning that if he was going to be unsuccessful he might as well be unsuccessful somewhere warm, that attracted him to Spain. The country, at that time, was still rising out of the ashes of a Civil War, staggering towards the end of the Franco dictatorship and into European Democracy. On learning of Chris's decision, his newly-found Spanish partner said, «The Spanish climate will certainly meet with your expectations but there is absolutely no way I can guarantee what else you might find». How right he was.

Lightning Source UK Ltd.
Milton Keynes UK
23 July 2010

157402UK00004B/66/P